Views of
Old Europe

Views of Old Europe

A Grand Tour Across
A Timeless Landscape

Bayard Taylor
Edited by Paul Dennis Sporer

ROLLRIGHT BOOKS

ANZA PUBLISHING, Chester, NY 10918
Rollright Books is an imprint of Anza Publishing
Copyright © 2005 by Anza Publishing

This work is a new, unabridged edition of *Views A-foot:
or Europe Seen with Knapsack and Staff* by J. Bayard Taylor,
originally published in 1850.

Library of Congress Cataloguing-in-Publication Data
Taylor, Bayard, 1825–1878.
  [Views a-foot]
  Views of old Europe / Bayard Taylor ;
  edited by Paul Dennis Sporer. — New, unabridged ed.
    p. cm.
  Originally published: Views a-foot, or, Europe seen with
  knapsack and staff. New York : G. P. Putnam, 1850.
  Includes index.
  ISBN 1-932490-31-0 (hardcover : alk. paper)
  1. Europe–Description and travel.
  2. Walking–Europe.
I. Sporer, Paul D. II. Title.
D919.T23 2005
914.04'283—dc22   2005021787

Visit AnzaPublishing.com for more information on outstanding
authors and titles. Please support our efforts to restore great
literature to a place of prominence in our culture.

ISBN 1-932490-31-0

∞ This book is printed on acid-free paper.

CONTENTS

Editor's Preface

This is a highly engaging and well-composed account by Bayard Taylor, of a two-year long journey in the 1840s, mostly on foot, through Britain, Ireland, Germany, Italy, France, Austria and Switzerland. A multitude of perceptive observations about European society are set against the background of the journey narrative, which keeps moving at a deliberate but very pleasant pace. In these observations, Taylor strikes just the right balance between panorama and detail. The communities of that time, in all their charm, ebullience, traditional customs, and protectiveness, are brought into clear focus, facilitated by the copious notes kept by the author. Such writings were made "partly by the wayside, when resting at midday, and partly on the rough tables of peasant inns, in the stillness of deserted ruins, or amid the sublime solitude of the mountain-top."

Over the long course, a variety of beauties both natural and man-made are encountered: mountains, rivers, lakes and woods, as well as galleries, museums, churches, mansions, and cathedrals. But the tour had its share of challenges, including fatiguing hikes on backroads, inadequate funds, and avoiding robbers. There was also a dearth of facilities conducive to material comfort and convenience, such as hotels, restaurants and shelters. Still, for Taylor, the advantages greatly outweighed the hardships. The fond recollections found in these pages betray a youthful idealism, one that came to fruition in his future multiple roles as diplomat, essayist, and poet.

The present volume is based on the ninth edition (1850), published by G. P. Putnam. Certain sections were altered to improve flow and clarity, but in general the original spellings of names and places were retained. We have also added a comprehensive index.

PAUL DENNIS SPORER

Views of Old Europe

Chapter I
THE VOYAGE

An enthusiastic desire of visiting the Old World haunted me from early childhood. I cherished a presentiment, amounting almost to belief, that I should one day behold the scenes, among which my fancy had so long wandered. The want of means was for a time a serious check to my anticipations; but I could not content myself to wait until I had slowly accumulated so large a sum as tourists usually spend on their travels. It seemed to me that a more humble method of seeing the world would place within the power of almost everyone, what has hitherto been deemed the privilege of the wealthy few. Such a journey, too, offered advantages for becoming acquainted with people as well as places—for observing more intimately, the effect of government and education, and more than all, for the study of human nature, in every condition of life. At length I became possessed of a small sum, to be earned by letters descriptive of things abroad, and on the 1st of July, 1844, set sail for Liverpool, with a relative and friend, whose circumstances were somewhat similar to mine. How far the success of the experiment and the object of our long pilgrimage were attained, these pages will show.

LAND AND SEA

There are springs that rise in the greenwood's heart,
  Where its leafy glooms are cast,
And the branches droop in the solemn air,
  Unstirred by the sweeping blast.

There are hills that lie in the noontide calm,
    On the lap of the quiet earth;
And, crown'd with gold by the ripened grain,
    Surround my place of birth.

Dearer are these to my pining heart,
    Than the beauty of the deep,
When the moonlight falls in a belt of gold
    On the waves that heave in sleep.
The rustling talk of the clustered leaves
    That shade a well-known door,
Is sweeter far than the booming sound
    Of the breaking wave before.

When night on the ocean sinks calmly down,
    I climb the vessel's prow,
Where the foam-wreath glows with its phosphor light,
    Like a crown on a sea-nymph's brow.
Above, through the lattice o' rope and spar,
    The stars in their beauty burn;
And the spirit longs to ride their beams,
    And back to the loved return.

They say that the sunset is brighter far
    When it sinks behind the sea;
That the stars shine out wits a softer fire —
    Not thus they seem to me.
Dearer the flush of the crimson west
    Through trees that my childhood knew,
When the star of love, with its silver lamp,
    Lights the homes of the tried and true!

Could one live on the sense of beauty alone, exempt from the necessity of "creature comforts," a sea-voyage would be delightful. To the landsman there is sublimity in the wild and ever-varied forms of the ocean; they fill his mind with living images of a glory he had only dreamed of before. But we would have been willing to forego all this and get back the comforts of the shore. At New York we took passage in the second cabin of the Oxford, which, as usual in the Liverpool packets, consisted of a small space amid ships, fitted up with rough, temporary berths. The communication with the deck is by an open hatchway, which in storms is closed down. As the passengers in this cabin furnish their own provisions, we made ourselves acquainted with the contents of certain storehouses on Pine St. wharf, and purchased a large box of provisions, which was stowed away under our narrow berth. The cook, for a small compensation, took on himself the charge of preparing them, and we made ourselves as comfortable as the close, dark dwelling would admit.

As we approached the Banks of Newfoundland, a gale arose, which for two days and nights carried us on, careering Mazeppa-like, up hill and down. The sea looked truly magnificent, although the sailors told us it was nothing at all in comparison with the storms of winter. But we were not permitted to pass the Banks, without experiencing one of the calms, for which that neighborhood is noted. For three days we lay almost motionless on the glassy water, sometimes surrounded by large flocks of sea-gulls. The weed brought by the gulf stream, floated around — some branches we fished up, were full of beautiful little shells. Once a large school of black-fish came around the vessel, and the carpenter climbed down on the fore-chains, with a harpoon to strike one. Scarcely had he taken his position, when they all darted off in a straight line, through the water, and were soon out of sight. He said they had smelt the harpoon.

We congratulated ourselves on having reached the Banks in seven days, as it is considered the longest third-part of the passage. But the hopes of reaching Liverpool in twenty days, were soon overthrown. A succession of southerly winds drove the vessel as far north as lat. 55 deg., without bringing us much nearer our destination. It was extremely cold, for we were but five degrees south of the latitude of Greenland, and the long northern twilights came on. The last glow of the evening twilight had scarcely faded, before the first glimmering of dawn appeared. I found it extremely easy to read, at 10 P. M., on the deck.

We had much diversion on board from a company of Iowa Indians, under the celebrated chief "White Cloud," who are on a visit to England. They are truly a wild enough looking company, and helped not a little to relieve the tedium of the passage. The chief was a grave and dignified person, but some of the braves were merry enough. One day we had a war-dance on deck, which was a most ludicrous scene. The chief and two braves sat upon the deck, beating violently a small drum and howling forth their war-song, while the others in full dress, painted in a grotesque style, leaped about, brandishing tomahawks and spears, and terminating each dance with a terrific yell. Some of the men are very fine-looking, but the squaws are all ugly. They occupied part of the second cabin, separated only by a board partition from our room. This proximity was any thing but agreeable. They kept us awake more than half the night, by singing and howling in the most dolorous manner, with the accompaniment of slapping their hands violently on their bare breasts. We tried an opposition, and a young German student, who was returning home after two years' travel in America, made our room ring with the chorus from Der Freischutz—but in vain. They would howl and beat their breasts, and the pappoose would squall. Any loss of temper is therefore not to be wondered at, when I state that I could scarcely turn in my berth, much less stretch myself out; my cramped limbs alone drove off half the night's slumber.

It was a pleasure, at least, to gaze on their strong athletic frames. Their massive chests and powerful limbs put to shame our dwindled proportions. One old man, in particular, who seemed the patriarch of the band, used to stand for hours on the quarter deck, sublime and motionless as a statue of Jupiter. An interesting incident occurred during the calm of which I spoke. They began to be fearful we were doomed to remain there forever, unless the spirits were invoked for a favorable wind. Accordingly, the prophet lit his pipe and smoked with great deliberation, muttering all the while in a low voice. Then, having obtained a bottle of beer from the captain, he poured it solemnly over the stern of the vessel into the sea. There were some indications of wind at the time, and accordingly the next morning we had a fine breeze, which the Iowas attributed solely to the Prophet's incantation and Eolus' love of beer.

After a succession of calms and adverse winds, on the 25th we were off the Hebrides, and though not within sight of land, the southern winds came to us strongly freighted with the "meadow freshness" of the Irish bogs, so we could at least smell it. That day the wind became more favorable, and the next morning we were all roused out of our berths by sunrise, at the long wished-for cry of "land!" Just under the golden flood of light that streamed through the morning clouds, lay far-off and indistinct the crags of an island, with the top of a lighthouse visible at one extremity. To the south of it, and barely distinguishable, so completely was it blended in hue with the veiling cloud, loomed up a lofty mountain. I shall never forget the sight! As we drew nearer, the dim and soft outline it first wore, was broken into a range of crags, with precipices jutting out to the sea, and sloping off inland. The white wall of the lighthouse shone in the morning's light, and the foam of the breakers dashed up at the foot of the airy cliffs. It was worth all the troubles of a long voyage, to feel the glorious excitement which this herald of new scenes and new adventures created. The lighthouse was on Tory Island, on the north-western coast of Ireland. The Captain decided on taking the North Channel, for, although rarely done, it was in our case nearer, and is certainly more interesting than the usual route.

We passed the Island of Ennistrahul, near the entrance of Londonderry harbor, and at sunset saw in the distance the islands of Islay and Jura, off the Scottish coast. Next morning we were close to the promontory of Fairhead, a bold, precipitous headland, like some of the Palisades on the Hudson; the highlands of the Mull of Cantire were on the opposite side of the Channel, and the wind being ahead, we tacked from shore to shore, running so near the Irish coast, that we could see the little thatched huts, stacks of peat, and even rows of potatoes in the fields. It was a panorama: the view extended for miles inland, and the fields of different colored grain were spread out before us, a brilliant mosaic. Towards evening we passed Ailsa Crag, the sea-bird's home, within sight, though about twenty miles distant.

On Sunday, the 28th, we passed the lofty headland of the Mull of Galloway and entered the Irish Sea. Here there was an occurrence of an impressive nature. A woman, belonging to the steerage, who had been ill the whole passage, died the morning before. She appeared to be of a very avaricious disposition, though this might indeed have been the result of self-denial, practised through filial affection. In the morning she was speechless, and while they were endeavoring to persuade her to give up her keys to the captain, died. In her pocket were found two parcels, containing forty sovereigns, sewed up with the most miserly care. It was ascertained she had a widowed mother in the north of Ireland, and judging her money could be better applied than to paying for a funeral on shore, the captain gave orders for committing the body to the waves. It rained drearily as her corpse, covered with starred bunting, was held at the gangway while the captain read the funeral service; then one plunge was heard, and a white object flashed up through the dark waters, as the ship passed on.

In the afternoon we passed the Isle of Man, having a beautiful view of the Calf, with a white stream tumbling down the rocks into the sea; and at night saw the sun set behind the mountains of Wales.

About midnight, the pilot came on board, and soon after sunrise I saw the distant spires of Liverpool. The Welsh coast was studded with windmills, all in motion, and the harbor spotted with buoys, bells and floating lights. How delightful it was to behold the green trees on the banks of the Mersey, and to know that in a few hours we should be on land! About 11 o'clock we came to anchor in the channel of the Mersey, near the docks, and after much noise, bustle and confusion, were transferred, with our baggage, to a small steamboat, giving a parting cheer to the Iowas, who remained on board. On landing, I stood a moment to observe the scene. The baggage-wagons, drawn by horses, mules and donkeys, were extraordinary; men were going about crying *"the celebrated Tralorum gingerbread!"* which they carried in baskets; and a boy in the University dress, with long blue gown and yellow knee-breeches, was running to the wharf to look at the Indians.

At last the carts were all loaded, the word was given to start, and then, what a scene ensued! Away went the mules, the horses and the donkeys; away ran men and women and children, carrying chairs and trunks, and boxes and bedding. The wind was blowing, and the dust whirled up as they dashed helter-skelter through the gate and started off on a hot race, down the dock to the depot. Two wagons came together, one of which was overturned, scattering the broken boxes of a Scotch family over the pavement; but while the poor woman was crying over her loss, the tide swept on, scarcely taking time to glance at the mishap.

Our luggage was "passed" with little trouble; the officer merely opening the trunks and pressing his hands on the top. Even some American reprints of English works which my companion carried, and feared would be taken from him, were passed over without a word. I was agreeably surprised at this, as from the accounts of some travellers, I had been led to fear horrible things of custom-houses. This over, we took a stroll about the city. I was first struck by seeing so many people walking in the middle of the streets, and so many gentlemen going about with pinks stuck in their button-holes. Then, the houses being all built of brown granite or dark brick, gives the town a sombre appearance, which the sunshine (when there is any) cannot really dispel. Of Liverpool we saw little. Before the twilight had wholly faded, we were again tossing on the rough waves of the Irish Sea.

Chapter II
A DAY IN IRELAND

On calling at the steamboat office in Liverpool, to take passage to Port Rush, we found that the fare in the fore cabin was but two shillings and a half, while in the chief cabin it was six times as much. As I had started to make the tour of all Europe with a sum little higher than is sometimes given for the mere passage to and fro, there was no alternative—the twenty-four hours' discomfort could be more easily endured than the expense, and as I expected to encounter many hardships, it was best to make a beginning. I had crossed the ocean with tolerable comfort for twenty-four dollars, and was determined to try whether England, where I had been told it was almost impossible to breathe without expense, might not also be seen by one of limited means.

The fore cabin was merely a bare room, with a bench along one side, which was occupied by half a dozen Irishmen in knee-breeches and heavy brogans. As we passed out of the Clarence Dock at 10 P.M., I went below and managed to get a seat on one end of the bench, where I spent the night in sleepless misery. The Irish bestowed themselves about the floor as they best could, for there was no light, and very soon the Morphean deepness of their breathing gave token of blissful unconsciousness.

The next morning was misty and rainy, but I preferred walking the deck and drying myself occasionally beside the chimney, to sitting in the dismal room below. We passed the Isle of Man, and through the whole forenoon were tossed about very disagreeably in the North Channel. In the afternoon we stopped at Larne, a little antiquated village, not far from Belfast, at the head of a crooked arm of the sea. There is an old ivy-grown tower near, and high green mountains rise up around. After leaving it, we had a beautiful panoramic view of the northern coast. Many of the precipices are of the same formation as the Causeway; Fairhead, a promontory of this kind, is grand in the extreme. The perpendicular face of fluted rock is about three hundred feet in height, and towering up sublimely from the water, seemed almost to overhang our heads.

My companion compared it to Niagara Falls petrified; and I think the simile very striking. It is like a cataract falling in huge waves, in some places leaping out from a projecting rock, in others descending in an unbroken sheet.

We passed the Giant's Causeway after dark, and about eleven o'clock reached the harbor of Port Rush, where, after stumbling up a strange old street, in the dark, we found a little inn, and soon forgot the Irish Coast and everything else.

In the morning when we arose it was raining, with little prospect of fair weather, but having expected nothing better, we set out on foot for the Causeway. The rain, however, soon came down in torrents, and we were obliged to take shelter in a cabin by the roadside. The whole house consisted of one room, with bare walls and roof, and earthen floor, while a window of three or four panes supplied the light. A fire of peat was burning on the hearth, and their breakfast, of potatoes alone, stood on the table. The occupants received us with rude but genuine hospitality, giving us the only seats in the room to sit upon; except a rickety bedstead that stood in one corner and a small table, there was no other furniture in the house. The man appeared intelligent, and although he complained of the hardness of their lot, he had no sympathy with O'Connell or the Repeal movement.

We left this miserable hut, as soon as it ceased raining — and, though there were many cabins along the road, few were better than this. At length, after passing the walls of an old church, in the midst of older tombs, — we saw the roofless towers of Dunluce Castle, on the sea-shore. It stands on an isolated rock, rising perpendicularly two hundred feet above the sea, and connected with the cliffs of the mainland by a narrow arch of masonry. On the summit of the cliffs were ire remains of the buildings where the ancient lords kept their vassals. An old man, who takes care of it for Lord Antrim, on whose property it is situated, showed us the way down to the castle. We walked across the narrow arch, entered the ruined hall, and looked down on the roaring sea below. It still rained, the wind swept furiously through the decaying arches of the banqueting hall and waved the long grass on the desolate battlements. Far below, the sea foamed white on the breakers and sent up an unceasing boom. It was the most mournful and desolate picture I eves beheld. There were some low dungeons yet entire, and rude stairways, where, by stooping down, I could ascend nearly to the top of one of the towers, and look out on the wild scenery of the coast.

Going back, I found a way down the cliff, to the mouth of a cavern in the rock, which extends under the whole castle to the sea. Sliding down a heap of sand and stones, I stood under an arch eighty feet high; in front the breakers dashed into the entrance, flinging the spray half-way to the roof, while the sound rang up through the arches like thunder. It seemed to me the haunt of the old Norsemen's sea-gods!

We left the road near Dunluce end walked along the smooth beach to the cliffs that surround the Causeway. Here we obtained a guide, and descended to one of the caves which can be entered from the shore. Opposite the entrance a bare rock called Sea Gull Isle, rises out of the sea like a church steeple. The roof at first was low, but we shortly came to a branch that opened or the sea, where the arch was forty-six feet in height. The breakers dashed far into the cave, and flocks of sea-birds circled round its mouth. The sound of a gun was like a deafening peal of thunder, crashing from arch to arch till it rolled out of the cavern.

On the top of the hill a splendid hotel is erected for visitors to the Causeway; after passing this we descended to the base of the cliffs, which are here upwards of four hundred feet high, and soon began to find, in the columnar formation of the rocks, indications of our approach. The guide pointed out some columns which appeared to have been melted and run together, from which Sir Humphrey Davy attributed the formation of the Causeway to the action of fire. Bear this is the Giant's Wall, a spring of the purest water, the bottom formed by three perfect hexagons, and the sides of regular columns. One of us observing that no giant had ever drunk from it, the old man answered — "Perhaps not, but it was made by a giant—God Almighty!"

From the well, the Causeway commences—a mass of columns, from triangular to octagonal, lying in compact forms, and extending into the sea. I was somewhat disappointed at first, having supposed the Causeway to be of great height, but I found the Giant's Loom, which is the highest part of it, to be but about fifty feet from the water. The singular appearance of the columns and the many strange forms which they assume, render it nevertheless, an object of the greatest interest. Walking out on the rocks we came to the Ladies' Chair, the seat, back, sides and footstool, being all regularly formed by the broken columns. The guide said that any lady who would take three drinks from the Giant's Well, then sit in this chair and think of any gentleman for whom she had a preference, would be married before a twelvemonth. I asked him if it would answer as well for gentlemen, for by a wonderful coincidence we had each drank three times at the well! He said it would, and thought he was confirming his statement.

A cluster of columns about half-way up the cliff is called the Giant's Organ—from its very striking resemblance to that instrument, and a single rock, worn by the waves into the shape of a rude seat, is his chair. A mile or two further along the coast, two cliffs project from the range, leaving a vast semicircular space between, which, from its resemblance to the old Roman theatres, was appropriated for that purpose by the Giant. Halfway down the crags are two or three pinnacles of rock, called the Chimneys, and the stumps of several others can be seen, which, it is said, were shot off by a vessel belonging to the Spanish Armada, in mistake for the towers of Dunluce Castle. The vessel was afterwards wrecked in the bay below, which has ever since been called Spanish Bay, and in calm weather the wreck may be still seen. Many of the columns of the Causeway have been carried off, and sold as pillars for mantels — and though a notice is put up threatening anyone with the rigor of the law, depredations are occasionally made.

Returning, we left the road at Dunluce, and took a path which led along the summit of the cliffs. The twilight was gathering, and the wind blew with perfect fury, which, combined with the black and stormy sky, gave the coast an air of extreme wildness. All at once, as we followed the winding path, the crags appeared to open before us, disclosing a yawning chasm, down which a large stream, falling in an unbroken sheet, was lost in the gloom below. Witnessed in a calm day, there may perhaps be nothing striking about it, but coming upon us at once, through the gloom of twilight, with the sea thundering below and a scowling sky above, it was absolutely startling.

The path at last wound, with many a steep and slippery bend, down the almost perpendicular crags, to the shore, at the foot of a giant isolated rock, having a natural arch through it, eighty feet in height. We followed the narrow strip of beach, having the bare crags on one side and a line of foaming breakers on the other. It soon grew dark; a furious storm came up and swept like a hurricane along the shore. I then understood what Horne means by "the lengthening javelins of the blast," for every drop seemed to strike with the force of an arrow, and our clothes were soon pierced in every part.

Then we went up among the sand hills, and lost each other in the darkness, when, after stumbling about among the gullies for half an hour, shouting for my companions, I found the road and heard my call answered; but it happened to be two Irishmen, who came up and said — "And is it another gintleman ye're callin' for? we heard someone cryin', and didn't know but somebody might be kilt."

Finally, about eleven o'clock we all arrived at the inn, dripping with rain, and before a warm fire concluded the adventures of our day in Ireland.

Chapter III
BEN LOMOND AND THE HIGHLAND LAKES

The steamboat Londonderry called the next day at Port Rush, and we left in her for Greenock. We ran down the Irish coast, past Dunluce Castle and the Causeway; the Giant's organ was very plainly visible, and the winds were strong enough to have sounded a storm-song upon it. Farther on we had a distant view of Carrick-a-Rede, a precipitous rock, separated by a yawning chasm from the shore, frequented by the catchers of sea-birds. A narrow swinging bridge, which is only passable in calm weather, crosses this chasm, 200 feet above the water.

The deck of the steamer was crowded with Irish, and certainly gave no very favorable impression of the condition of the peasantry of Ireland. On many of their countenances there was scarcely a mark of intelligence—they were a most brutalized and degraded company of beings. Many of them were in a beastly state of intoxication, which, from the contents of some of their pockets, was not likely to decrease. As evening drew on, two or three began singing, and the others collected in groups around them. One of them who sang with great spirit, was loudly applauded, and poured forth song after song, of the most rude and unrefined character.

We took a deck passage for three shillings, in preference to paying twenty for the cabin, and having secured a vacant place near the chimney, kept it during the whole passage. The waves were as rough in the Channel as I ever saw them in the Atlantic, and our boat was tossed about like a plaything. By keeping still we escaped sickness, but we could not avoid the sight of the miserable beings who filled the deck. Many of them spoke in the Irish tongue, and our German friend (the student whom I have already mentioned) noticed in many of the words a resemblance to his mother tongue. I procured a bowl of soup from the steward, but as I was not able to eat it, I gave it to an old man whose hungry look and wistful eyes convinced me it would not be lost on him. He swallowed it with ravenous avidity, together with a crust of bread, which was all I had to give him, and seemed for the time as happy and cheerful as if all his earthly wants were satisfied.

We passed by the foot of Goat Fell, a lofty mountain on the island of Arran, and sped on through the darkness past the hills of Bute, till we entered the Clyde. We arrived at Greenock at one o'clock at night, and walking at random through its silent streets, met a police-man, whom we asked to show us where we might find lodgings. He took my cousin and myself to the house of a poor widow, who had a spare bed which she let to strangers, and then conducted our comrade and the German to another lodging-place.

An Irish strolling musician, who was on board the Dumbarton boat, commenced playing soon after we left Greenock, and, to my surprise, struck at once into "Hail Columbia." Then he gave "the Exile of Erin," with the most touching sweetness; and I noticed that always after playing any air that was desired of him, he would invari-ably return to the sad lament, which I never heard executed with more feeling. It might have been the mild, soft air of the morning, or some peculiar mood of mind that influenced me, but I have been far less affected by music which would be considered immeasurably superior to his. I had been thinking of America, and going up to the old man, I quietly bade him play "Home." It thrilled with a painful delight that almost brought tears to my eyes. My companion started as the sweet melody arose, and turned towards me, his face kindling with emotion.

Dumbarton Rock rose higher and higher as we went up the Clyde, and before we arrived at the town I hailed the dim outline of Ben Lomond, rising far off among the highlands. The town is at the head of a small inlet, a short distance from the rock, which was once surrounded by water. We went immediately to the Castle. The rock is nearly 500 feet high, and from its position and great strength as a fortress, has been called the Gibraltar of Scotland. The top is surrounded with battlements, and the armory and barracks stand in a cleft between the two peaks. We passed down a green lane, around the rock, and entered the castle on the south side. A soldier conducted us through a narrow cleft, overhung with crags, to the summit. Here, from the remains of a round building, called Wallace's Tower, from its having been used as a look-out station by that chieftain, we had a beautiful view of the whole of Leven Vale to Loch Lomond, Ben Lomond and the Highlands, and on the other hand, the Clyde and the Isle of Bute. In the soft and still balminess of the morning, it was a lovely picture. In the armory, I lifted the sword of Wallace, a two-handed weapon, five feet in length. We were also shown a Lochaber battle-axe, from Bannockburn, and several ancient claymores.

We lingered long upon the summit before we forsook the stern fortress for the sweet vale spread out before us. It was indeed a glorious walk, from Dumbarton to Loch Lomond, through this enchanting valley. The air was mild and clear; a few light clouds occasionally crossing the sun, chequered the hills with sun and shade. I have as yet seen nothing that in pastoral beauty can compare with its glassy winding stream, its mossy old woods, and guarding hills—and the ivy-grown, castellated towers embosomed in its forests, or standing on the banks of the Leven—the purest of rivers. At a little village called Renton, is a monument to Smollett, but the inhabitants seem to neglect his memory, as one of the tablets on the pedestal is broken and half fallen away. Further up the vale, a farmer showed us an old mansion in the midst of a group of trees on the bank of the Leven, which he said belonged to Smollett—or Roderick Random, as he called him. Two or three old pear trees were still standing where the garden had formerly been, under which he was accustomed to play in his childhood.

At the head of Leven Vale, we set off in the steamer "Water Witch" over the crystal waters of Loch Lomond, passing Inch Murrin, the deer-park of the Duke of Montrose, and Inch Caillach,

> — "where gray pines wave
> Their shadows o'er Clan Alpine's grave."

Under the clear sky and golden light of the declining sun, we entered the Highlands, and heard on every side names we had learned long ago in the lays of Scott. Here were Glen Fruin and Bannochar, Ross Dhu and the pass of Beal-ma-na. Further still, we passed Rob Roy's rock, where the lake is locked in by lofty mountains. The cone-like peak of Ben Lomond rises far above on the right, Ben Voirlich stands in front, and the jagged crest of Ben Arthur looks over the shoulders of the western hills. A Scotchman on board pointed out to us the remarkable places, and related many interesting legends. Above Inversnaid, where there is a beautiful waterfall, leaping over the rock and glancing out from the overhanging birches, we passed McFarland's Island, concerning the origin of which name, he gave a history. A nephew of one of the old Earls of Lennox, the ruins of whose castle we saw on Inch Murrin, having murdered his uncle's cook in a quarrel, was obliged to flee for his life. Returning after many years, he built a castle upon this island, which was always after named, on account of his exile, *Far-land*. On a precipitous point above Inversnaid, are two caves in the rock; one near the water is called Rob Roy's, though the guides generally call it Bruce's also, to avoid trouble, as the real Bruce's Cave is high up the hill. It is so called, because Bruce hid there one night, from the pursuit of his enemies. It is related that a mountain goat, who used this probably for a sleeping place, entered, trod on his mantle, and aroused him. Thinking his enemies were upon him, he sprang up, and saw the silly animal before him. In token of gratitude for this agreeable surprise, when he became king, a law was passed, declaring goats free throughout all Scotland—unpunishable for whatever trespass they might commit, and the legend further says, that not having been repealed, it continues in force at the present day.

On the opposite shore of the lake is a large rock, called "Bull's Rock," having a door in the side, with a stairway cut through the interior to a pulpit on the top, from which the pastor at Arroquhar preaches a monthly discourse. The Gaelic legend of the rock is, that it once stood near the summit of the mountain above, and was very nearly balanced on the edge of a precipice. Two wild bulls, fighting violently, dashed with great force against the rock, which, being thrown from its balance, was tumbled down the side of the mountain, till it reached its present position. The Scot was speaking with great bitterness of the betrayal of Wallace, when I asked him if it was still considered an insult to turn a loaf of bread bottom upwards in the presence of a Montieth.

"Indeed it is, sir," said he, "I have often done it myself."

Until last May, travellers were taken no higher up the lake than Rob Roy's Cave, but another boat having commenced running, they can now go beyond Loch Lomond, two miles up Glen Falloch, to the Inn of Inverarnan, thereby visiting some of the finest scenery in that part of the Highlands. It was ludicrous, however, to see the steamboat on a river scarcely wider than herself, in a little valley, hemmed in completely with lofty mountains. She went on, however, pushing aside the thickets which lined both banks, and I almost began to think she was going to take the shore for it, when we came to a place widened out for her to be turned around in; here we jumped ashore into a green meadow, on which the cool mist was just beginning to descend.

When we arose in the morning, at 4 o'clock, to return with the boat, the sun was already shining upon the westward hills, scarcely a cloud was in the sky, and the air was pure and cool. To our great delight Ben Lomond was unshrouded, and we were told that a more favorable day for the ascent had not occurred for two months. We left the boat at Rowardennan, an inn at the southern base of Ben Lomond. After breakfasting on Loch Lomond trout, I stole out to the shore while my companions were preparing for the ascent, and made a hasty sketch of the lake.

We purposed descending on the northern side and crossing the Highlands to Loch Katrine; though it was represented as difficult and dangerous by the guide who wished to accompany us, we determined to run the risk of being enveloped in a cloud on the summit, and so set out alone, the path appearing plain before us. We had no difficulty in following it up the lesser heights, around the base. It wound on, over rock and bog, among the heather and broom with which the mountain is covered, sometimes running up a steep acclivity, and then winding zigzag round a rocky ascent. The rains two days before, had made the bogs damp and muddy, but with this exception, we had little trouble for some time. Ben Lomond is a doubly formed mountain. For about three-fourths of the way there is a continued ascent, when it is suddenly terminated by a large barren plain, from one end of which the summit shoots up abruptly, forming at the north side, a precipice 500 feet high. As we approached the summit of the first part of the mountain, the way became very steep and toilsome; but the prospect, which had before been only on the south side, began to open on the east, and we saw suddenly spread out below us, the vale of Menteith, with a "far Loch Ard and Aberfoil" in the centre, and the huge front of Benvenue filling up the picture. Taking courage from this, we hurried on. The heather had become stunted and dwarfish, and the ground was covered with short brown grass. The mountain sheep, which we saw looking at us from the rock above, had worn so many paths along the side, that we could not tell which to take, but pushed on in the direction of the summit, till thinking it must be near at hand, we found a mile and a half of plain before us, with the top of Ben Lomond at the farther end. The plain was full of wet moss, crossed in all directions by deep ravines or gullies worn in it by the mountain rains, and the wind swept across with a tempest-like force.

I met, near the base, a young gentleman from Edinburgh, who had left Rowardennan before us, and we commenced ascending together. It was hard work, but neither liked to stop, so we climbed up to the first resting place, and found the path leading along the brink of a precipice. We soon attained the summit, and climbing up a little mound of earth and stones, I saw the half of Scotland at a glance. The clouds hung just above the mountain tops, which rose all around like the waves of a mighty sea. On every side—near and far—stood their misty summits, but Ben Lomond was the monarch of them all. Loch Lomond lay unrolled under my feet like a beautiful map, and just opposite, Loch Long thrust its head from between the feet of the crowded hills, to catch a glimpse of the giant. We could see from Ben Nevis to Ayr—from Edinburgh to Staffa. Stirling and Edinburgh Castles would have been visible, but that the clouds hung low in the valley of the Forth and hid them from our sight.

The view from Ben Lomond is nearly twice as extensive as that from Catskill, being uninterrupted on every side, but it wants the glorious forest scenery, clear, blue sky, and active, rejoicing charac-ter of the latter. We stayed about two hours upon the summit, taking refuge behind the cairn, when the wind blew strong. I found the smallest of flowers under a rock, and brought it away as a memento. In the middle of the precipice there is a narrow ravine or rather cleft in the rock, to the bottom, from whence the mountain slopes regu-larly but steeply down to the valley. At the bottom we stopped to awake the echoes, which were repeated four times; our German companion sang the Hunter's Chorus, which resounded magnificently through this Highland hall. We drank from the river Forth, which starts from a spring at the foot of the rock, and then commenced descending. This was also toilsome enough. The mountain, was quite wet and covered with loose stones, which, dislodged by our feet, went rattling down the side, oftentimes to the danger of the foremost ones; and when we had run or rather slid down the three miles to the bottom, our knees trembled so as barely to support us.

Here, at a cottage on the farm of Coman, we procured some oat cakes and milk for dinner, from an old Scotch woman, who pointed out the direction of Loch Katrine, six miles distant; there was no road, nor indeed a solitary dwelling between. The hills were bare of trees, covered with scraggy bushes and rough heath, which in some places was so thick we could scarcely drag our feet through. Added to this, the ground was covered with a kind of moss that retained the moisture like a sponge, so that our boots ere long became thoroughly soaked. Several considerable streams were rushing down the side, and many of the wild breed of black Highland cattle were grazing around. After climbing up and down one or two heights, occasionally startling the moorcock and ptarmigan from their heathery coverts, we saw the valley of Loch Con; while in the middle of the plain on the top of the mountain we had ascended, was a sheet of water which we took to be Loch Ackill. Two or three wild fowl swimming on its surface were the only living things in sight. The peaks around shut it out from all view of the world; a single decayed tree leaned over it from a mossy rock, which gave the whole scene an air of the most desolate wildness. I forget the name of the lake; but we learned afterwards that the Highlanders consider it the abode of the fairies, or "men of peace," and that it is still superstitiously shunned by them after nightfall.

From the next mountain we saw Loch Ackill and Loch Katrine below, but a wet and weary descent had yet to be made. I was about throwing off my knapsack on a rock, to take a sketch of Loch Katrine, which appeared very beautiful from this point, when we discerned a cavalcade of ponies winding along the path from Inversnaid, to the head of the lake, and hastened down to take the boat when they should arrive. Our haste turned out to be unnecessary, however, for they had to wait for their luggage, which was long in coming. Two boatmen then offered to take us for two shillings and sixpence each, with the privilege of stopping at Ellen's Isle; the regular fare being two shillings. We got in, when, after exchanging a few words in Gaelic, one of them called to the travellers, of whom there were a number, to come and take passage at two shillings—then at one and sixpence, and finally concluded by requesting them all to step on board the shilling boat! At length, having secured nine at this reduced price, we pushed off; one of the passengers took the helm, and the boat glided merrily over the clear water.

It appears there is some opposition among the boatmen this summer, which is all the better for travelers. They are a bold race, and still preserve many of the characteristics of the clan from which they sprung. One of ours, who had a chieftain-like look, was a MacGregor, related to Rob Roy. The fourth descendant in a direct line, now inhabits the Rob Roy mansion, at Glengyle, a valley at the head of the lake. A small steamboat was put upon Loch Katrine a short time ago, but the boatmen, jealous of this new invasion of their privilege, one night towed her out to the middle of the lake and there sunk her.

Near the point of Brianchoil is a very small island with a few trees upon it, of which the boatman related a story that was new to me. He said an eccentric individual, many years ago, built his house upon it — but it was soon beaten down by the winds and waves. Having built it up with like fortune several times, he at last desisted, saying, "bought wisdom was the best;" since when it has been called the Island of Wisdom. On the shore below, the boatman showed us his cottage. The whole family were out at the door to witness our progress; he hoisted a flag, and when we came opposite, they exchanged shouts in Gaelic. As our men resumed their oars again, we assisted in giving three cheers, which made the echoes of Benvenue ring again. Someone observed his dog, looking after us from a projecting rock, when he called out to him, "go home, you brute!" We asked him why he did not speak Gaelic also to his dog.

"Very few dogs, indeed," said he, "understand Gaelic, but they all understand English. And we therefore all use English when speaking to our dogs; indeed, I know some persons, who know nothing of English, that speak it to their dogs!"

They then sang, in a rude manner, a Gaelic song. The only words I could distinguish was Inch Caillach, the burying place of Clan Alpine. They told us it was the answer of a Highland girl to a foreign lord, who wished to make her his bride. Perhaps, like the American Indian, she would not leave the graves of her fathers. As we drew near the eastern end of the lake, the scenery became far more beautiful. The Trosachs opened before us. Ben Ledi looked down over the "forehead bare" of Ben An, and, as we turned a rocky point, Ellen's isle rose up in front. It is a beautiful little turquoise in the silver setting of Loch Katrine. The northern side alone is accessible, all the others being rocky and perpendicular, and thickly grown with trees. We rounded the island to the little bay, bordered by the silver strand, above which is the rock from which Fitz-James wound his horn, and shot under an ancient oak which flung its long grey arms over the water; we here found a flight of rocky steps, leading to the top, where stood the bower erected by Lady Willoughby D'Eresby, to correspond with Scott's description. Two or three blackened beams are all that remain of it, having been burned down some years ago, by the carelessness of a traveler.

The mountains stand all around, like giants, to "sentinel this enchanted land." On leaving the island, we saw the Goblin's Cave, in the side of Benvenue, called by the Gaels, "Coirnan-Uriskin." Near it is Beal-nam-bo, the pass of cattle, overhung with grey weeping birch trees. Here the boatmen stopped to let us hear the fine echo, and the names of "Rob Roy," and "Roderick Dhu," were sent back to us apparently as loud as they were given. The description of Scott is wonderfully exact, though the forest that feathered over the sides of Benvenue, has since been cut down and sold by the Duke of Montrose. When we reached the end of the lake it commenced raining, and we hastened on through the pass of Beal-an-Duine, scarcely taking time to glance at the scenery, till Loch Achray appeared through the trees, and on its banks the ivy-grown front of the inn of Ardcheancrochan, with its unpronounceable name.

Chapter IV
THE BURNS' FESTIVAL

We passed a glorious summer morning over on the banks of Loch Katrine. The air was pure, fresh and balmy, and the warm sunshine glowed upon forest and lake, upon dark crag and purple mountain-top. The lake was a scene in fairy-land. Returning over the rugged battle-plain in the jaws of the Trosachs, we passed the wild, lonely valley of Glenfinlas and Lanric Mead, at the head of Loch Vennachar, rounding the foot of Ben Ledi to Coilantogle Ford. We saw the desolate hills of Uam-var over which the stag fled from his lair in Glenartney, and keeping on through Callander, stopped for the night at a little inn on the banks of the Teith.

The next day we walked through Doune, over the lowlands to Stirling. Crossing Allan Water and the Forth, we climbed Stirling Castle and looked on the purple peaks of the Ochill Mountains, the far Grampians, and the battlefields of Bannockburn and Sheriff Muir. Our German comrade, feeling little interest in the memory of the poet-ploughman, left in the steamboat for Edinburg; we mounted an English coach and rode to Falkirk, where we took the cars for Glasgow in order to attend the Burns Festival, on the 6th of August.

This was a great day for Scotland—the assembling of all classes to do honor to the memory of her peasant-bard. And right fitting was it, too, that such a meeting should be held on the banks of the Doon, the stream of which he has sung so sweetly, within sight of the cot where he was born, the beautiful monument erected by his country-men, and more than all, beside "Alloway's witch-haunted wall!" One would think old Albyn would rise up at the call, and that from the wild hunters of the northern hills to the shepherds of the Cheviots, half her honest yeomanry would be there, to render gratitude to the memory of the sweet bard who was one of them, and who gave their wants and their woes such eloquent utterance.

For months before had the proposition been made to hold a meet-ing on the Doon, similar to the Shakespeare Festival on the Avon, and the 10th of July was first appointed for the day, but owing to the necessity of further time for preparation, it was postponed until the 6th of August. The Earl of Eglintoun was chosen Chairman, and Professor Wilson Vice-Chairman; in addition to this, all the most eminent British authors were invited to attend. A pavilion, capable of containing two thousand persons, had been erected near the monument, in a large field, which was thrown open to the public. Other preparations were made and the meeting was expected to be of the most interesting character.

When we arose it was raining, and I feared that the weather might dampen somewhat the pleasures of the day, as it had done to the celebrated tournament at Eglintoun Castle. We reached the station in time for the first train, and sped in the face of the wind over the plains of Ayrshire, which, under such a gloomy sky, looked most desolate. We ran some distance along the coast, having a view of the Hills of Arran, and reached Ayr about nine o'clock. We came first to the New Bridge, which had a triumphal arch in the middle, and the lines, from the "Twa Brigs of Ayr":

"Will your poor narrow footpath of a street,
  Where twa wheel-barrows tremble when they meet,
  Your ruin'd, formless bulk d stane and lime,
  Compare wi' bonnie brigs o' modern time?"

While on the arch of the 'old brig' was the reply:

"I'll be a brig when ye're a shapeless stave."

As we advanced into the town, the decorations became more frequent. The streets were crowded with people carrying banners and
wreaths, many of the houses were adorned with green boughs and
the vessels in the harbor hung out all their flags. We saw the Wallace
Tower, a high Gothic building, having in front a statue of Wallace
leaning on his sword, by Thom, a native of Ayr, and on our way to
the green, where the procession was to assemble, passed under the
triumphal arch thrown across the street opposite the inn where Tam
O'Shanter caroused so long with Souter Johnny. Leaving the companies to form on the long meadow bordering the shore, we set out for
the Doon, three miles distant. Beggars were seated at regular distances along the road, uttering the most dolorous whinings. Both
bridges were decorated in the same manner, with miserable looking
objects, keeping up, during the whole day, a continual lamentation.
Persons are prohibited from begging in England and Scotland, but
I suppose, this being an extraordinary day, license was given them
as a favor, to beg free. I noticed that the women, with their usual
kindness of heart, bestowed nearly all the alms which these unfortunate objects received. The night before, as I was walking through the
streets of Glasgow, a young man of the poorer class, very scantily
dressed, stepped up to the and begged me to listen to him for a
moment. He spoke hurriedly, and agitatedly, begging me, in Gods
name, to give him something, however little. I gave him what few
pence I had with me, when he grasped my hand with a quick

motion, saying "Sir, you little think how much you have done for me." I was about to inquire more particularly into his situation, but he had disappeared among the crowd.

We passed the "cairn where hunters found the murdered bairn," along a pleasant road to the Burns cottage, where it was spanned by a magnificent triumphal arch of evergreens and flowers. To the disgrace of Scotland, this neat little thatched cot, where Burns passed the first seven years of his life, is now occupied by somebody, who has stuck up a sign over the door, *licensed to retail spirits, to be drunk on the premises;*" and accordingly the rooms were crowded full of people, all drinking. There was a fine original portrait of Burns in one room, and in the old fashioned kitchen we saw the recess where he was born. The hostess looked towards us as if to inquire what we would drink, and I hastened away—there was profanity in the thought. But by this time, the bell of Old Alloway, which still hangs in its accustomed place, though the walls only are left, began tolling, and we obeyed the call. The attachment of the people for this bell, is so great, that a short time ago, when it was ordered to be removed, the inhabitants rose en masse, and prevented it. The ruin, which is close by the road, stands in the middle of the church-yard, and the first thing I saw, on going in the gate, was the tomb of the father of Burns. I looked in the old window, but the interior was filled with rank weeds, and overshadowed by a young tree, which had grown nearly to the eaves.

The crowd was now fast gathering in the large field, in the midst of which the pavilion was situated. We went down by the beautiful monument to Burns, to the "Auld Brig o' Doon," which was spanned by an arch of evergreens, and contained a representation of Tam O'Shanter and his grey mare, pursued by the witches. It had been arranged that the procession was to pass over the old and new bridges, and from thence by a temporary bridge over the hedge into the field. At this latter place a stand was erected for the sons of Burns, the officers of the day, and distinguished guests. Here was a beautiful specimen of English exclusiveness. The space adjoining the pavilion was fenced around, and admittance denied at first to any, except those who had tickets for the dinner, which, the price being fifteen shillings, entirely prevented the humble laborers, who, more than all, should participate on the occasion, from witnessing the review of the procession by the sons of Burns, and hearing the eloquent speeches of Professor Wilson and Lord Eglintoun. Thus, of the many thousands who were in the field, but a few hundred who were crowded between the bridge and the railing around the pavilion, enjoyed the interesting spectacle. By good fortune, I obtained a stand, where I had an excellent view of the scene. The sons of Burns were in the middle of the platform, with Eglintoun on the right, and Wilson on their left. Mrs. Begg, sister of the Poet, with her daughters, stood by the Countess of Eglintoun. She was a plain, benevolent looking woman, dressed in black, and appearing still active and vigorous, though she is upwards of eighty years old. She bears some likeness, especially in the expression of her eye, to the Poet. Robert Burns, the oldest son, appeared to me to have a strong resemblance of his father, and it is said he is the only one who re-members his face. He has for a long time had an office under Government, in London. The others have but lately returned from a residence of twenty years in India. Professor Wilson appeared to enter into the spirit of the scene better than any of them. He shouted and waved his hat, and, with his fine, broad forehead, his long brown locks already mixed with gray, streaming over his shoulders, and that eagle eye glancing over the vast assemblage, seemed a real Christopher North, yet full of the fire and vigor of youth — "a gray-haired, happy boy!"

About half of the procession consisted of lodges of masons, all of whom turned out on the occasion, as Burns was one of the fraternity. I was most interested in several companies of shepherds, from the hills, with their crooks and plaids; a body of archers in Lincoln green, with a handsome chief at their head, and some Highlanders in their most picturesque of costumes. As one of the companies, which carried a mammoth thistle in a box, came near the platform, Wilson snatched a branch, regardless of its pricks, and placed it on his coat. After this pageant, which could not have been much less than three miles long, had passed, a band was stationed on the platform in the centre of the field, around which it formed in a circle, and the whole company sang, "Ye Banks and Braes o' Bonnie Doon." Just at this time, a person dressed to represent Tam O'Shanter, mounted on a gray mare, issued from a field near the Burns Monument and rode along towards Alloway Kirk, from which, when he approached it, a whole legion of witches sallied out and commenced a hot pursuit. They turned back, however, at the keystone of the bridge, the witch with the "cutty sark" holding up in triumph the abstracted tail of Maggie. Soon after this the company entered the pavilion, and the thousands outside were entertained, as an especial favor, by the band of the 87th Regiment, while from the many liquor booths around the field, they could enjoy themselves in another way.

We went up to the Monument, which was of more particular interest to us, from the relics within, but admission was denied to all. Many persons were collected around the gate, some of whom, having come from a great distance, were anxious to see it; but the keeper only said, such were the orders and he could not disobey them. Among the crowd, a grandson of the original Tam O'Shanter was shown to us. He was a raw-looking boy of nineteen or twenty, wearing a shepherd's cap and jacket, and muttered his disapprobation very decidedly, at not being able to visit the Monument.

There were one or two showers during the day, and the sky, all the time, was dark and lowering, which was unfavorable for the celebration; but all were glad enough that the rain kept aloof till the ceremonies were nearly over. The speeches delivered at the dinner, which appeared in the papers next morning, are undoubtedly very eloquent. I noticed in the remarks of Robert Burns, in reply to Professor Wilson, an acknowledgment which the other speakers forgot. He said, "The Sons of Burns have grateful hearts, and to the last hour of their existence, they will remember the honor that has been paid them this day, by the noble, the lovely and the talented, of their native land — by men of genius and kindred spirit from our sister land — and lastly, they owe their thanks to the inhabitants of the far distant west, a country of a great, free, and kindred people! (loud cheers.)" In regard with this subject, I saw an anecdote of the Poet, yesterday, which is not generally known. During his connection with the Excise, he was one day at a party, where the health of Pitt, then minister, was proposed, as "his master and theirs." He immediately turned down his glass and said, "I will give you the health of a far greater and better man — George Washington!"

We left the field early and went back through the muddy streets of Ayr. The street before the railway office was crowded, and there was so dense a mass of people on the steps, that it seemed almost impossible to get near. Seeing no other chance, I managed to take my stand on the lowest steps, where the pressure of the crowd behind and the working of the throng on the steps, raised me off my feet, and in about a quarter of an hour carried me, compressed into the smallest possible space, up the steps to the door, where the crowd burst in by fits, like water rushing out of a bottle. We esteemed ourselves fortunate in getting room to stand in an open car, where, after a two hours' ride through the wind and pelting rain, we arrived at Glasgow.

Chapter V
WALK FROM EDINBURG OVER THE BORDER AND ARRIVAL AT
  LONDON

We left Glasgow on the morning after returning from the Burns
Festival, taking passage in the open cars for Edinburg, for six shillings. On leaving the depot, we plunged into the heart of the hill on
which Glasgow Cathedral stands and were whisked through darkness and sulphury smoke to daylight again. The cars bore us past a
spur of the Highlands, through a beautiful country where women
were at work in the fields, to Linlithgow, the birthplace of Queen
Mary. The majestic ruins of its once proud palace, stand on a green
meadow behind the town. In another hour we were walking through
Edinburg, admiring its palace-like edifices, and stopping every few
minutes to gaze up at some lofty monument. Really, thought I, we
call Baltimore the "Monumental City" for its two marble columns,
and here is Edinburg with one at every street-corner! These, too, not
in the midst of glaring red buildings, where they seem to have been
accidentally dropped, but framed in by lofty granite mansions,
whose long vistas make an appropriate background to the picture.

We looked from Calton Hill on Salisbury Crags and over the Frith
of Forth, then descended to dark old Holyrood, where the memory
of lovely Mary lingers like a stray sunbeam in her cold halls, and the
fair, boyish face of Rizzio looks down from the canvas on the armor
of his murderer. We threaded the Canongate and climbed to the
Castle; and finally, after a day and a half's sojourn, buckled on our
knapsacks and marched out of the Northern Athens. In a short time
the tall spire of Dalkeith appeared above the green wood, and we
saw to the right, perched on the steep banks of the Esk, the picturesque cottage of Hawthornden, where Drummond once lived in
poetic solitude. We made haste to cross the dreary waste of the

Muirfoot Hills before nightfall, from the highest summit of which we took a last view of Edinburgh Castle and the Salisbury Crags, then blue in the distance. Far to the east were the hills of Lammermuir and the country of Mid-Lothian lay before us. It was all Scotland. The inn of Torsonce, beside the Gala Water, was our resting-place for the night. As we approached Galashiels the next morning, where the bed of the silver Gala is nearly emptied by a number of dingy manufactories, the hills opened, disclosing the sweet vale of the Tweed, guarded by the triple peak of the Eildon, at whose base lay nestled the village of Melrose.

I stopped at a bookstore to purchase a view of the Abbey; to my surprise nearly half the works were by American authors. There were Bryant, Longfellow, Channing, Emerson, Dana, Ware and many others. The bookseller told me he had sold more of Ware's Letters than any other book in his store, "and also," to use his own words, "an immense number of the great Dr. Channing." I have seen English editions of Percival, Willis, Whittier and Mrs. Sigourney, but Bancroft and Prescott are classed among the "standard *British* historians."

Crossing the Gala we ascended a hill on the road to Selkirk, and behold! the Tweed ran below, and opposite, in the midst of embowering trees planted by the hand of Walter Scott, rose the grey halls of Abbotsford. We went down a lane to the banks of the swift stream, but finding no ferry, B —— and I, as it looked very shallow, thought we might save a long walk by wading across. F —— preferred hunting for a boat; we two set out together, with our knapsacks on our backs, and our boots in our hands. The current was ice-cold and very swift, and as the bed was covered with loose stones, it required the greatest care to stand upright. Looking at the bottom, through the rapid water, made my head so giddy, I was forced to stop and shut my eyes; my friend, who had firmer nerves, went plunging on to a deeper and swifter part, where the strength of the current made him stagger very unpleasantly. I called to him to return; the next thing I saw, he gave a plunge and went down to the shoulder in the cold flood. While he was struggling with a frightened expression of face to recover his footing, I leaned on my staff and laughed till I was on the point of falling also. To crown our mortification, F —— had found a ferry a few yards higher up and was on the opposite shore, watching us wade back again, my friend with dripping clothes and boots full of water. I could not forgive the pretty Scotch damsel who rowed us across, the mischievous lurking smile which told that she too had witnessed the adventure.

We found a footpath on the other side, which led through a young forest to Abbotsford. Rude pieces of sculpture, taken from Melrose Abbey, were scattered around the gate, some half-buried in the earth and overgrown with weeds. The niches in the walls were filled with pieces of sculpture, and an antique marble greyhound reposed in the middle of the court yard. We rang the bell in an outer vestibule, ornamented with several pairs of antlers, when a lady appeared, who, from her appearance, I have no doubt was Mrs. Ormand, the "Duenna of Abbotsford," so humorously described by D'Arlincourt, in his "Three Kingdoms." She ushered us into the entrance hall, which has a magnificent ceiling of carved oak and is lighted by lofty stained windows. An effigy of a knight in armor stood at either end, one holding a huge two-handed sword found on Bosworth Field; the walls were covered with helmets and breastplates of the olden time.

Among the curiosities in the Armory are Napoleon's pistols, the blunderbuss of Hofer, Rob Roy's purse and gun, and the offering box of Queen Mary. Through the folding doors between the dining-room, drawing-room and library, is a fine vista, terminated by a niche, in which stands Chantrey's bust of Scott. The ceilings are of carved Scottish oak and the doors of American cedar. Adjoining the library is his study, the walls of which are covered with books; the doors and windows are double, to render it quiet and undisturbed. His books and inkstand are on the table and his writing-chair stands before it, as if he had left them but a moment before. In a little closet adjoining, where he kept his private manuscripts, are the clothes he last wore, his cane and belt, to which a hammer and small axe are attached, and his sword. A narrow staircase led from the study to his sleeping room above, by which he could come down at night and work while his family slept. The silence about the place is solemn and breathless, as if it waited to be broken by his returning footstep. I felt an awe in treading these lonely halls, like that which impressed me before the grave of Washington — a feeling that hallowed the spot, as if there yet lingered a low vibration of the lyre, though the minstrel had departed forever!

Plucking a wild rose that grew near the walls, I left Abbotsford, embosomed among the trees, and turned into a green lane that led down to Melrose. We went immediately to the Abbey, in the lower part of the village, near the Tweed. As I approached the gate, the porteress came out, and having scrutinized me rather sharply, asked my name. I told her;—"well," she added, "there is a *prospect* here for you." Thinking she alluded to the ruin, I replied: "Yes, the view is certainly very fine." "Oh! I don't mean that," she replied, "a young gentleman left, a prospect here for you!"—whereupon she brought out a spy-glass, which I recognized as one that our German comrade had given to me. He had gone on, and hoped to meet us at Jedburgh.

Melrose is the finest remaining specimen of Gothic architecture in Scotland. Some of the sculptured flowers in the cloister arches are remarkably beautiful and delicate, and the two windows—the south and east oriels—are of a lightness and grace of execution really surprising. We saw the tomb of Michael Scott, of King Alexander II, and that of the Douglas, marked with a sword. The heart of Bruce is supposed to have been buried beneath the high altar. The chancel is all open to the sky, and rooks build their nests among the wild ivy that climbs over the crumbling arches. One of these came tamely down and perched upon the hand of our fair guide. By a winding stair in one of the towers we mounted to the top of the arch and looked down on the grassy floor. I sat on the broken pillar, which Walter Scott always used for a seat when he visited the Abbey, and read the disinterring of the magic book, in the "Lay of the Last Minstrel." I never comprehended its full beauty till then; the memory of Melrose will give it a thrilling interest, in the future. When we left, I was willing to say, with the Minstrel:

"Was never scene so sad and fair!"

After seeing the home and favorite haunt of Scott, we felt a wish to stand by his grave, but we had Ancrum Moor to pass before night, and the Tweed was between us and Dryburgh Abbey. We did not wish to try another watery adventure, and therefore walked on to the village of Ancrum, where a gate-keeper on the road gave us lodging and good fare, for a moderate price. Many of this class practise this double employment, and the economical traveller, who looks more to comfort than luxury, will not fail to patronize them.

Next morning we took a footpath over the hills to Jedburgh. From the summit there was a lovely view of the valley of the Teviot, with the blue Cheviots in the distance. I thought of Pringle's beautiful farewell:

"Our native land, our native vale,
    A long, a last adieu,
Farewell to bonny Teviot-dale,
    And Cheviots mountains blue"

The poet was born in the valley below, and one that looks upon its beauty cannot wonder how his heart clung to the scenes he was leaving. We saw Jedburgh and its majestic old Abbey, and ascended the valley of the Jed towards the Cheviots. The hills, covered with woods of a richness and even gorgeous beauty of foliage, shut out this lovely glen completely from the world. I found myself continually coveting the lonely dwellings that were perched on the rocky heights, or nestled, like a fairy pavilion, in the lap of a grove. These forests formerly furnished the wood for the celebrated Jed wood axe, used in the Border forays.

As we continued ascending, the prospect behind us widened, till we reached the summit of the Carter Fell, whence there is a view of great extent and beauty. The Eildon Hills, though twenty-five miles distant, seemed in the foreground of the picture. With a glass, Edinburgh Castle might be seen over the dim outline of the Muirfoot Hills. After crossing the border, we passed the scene of the encounter between Percy and Douglass, celebrated in "Chevy Chase," and at the lonely inn of Whitelee, in the valley below, took up our quarters for the night.

Travellers have described the Cheviots as being bleak and uninteresting. Although they are bare and brown, to me the scenery was of a character of beauty entirely original. They are not rugged and broken like the Highlands, but lift their round backs gracefully from the plain, while the more distant ranges are clad in many an airy hue. Willis quaintly and truly remarks, that travellers only tell you the picture produced in their own brain by what they see, otherwise the world would be like a pawnbroker's shop, where each traveller wears the cast-off clothes of others. Therefore let no one, of a gloomy temperament, journeying over the Cheviots in dull November, arraign me for having falsely praised their beauty.

I was somewhat amused with seeing a splendid carriage with footmen and outriders, crossing the mountain, the glorious landscape full in view, containing a richly dressed lady, fast asleep! It is no uncommon thing to meet carriages in the Highlands, in which the occupants are comfortably reading, while being whirled through the finest scenery. And apropos of this subject, my German friend related to me an incident. His brother was travelling on the Rhine, and when in the midst of the grandest scenes, met a carriage containing an English gentleman and lady, both asleep, while on the seat behind was stationed an artist, sketching away with all his might. He asked the latter the reason of his industry, when he answered, "Oh! my lord wishes to see every night what he has passed during the day, and so I sketch as we go along!"

The hills, particularly on the English side, are covered with flocks of sheep, and lazy shepherds lay basking in the sun, among the purple heather, with their shaggy black dogs beside them. On many of the hills are landmarks, by which, when the snow has covered all the tracks, they can direct their way. After walking many miles through green valleys, down which flowed the Red Water, its very name telling of the conflicts which had crimsoned its tide, we came to the moors, and ten miles of blacker, drearier waste I never saw. Before entering them we passed the pretty little village of Otterburn, near the scene of the battle. I brought away a wild flower that grew on soil enriched by the blood of the Percys. On the village inn, is their ancient coat of arms, a lion rampant, on a field of gold, with the motto, "*Esperance en Dieu.*" Scarcely a house or a tree enlivened the black waste, and even the road was marked on each side by high poles, to direct the traveller in winter. We were glad when at length the green fields came again in sight, and the little village of Whelpington Knowes, with its old ivy-grown church tower, welcomed us after the lonely walk.

At the only inn in the place, I found it quite impossible to understand the servants, who spoke the rugged Northumbrian dialect. The landlady, who spoke tolerable English, came to our assistance, and received us with more cordiality than our knapsacks and dusty garments led us to expect. She quartered us for the night in an outbuilding, which appeared to be a kind of hunting lodge. It was a single room, with two beds, fowling-pieces and shot-belts hanging on the walls, and some stuffed grouse on the top of a quaint old wardrobe. The evening was cool, and the unintelligible servants made a cheerful fire on the hearth. Our supper was served in a room of the inn, which was occupied by a young lady, whose appearance contrasted strangely with her situation. She was pale, but handsome, dressed with perfect taste, and the few words she spoke gave evidence of thorough refinement and cultivation. Her face was very sad, her manner subdued, yet with a quiet dignity which forced the landlady, who made very unceremonious use of her room, to treat her with respect. A shelf of classic authors, and some flower-pots in the window, were the tokens of her tastes. Here is a romance, if not a tragedy, I thought, but I did not venture to ask any questions.

As one specimen of the intelligence of this part of England, we saw a board conspicuously posted at the commencement of a private road, declaring that "all persons travelling this way will be *persecuted.*" As it led to a church, however, there may have been a design in the expression.

On the fifth day after leaving Edinburgh, we reached a hill, overlooking the valley of the Tyne and the German Ocean, as sunset was reddening in the west. A cloud of coal-smoke made us aware of the vicinity of Newcastle. On the summit of the hill a large cattle fair was being held, and crowds of people were gathered in and around a camp of gaudily decorated tents. Fires were kindled here and there, and drinking, carousing and horse-racing were flourishing in full vigor. After entering the town, we applied to a policeman to conduct us to a cheap lodging-place. He readily took us to a house in a dingy street near the river, inhabited by a poor family, who furnished us with beds (probably their own), and cooked us frugal meals, during the two days that we were obliged to await the departure of a steamer for London.

We set out one morning to hunt the Roman Wall. Passing the fine buildings in the centre of the city and the lofty monument to Earl Grey, we went towards the western gate and soon came to the ruins of a building, about whose origin there could be no doubt. It stood there, blackened by the rust of ages, a remnant of power passed away. There was no mistaking the massive round tower, with its projecting ornaments, such as are often seen in the ruder works of the

Romans. On each side a fragment of wall remained standing, and there appeared to be a chamber in the interior, which was choked up with rubbish. There is another tower, much higher, in a public square in another part of the city, a portion of which is fitted up as a dwelling for the family which takes care of it; but there was such a ridiculous contrast between the ivy-grown top, and the handsome modern windows and doors of the lower story, that it did not impress me half as much as the other, with all its neglect. These are the farthest limits of that power whose mighty works I hope hereafter to view at the seat of her grandeur and glory.

I witnessed a scene at Newcastle that cannot soon be forgotten; as it showed more plainly than I had before an opportunity of observing, the state to which the laboring classes of England are reduced. Hearing singing in the street, under my window, one morning, I looked out and saw a body of men, apparently of the lower class, but decent and sober looking, who were singing in a rude and plaintive strain some ballad, the purport of which I could not understand. On making inquiry, I discovered it was part of a body of miners, who, about eighteen weeks before, in consequence of not being. able to support their families with the small pittance allowed them, had "struck" for higher wages. This their employers refused to give them, and sent to Wales, where they obtained workmen at the former price. The houses these laborers had occupied were all taken from them, and for eighteen weeks they had no other means of subsistence than the casual charity given them for singing the story of their wrongs. It made my blood boil to hear those tones, wrung from the heart of poverty by the hand of tyranny. The ignorance, permitted by the government, causes an unheard amount of misery and degradation. We heard afterwards in the streets, another company who played on musical instruments. Beneath the proud swell of England's martial airs, there sounded to my ears a tone whose gathering murmur will make itself heard not before long by the dull ears of Power.

At last at the appointed time, we found ourselves on board the "London Merchant," in the muddy Tyne, waiting for the tide to rise high enough to permit us to descend the river. There is great competition among the steamboats this summer, and the price of passage to London is reduced to five and ten shillings. The second cabin, however, is a place of tolerable comfort, and as the steward had promised to keep berths for us, we engaged passage. Following the windings of the narrow river, we passed Sunderland and Tynemouth, where it expands into the German Ocean. The water was barely stirred by a gentle wind, and little resembled the stormy sea I expected to find it. We glided over the smooth surface, watching the blue line of the distant shore till dark, when I went below expecting to enjoy a few hours' oblivion. But the faithless steward had given up the promised berth to another, and it was only with difficulty that I secured a seat by the cabin table, where I dozed half the night with my head on my arms. It grew at last too close and wearisome; I went up on deck and lay down on the windlass, taking care to balance myself well before going to sleep. The earliest light of dawn awoke me to a consciousness of damp clothes and bruised limbs. We were in sight of the low shore the whole day, sometimes seeing the dim outline of a church, or group of trees over the downs or flat beds of sand, which border the eastern coast of England. About dark, the red light of the Nore was seen, and we hoped before many hours to be in London. The lights of Gravesend were passed, but about ten o'clock, as we entered the narrow channel of the Thames, we struck another steamboat in the darkness, and were obliged to cast anchor for some time.

When I went on deck in the gray light of morning again, we were gliding up a narrow, muddy river, between rows of gloomy buildings, with many vessels lying at anchor. It grew lighter, till, as we turned a point, right before me lay a vast crowd of vessels, and in the distance, above the wilderness of buildings, stood a dim, gigantic dome in the sky; what a bound my heart gave at the sight! And the tall pillar that stood near it—I did not need a second glance to recognize the Monument. I knew the majestic bridge that spanned the river above; but on the right bank stood a cluster of massive buildings, crowned with many a turret, that attracted my eye. A crowd of old associations pressed bewilderingly upon the mind, to see standing there, grim and dark with many a bloody page of England's history—the Tower of London! The morning sky was as yet but faintly obscured by the coal-smoke, and in the misty light of coming sunrise, all objects seemed grander than their wont. In spite of the thrilling interest of the scene, I could not help thinking of Byron's ludicrous but most expressive description:

"A mighty mass of brick and smoke and shipping,
　　Dirty and dusky, but as wide as eye
　　Can reach; with here and there a sail just skipping
　　In sight, then lost amidst the forestry
　　Of masts; a wilderness of steeples peeping
　　On tiptoe through their sea-coal canopy;
　　A huge dun cupola, like a fool's-cap crown
　　On a fool's head, —and there is London town"

Chapter VI
SOME OF THE "SIGHTS" OF LONDON

In the course of time we came to anchor in the stream; skiffs from the shore pulled alongside, and after some little quarrelling, we were safely deposited in one, with a party who desired to be landed at the Tower Stairs. The dark walls frowned above us as we mounted from the water and passed into an open square on the outside of the moat. The laborers were about commencing work, the fashionable day having just closed, but there was still noise and bustle enough in the streets, particularly when we reached Whitechapel, part of the great thoroughfare, extending through the heart of London to Westminster Abbey and the Parliament buildings. Further on, through Leadenhall street and Fleet street — what a world! Here come the ever-thronging, ever-rolling waves of life, pressing and whirling on in their tumultuous career. Here day and night pours the stream of human beings, seeming amid the roar and din and clatter of the passing vehicles, like the tide of some great combat. How lonely it makes one to stand still and feel that of all the mighty throng which divides itself around him, not a being knows or cares for him! What knows he too of the thousands who pass him by? How many who bear the impress of godlike virtue, or hide beneath a goodly countenance a heart black with crime? How many fiery spirits, all glowing with hope for the yet unclouded future, or brooding over a darkened and desolate past in the agony of despair? There is a sublimity in this human Niagara that makes one look on his own race with something of awe.

We walked down the Thames, through the narrow streets of Wapping. Over the mouth of the Tunnel is a large circular building, with a dome to light the entrance below. Paying the fee of a penny, we descended by a winding staircase to the bottom, which is seventy-three feet below the surface. The carriageway, still unfinished, will extend further into the city. From the bottom the view of the two arches of the Tunnel, brilliantly lighted with gas, is very fine; it has a much less heavy and gloomy appearance than I expected. As we walked along under the bed of the river, two or three girls at one end began playing on the French horn and bugle, and the echoes, when not too deep to confuse the melody, were remarkably beautiful. Between the arches of the division separating the two passages, are shops, occupied by venders of fancy articles, views of the Tunnel, engravings, &c. In the middle is a small printing press, where a sheet containing a description of the whole work is printed for those who desire it. As I was no stranger to this art, I requested the boy to let me print one myself, but he had such a bad roller I did not succeed in getting a good impression. The air within is somewhat damp, but fresh and agreeably cool, and one can scarcely realize in walking along the light passage, that a river is rolling above his head. The immense solidity and compactness of the structure precludes the danger of accident, each of the sides being arched outwards, so that the heaviest pressure only strengthens the whole. It will long remain a great noble monument of human daring and ingenuity.

St. Paul's is on a scale of grandeur excelling everything I have yet seen. The dome seems to stand in the sky, as you look up to it; the distance from which you view it, combined with the atmosphere of London, give it a dim, shadowy appearance, that perfectly startles one with its immensity. The roof from which the dome springs is itself as high as the spires of most other churches—blackened for two hundred years with the coal-smoke of London, it stands like a relic of the giant architecture of the early world. The interior is what one would expect to behold, after viewing the outside. A maze of grand arches on every side, encompasses the dome, which you gaze up at, as at the sky; and from every pillar and wall look down the marble forms of the dead. There is scarcely a vacant niche left in all of this mighty hall, so many are the statues that one will meet on every side. With the exceptions of John Howard, Sir Astley Cooper and Wren, whose monument is the church itself, they are all to military men. I thought if they had all been removed except Howard's, it would better have suited such a temple, and the great soul it commemorated.

I never was more impressed with the grandeur of human invention, than when ascending the dome. I could with difficulty conceive the means by which such a mighty edifice had been lifted into the air. That small frame of Sir Christopher Wren must have contained a mind capable of vast conceptions. The dome is like the summit of a mountain; so wide is the prospect, and so great the pile upon which you stand. London lay beneath us, like an ant-hill, with the black insects swarming to and fro in their long avenues, the sound of their employments coming up like the roar of the sea. A cloud of coal-smoke hung over it, through which many a pointed spire was thrust up; sometimes the wind would blow it aside for a moment, and the thousands of red roofs would shine out clearer. The bridged Thames, covered with craft of all sizes, wound beneath us like a ringed and spotted serpent. The scene was like an immense circular picture in the blue frame of the hills around.

Continuing our way up Fleet street, which, notwithstanding the gaiety of its shops and its constant bustle, has an antique appearance, we came to the Temple Bar, the western boundary of the ancient city. In the inside of the middle arch, the old gates are still standing. From this point we entered the new portion of the city, which wore an air of increasing splendor as we advanced. The appearance of the Strand and Trafalgar Square is truly magnificent. Fancy every house in Broadway a store, all built of light granite, the Park stripped of all its trees and paved with granite, and a lofty column in the centre, double the crowd and the tumult of business, and you will have some idea of the view.

It was a relief to get into St. James's Park, among the trees and flowers again. Here, beautiful winding walks led around little lakes, in which were hundreds of water-fowl, swimming. Groups of merry children were sporting on the green lawn, enjoying their privilege of roaming everywhere at will, while the older bipeds were confined to the regular walks. At the western end stood Buckingham Palace, looking over the trees towards St. Paul's; through the grove on the eminence above, the towers of St. James's could be seen. But there was a dim building, with two lofty square towers, decorated with a profusion of pointed Gothic pinnacles, that I looked at with more interest than these appendages of royalty. I could not linger long in its vicinity, but going back again by the Horse Guards, took the road to Westminster Abbey.

We approached by the general entrance, Poet's Corner. I hardly stopped to look at the elaborate exterior of Henry VIIth's Chapel, but passed on to the door. On entering, the first thing that met my eyes were the words, "OH RARE BEN JONSON" under his bust. Near by stood the monuments of Spenser and Gay, and a few paces further looked down the sublime countenance of Milton. Never was a spot so full of intense interest. The light was just dim enough to give it a solemn, religious appearance, making the marble forms of poets and philosophers so shadowy and impressive, that I felt as if standing in their living presence. Every step called up some mind linked with the associations of my childhood. There was the gentle feminine countenance of Thompson, and the majestic head of Dryden; Addison with his classic features, and Gray full of the fire of lofty thought. In another chamber, I paused long before the ashes of Shakespeare; and while looking at the monument of Garrick, started to find that I stood upon his grave. What a glorious galaxy of genius is here collected—what a constellation of stars whose light is immortal! The mind is completely fettered by their spirit. Everything is forgotten but the mighty dead, who still "rule us from their urns."

The Chapel of Henry VII., which we next entered, is one of the most elaborate specimens of Gothic workmanship in the world. If the first idea of the Gothic arch sprung from observing the forms of trees, this chapel must resemble the first conceptions of that order, for the fluted columns rise up like tall trees, branching out at the top into spreading capitals covered with leaves, and supporting arches of the ceiling resembling a leafy roof.

The side-chapels are filled with tombs of knightly families, the husband and wife lying on their backs on the tombs, with their hands clasped, while their children, about the size of dolls, are kneeling around. Numberless are the Barons and Earls and Dukes, whose grim effigies stare from their tombs. In opposite chapels are the tombs of Mary and Elizabeth, and near the former that of Darnley. After having visited many of the scenes of her life, it was with no ordinary emotion that I stood by the sepulchre of Mary. How differently one looks upon it and upon that of the proud Elizabeth!

We descended to the Chapel of Edward the Confessor, within the splendid shrine of which repose his ashes. Here we were shown the chair on which the English monarchs have been crowned for several hundred years. Under the seat is the stone, brought from the Abbey of Scone, whereon the Kings of Scotland were crowned. The chair is of oak, carved and hacked over with names, and on the bottom someone has recorded his name with the fact that he once slept in it. We sat down and rested in it without ceremony. Passing along an aisle leading to the grand hall, we saw the tomb of Aymer de Valence, a knight of the Crusades. Near here is the hall where the Knights of the order of Bath met. Over each seat their dusty banners are still hanging, each with its crest, and their armor is rusting upon the wall. It seemed like a banqueting ball of the olden time, where the knights had left their seats for a moment vacant. Entering the nave, we were lost in the wilderness of sculpture. Here stood the forms of Pitt, Fox, Burke, Sheridan and Watts, from the chisels of Chantry, Bacon and Westmacott. Further down were Sir Isaac Newton and Sir Godfrey Kneller—opposite Andre, and Paoli, the Italian, who died here in exile. How can I convey an idea of the scene? Notwithstanding all the descriptions I had read, I was totally unprepared for the reality, nor could I have anticipated the hushed and breathless interest with which I paced the dim aisles, gazing, at every step, on the last resting place of some great and familiar name. A place so sacred to all who inherit the English tongue, is worthy of a special pilgrimage across the deep. To those who are unable to visit it, a description may be interesting; but so far does it fall short of the scene itself, that if I thought it would induce a few of our wealthy idlers, or even those who, like myself, must travel with toil and privation to come hither, I would write till the pen dropped from my hand.

More than twenty grand halls of the British Museum are devoted to antiquities, and include the Elgin Marbles — the spoils of the Parthenon — the Fellows Marbles, brought from the ancient city of Xanthus, and Sir William Hamilton's collection of Italian antiquities. It was painful to see the friezes of the Parthenon, broken and defaced as they are, in such a place. Rather let them moulder to dust on the ruin from which they were torn, shining through the blue veil of the Grecian atmosphere, from the summit of the Acropolis!

The National Gallery, on Trafalgar Square, is open four days in the week, to the public. The "Raising of Lazarus," by Sebastian del Piombo, is considered the gem of the collection, but my unschooled eyes could not view it as such. It is also remarkable for having been transferred from wood to canvas, without injury. This delicate operation was accomplished by gluing the panel on which it was painted, flat on a smooth table, and planing the wood gradually away till the coat of hardened paint alone remained. A proper canvass was then prepared, covered with a strong cement, and laid on the back of the picture, which adhered firmly to it. The owner's nerves must have had a severe trial, if he had courage to actually watch the operation. I was enraptured with Murillo's pictures of St. John and the Holy Family. St. John is represented as a boy in the woods, fondling a lamb. It is a glorious head. The dark curls cluster around his fair brow, and his eyes seem already glowing with the fire of future inspiration. There is an innocence, a childish sweetness of expression in the countenance, which makes one love to gaze upon it. Both of these paintings were constantly surrounded by ladies, and they certainly deserved the preference. In the rooms devoted to the English artists, there are many of the finest works of West, Reynolds, Hogarth and Wilkie.

We spent a day in visiting the *lungs of London,* as the two grand parks have been called. From the Strand through the Regent Circus, the centre of the fashionable part of the city, we passed to Piccadilly, calling on our way to see our old friends, the Iowas. They were at the Egyptian Hall, in connection with Catlin's Indian collection. The old braves knew us at once, particularly Blister Feet, who used often to walk a line on deck with me, at sea. Further along Piccadilly is Wellington's mansion of Apsley House, and nearly opposite it, in the corner of Hyde Park, stands the colossal statue of Achilles, cast from cannon taken at Salamanca and Vittoria. The Park resembles an open common, with here and there a grove of trees, intersected by carriage roads. It is like getting into the country again to be out on its broad, green field, with the city seen dimly around through the smoky atmosphere. We walked for a mile or two along the shady avenues and over the lawns, having a view of the princely terraces and gardens on one hand, and the gentle outline, of Primrose Hill on the other. Regent's Park itself covers a space of nearly four hundred acres!

But if London is unsurpassed in splendor, it has also its corresponding share of crime. Notwithstanding the large and efficient body of police, who do much towards the control of vice, one sees enough of degradation and brutality in a short time, to make his heart sick. Even the public thoroughfares are thronged at night with characters of the lowest description, and it is not expedient to go through many of the narrow bye-haunts of the old city in the daytime. The police, who are ever on the watch, immediately seize and carry off any offender, but from the statements of persons who have had an opportunity of observing, as well as from my own slight experience, I am convinced that there is an untold amount of misery and crime. London is one of the wonders of the world, but there is reason to believe it is one of the curses of the world also; though, in fact, nothing but an active and unceasing philanthropy can prevent any city from becoming so.

Aug. 22. — I have now been six days in London, and by making good use of my feet and eyes, have managed to become familiar with almost every object of interest within its precincts. Having a plan mapped out for the day, I started from my humble lodgings at the Aldgate Coffee House, where I slept off fatigue for a shilling a night, and walked up Cheapside or down Whitechapel, as the case might be, hunting out my way to churches, halls and theatres. In this way, at a trifling expense, I have perhaps seen as much as many who spend here double the time and ten times the money. Our whole tour from Liverpool hither, by way of Ireland and Scotland, cost us but twenty-five dollars each! although, except in one or two cases, we denied ourselves no necessary comfort. This shows that the glorious privilege of looking on the scenes of the old world need not be confined to people of wealth and leisure. It may be enjoyed by all who can occasionally forego a little bodily comfort for the sake of mental and spiritual gain. We leave this afternoon for Dover. Tomorrow I shall dine in Belgium!

Chapter VII
FLIGHT THROUGH BELGIUM

Bruges. — On the Continent at last! How strangely look the century-old towers, antique monuments, and quaint, narrow streets of the Flemish cities! It is an agreeable and yet a painful sense of novelty to stand for the first time in the midst of a people whose language and manners are quite different from one's own. The old buildings around, linked with many stirring associations of past history, gratify the glowing anticipations with which one has looked forward to seeing them, and the fancy is busy at work reconciling the *real* scene with the *ideal;* but the want of a communication with the living world about, walls one up with a sense of loneliness one could not before have conceived. I envy the children in the streets of Bruges their childish language.

Yesterday afternoon we came from London through the green wooded lawns and vales of England, to Dover, which we reached at sunset, passing by a long tunnel through the lofty Shakespeare Cliff.

We had barely time before it grew dark to ascend the cliff. The glorious coast view looked still wilder in the gathering twilight, which soon hid from our sight the dim hills of France. On the cliff opposite frowned the massive battlements of the Castle, guarding the town, which lay in a nook of the rocks below. As the Ostend boat was to leave at four in the morning, my cousin aroused us at three, and we felt our way down stairs in the dark. But the landlord was reluctant to part with us; we stamped and shouted and rang bolls, till the whole house was in an uproar, for the door was double-locked, and the steamboat bell began to sound. At last he could stand it no longer; we gave a quick utterance to our overflowing wrath and rushed down to the boat but a second or two before it left.

The water of the Channel was smooth as glass and as the sun rose, the far chalky cliffs gleamed along the horizon, a belt of fire. I waved a goodbye to Old England and then turned to see the spires of Dunkirk, which were visible in the distance before us. On the low Belgian coast we could see trees and steeples, resembling a mirage over the level surface of the sea; at length, about ten o'clock, the square tower of Ostend came in sight. The boat passed into a long muddy basin, in which many unwieldy, red-sailed Dutch craft were lying, and stopped beside a high pier. Here amid the confusion of three languages, an officer came on board and took charge of our passports and luggage. As we could not get the former for two or three hours, we did not hurry the passing of the latter, and went on shore quite unincumbered, for a stroll about the city, disregarding the cries of the hackney-coachmen on the pier, "*Hôtel d'Angleterre,*" "*Hôtel des Bains!*" and another who called out in English, "I recommend you to the Royal Hotel, sir!"

There is little to be seen in Ostend. We wandered through long rows of plain yellow houses, trying to read the French and low Dutch signs, and at last came out on the wall near the sea. A soldier motioned us back as we attempted to ascend it, and muttering some unintelligible words, pointed to a narrow street near. Following this out of curiosity, we crossed the moat and found ourselves on the great bathing beach. To get out of the hands of the servants who immediately surrounded us, we jumped into one of the little wagons and were driven out into the surf.

To be certain of fulfilling the railroad regulations, we took our seats quarter of an hour before the time. The dark walls of Ostend soon vanished and we were whirled rapidly over a country perfectly level, but highly fertile and well-cultivated. Occasionally there was a ditch or row of trees, but otherwise there was no division between the fields, and the plain stretched unbroken away into the distance. The twenty miles to Bruges we made in forty minutes. The streets of this antique city are narrow and crooked, and the pointed, orna-mented gables of the houses, produce a novel impression on one who has been accustomed to the green American forests. Then there was the endless sound of wooden shoes clattering over the rough pavements, and people talking in that most unmusical of all lan-guages, low Dutch. Walking at random through the streets, we came by chance upon the Cathedral of Notre Dame. I shall long remember my first impression of the scene within. The lofty gothic ceiling arched far above my head and through the stained windows the light came but dimly—it was all still, solemn and religious. A few wor-shippers were kneeling in silence before some of the shrines and the echo of my tread seemed like a profaning sound. On every side were pictures, saints and gilded shrines. A few steps removed one from the bustle and din of the crowd to the stillness and solemnity of the holy retreat.

We learned from the guide, whom we had engaged because he spoke a few words of English, that there was still a *treckshuyt* line on the canals, and that one boat leaves tonight at ten o'clock for Ghent. Wishing to try this old Dutch method of travelling, he took us about half a mile along the Ghent road to the canal, where a moderate sized boat was lying. Our baggage deposited in the plainly furnished cabin, I ran back to Bruges, although it was beginning to grow dark, to get a sight of the belfry; for Longfellow's lines had been running through my head all day:

"In the market place of Bruges,
  stands the belfry old and brown,
  Thrice consumed and thrice rebuilded,
  still it watches o'er the town."

And having found the square, brown tower in one corner of the open market square, we waited to hear the chimes, which are said to be the finest in Europe. They rang out at last with a clear silvery tone, most beautifully musical indeed. We then returned to the boat in the twilight. We were to leave in about an hour, according to the arrangement, but as yet there was no sound to be heard, and we were the only tenants. However, trusting to Dutch regularity, we went to sleep in the full confidence of awakening in Ghent.

I awoke once in the night and saw the dark branches of trees passing before the window, but there was no perceptible sound nor motion; the boat glided along like a dream, and we were awakened next morning by its striking against the pier at Ghent. After paying three francs for the whole night journey, the captain gave us a guide to the railroad station, and as we had nearly an hour before the train left, I went to see the Cathedral of St. Bavon. After leaving Ghent, the road passes through a beautiful country, cultivated like a garden. The Dutch passion for flowers is displayed in the gardens around the cottages; even every vacant foot of ground along the railway is plant-ed with roses and dahlias. At Ghent, the morning being fair, we took seats in the open cars. About noon it commenced raining and our situation was soon anything but comfortable. My cousin had fortu-nately a waterproof Indian blanket with him, which he had pur-chased in the "Far West," and by wrapping this around all three of us, we kept partly dry. I was much amused at the plight of a party of young Englishmen, who were in the same car; one of them held a little parasol which just covered his hat, and sent the water in streams down on his back and shoulders.

We had a misty view of Liege, through the torrents of rain, and then dashed away into the wild, mountain scenery of the Meuse. Steep, rocky hills, covered with pine and crowned with ruined towers, hemmed in the winding and swollen river, and the wet, cloudy sky seemed to rest like a canopy on their summits. Instead of threading their many tight passages, we plunged directly into the mountain's heart, flew over the narrow valley on lofty and light-sprung arches, and went again into the darkness. At Verviers, our baggage was weighed, examined and transferred, with ourselves, to a Prussian train. There was a great deal of disputing on the occasion. A lady, who had a dog in a large willow basket, was not allowed to retain it, nor would they take it as baggage. The matter was finally compromised by their sending the basket, obliging tier to carry the dog, which was none of the smallest, in her arms! The next station bore the sign of the black eagle, and here our passports were obliged to be given up. Advancing through long ranges of wooded hills, we saw at length, in the dull twilight of a rainy day, the old kingly city of Aix la Chapelle on a plain below us. After a scene at the custom-house, where our baggage was reclaimed with tickets given at Verviers, we drove to the *Hôtel du Rhin,* and while warming our shivering limbs and drying our damp garments, felt tempted to exclaim with the old Italian author: "O! holy and miraculous tavern!"

The Cathedral with its lofty Gothic tower, was built by the emperor Otho in the tenth century. It seems at present to he undergoing repairs, for a large scaffold shut out the dome. The long hall was dim with incense smoke as we entered, and the organ sounded through the high arches with an effect that startled me. The windows glowed with the forms of kings and saints, and the dusty and mouldering shrines which rose around were colored with the light that came through. The music pealed out like a triumphal march, sinking at times into a mournful strain, as if it celebrated and lamented the heroes who slept below. In the stone pavement nearly under my feet was a large square marble slab, with words "CAROLO MAGNO." It was like a dream, to stand there on the tomb of the mighty warrior, with the lofty arches of the Cathedral above, filled with the sound of the divine anthem. I mused above his ashes till the music ceased and then left the Cathedral, that nothing might break the romantic spell associated with that crumbling pile and the dead it covered. I have always revered the memory of Charlemagne. He lived in a stern age, but he was in mind and heart a man, and like Napoleon, who placed the iron crown which had lain with him centuries in the tomb, upon his own brow, he had an Alpine grandeur of mind, which the world was forced to acknowledge.

At noon we took the *chars-à-banc, or* second-class carriages, for fear of rain, and continued our journey over a plain dotted with villages and old chateaux. Two or three miles from Cologne we saw the spires of the different churches, conspicuous among which were the unfinished towers of the Cathedral, with the enormous crane standing as it did when they left off building, two hundred years ago or more. On arriving, we drove to the Bonn railway, where finding the last train did not leave for four hours, we left our baggage and set out for the Cathedral. Of all Gothic buildings, the plan of this is certainly the most stupendous; even ruin as it is, it cannot fail to excite surprise and admiration. The King of Prussia has undertaken to complete it according to the original plan, which was lately found in the possession of a poor man, of whom it was purchased for 40,000 florins, but he has not yet finished repairing what is already built. The legend concerning this plan may not be known to everyone. It is related of the inventor of it, that in despair of finding any sufficiently great, he was walking one day along the river, sketching with his stick upon the sand, when he finally hit upon one which pleased him so much that he exclaimed: "This must be the plan!" "I will show you a better one than that!" said a voice suddenly behind him, and a certain black gentleman who figures in all German legends stood by him, and pulled from his pocket a roll containing the present plan of the Cathedral. The architect, amazed at its grandeur, asked an explanation of every part. As he knew his soul was to be the price of it, he occupied himself while the devil was explaining, in committing its proportions carefully to memory. Having done this, he remarked that it did not please him and he would not take it. The devil, seeing through the cheat, exclaimed in his rage: "You may build your Cathedral according to this plan, but you shall never finish it!" This prediction seems likely to be verified, for though it was commenced in 1248, and built for 250 years, only the choir and nave and one tower to half its original height, are finished.

We visited the chapel of the eleven thousand virgins, the walls of which are full of curious grated cells, containing their bones, and then threaded the narrow streets of Cologne, which are quite dirty enough to justify Coleridge's lines:

"The river Rhine, it is well known
  Doth wash the city of Cologne;
  But tell me nymphs, what power divine
  Shall henceforth wash the river Rhine!"

Chapter VIII
THE RHINE TO HEIDELBERG

HEIDELBERG, August 30.

Here at last! and a most glorious place it is. This is our first morning in our new rooms, and the sun streams warmly in the eastern windows, as I write, while the old castle rises through the blue vapor on the side of the Kaiserstuhl. The Neckar rushes on below; and the Odenwald, before me, rejoices with its vineyards in the morning light. The bells of the old chapel near us are sounding most musically, and a confused sound of voices and the rolling of vehicles comes up from the street. It is a place to live in!

I must go back five or six days and take up the record of our journeyings at Bonn. We had been looking over Murray's infallible "Handbook," and observed that he recommended the "Star" hotel in that city, as "the most moderate in its prices of any on the Rhine;" so when the train from Cologne arrived and we were surrounded, in the darkness and confusion, by porters and valets, I sung out: *"Hôtel de l'Etoile d'or!"* our baggage and ourselves were transferred to a stylish omnibus, and in five minutes we stopped under a brilliantly-lighted archway, where Mr. Joseph Schmidt received us with the usual number of smiles and bows bestowed upon untitled guests. We were furnished with neat rooms in the summit of the house, and then descended to the *salle à manger*. I found a folded note by my plate, which I opened—it contained an engraving of the front of the hotel, a plan of the city and catalogue of its lions, together with a list of the titled personages who have, from time to time, honored the "Golden Star" with their custom. Among this number were "Their Royal Highnesses the Duke and Duchess of Cambridge, Prince Albert," etc. Had it not been for fatigue, I should have spent an uneasy night, thinking of the heavy bill which was to be presented on the morrow. We escaped, however, for seven francs apiece, three of which were undoubtedly for the honor of breathing an aristocratic atmosphere.

I was glad when we were really in motion on the swift Rhine, the next morning, and nearing the chain of mountains that rose up before us. We passed Godesberg on the right, while on our left was the group of the seven mountains which extend back from the Drachenfels to the Wolkenberg, or Castle of the Clouds. Here we begin to enter the enchanted land. The Rhine sweeps around the foot of the Drachenfels, while opposite the precipitous rock of Rolandseck, crowned with the castle of the faithful knight, looks down upon the beautiful Island of Nonnenwerth, the white walls of the convent still gleaming through the trees, as they did when the warrior's weary eyes looked upon them for the last time. I shall never forget the enthusiasm with which I saw this scene in the bright, warm sunlight, the rough crags softened in the haze which filled the atmosphere, and the wild mountains springing up in the midst of vineyards, and crowned with crumbling towers, filled with the memories of a thousand years.

After passing Andernach, we saw in the distance the highlands of the middle Rhine, which rise above Coblentz, guarding the entrance to its wild scenery, and the mountains of the Moselle. They parted as we approached; from the foot shot up the spires of Coblentz, and the battlements of Ehrenbreitstein crowning the mountain opposite, grew larger and broader. The air was slightly hazy, and the clouds seemed laboring among the distant mountains to raise a storm. As we came opposite the mouth of the Moselle and under the shadow of the mighty fortress, I gazed up with awe at its massive walls. Apart from its magnitude and almost impregnable situation on a perpendicular rock, it is filled with the recollections of history and hallowed by the voice of poetry. The scene went past like a panorama, the bridge of boats opened, the city glided behind us and we entered the highlands again.

Above Coblentz almost every mountain has a ruin and a legend. One feels everywhere the spirit of the past, and its stirring recollections come back upon the mind with irresistible force. I sat upon the deck the whole afternoon, as mountains, towns and castles passed by on either side, watching them with a feeling of the most enthusiastic enjoyment. Every place was familiar to me in memory, and they seemed like friends I had long communed with in spirit and now met face to face.

The English tourists, with whom the deck was covered, seemed interested too, but in a different manner. With Murray's Handbook open in their hands, they sat and read about the very towns and towers they were passing, scarcely lifting their eyes to the real scenes, except now and then, to observe that it was "very nice."

As we passed Boppart, I sought out the Inn of the "Star," mentioned in "Hyperion"; there was a maiden sitting on the steps who might have been Paul Flemming's fair boat-woman. The clouds which had here gathered among the hills, now came over the river, and the rain cleared the deck of its crowd of admiring tourists. As we were approaching Lurlei Berg, I did not go below, and so enjoyed some of the finest scenery on the Rhine alone. The mountains approach each other at this point, and the Lurlei Rock rises up for six hundred feet from the water. This is the haunt of the water nymph, Lurlei, whose song charmed the ear of the boatman while his barque was dashed to pieces on the rocks below. It is also celebrated for its remarkable echo. As we passed between the rocks, a guard, who has a little house built on the road-side, blew a flourish on his bugle, which was instantly answered by a blast from the rocky battlements of Lurlei. The German students have a witty trick with this echo: they call out, "Who is the Burgomaster of Oberwesel?" a town just above. The echo answers with the last syllable "Esel!" which is the German for ass.

The sun came out of the cloud as we passed Oberwesel, with its tall round tower, and the light shining through the ruined arches of Schonberg castle, made broad bars of light and shade in the still misty air. A rainbow sprang up out of the Rhine, and lay brightly on the mountain side, coloring vineyard and crag, in the most singular beauty, while its second reflection faintly arched like a glory above the high summits. In the bed of the river were the seven countesses of Schonberg, turned into seven rocks for their cruelty and hard-heartedness towards the knights whom their beauty had made captive. In front, at a little distance was the castle of Pfalz, in the middle of the river, and from the heights above Caub frowned the crumbling citadel of Gutenfels. Imagine all this, and tell me if it is not a picture whose memory should last a lifetime!

We came at last to Bingen, the southern gate of the Highlands,

Here, on an island in the middle of the stream, is the old Mouse tower where Bishop Hatto of Mayence was eaten up by the rats for his wicked deeds. Passing Rudesheim and Geissenheim, celebrated for their wines, at sunset, we watched the varied shore in the growing darkness, till like a line of stars across the water, we saw before us the bridge of Mayence.

The next morning I parted from my friends, who were going to Heidelberg by way of Mannheim, and set out alone for Frankfort. The cars passed through Hochheim, whose wines are celebrated all over the world; there is little to interest the traveler till he arrives at Frankfort, whose spires are seen rising from groves of trees as he approaches. I left the cars, unchallenged for my passport, greatly to my surprise, as it had cost me a long walk and five shillings in London, to get the signature of the Frankfort Consul. I learned afterwards it was not at all necessary. Before leaving America, N. P. Willis had kindly given me a letter to his brother, Richard S. Willis, who is now cultivating a naturally fine taste for music in Frankfort, and my first care was to find the American Consul, in order to learn his residence. I discovered at last, from a gentleman who spoke a little French, that the Consul's office was in the street *Bellevue,* which street I not only looked for through the city, but crossed over the bridge to the suburb of Sachsenhausen, and traversed its narrow, dirty alleys three several times, but in vain. I was about giving up the search, when I stumbled upon the office accidentally. The name of the street had been given to me in French and very naturally it was not to be found. Willis received me very kindly and introduced me to the amiable German family with whom he resides.

After spending a delightful evening with my newly-found friends, I left the next morning in the omnibus for Heidelberg. We passed through Sachsenhausen and ascended a long hill to the watchtower, whence there is a beautiful view of the Main valley. Four hours' driving over the monotonous plain, brought me to Darmstadt. The city wore a gay look, left by the recent *fêtes.* The monu-

ment of the old Duke Ludwig had just been erected in the centre of
the great square, and the festival attendant upon the unveiling of it,
which lasted three days, had just closed. The city was hung with
garlands, and the square filled with the pavilions of the royal family
and the musicians, of whom there were a thousand present, while
everywhere were seen red and white flags—the colors of Darmstadt.
We met wagons decorated with garlands, full of pleasant girls, in the
odd dress which they have worn for three hundred years.

After leaving Darmstadt we entered upon the Bergstrasse, or
Mountain-way, leading along the foot of the mountain chain which
extends all the way to Heidelberg on the left, while on the right
stretches far away the Rhine-plain, across which we saw the dim
outline of the Donnersberg, in France. The hills are crowned with
castles and their sides loaded with vines; along the road the rich
green foliage of the walnut trees arched and nearly met above us.
The sun shone warm and bright, and everybody appeared busy and
contented and happy. All we met had smiling countenances. In
some places we saw whole families sitting under the trees shelling
the nuts they had beaten down, while others were returning from
the vineyards, laden with baskets of purple and white grapes. The
scene seemed to realize all I had read of the happiness of the German peasantry, and the pastoral beauty of the German plains.

With the passengers in the omnibus I could hold little conversation. One, who knew about as much French as I did, asked me
where I came from, and I shall not soon forget his expression of
incredulity, as I mentioned America. "Why," said he, "you are white
—the Americans are all black!"

We passed the ruined castles of Auerback and Starkenburg, and
Burg Windeck, on the summit of a mountain near Weinheim, formerly one of the royal residences of Charlemagne, and finally came
to the Heiligenberg or Holy Mountain, guarding the entrance into
the Odenwald by the valley of the Neckar. As we wound around its
base to the river, the Kaiserstuhl rose before us, with the mighty

castle hanging upon its side and Heidelberg at its feet. It was a most strikingly beautiful scene, and for a moment I felt inclined to assent to the remark of my French acquaintance—, "America is not beautiful—Heidelberg is beautiful!" The sun had just set as we turned the corner of the Holy Mountain and drove up the bank of the Neckar; all the chimes of Heidelberg began suddenly to ring and a cannon by the riverside was fired off every minute—the sound echoing five times distinctly from mountain back to mountain, and finally crashing far off, along the distant hills of the Odenwald. It was the birthday of the Grand Duke of Baden, and these rejoicings were for the closing *fête.*

Chapter IX
SCENES IN AND AROUND HEIDELBERG

Sept. 30.—There is so much to be seen around this beautiful place, that I scarcely know where to begin a description of it. I have been wandering among the wild paths that lead up and down the mountain side, or away into the forests and lonely meadows in the lap of the Odenwald. My mind is filled with images of the romantic German scenery, whose real beauty is beginning to displace the imaginary picture which I had painted with the enthusiastic words of Howitt. I seem to stand now upon the Kaiser-stuhl, which rises above Heidelberg, with that magnificent landscape around me, from the Black Forest and Strasburg to Mainz, and from the Vosges in France to the hills of Spessart in Bavaria. What a glorious panorama! and not less rich in associations than in its natural beauty. Below me had moved the barbarian hordes of old, the triumphant followers of Arminius, and the Cohorts of Rome; and later, full many a warlike host bearing the banners of the red cross to the Holy Land,—many a knight returning with his vassals from the field, to lay at the feet of his lady-love the scarf he had worn in a hundred battles and claim the reward of his constancy and devotion. But brighter spirits had also toiled below. That plain had witnessed the presence of Luther, and a host who strove with him to free the world from the chains of a corrupt and oppressive religion. There had also trodden the master spirits of German song the giant twain, with their scarcely less harmonious brethren; they, too, had gathered inspiration from those scenes—more fervent worship of nature and a deeper love for their beautiful fatherland! Oh! what waves of crime and bloodshed have swept like the waves of a deluge down the valley of the Rhine! War has laid his mailed hand on those desolate towers and ruthlessly torn down what time has spared, yet he could not mar the beauty of the shore, nor could Time himself hurl down the mountains that guard it. And what if I feel a new inspiration on beholding the scene? Now that those ages have swept by, like the red waves of a tide of blood, we see not the darkened earth, but the golden sands which the flood has left behind. Besides, I have come from a new world, where the spirit of man is untrammeled by the mouldering shackles of the past, but in its youthful and joyous freedom, goes on to make itself a noble memory for the ages that are to come!

Then there is the Wolfsbrunnen, which one reaches by a beautiful walk up the hank of the Neckar, to a quiet dell in the side of the mountain. Through this the roads lead up by rustic mills, always in motion, and orchards laden with ripening fruit, to the commencement of the forest, where a quaint stone fountain stands, commemorating the abode of a sorceress of the olden time, who was torn in pieces by a wolf. There is a handsome rustic inn here, where every Sunday afternoon a band plays in the portico, while hundreds of people are scattered around in the cool shadow of the trees, or feeding the splendid trout in the basin formed by the little stream. They generally return to the city by another walk leading along the mountain side, to the eastern terrace of the castle, where they have fine views of the great Rhine plain, terminated by the Alsatian hills, stretching along the western horizon like the long crested swells on the ocean. We can even see these from the windows of our room on the bank of the Neckar; and I often look with interest on one sharp peak, for on its side stands the Castle of Trifels, where Coeur de Lion was imprisoned by the Duke of Austria, and where Blondel, his faithful minstrel, sang the ballad which discovered the retreat of the noble captive.

The people of Heidelberg are rich in places of pleasure and amusement. From the Carl Platz, an open square at the upper end of the city, two paths lead directly up to the castle. By the first walk we ascend a flight of steps to the western gate, passing through which, we enter a delightful garden, between the outer walls of the Castle, and the huge moat which surrounds it. Great linden, oak and beach trees shadow the walk, and in secluded nooks, little mountain streams spring from the side of the wall into stone basins. There is a tower over the moat on the south side, next the mountain, where the portcullis still hangs with its sharp teeth as it was last drawn up; on each side stand two grim knights guarding the entrance. In one of the wooded walks is an old tree brought from America in the year 1618. It is of the kind called *arbor vitæ,* and uncommonly tall and slender for one of this species; yet it does not seem to thrive well in a foreign soil. I noticed that persons had cut many slips off the lower branches, and I would have been tempted to do the same myself if there had been any I could reach. In the curve of the mountain is a handsome pavilion, surrounded with beds of flowers and fountains; here all classes meet together in the afternoon to sit with their re-freshments in the shade, while frequently a fine band of music gives them their invariable recreation. All this, with the scenery around them, leaves nothing unfinished to their present enjoyment. The Germans enjoy life under all circumstances, and in this way they make themselves much happier than we, who have far greater means of being so.

At the end of the terrace built for the princess Elizabeth, of Eng-land, is one of the round towers, which was split in twain by the

French. Half has fallen entirely away, and the other semicircular shell which joins the terrace and part of the Castle buildings, clings firmly together, although part of its foundation is gone, so that its outer ends actually hang in the air. Some idea of the strength of the castle may be obtained when I state that the walls of this tower are twenty-two feet thick, and that a staircase has been made through them to the top, where one can sit under he lindens growing upon it, or look down from the end on the city below with the pleasant consciousness that the great mass upon which he stands is only prevented from crashing down with him by the solidity of its masonry. On one side, joining the garden, the statue of the Archduke Louis, in his breastplate and flowing beard, looks out from among the ivy.

There is little to be seen about the Castle except the walls themselves. The guide conducted us through passages, in which were heaped many of the enormous cannon ball, which it had received in sieges, to some chambers in the foundation. This was the oldest part of the Castle, built in the thirteenth century. We also visited the chapel, which is in a tolerable state of preservation. A kind of narrow bridge crosses it, over which we walked, looking down on the empty pulpit and deserted shrines. We then went into the cellar to see the celebrated Tun. In a large vault are kept several enormous hogsheads, one of which is three hundred years old, but they are nothing in comparison with the tun, which itself fills a whole vault. It is as high as a common two story house; on the top is a platform upon which the people used to dance after it was filled, to which one ascends by two flights of steps. I forgot exactly how many casks it holds, but I believe eight hundred. It has been empty for fifty years.

We are very pleasantly situated here. My friends, who arrived a day before me, hired three rooms (with the assistance of a courier) in a large house on the banks of the Neckar. We pay for them, with attendance, thirty florins— about twelve dollars—a month, and Frau Dr. Grosch, our polite and talkative landlady, gives us a student's

breakfast— coffee and biscuit—for about seven cents apiece. We are
often much amused to hear her endeavors to make us understand.
As if to convey her meaning plainer, she raises both thumbs and
forefingers to her mouth and pulls out the words like a long string;
her tongue goes so fast that it keeps my mind always on a painful
stretch to comprehend an idea here and there. Dr. S——, from
whom we take lessons in German, has kindly consented to our
dining with his family for the sake of practice in speaking. We have
taken several long walks with them along the banks of the Neckar,
but I should be puzzled to repeat any of the conversations that took
place. The language, however, is fast growing more familiar, since
women are the principal teachers.

Opposite my window rises the Heiligenberg, on the other side of
the Neckar. The lower part of it is rich with vineyards, and many cottages stand embosomed in shrubbery among them. Sometimes we
see groups of maidens standing under the grape arbors, and every
morning the peasant women go toiling up the steep paths with baskets on their heads, to labor among the vines. On the Neckar below
us, the fishermen glide about in their boats, sink their square nets
fastened to a long pole, and haul them up with the glittering fish, of
which the stream is full. I often lean out of the window late at night,
when the mountains above are wrapped in dusky obscurity, and listen to the low, musical ripple of the river. It tells to my excited fancy
a knightly legend of the old German time. Then comes the bell, rung
for closing the inns, breaking the spell with its deep clang, which
vibrates far away on the night air, till it has roused all the echoes of
the Odenwald. I then shut the window, turn into the narrow box
which the Germans call a bed, and in a few minutes am wandering
in America. Half-way up the Heiligenberg runs a beautiful walk,
dividing the vineyards from the forest above. This is called the Philosopher's Way, because it was the favorite ramble of the old Profes-
sors of the University. It can be reached by a toilsome, winding path
among the vines, called the Snake-way, and when one has ascended

to it he is well rewarded by the lovely view. In the evening, when the sun has got behind the mountain, it is delightful to sit on the stone steps and watch the golden light creeping up the side of the Kaiser-stuhl, till at last twilight begins to darken in the valley and a mantle of mist gathers above the Neckar.

We ascended the mountain a few days ago. There is a path which leads up through the forest, but we took the shortest way, directly up the side, though it was at an angle of nearly fifty degrees. It was hard enough work, scrambling through the thick broom and heather, and over stumps and stones. In one of the stone-heaps I dislodged a large orange-colored salamander, seven or eight inches long. They are sometimes found on these mountains, as well as a very large kind of lizard, called the *eidechse,* which the Germans say is perfectly harmless, and if one whistles or plays a pipe, will come and play around him. The view from the top reminded me of that from Catskill Mountain House, but is on a smaller scale. The mountains stretch off sideways, confining the view to but half the horizon, and in the middle of the picture the Hudson is well represented by the lengthened windings of the "abounding Rhine." Nestled at the base below us, was the little village of Handschuhheim, one of the oldest in this part of Germany. The castle of its former lords has nearly all fallen down, but the massive solidity of the walls which yet stand, proves its antiquity. A few years ago, a part of the outer walls which was remarked to have a hollow sound, was taken down, when there fell from a deep niche built therein, a skeleton, clad in a suit of the old German armor. We followed a road through the woods to the peak on which stand the ruins of St. Michael's chapel, which was built in the tenth century and inhabited for a long time by a sect of white monks. There is now but a single tower remaining, and all around is grown over with tall bushes and weeds. It had a wild and romantic look, and I sat on a rock and sketched at it, till it grew dark, when we got down the mountain the best way we could.

We lately visited the great University Library. You walk through one hall after another, filled with books of all kinds, from the monk's manuscript of the Middle Ages, to the most elegant print of the present day. There is something to me more impressive in a library like this than a solemn Cathedral. I think involuntarily of the hundreds of mighty spirits who speak from these three hundred thousand volumes — of the toils and privations with which genius has ever struggled, and of his glorious reward. As in a church, one feels as it were, the presence of God; not because the place has been hallowed by his worship, but because all around stand the inspirations of his spirit, breathed through the mind of genius, to men. And if the mortal remains of saints and heroes do not repose within its walls, the great and good of the whole earth are there, speaking their counsels to the searcher for truth, with voices whose last reverberation will die away only when the globe falls into ruin.

A few nights ago there was a wedding of peasants across the river. In order to celebrate it particularly, the guests went to the house where it was given, by torchlight. The night was quite dark, and the bright red torches glowed on the surface of the Neckar, as the two couriers galloped along the banks to the bridegroom's house. Here, after much shouting and confusion, the procession was arranged, the two riders started back again with their torches, and the wagons containing the guests followed after with their flickering lights glancing on the water, till they disappeared around the foot of the mountain. The choosing of Conscripts also took place lately. The law requires one person out of every hundred to become a soldier, and this, in the city of Heidelberg, amounts to nearly 150. It was a sad spectacle. The young men, or rather boys, who were chosen, went about the city with cockades fastened on their hats, shouting and singing, many of them quite intoxicated. I could not help pitying them because of the dismal, mechanical life they are doomed to follow. Many were rough, ignorant peasants, to whom nearly any kind of life would be agreeable; but there were some whose countenances spoke otherwise, and I thought involuntarily, that their drunken gaiety was only affected to conceal their real feelings with regard to the lot which had fallen upon them.

We are gradually becoming accustomed to the German style of living, which is very different from our own. Their cookery is new to us, but is, nevertheless, good. We have everyday a different kind of soup, so I have supposed they keep a regular list of three hundred and sixty-five, one for everyday in the year! Then we have potatoes "done up" in oil and vinegar, veal flavored with orange peel, barley pudding, and all sorts of pancakes, boiled artichokes, and always rye bread, in loaves a yard long! Nevertheless, we thrive on such diet, and I have rarely enjoyed more sound and refreshing sleep than in their narrow and coffin-like beds, uncomfortable as they seem. Many of the German customs are amusing. We never see oxen working here, but always cows, sometimes a single one in a cart, and sometimes two fastened together by a yoke across their horns. The women labor constantly in the fields; from our window we can hear the nut-brown maidens singing their cheerful songs among the vineyards on the mountain side. Their costume, too, is odd enough. Below the tight-fitting vest they wear such a number of short skirts, one above another, that it reminds one of an animated hogshead, with a head and shoulders starting out from the top. I have heard it gravely asserted that the wealth of a German damsel may be known by counting the number of her "kirtles." An acquaintance of mine remarked, that it would be an excellent costume for falling down a precipice!

We have just returned from a second visit to Frankfort, where the great annual fair filled the streets with noise and bustle. On our way back, we stopped at the village of Zwingenberg, which lies at the foot of the Melibochus, for the purpose of visiting some of the scenery of the Odenwald. Passing the night at the inn there, we slept with one bed under and two above, and started early in the morning to climb up the side of the Melibochus. After a long walk through the forests, which were beginning to change their summer foliage for a brighter garment, we reached the summit and ascended the stone tower which stands upon it. This view gives one a better idea of the Odenwald, than that from the Kaiser-stuhl at Heidelberg. In the soft autumn atmosphere it looked even more beautiful. After an hour in that heaven of uplifted thought, into which we step from the mountaintop, our minds went with the path downward to earth, and we descended the eastern side into the wild region which contains the *Felsenmeer,* or Sea of Rocks.

We met on the way a student from Fulda—a fine specimen of that free-spirited class, and a man whose smothered aspiration was betrayed in the flashing of his eye, as he spoke of the present painful and oppressed condition of Germany. We talked so busily together that without noticing the path, which had been bringing us on, up hill and down, through forest and over rock, we came at last to a halt in a valley among the mountains. Making inquiries there, we found we had gone wrong, and must ascend by a different path the mountain we had just come down. Near the summit of this, in a wild pine wood, was the Felsenmeer—a great collection of rocks heaped together like pebbles on the sea shore, and worn and rounded as if by the action of water; so much do they resemble waves, that one standing at the bottom and looking up, cannot resist the idea, that they will flow down upon him. It must have been a mighty tide whose receding waves left these masses piled up together! The same formation continues at intervals, to the foot of the mountains. It reminded me of a *glacier* of rocks instead of ice. A little higher up, lies a massive block of granite called the "Giant's Column." It is thirty-two feet long and three to four feet in diameter, and still bears the mark of the chisel. When or by whom it was made, remains a mystery. Some have supposed it was intended to be erected for the worship of the Sun, by the wild Teutonic tribes who inhabited this forest; it is more probably the work of the Romans. A project was once started, to erect it as a monument on the battlefield of Leipsic, but it was found too difficult to carry into execution.

After dining at the little village of Reichelsdorf in the valley below, where the merry landlord charged my friend two kreutzers less than myself because he was not so tall, we visited the Castle of Schönberg, and joined the Bergstrasse again. We walked the rest of the way here; long before we arrived, the moon shone down on us over the mountains, and when we turned around the foot of the Heiligenberg, the mist descending in the valley of the Neckar, rested like a light cloud on the church spires.

Chapter X
A WALK THROUGH THE ODENWALD

B —— and I are now comfortably settled in Frankfort, having, with Mr. Willis's kind assistance, obtained lodgings with the amiable family, with whom he has resided for more than two years. My cousin remains in Heidelberg to attend the winter course of lectures at the University.

Having forwarded our baggage by the omnibus, we came hither on foot, through the heart of the Odenwald, a region full of interest, yet little visited by travellers. Dr. S —— and his family walked with us three or four miles of the way, and on a hill above Ziegelhausen, with a splendid view behind us, through the mountain-door, out of which the Neckar enters on the Rhine-plain, we parted. This was a first, and I must confess, a somewhat embarrassing experience in German leave-taking. After bidding adieu three or four times, we started to go up the mountain and they down it, but at every second step we had to turn around to acknowledge the waving of hands and handkerchiefs, which continued so long that I was glad when we were out of sight of each other. We descended on the other side into a wild and romantic valley, whose meadows were of the brightest green; a little brook which wound through them, put now and then its "silvery shoulder" to the wheel of a rustic mill. By the road-side two or three wild-looking gypsies sat around a fire, with some goats feeding near them.

Passing through this valley and the little village of Schönau, we commenced ascending one of the loftiest ranges of the Odenwald. The side of the mountain was covered with a thick pine forest. There was no wind to wake its solemn anthem; all was calm and majestic, and even awful. The trees rose all around like the pillars of a vast Cathedral, whose long arched aisles vanished far below in the deepening gloom.

> "Nature with folded hands seemed there,
>   Kneeling at her evening prayer,"

for twilight had already begun to gather. We went on and up and ever higher, like the youth in "Excelsior;" the beech and dwarf oak took the place of the pine, and at last we arrived at a cleared summit whose long brown grass waved desolately in the dim light of evening. A faint glow still lingered over the forest-hills, but down in the valley the dusky shades hid every vestige of life, though its sounds came up softened through the long space. When we reached the top a bright planet stood like a diamond over the brow of the eastern hill, and the sound of a twilight bell came up clearly and sonorously on the cool damp air. The white veil of mist slowly descended down the mountain side, but the peaks rose above it like the wrecks of a world, floating in space. We made our way in the dusk down the long path, to the rude little dorf of Elsbach. I asked at the first inn for lodging, where we were ushered into a great room, in which a number of girls who had been at work in the fields, were assembled. They were all dressed in men's jackets, and short gowns, and some had their hair streaming down their back. The landlord's daughter, however, was a beautiful girl, whose modest, delicate features contrasted greatly with the coarse faces of the others. I thought of Uhland's beautiful little poem of "The Landlady's Daughter," as I looked on her. In the room hung two or three pair of antlers, and they told us deer were still plenty in the forests.

When we left the village the next morning, we again commenced ascending. Over the whole valley and half-way up the mountain, lay a thick white frost, almost like snow, which contrasted with the green trees and bushes scattered over the meadows, produced the most singular effect. We plucked blackberries ready iced from the bushes by the road-side, and went on in the cold, for the sun shone only on the top of the opposite mountain, into another valley, down which rushed the rapid Ulver. At a little village which bears the beautiful name Anteschönmattenwag, we took a footpath directly over a steep mountain to the village of Finkenbach. Near the top I found two wild-looking children, cutting grass with knives, both of whom I prevailed upon for a few kreutzers to stand and let me sketch them. From the summit the view on the other side was very striking. The hills were nearly every one covered with wood, and not a dwelling in sight. It reminded me of our forest scenery at home. The principal difference is, that our trees are two or three times the size of theirs.

At length, after scaling another mountain, we reached a wide, elevated plain, in the middle of which stood the old dorf of Beer-felden. It was then crowded with people, on account of a great cat-tle-fair being held there. All the farmers of the neighborhood were assembled, clad in the ancient country costume—broad cocked hats and blue frocks. An orchard near the town was filled with cattle and horses, and near by, in the shade, a number of pedlars had arranged their wares.

The cheerful looking country people touched their hats to us as we passed. This custom of greeting travellers, universal in Germany, is very expressive of their social, friendly manners. Among the mountains, we frequently met groups of children, who sang together their simple ballads as we passed by.

From Beerfelden we passed down the valley of the Mimling to

Erbach, the principal city in the Odenwald, and there stopped a short time to view the Rittersaal in the old family castle of the Counts of Erbach. An officer, who stood at the gates, conducted us to the door, where we were received by a noble-looking, gray-headed steward. He took us into the Rittersaal at once, which was like stepping back three hundred years. The stained windows of the lofty Gothic hall, let in a subdued light which fell on the forms of kings and knights, clad in the armor they wore during life. On the left as we entered, were mail-covered figures of John and Cosmo de Medici; further on stood the Emperor Maximilian, and by his side the celebrated dwarf who was served up in a pie at one of the imperial feasts. His armor was most delicate and beautiful, but small as it was, General Thumb would have had room in it. Gustavus Adolphus and Wallenstein looked down from the neighboring pedestals, while at the other end stood Goetz von Berlichingen and Albert of Brunswick. Guarding the door were Hans, the robber-knight of Nuremberg, and another from the Thuringian forest. The steward told me that the iron hand of Goetz was in possession of the family, but not shown to strangers; he pointed out, however, the buckles on the armor, by which it was fastened. Adjoining the hall is an antique chapel, filled with rough old tombs, and containing the sarcophagus of Count Eginhard of Denmark, who lived about the tenth century. There were also monks' garments five hundred years old hanging up in it.

The collection of antiquities is large and interesting; but it is said that the old Count obtained some of them in rather a questionable manner. Among other incidents, they say that when in Rome he visited the Pope, taking with him an old servant who accompanied him in all his travels, and was the accomplice in most of his antiquarian thefts. In one of the outer halls, among the curiosities, was an antique shield of great value. The servant was left in this hall while the Count had his audience, and in a short time this shield was missed. The servant who wore a long cloak, was missed also; orders were given to close the gates and search everybody, but it was too late—the thief was gone.

Leaving Erbach we found out the direction of Snellert, the Castle of the Wild Huntsman, and took a road that led us for two or three hours along the top of a mountain ridge. Through the openings in the pine and larch forests, we had glimpses of the hills of Spessart, beyond the Main. When we finally left the by-road we had chosen it was quite dark, and we missed the way altogether among the lanes and meadows. We came at last to a full stop at the house of a farmer, who guided us by a foot path over the fields to a small village. On entering the only inn, kept by the Burgomaster, the people finding we were Americans, regarded us with a curiosity quite uncomfortable. They crowded around the door, watching every motion, and gazed in through the windows. The wild huntsman himself could scarcely have made a greater sensation. The news of our arrival seemed to have spread very fast, for the next morning when we stopped at a prune orchard some distance from the village to buy some fruit, the farmer cried out from a tree, "they are the Americans; give them as many as they want for nothing!"

With the Burgomaster's little son for a guide, we went back a mile or two of our route to Snellert, which we had passed the night before, and after losing ourselves two or three times in the woods, arrived at last at the top of the mountain, where the ruins of the castle stand. The walls are nearly level with the ground. The interest of a visit rests entirely on the romantic legend, and the wild view over the hills around, particularly that in front, where on the opposite mountain are the ruins of Rodenstein, to which the wild Huntsman was wont to ride at midnight—where he now rides no more. The echoes of Rodenstein are no longer awakened by the sound of his bugle, and the hoofs of his demon steed clanging on the battlements. But the hills around are wild enough, and the roar of the pine forests deep enough to have inspired the simple peasants with the romantic tradition.

Stopping for dinner at the town of Rheinheim, we met an old man, who, on learning we were Americans, walked with us as far as the next village. He had a daughter in America and was highly gratified to meet anyone from the country of her adoption. He made me promise to visit her, if I ever should go to St. Louis, and say that I had walked with her father from Rheinheim to Zwangenburg. To satisfy his fears that I might forget it, I took down his name and that of his daughter. He shook me warmly by the hand at parting, and was evidently made happier for that day.

We reached Darmstadt just in time to take a seat in the omnibus for Frankfort. Among the passengers were a Bavarian family, on their way to Bremen, to ship from thence to Texas. I endeavored to discourage the man from choosing such a country as his home, by telling him of its heat and pestilences, but he was too full of hope to be shaken in his purpose. I would have added that it was a slave-land, but I thought on our own country's curse, and was silent. The wife was not so sanguine; she seemed to mourn in secret at leaving her beautiful fatherland. It was saddening to think how lonely they would feel in that far home, and how they would long, with true German devotion, to look again on the green vintage-hills of their forsaken country. As night drew on, the little girl crept over to her father for his accustomed evening kiss, and then sank back to sleep in a corner of the wagon. The boy, in the artless confidence of childhood, laid his head on my breast, weary with the day's travel, and soon slept also. Thus we drove on in the dark, till at length the lights of Frankfort glimmered on the breast of the rapid Main, as we passed over the bridge, and when we stopped near the Cathedral, I delivered up my little charge and sent my sympathy with the wanderers on their lonely way.

Chapter XI
SCENES IN FRANKFORT — AN AMERICAN COMPOSER — THE
   POET FREILIGRATH

Dec. 4— This is a genuine old German city. Founded by Charlemagne, afterwards a rallying point of the Crusaders, and for a long time the capital of the German empire, it has no lack of interesting historical recollections, and notwithstanding it is fast becoming modernized, one is everywhere reminded of the Past. The Cathedral, old as the days of Peter the Hermit, the grotesque street of the Jews, the many quaint, antiquated dwellings and the mouldering watchtowers on the hills around, give it a more interesting character than any German city I have yet seen.

The house we dwell in, on the Markt Platz, is more than two hundred years old; directly opposite is a great castellated building, gloomy with the weight of six centuries, and a few steps to the left brings me to the square of the Roemerberg, where the Emperors were crowned, in a corner of which is a curiously ornamented house, formerly the residence of Luther. There are legends innumerable connected with all these buildings, and even yet discoveries are frequently made in old houses, of secret chambers and staircases. When you add to all this, the German love of ghost stories, and, indeed, their general belief in spirits, the lover of romance could not desire a more agreeable residence.

I often look out on the singular scene below my window. On both sides of the street, leaving barely room to enter the houses, sit the market women, with their baskets of vegetables and fruit. The middle of the street is filled with women buying, and every cart or carriage that comes along, has to force its way through the crowd, sometimes rolling against and overturning the baskets on the side, when for a few minutes there is a Babel of unintelligible sounds. The

country women in their jackets and short gowns go backwards and
forwards with great loads on their heads, sometimes nearly as high
as themselves. It is a most singular scene, and so varied that one
never tires of looking upon it. These women sit here from sunrise till
sunset, day after day, for years. They have little furnaces for cooking
and for warmth in winter, and when it rains they sit in large wooden
boxes. One or two policemen are generally on the ground in the
morning to prevent disputing about their places, which often gives
rise to interesting scenes.

Perhaps this kind of life in the open air is conducive to longevity;
for certainly there is no country on earth that has as many old
women. Many of them look like walking machines made of leather;
and to judge from what I see in the streets here, I should think they
work till they die.

On the 21st of October a most interesting fete took place. The
magnificent monument of Goethe, modelled by the sculptor
Schwanthaler, at Munich, and cast in bronze, was unveiled. It arrived a few days before, and was received with much ceremony and
erected in the destined spot, an open square in the western part of
the city, planted with acacia trees. I went there at ten o'clock, and
found the square already full of people. Seats had been erected
around the monument for ladies, the singers and musicians. A company of soldiers was stationed to keep an entrance for the procession, which at length arrived with music and banners, and entered
the enclosure. A song for the occasion was sung by the choir; it
swelled up gradually, and with such perfect harmony and unity, that
it seemed like some glorious instrument touched by a single hand.
Then a poetical address was delivered; after which four young men
took their stand at the corners of the monument; the drums and
trumpets gave a flourish, and the mantle fell. The noble figure
seemed to rise out of the earth, and thus amid shootings and the
triumphal peal of the band, the form of Goethe greeted the city of
his birth. He is represented as leaning on the trunk of a tree, holding

in his right hand a roll of parchment, and in his left a wreath. The pedestal, which is also of bronze, contains bas reliefs, representing scenes from Faust, Wilhelm Meister and Egmont. In the evening Goethe's house, in a street near, was illuminated by arches of lamps between the windows, and hung with wreaths of flowers. Four pillars of colored lamps lighted the statue. At nine o'clock the choir of singers came again in a procession, with colored lanterns, on poles, and after singing two or three songs, the statue was exhibited in the red glare of the Bengal light. The trees and houses around the square were covered with the glow, which streamed in broad sheets up against the dark sky.

I have lately heard one of the most perfectly beautiful creations that ever emanated from the soul of genius — the opera of Fidelio. I have caught faint glimpses of that rich world of fancy and feeling, to which music is the golden door. Surrendering myself to the grasp of Beethoven's powerful conception, I read in sounds far more expressive than words, the almost despairing agony of the strong-hearted, but still tender and womanly Fidelio—the ecstatic joy of the wasted prisoner, when he rose from his hard couch in the dungeon, seeming to feel, in his manic brain, the presentiment of a bright being who would come to unbind his chains—and the sobbing and wailing, almost human, which came from the orchestra, when they dug his grave, by the dim lantern's light. When it was done, the murderer stole into the dungeon, to gloat on the agonies of his victim, ere he gave the death-blow. Then, while the prisoner is waked to reason by that sight, and Fidelio throws herself before the uplifted dagger, rescuing her husband with the courage which love gives to a woman's heart, the storm of feeling which has been gathering in the music, swells to a height beyond which it seemed impossible for the soul to pass. My nerves were thrilled till I could bear no more. A mist seemed to come before my eyes and I scarcely knew what followed, till the rescued kneeled together and poured forth in the closing hymn the painful fullness of their joy. I dreaded the sound of voices after the close, and the walk home amid the harsh rattling of vehicles on the rough streets. For days afterwards my brain was filled with a mingled and confused sense of melody, like the half-remembered music of a dream.

Why should such magnificent creations of art be denied the new world? There is certainly enthusiasm and refinement of feeling enough at home to appreciate them, were the proper direction given to the popular taste. What country possesses more advantages to foster the growth of such an art, than ours? Why should not the composer gain mighty conceptions from the grandeur of our mountain scenery, from the howling of the storm through our giant forests, from the eternal thunder of Niagara? All these collateral influences, which more or less tend to the development and expansion of genius, are characteristics of our country; and a taste for musical compositions of a refined and lofty character, would soon give birth to creators.

Fortunately for our country, this missing star in the crown of her growing glory, will probably soon be replaced. Richard S. Willis, with whom we have lived in delightful companionship, since coming here, has been for more than two years studying and preparing himself for the higher branches of composition. The musical talent he displayed while at college, and the success following the publication of a set of beautiful waltzes he there composed, led him to choose this most difficult but lofty path; the result justifies his early promise and gives the most sanguine anticipations for the future. He studied the first two years here under Schnyder von Wartensee, a distinguished Swiss composer; and his exercises have met with the warmest approval from Mendelsohn, at present the first German composer, and Rinck, the celebrated organist. The enormous labor and application required to go through the preparatory studies alone, would make it seem almost impossible for ne with the restless energy of the American character, to undertake it; but as this very energy gives genius its greatest power, we may now trust with confidence that Willis, since he has nearly completed his studies, will win himself and his country honor in the difficult path he has chosen.

Since I have been in Frankfort, an event has occurred, which shows very distinctly the principles at work in Germany, and gives us some foreboding of the future. Ferdinand Freiligrath, the first living poet with the exception of Uhland, has within a few weeks published a volume of poems entitled, "My Confession of Faith, or Poems for the Times." It contains some thrilling appeals to the free spirit of the German people, setting forth the injustice under which they labor, in simple but powerful language, and with the most forcible illustrations, adapted to the comprehension of every one. Viewed as a work of genius alone, it is strikingly powerful and original: but when we consider the effect it is producing among the people—the strength it will add to the rising tide of opposition to every form of tyranny, it has a still higher interest. Freiligrath had three or four years before, received a pension of three hundred thalers from the King of Prussia, soon after his accession to the throne: he ceased to draw this about a year ago, stating in the preface to his volume that it was accepted in the belief the King would adhere to his promise of giving the people a new constitution, but that now since time has proved there is no dependence to be placed on the King's word, he must speak for his people and for his land.

The book has not only been prohibited, but Freiligrath has exiled himself voluntarily, to escape imprisonment. He is now in Paris, where Heine and Herwegh, two of Germany's finest poets, both banished for the same reason, are living. The free spirit which characterises these men, who come from among the people, shows plainly the tendency of the times; and it is only the great strength with which tyranny here has environed himself, and the almost lethargic slowness of the Germans, which has prevented a change before this.

Chapter XII
A WEEK AMONG THE STUDENTS

Receiving a letter from my cousin one bright December morning, the idea of visiting him struck me, and so, within an hour, B —— and I were on our way to Heidelberg. It was delightful weather; the air was mild as the early days of spring, the pine forests around wore a softer green, and though the sun was but a hand's breadth high, even at noon, it was quite warm on the open road. We stopped for the night at Bensheim; the next morning was as dark as a cloudy day in the north can be, wearing a heavy gloom I never saw elsewhere. The wind blew the snow down from the summits upon us, but being warm from walking, we did not heed it. The mountains looked higher than in summer, and the old castles more grim and frowning. From the hard roads and freezing wind, my feet became very sore, and after limping along in excruciating pain for a league or two, I filled my boots with brandy, which deadened the wounds so much, that I was enabled to go on in a kind of trot, which I kept up, only stopping ten minutes to dinner, till we reached Heidelberg.

The same evening there was to be a general *commers,* or meeting of the societies among the students, and I determined not to omit witnessing one of the most interesting and characteristic features of student life. So borrowing a cap and coat, I looked the student well enough to pass for one of them, though the former article was somewhat of the *Philister* form. Baader, a young poet of some note, and president of the "Palatia" Society, having promised to take us there, we met at eight o'clock at an inn frequented by the students, and went to the rendezvous, near the Markt Platz.

A confused sound of voices came from the inn, as we drew near; groups of students were standing around the door. In the entry we saw the Red Fisherman, one of the most conspicuous characters about the University. He is a small, stout man, with bare neck and breast, red hair, whence his name, and a strange mixture of roughness and benevolence in his countenance. He has saved many persons at the risk of his own life, from drowning in the Neckar, and on that account is leniently dealt with by the faculty whenever he is arrested for assisting the students in any of their unlawful proceedings. Entering the room I could scarcely see at first, on account of the smoke that ascended from a hundred pipes. All was noise and confusion. Near the door sat some half dozen musicians who were getting their instruments ready for action, and the long room was filled with tables, all of which seemed to be full and the students were still pressing in. The tables were covered with great stone jugs and long beer glasses; the students were talking and shouting and drinking. One who appeared to have the arrangement of the meeting, found seats for us together, and having made a slight acquaintance with those sitting next us, we felt more at liberty to witness their proceedings. They were all talking in a sociable, friendly way, and I saw no one who appeared to be intoxicated. The beer was a weak mixture, which I should think would make one fall over from its weight before it would intoxicate him. Those sitting near me drank but little, and that principally to make or return compliments. One or two at the other end of the table were more boisterous, and more than one glass was overturned on the legs below it. Leaves containing the songs for the evening lay at each seat, and at the head, where the President sat, were two swords crossed, with which he occasionally struck upon the table to preserve order. Our President was a fine, romantic-looking young man, dressed in the old German costume, which is far handsomer than the modern. I never saw in any company of young men, so many handsome, manly countenances. If their faces were any index of their characters, there were many noble, free souls among them. Nearly opposite to me sat a young poet, whose dark eyes flashed with feeling as he spoke to those near him. After some time passed in talking and drinking together, varied by an occasional air from the musicians, the President beat order with the sword, and the whole company joined in one of their glorious songs, to a melody at the same time joyous and solemn. Swelled by so many manly voices it rose up like a hymn of triumph — all other sounds were stilled. Three times during the singing all rose up, clashed their glasses together around the tables and drank to their Fatherland, a health and blessing to the patriot, and honor to those who struggle in the cause of freedom, at the close thundering out their motto:

"Fearless in strife, to the banner still true!"

After this song the same order as before was continued, except that students from the different societies made short speeches, accompanied by some toast or sentiment. One spoke of Germany — predicting that all her dissensions would be overcome, and she would rise up at last, like a phoenix among the nations of Europe; and at the close gave 'strong, united, regenerated Germany!' Instantly all sprang to their feet, and clashing the glasses together, gave a thundering *"hoch!"* This enthusiasm for their country is one of the strongest characteristics of the German students; they have ever been first in the field for her freedom, and on them mainly depends her future redemption.

Cloths were passed around, the tables wiped off and preparations made to sing the "*Landsfather*" or consecration song. This is one of the most important and solemn of their ceremonies, since by performing it the new students are made *burschen,* and the bands of brotherhood continually kept fresh and sacred. All became still a moment, then they commenced the lofty song:

"Silent bending, each one lending
  To the solemn tones his ear,
Hark, the song of songs is sounding

Back from joyful choir resounding,
  Hear it, German brothers, hear!

"German proudly, raise it loudly,
  Singing of your fatherland
Fatherland! thou land of story,
To the altars of thy glory
  Consecrate us, sword in hand

"Take the beaker, pleasure seeker,
  With thy country's drink brimmed o'er!
In thy left the sword is blinking,
Pierce it through the cap, while drinking
  To thy Fatherland once more!"

With the first line of the last stanza, the Presidents sitting at the
head of the table, take their glasses in their right hands, and at the
third line, the sword in their left, at the end striking their glasses
together and drinking.

"In left hand gleaming, thou art beaming,
  Sword from all dishonor free!
Thus I pierce the cap, while swearing,
It in honor ever wearing,
  I, a valiant Bursch will be!"

They clash their swords together till the third line is sung, when
each takes his cap, and piercing the point of the sword through the
crown, draws it down to the guard. Leaving their caps on the swords,
the Presidents stand behind the two next students, who go through
the same ceremony, receiving the swords at the appropriate time,
and giving it back loaded with their caps also. This ceremony is
going on at every table at the same time. These two stanzas are

repeated for every pair of students, till all have gone through with it, and the Presidents have arrived at the bottom of the table, with their swords strung full of caps. Here they exchange swords, while all sing:

"Come thou bright sword, now made holy,
    Of free men the weapon free;
Bring it solemnly and slowly,
    Heavy with pierced caps, to me!
From its burden now divest it;
    Brothers be ye covered all,
    And till our next festival,
Hallowed and unspotted rest it!

"Up, ye feast companions! ever
    Honor ye our holy band!
And with heart and soul endeavor
    E'er as high-souled men to stand!
Up to feast, ye men united!
    Worthy be your fathers' fame,
    And the sword may no one claim,
Who to honor is not plighted!"

Then each President, taking a cap off his sword, reached it to the student opposite, and they crossed their swords, the ends resting on the two students' heads, while they sang the next stanza:

"So take it back; thy head I now will cover
    And stretch the bright sword over.
Live also then this Bursche, hoch!
    Wherever we may meet him,
    Will we, as Brother greet him
Live also this, our Brother, hoch!"

This ceremony was repeated till all the caps were given back, and they then concluded with the following:

"Rest, the Burschen-feast is over,
   Hallowed sword and thou art free!
Each one strive a valiant lover
   Of his fatherland to be!
Hail to him, who, glory-haunted,
   Follows still his fathers bold;
   And the sword may no one hold
But the noble and undaunted!"

The Landsfather being over, the students were less orderly; the smoking and drinking began again and we left, as it was already eleven o'clock, glad to breathe the pure cold air.

In the University I heard Gervinus, who was formerly professor in Göttingen, but was obliged to leave on account of his liberal principles. He is much liked by the students and his lectures are very well attended. They had this winter a torchlight procession in honor of him. He is a stout, round-faced man, speaks very fast, and makes them laugh continually with his witty remarks. In the room I saw a son of Rückert, the poet, with a face strikingly like his father's. The next evening I went to hear Schlosser, the great historian. Among his pupils are the two princes of Baden, who are now at the University. He came hurriedly in, threw down his portfolio and began instantly to speak. He is an old, gray-headed man, but still active and full of energy. The Germans find him exceedingly difficult to understand, as he is said to use the English construction almost entirely; for this reason, perhaps, I understood him quite easily. He lectures on the French Revolution, but is engaged in writing a Universal History, the first numbers of which are published.

Two or three days after, we heard that a duel was to take place at Neuenheim, on the opposite side of the Neckar, where the students have a house hired for that purpose. In order to witness the spectacle, we started immediately with two or three students. Along the road were stationed old women, at intervals, as guards, to give notice of the approach of the police, and from these we learned that one duel had already been fought, and they were preparing for the other. The Red Fisherman was busy in an outer room grinding the swords, which are made as sharp as razors. In the large room some forty or fifty students were walking about, while the parties were preparing. This was done by taking off the coat and vest and binding a great thick leather garment on, which reached from the breast to the knees, completely protecting the body. They then put on a leather glove reaching nearly to the shoulder, tied a thick cravat around the throat, and drew on a cap with a large vizor. This done, they were walked about the room a short time, the seconds holding out their arms to strengthen them; their faces all this time betrayed considerable anxiety.

All being ready, the seconds took their stations immediately behind them, each armed with a sword, and gave the words: "*ready—bind your weapons—loose!*" They instantly sprang at each other, exchanged two or three blows, when the seconds cried "halt!" and struck their swords up. Twenty-four rounds of this kind ended the duel, without either being hurt, though the cap of one of them was cut through and his forehead grazed. All their duels do not end so fortunately, however, as the frightful scars on the faces of many of those present, testified. It is a gratification to know that but a small portion of the students keep up this barbarous custom. The great body is opposed to it; in Heidelberg, four societies, comprising more than one half the students, have been formed against it. A strong desire for such a reform seems to prevail, and the custom will probably be totally discontinued in a short time.

This view of the student-life was very interesting to me; it appeared in a much better light than I had been accustomed to view it. Their peculiar customs, except duelling and drinking, of course, may be the better tolerated when we consider their effect on the liberty of Germany. It is principally through them that a free spirit is kept alive; they have ever been foremost to rise up for their Fatherland, and bravest in its defence. And though many of their customs have so often been held up to ridicule, among no other class can one find warmer, truer or braver hearts.

Chatper XIII
CHRISTMAS AND NEW YEAR IN GERMANY

Jan. 2, 1845. — I have lately been computing how much my travels have cost me up to the present time, and how long I can remain abroad to continue the pilgrimage, with my present expectations. The result has been most encouraging to my plan. Before leaving home, I wrote to several gentlemen who had visited Europe, requesting the probable expense of travel and residence abroad. They sent different accounts; E. Joy Morris said I must calculate to spend at least $1500 a year; another suggested $1000, and the most moderate of all, said that it was *impossible* to live in Europe a year on less than $500. Now, six months have elapsed since I left home — six months of greater pleasure and profit than any year of my former life — and my expenses, in full, amount to $130! This, however, nearly exhausts the limited sum with which I started, but through the kindness of the editorial friends who have been publishing my sketches of travel, I trust to receive a remittance shortly. Printing is a business attended with so little profit here, as there are already so many workmen, that it is almost useless for a stranger to apply. Besides, after a tough grapple, I am just beginning to master the language, and it seems so necessary to devote every minute to study, that I would rather undergo some privation, than neglect turning these fleeting hours into gold, for the miser Memory to stow away in the treasure-vaults of the mind.

We have lately witnessed the most beautiful and interesting of all German festivals — Christmas. This is here peculiarly celebrated. About the commencement of December, the Christmarkt or fair, was opened in the Roemerberg, and has continued to the present time. The booths, decorated with green boughs, were filled with toys of various kinds, among which during the first days the figure of St. Nicholas was conspicuous. There were bunches of wax candles to illuminate the Christmas tree, gingerbread with printed mottos in poetry, beautiful little earthenware, basket-work, and a wilderness of playthings. The 5th of December, being Nicholas evening, the booths were lighted up, and the square was filled with boys, running from one stand to another, all shouting and talking together in the most joyous confusion. Nurses were going around, carrying the smaller children in their arms, and parents bought presents decorated with sprigs of pine and carried them away. Some of the shops had beautiful toys, as for instance, a whole grocery store in miniature, with barrels, boxes and drawers, all filled with sweetmeats, a kitchen with a stove and all suitable utensils, which could really be used, and sets of dishes of the most diminutive patterns. All was a scene of activity and joyous feeling.

Many of the tables had bundles of rods with gilded bands, which were to be used that evening by the persons who represented St. Nicholas. In the family with whom we reside, one of our German friends dressed himself very comically, with a mask, fur robe and long tapering cap. He came in with a bunch of rods and a sack, and a broom for a sceptre. After we all had received our share of the beating, he threw the contents of his bag on the table, and while we were scrambling for the nuts and apples, gave us many smart raps over the fingers. In many families the children are made to say, "I thank you, Herr Nicolaus," and the rods are hung up in the room till Christmas to keep them in good behavior. This was only a forerunner of the Christ-kindchen's coming. The Nicolaus is the punishing spirit, the Christ-kindchen the rewarding one.

When this time was over, we all began preparing secretly our presents for Christmas. Everyday there were consultations about the things which should be obtained. It was so arranged that all should interchange presents, but nobody must know beforehand what he would receive. What pleasure there was in all these secret purchases and preparations! Scarcely anything was thought or spoken of but Christmas, and everyday the consultations became more numerous and secret. The trees were bought sometime beforehand, but as we were to witness the festival for the first time, we were not allowed to see them prepared, in order that the effect might be as great as possible. The market in the Roemerberg Square grew constantly larger and more brilliant. Every night it was lit up with lamps and thronged with people. Quite a forest sprang up in the street before our door. The old stone house opposite, with the traces of so many centuries on its dark face, seemed to stand in the midst of a garden. It was a pleasure to go out every evening and see the children rushing to and fro, shouting and seeking out toys from the booths, and talking all the time of the Christmas that was so near. The poor people went by with their little presents hid under their cloaks, lest their children might see them; every heart was glad and every countenance wore a smile of secret pleasure.

Finally, the day before Christmas arrived. The streets were so full I could scarce make my way through, and the sale of trees went on more rapidly than ever. These were commonly branches of pine or fir, set upright in a little miniature garden of moss. When the lamps were lighted at night, our street had the appearance of an illuminated garden. We were prohibited from entering the rooms up stairs in which the grand ceremony was to take place, being obliged to take our seats in those arranged for the guests, and wait with impatience the hour when Christ-kindchen should call. Several relations of the family came, and what was more agreeable, they brought with them five or six children. I was anxious to see how they would view the ceremony. Finally, in the middle of an interesting conversation, we heard the bell ringing up stairs. We all started up, and made for the door. I ran up the steps with the children at my heels, and at the top met a blaze of light coming from the open door, that dazzled me. In each room stood a great table, on which the presents were arranged, amid flowers and wreaths. From the centre, rose the beautiful Christmas tree covered with wax tapers to the very top, which made it nearly as light as day, while every bough was hung with sweetmeats and gilded nuts. The children ran shouting around the table, hunting their presents, while the older persons had theirs pointed out to them. I had quite a little library of German authors as my share; and many of the others received quite valuable gifts.

But how beautiful was the heart-felt joy that shone on every countenance! As each one discovered he embraced the givers, and all was a scene of the purest feelings. It is a glorious feast, this Christmas time! What a chorus from happy hearts went up on that evening to Heaven! Full of poetry and feeling and glad associations, it is here anticipated with joy, and leaves a pleasant memory behind it. We may laugh at such simple festivals at home, and prefer to shake ourselves loose from every shackle that bears the rust of the Past, but we would certainly be happier if some of these beautiful old customs were better honored. They renew the bond of feeling between families and friends, and strengthen their kindly sympathy; even lifelong friends require occasions of this kind to freshen the wreath that binds them together.

New Year's Eve is also favored with a peculiar celebration in Germany. Everybody remains up and makes himself merry till midnight. The Christmas trees are again lighted, and while the tapers are burning down, the family play for articles which they have purchased and hung on the boughs. It is so arranged that each one shall win as much as he gives, which change of articles makes much amusement. One of the ladies rejoiced in the possession of a red silk handkerchief and a cake of soap, while a cup and saucer and a pair of scissors fell to my lot! As midnight drew near, it was louder in the streets, and companies of people, some of them singing in chorus, passed by on their way to the Zeil. Finally three-quarters struck, the windows were opened and everyone waited anxiously for the clock to strike. At the first sound, such a cry arose as one may imagine, when thirty or forty thousand persons all set their lungs going at once. Everybody in the house, in the street, over the whole city, shouted, "Prosst Neu Jahr?" In families, all the members embrace each other, with wishes of happiness for the new year. Then the windows are thrown open, and they cry to their neighbors or those passing by.

After we had exchanged congratulations, Dennett, B —— and I set out for the Zeil. The streets were full of people, shouting to one another and to those standing at the open windows. We failed not to cry, *"Prosst Neu Jahr!"* wherever we saw a damsel at the window, and the words came back to us more musically than we sent them. Along the Zeil the spectacle was most singular. The great wide street was filled with companies of men, marching up and down, while from the mass rang up one deafening, unending shout, that seemed to pierce the black sky above. The whole scene looked stranger and wilder from the flickering light of the swinging lamps, and I could not help thinking it must resemble a night in Paris during the French Revolution. We joined the crowd and used our lungs as well as any of them. For some time after we returned home, companies passed by, singing "with us 'tis ever so!" but at three o'clock all was again silent.

Chapter XIV
WINTER IN FRANKFORT—A FAIR, AN INUNDATION AND A FIRE

After New Year, the Main, just above the city, and the lakes in the promenades, were frozen over. The ice was tried by the police, and having been found of sufficient thickness, to the great joy of the schoolboys, permission was given to skate. The lakes were soon covered with merry skaters, and every afternoon the banks were crowded with spectators. It was a lively sight to see two or three hundred persons darting, about, turning and crossing like a flock of crows, while, by means of armchairs mounted on runners, the ladies were enabled to join in the sport, and whirl around among them. Some of the broad meadows near the city, which were covered with water, were the resort of the schools. I went there often in my walks, and always found two or three schools, with the teachers, all skating together, and playing their winter games on the ice. I have often seen them on the meadows along the Main; the teachers generally made quite as much noise as the scholars in their sports.

In the Art Institute I saw the picture of "Huss before the Council of Constance," by the painter Lessing. It contains upwards of twenty figures. The artist has shown the greatest skill in the expression and grouping of these. Bishops and Cardinals in their splendid robes are seated around a table, covered with parchment folios, and before them stands Huss alone. His face, pale and thin with long imprisonment, he has lain one hand on his breast, while with the other he has grasped one of the volumes on the table; there is an air of majesty, of heavenly serenity on his lofty forehead and calm eye. One feels instinctively that he has truth on his side. There can be no deception, no falsehood in those noble features. The three Italian cardinals before him appear to be full of passionate rage; the bishop in front, who holds the imperial pass given to Huss, looks on with an expression of scorn, and the priests around have an air of mingled curiosity and hatred. There is one, however, in whose mild features and tearful eye is expressed sympathy and pity for the prisoner. It is said this picture has had a great effect upon Catholics who have seen it, in softening the bigotry with which they regarded the early reformers; and if so, it is a triumphant proof how much art can effect in the cause of truth and humanity. I was much interested in a cast of the statue of St. George, by the old Italian sculptor Donatello. It is a figure full of youth and energy, with a countenance that seems to breathe. Donatello was the teacher of Michael Angelo, and when the young sculptor was about setting off for Rome, he showed him the statue, his favorite work. Michael gazed at it long and intensely, and at length, on parting, said to Donatello, "It wants but one thing." The artist pondered long over this expression, for he could not imagine what could fail the matchless figure. At length, after many years, Michael Angelo, in the noon of his renown, visited the death-bed of his old master. Donatello begged to know, before he died, what was wanting to his St. George. Angelo answered, *"the gift of speech!"* and a smile of triumph lighted the old man's face, as he closed his eyes forever.

The Eschernheim Tower, at the entrance of one of the city gates, is universally admired by strangers, on account of its picturesque appearance, overgrown with ivy and terminated by the little pointed turrets, which one sees so often in Germany, on buildings three or four centuries old. There are five other watch towers of similar form, which stand on different sides of the city, at the distance of a mile or two, and generally upon an eminence overlooking the country. They were erected several centuries ago, to discern flow afar the approach of an enemy, and protect the caravans of merchants, which at that time travelled from city to city, from the attacks of robbers. The Eschernheim Tower is interesting from another circumstance, which, whether true or not, is universally believed. When Frankfort was under the sway of a prince, a Swiss hunter, for some civil offence, was condemned to die. He begged his life from the prince, who granted it only on condition that he should fire the figure 9 with his rifle through the vane of this tower. He agreed, and did it; and at the present time, one can distinguish a rude '9' on the vane, as if cut with bullets, while two or three marks at the side appear to be from shots that failed.

The promise of spring which has lately visited us, was not destined for fulfilment. Shortly afterwards it grew cold again, with a succession of snows and sharp northerly winds. Such weather at the commencement of spring is not uncommon at home; but here they say there has not been such a winter known for 150 years. In the north of Prussia many persons have been starved to death on account of provisions becoming scarce. Among the Hartz also, the suffering is very great. We saw something of the misery even here. It was painful to walk through the streets and see so many faces hearing plainly the marks of want, so many pale, hollow-eyed creatures, with suffering written on every feature. We were assailed with petitions for help which could not be relieved, though it pained and saddened the heart to deny. The women, too, labor like brutes, day after day. Many of them appear cheerful and contented, and are no doubt, tolerably happy, for the Germans have all true, warm hearts, and are faithful to one another, as far as poverty will permit; but one cannot see old, gray-headed woman, carrying loads on their heads as heavy as themselves, exposed to all kinds of weather and working from morning till night, without pity and indignation.

So unusually severe has been the weather, that the deer and hares in the mountains near, came nearly starved and tamed down by hunger, into the villages to hunt food. The people fed them everyday, and also carried grain into the fields for the partridges and pheasants, who flew up to them like domestic fowls. The poor ravens made me really sorry; some lay dead in the fields and many came into the city perfectly tame, dying along the Main with wings hardly strong enough to bear up their skeleton bodies. The storks came at the usual time, but went back again. I hope the year's blessing has not departed with them, according to the old German superstition.

March 26. — We have hopes of spring at last. Three days ago the rain began and has continued with little intermission till now. The air is warm, the snow goes fast, and everything seems to announce that the long winter is breaking up. The Main rises fast, and goes by the city like an arrow, whirling large masses of ice upon the banks. The hills around are coming out from under the snow, and the lilac-buds in the promenades begin to expand for the second time.

The Fair has now commenced in earnest, and it is a most singular and interesting sight. The open squares are filled with booths, leaving narrow streets between them, across which canvas is spread. Every booth is open and filled with a dazzling display of wares of all kinds. Merchants assemble from all parts of Europe. The Bohemians come with their gorgeous crystal-ware; the Nurembergers with their toys, quaint and fanciful as the old city itself; men from the Thüringian forest, with minerals and canes, and traders from Berlin, Vienna, Paris and Switzerland, with dry goods and wares of all kinds. Near the Exchange are two or three companies of Tyrolese, who attract much of my attention. Their costume is exceedingly picturesque. The men have all splendid manly figures, and honor and bravery are written on their countenances. One of the girls is a really handsome mountain maiden, and with her pointed, broad-brimmed black hat, as romantic looking as one could desire. The musicians have arrived, and we are entertained the whole day long by wandering hands, some of whom play finely. The best, which is also the favorite company, is from Saxony, called "The Mountain Boys." They are now playing in our street, and while I write, one of the beautiful choruses from Norma comes up through the din of the crowd. In fact, music is heard over the whole city, and the throngs that fill every street with all sorts of faces and dresses, somewhat relieve the monotony that was beginning to make Frankfort tiresome.

We have an ever-varied and interesting scene from our window. Besides the motley crowd of passers-by, there are booths and tables stationed thick below. One man in particular is busily engaged in selling his store of blacking in the auction-style, in a manner that would do credit to a real Down-easter. He has flaming certificates exhibited, and prefaces his calls to buy with a high-sounding description of its wonderful qualities. He has a bench in front, where he tests it on the shoes of his customers, or if none of these are disposed to try it, he rubs it on his own, which shine like mirrors. So he rattles on with amazing fluency in French, German and Italian, and this, with his black beard and moustache and his polite, graceful manner, keeps a crowd of customers around him, so that the wonderful blacking goes off as fast as he can supply it.

April 6.—Old Winter's gates are shut close behind us, and the sun looks down with his summer countenance. The air, after the long cold rain, is like that of Paradise. All things are gay and bright, and everybody is in motion. Spring commenced with yesterday in earnest, and lo! before night the roads were all dry and fine as if there had been no rain for a month; and the gardeners dug and planted in ground which, eight days before, was covered with snow!

After having lived through the longest winter here, for one hundred and fifty years, we were destined to witness the greatest flood for sixty, and little lower than any within the last three hundred years. On the 28th of March, the river overflooded the high pier along the Main, and rising higher and higher, began to come into the gates and alleys. Before night the whole bank was covered and the water intruded into some of the booths in the Römerberg. When I went there the next morning, it was a sorrowful sight. Persons were inside the gate with boats; so rapidly had it risen, that many of the merchants had no time to move their wares, and must suffer great damage. They were busy rescuing what property could be seized in the haste, and constructing passages into the houses which were surrounded. No one seemed to think of buying or selling, but only on the best method to escape the danger. Along the Main it was still worse. From the measure, it had risen seventeen feet above its usual level, and the arches of the bridge were filled nearly to the top. At the Upper-Main gate, everything was flooded—houses, gardens, workshops, &c.; the water had even overrun the meadows above and attacked the city from behind, so that a part of the beautiful promenades lay deep under water. On the other side, we could see houses standing in it up to the roof. It came up through the sewers into the middle of Frankfort; a large body of men were kept at work constructing slight bridges to walk on, and transporting boats to places where they were needed. This was all done at the expense of the city; the greatest readiness was everywhere manifested to render all possible assistance. In the Fischergasse, I saw them taking provisions to the people in boats; one man even fastened a loaf of bread to the end of a broomstick and reached it across the narrow street from an upper story window, to the neighbor opposite. News came that Hausen, a village towards the Taunus, about two miles distant, was quite underwater, and that the people clung to the roofs and cried for help; but it was fortunately false. About noon, cannon shots were heard, and twenty boats were sent out from the city.

In the afternoon I ascended the tower of the Cathedral, which commands a wide view of the valley, up and down. Just above the city the whole plain was like a small lake—between two and three miles wide. A row of new-built houses stretched into it like a long promontory, and in the middle, like an island, stood a country-seat with large out-buildings. The river sent a long arm out below, that reached up through the meadows behind the city, as if to clasp it all and bear it away together. A heavy storm was raging along the whole extent of the Taunus; but a rainbow stood in the eastern sky. I thought of its promise, and hoped, for the sake of the hundreds of poor people who were suffering by the waters, that it might herald their fall.

We afterwards went over to Sachsenhausen, which was, if possible, in a still more unfortunate condition. The water had penetrated the passages and sewers, and from these leaped and rushed lip into the streets, as out of a fountain. The houses next to the Main, which were first filled, poured torrents out of the doors and windows into the street below. These people were nearly all poor, and could ill afford the loss of time and damage of property it occasioned them. The stream was filled with wood and boards, and even whole roofs, with the tiles on, went floating down. The bridge was crowded with people; one saw everywhere mournful countenances, and heard lamentations over the catastrophe. After sunset, a great cloud, filling half the sky, hung above; the reflection of its glowing crimson tint, joined to the brown hue of the water, made it seem like a river of fire.

What a difference a little sunshine makes! I could have for gotten the season the next day, but for the bare trees and swelling; Main, as I threaded my way through the hundreds of people who thronged its banks. It was that soft warmth that comes with the first spring days, relaxing the body and casting a dreamy hue over the mind. I leaned over the bridge in the full enjoyment of it, and listening to the roaring of the water under the arches, forgot everything else for a time. It was amusing to walk up and down the pier and look at the countenances passing by, while the fantasy was ever ready, weaving a tale for all. My favorite Tyrolese were there, and I saw a Greek leaning over the stone balustrade, wearing the red cap and white frock, and with the long dark hair and fiery eye of the Orient. I could not but wonder, as he looked at the dim hills of the Odenwald, along the eastern horizon, whether they called up in his mind the purple isles of his native Archipelago.

The general character of a nation is plainly stamped on the countenances of its people. One who notices the faces in the streets, can soon distinguish, by the glance he gives in going by, the Englishman or the Frenchman from the German, and the Christian from the Jew. Not less striking is the difference of expression between the Germans themselves; and in places where all classes of people are drawn together, it is interesting to observe how accurately these distinctions are drawn. The boys have generally handsome, intelligent faces, and like all boys, they are full of life and spirit, for they know nothing of the laws by which their country is chained down, and would not care for them, if they did. But with the exception of the students, who talk, at least, of Liberty and Right, the young men lose this spirit and at last settle down into the calm, cautious, *lethargic* citizen. One distinguishes an Englishman and I should think an American, also, in this respect, very easily; the former, moreover, by a certain cold stateliness and reserve. There is something, however, about a Jew, whether English or German, which marks him from all others. However different their faces, there is a family character which runs through the whole of them. It lays principally in their high cheek-bones, prominent nose and thin, compressed lips; which, especially in elderly men, gives a peculiar miserly expression that is unmistakeable. I regret to say, one looks almost in vain, in Germany, for a handsome female countenance. Here and there, perhaps, is a woman with regular features, but that intellectual expression, which gives such a charm to the most common face, is wanting. I have seen more beautiful women in one night, in a public assembly in America, than during the seven months I have been on the Continent. Some of the young Jewesses, in Frankfort, are considered handsome, but their features soon become too strongly marked. In a public walk, the number of positively ugly faces is really astonishing.

About ten o'clock that night, I heard a noise of persons running in the street, and going to the Römerberg, found the water had risen, all at once, much higher, and was still rapidly increasing. People were setting up torches and lengthening the rafts, which had been already formed.

The lower part of the city was a real Venice—the streets were full of boats and people could even row about in their own houses; though it was not quite so bad as the flood in Georgia, where they went upstairs to bed in boats! I went to the bridge. Persons were calling around — "The water! The water! It rises continually!" The river rushed through the arches, foaming and dashing with a noise like thunder, and the red light of the torches along the shore cast a flickering glare on the troubled waves. It was then twenty-one feet above its usual level. Men were busy all around, carrying boats and ladders to the places most threatened, or emptying cellars into which it was penetrating. The sudden swelling was occasioned by the coming down of the floods from the mountains of Spessart.

Part of the upper quay cracked next morning and threatened to fall in, and one of the projecting piers of the bridge sunk away from the main body three or four inches. In Sachsenhausen the desolation occasioned by the flood is absolutely frightful; several houses have fallen into total ruin. All business was stopped for the day; the Exchange was even shut up. As the city depends almost entirely on pumps for its supply of water, and these were filled with the flood, we have been drinking the muddy current of the Main ever since. The damage to goods is very great. The fair was stopped at once, and the loss in this respect alone, must be several millions of florins. The water began to fall on the 1st, and has now sunk about ten feet, so that most of the houses are again released, although unfortunately in a bad condition.

Yesterday afternoon, as I was sitting in my room, writing, I heard all at once an explosion like a cannon in the street, followed by loud and continued screams. Looking out the window, I saw the people rushing by with goods in their arms, some wringing their hands and crying, others running in all directions. Imagining that it was nothing less than the tumbling down of one of the old houses, we ran down and saw a store a few doors distant in flames. The windows were bursting and flying out, and the mingled mass of smoke and red flame reached half-way across the street. We learned afterwards it was occasioned by the explosion of a jar of naphtha, which instantly enveloped the whole room in fire, the people barely escaping in time. The persons who had booths near were standing still in despair, while the flames were beginning to touch their property. A few butchers who first came up, did almost everything. A fire engine arrived soon, but it was ten minutes before it began to play, and by that time the flames were coming out of the upper stories. Then the supply of water soon failed, and though another engine came up shortly after, it was sometime before it could be put in order, so that by the time they got fairly to work, the fire had made its way nearly through the house. The water was first brought in barrels drawn by horses, till some officer came and opened the fire plug. The police were busy at work seizing those who came by and setting them to work; and as the alarm had drawn a great many together, they at last began to effect something. All the military are obliged to be out, and the officers appeared eager to use their authority while they could, for everyone was ordering and commanding, till all was a scene of perfect confusion and uproar. I could not help laughing heartily, so ludicrous did the scene appear. There were little, miserable engines, not much bigger than a hand-cart, and looking as if they had not been used for half a century, the horses running backwards and forwards, dragging barrels which were emptied into tubs, after which the water was finally dipped up in buckets, and emptied into the engines! These machines can only play into the second or third story, after which the hose was taken up in the houses on the opposite side of the street, and made to play across. After four hours the fire was overcome, the house being thoroughly burnt out; it happened to have double fire walls, which prevented those adjoining from catching easily.

Chapter XV
THE DEAD AND THE DEAF—MENDELSSOHN THE COMPOSER

It is now a luxury to breathe. These spring days are the perfection of delightful weather. Imagine the delicious temperature of our Indian summer joined to the life and freshness of spring, add to this a sky of the purest azure, and a breeze filled with the odor of violets, —the most exquisite of all perfumes—and you have some idea of it. The meadows are beginning to bloom, and I have already heard the larks singing high up in the sky. Those sacred birds, the storks, have returned and taken possession of their old nests on the chimney-tops; they are sometimes seen walking about in the fields, with a very grave and serious air, as if conscious of the estimation in which they are held. Everybody is out in the open air; the woods, although they still look wintry, are filled with people, and the boat-men on the Main are busy ferrying gay parties across. The spring has been so long in coming, that all are determined to enjoy it well, while it lasts.

We visited the cemetery a few days ago. The dead-house, where corpses are placed in the hope of resuscitation, is an appendage to cemeteries found only in Germany. We were shown into a narrow chamber, on each side of which were six cells, into which one could distinctly see, by means of a large plate of glass. In each of these is a bier for the body, directly above which hangs a cord, having on the end ten thimbles, which are put upon the fingers of the corpse, so that the slightest motion strikes a bell in the watchman's room. Lamps are lighted at night, and in winter the rooms are warmed. In the watchman's chamber stands a clock with a dial-plate of twenty-four hours, and opposite every hour is a little plate, which can only be moved two minutes before it strikes. If then the watchman has slept or neglected his duty at that time, he cannot move it after-wards, and his neglect is seen by the superintendent. In such a case, he is severely fined, and for the second or third offence, dismissed. There are other rooms adjoining, containing beds, baths, galvanic battery, &c. Nevertheless, they say there has been no resuscitation during the fifteen years it has been established.

We afterwards went to the end of the cemetery to see the bas-reliefs of Bertel Thorwaldsen, in the vault of the Bethmann family. They are three in number, representing the death of a son of the present banker, Moritz von Bethmann, who tragically drowned in the Arno about fourteen years ago. The middle one represents the young man drooping in his chair, the beautiful Greek Angel of Death standing at his back, with one arm over his shoulder, while his youn-ger brother is sustaining him, and receiving the wreath that drops from his sinking hand. The young woman who showed us these, told us of Thorwaldsen's visit to Frankfort, about three years ago. She described him as a beautiful and venerable old man, with long white locks hanging over his shoulders, still vigorous and active for his years. There seems to have been much resemblance between him and Dannecker—not only in personal appearance and character, but in the simple and classical beauty of their works.

The cemetery contains many other monuments; with the exception of one or two by Launitz, and an exquisite Death Angel in sandstone, from a young Frankfort sculptor, they are not remarkable. The common tombstone is a white wooden cross; opposite the entrance is a perfect forest of them, involuntarily reminding one of a company of ghosts, with outstretched arms. These contain the names of the deceased with mottoes, some of which are beautiful and touching, as for instance: *"Through darkness unto light;" "Weep not for her; she is not dead, but sleepeth;" "Slumber sweet!"* etc. The graves are neatly bordered with grass, and planted with flowers, and many of the crosses have withered wreaths hanging upon them. In summer it is a beautiful place; in fact, the very name of cemetery in German — *Friedhof* or Court of Peace—takes away the idea of death; the beautiful figure of the youth, with his inverted torch, makes one think of the grave only as a place of repose.

On our way back we stopped at the Institute for the Deaf, for by the new method of teaching they are no longer dumb. It is a handsome building in the gardens skirting the city. We applied, and on learning we were strangers, they gave us permission to enter. On finding we were Americans, the instructress immediately spoke of Dr. Howe, who had visited the Institute a year or two before, and was much pleased to find that Mr. Dennett was acquainted with him. She took us into a room where about fifteen small children were assembled, and addressing one of the girls, said in a distinct tone: "These gentlemen are from America; the deaf children there speak with their fingers—canst thou speak so?" To which the child answered distinctly, but with some effort: "No, we speak with our mouths." She then spoke to several others with the same success;

one of the boys in particular, articulated with astonishing success. It was interesting to watch their countenances, which were alive with eager attention, and to see the apparent efforts they made to utter the words.

They spoke in a monotonous tone, slowly and deliberately, but their voices had a strange, sepulchral sound, which was at first unpleasant to the ear. I put one or two questions to a little boy, which he answered quite readily; as I was a foreigner, this was the best test that could be given of the success of the method. We conversed afterwards with the director, who received us kindly, and appointed a day for us to come and witness the system more fully. He spoke of Dr. Howe and Horace Mann, of Boston, and seemed to take a great interest in the introduction of his system in America.

We went again at the appointed time, and as their drawing teacher was there, we had an opportunity of looking over their sketches, which were excellent. The director showed us the manner of teaching them, with a looking-glass, in which they were shown the different positions of the organs of the mouth, and afterwards made to feel the vibrations of the throat and breast, produced by the sound. He took one of the youngest scholars, covered her eyes, and placing her hand upon his throat, articulated the second sound of A. She followed him, making the sound softer or louder as he did. All the consonants were made distinctly, by placing her hand before his mouth. Their exercises in reading, speaking with one another, and writing from dictation, succeeded perfectly. He treated them all like his own children, and sought by jesting and playing to make the exercise appear much like a sport. They call him father and appear to be much attached to him.

One of the pupils, about fourteen years old, interested me through his history. He and his sister were found in Sachsenhausen, by a Frankfort merchant, in a horrible condition. Their mother had died about two years and a half before, and during all that time their father had neglected them till they were near dead through privation and filth. The boy was placed in this Institute, and the girl in that of the Orphans. He soon began to show a talent for modelling figures, and for some time he has been taking lessons of the sculptor Launitz. I saw a beautiful copy of a bas-relief of Thorwaldsen which he made, as well as an original, very interesting, from its illustration of his history. It was in two parts; the first represented himself and his sister, kneeling in misery before a ruined family altar, by which an angel was standing, who took him by one hand, while with the other he pointed to his benefactor, standing near. The other represented the two kneeling in gratitude before a restored altar, on which was the anchor of Hope. From above streamed down a light, where two angels were rejoicing over their happiness. For a boy of fourteen, deprived of one of the most valuable senses, and taken from such a horrible condition of life, it is a surprising work and gives brilliant hopes for his future.

We went lately into the Roemerberg, to see the Kaisersaal and the other rooms formerly used by the old Emperors of Germany, and their Senates. The former is now in the process of restoration. The ceiling is in the gorgeous illuminated style of the Middle Ages; along each side are rows of niches for the portraits of the Emperors, which have been painted by the best artists in Berlin, Dresden, Vienna and Munich. It is remarkable that the number of the old niches in the hall should exactly correspond with the number of the German Emperors, so that the portrait of the Emperor Francis of Austria, who was the last, will close the long rank coming down from Charlemagne. The pictures, or at least such of them as are already finished, are kept in another room; they give one a good idea of the changing styles of royal costumes, from the steel shirt and helmet to the jewelled diadem and velvet robe. I looked with interest on a painting of Frederic Barbarossa, by Lessing, and mused over the popular tradition that he sits with his paladins in a mountain cave under the Castle of Kyffhauser, ready to come forth and assist his Fatherland in the hour of need. There was the sturdy form of Maximilian; the

martial Conrad; and Ottos, Siegfrieds and Sigismunds in plenty—
many of whom moved a nation in their day, but are now dust and
forgotten.

I yesterday visited Mendelssohn, the celebrated composer.
Having heard some of his impressive music this winter, particularly
that magnificent creation, the "Walpurgisnacht," I wanted to obtain
his autograph before leaving, and sent a note for that purpose. He
sent a kind note in answer, adding a chorus out of the Walpurgisnacht from his own hand. After this, I could not repress the desire
of speaking with him. He received me with true German cordiality,
and on learning I was an American, spoke of having been invited to
attend a musical festival in New York. He invited me to call on him
if he happened to be in Leipsic or Dresden when we should pass
through, and spoke particularly of the fine music there. I have rarely
seen a man whose countenance bears so plainly the stamp of genius. He has a glorious dark eye, and Byron's expression of a "dome
of thought," could never be more appropriately applied than to his
lofty and intellectual forehead, the marble whiteness and polish of
which are heightened by the raven hue of his hair. He is about forty
years of age, in the noon of his fame and the full maturity of his
genius. Already as a boy of fourteen he composed an opera, which
was played with much success at Berlin; he is now the first living
composer of Germany. Moses Mendelssohn, the celebrated Jewish
philosopher, was his grandfather; and his father, now living, is
accustomed to say that in his youth he was spoken of as the *son* of
the great Mendelssohn; *now* he is known as the *father* of the great
Mendelssohn!

Chapter XVI
JOURNEY ON FOOT FROM FRANKFORT TO CASSEL

The day for leaving Frankfort came at last, and I bade adieu to the gloomy, antique, but still quaint and pleasant city. I felt like leaving a second home, so much had the memories of many delightful hours spent there attached me to it. I shall long retain the recollection of its dark old streets, its massive, devil-haunted bridge and the ponderous cathedral, telling of the times of the Crusaders. I toiled up the long hill on the road to Friedberg, and from the tower at the top took a last look at the distant city, with a heart heavier than the knapsack whose unaccustomed weight rested uneasily on my shoulders. Being alone—starting out into the wide world, where as yet I knew no one, —I felt much deeper what it was to find friends in a strange land. But such is the wanderer's lot.

We had determined on making the complete tour of Germany on foot, and in order to vary it somewhat, my friend and I proposed taking different routes from Frankfort to Leipsic. He choose a circuitous course, by way of Nuremberg and the Thuringian forests; while I, whose fancy had been running wild with Goethe's witches, preferred looking on the gloom and grandeur of the rugged Hartz. We both left Frankfort on the 23d of April, each bearing a letter of introduction to the same person in Leipsic, where we agreed to meet in fourteen days. As we were obliged to travel as cheaply as possible, I started with but seventy-nine florins, (a florin is forty cents American) well knowing that if I took more, I should, in all probability, spend proportionably more also. Thus, armed with my passport, properly viséd, a knapsack weighing fifteen pounds and a cane from the Kentucky Mammoth Cave, I began my lonely walk through Northern Germany.

The warm weather of the week before had brought out the foliage of the willows and other early trees — violets and cowslips were springing up in the meadows. Keeping along the foot of the Taunus, I passed over great, broad hills, which were brown with the spring ploughing, and by sunset reached Friedberg — a large city, on the summit of a hill. The next morning, after sketching its old, baronial castle, I crossed the meadows to Nauheim, to see the salt springs there. They are fifteen in number; the water, which is very warm, rushes up with such force as to leap several feet above the earth. The buildings made for evaporation are nearly two miles in length; a walk along the top gives a delightful view of the surrounding valleys. After reaching the *chaussée* again, I was hailed by a wandering journeyman, or *handwerker,* as they are called, who wanted company. As I had concluded to accept all offers of this kind, we trudged along together very pleasantly. He was from Holstein, on the borders of Denmark and was just returning home, after an absence of six years, having escaped from Switzerland after the late battle of Luzerne, which he had witnessed. He had his knapsack and tools fastened on two wheels, which he drew after him quite conveniently. I could not help laughing at the adroit manner in which he begged his way along, through every village. He would ask me to go on and wait for him at the other end; after a few minutes he followed, with a handful of small copper money, which he said he had *fought for,* —the handwerker's term for *begged.*

We passed over long ranges of hills, with an occasional view of the Vogelsgebirge, or Bird's Mountains, far to the east. I knew at length, by the pointed summits of the hills, that we were approaching Giessen and the valley of the Lahn. Finally, two sharp peaks appeared in the distance, each crowned with a picturesque fortress, while the spires of Giessen rose from the valley below. Parting from my companion, I passed through the city without stopping, for it was the time of the university vacation, and Dr. Liebeg, the world-renowned chemist, whom I desired to see, was absent.

Crossing a hill or two, I came down into the valley of the Lahn, which flows through meadows of the brightest green, with red-roofed cottages nestled among gardens and orchards upon its banks. The women here wear a remarkable costume, consisting of a red bodice with white sleeves, and a dozen skirts, one above another, reaching only to the knees. I slept again at a little village among the hills, and started early for Marburg. The meadows were of the purest emerald, through which the stream wound its way, with even borders, covered to the water's edge with grass so smooth and velvety, that a fairy might have danced along on it for miles without stumbling over an uneven tuft. This valley is one of the finest districts in Germany. I thought, as I saw the peaceful inhabitants at work in their fields, I had most probably, on the battlefield of Brandywine, walked over the bones of some of their ancestors, whom a despotic prince had torn from their happy homes, to die in a distant land, fighting against the cause of freedom.

I now entered directly into the heart of Hesse Cassel. The country resembled a collection of hills thrown together in confusion—sometimes a wide plain left between them, sometimes a clustre of wooded peaks, and here and there a single pointed summit rising above the rest. The valleys were green as ever, the hillsides freshly ploughed and the forests beginning to be colored by the tender foliage of the larch and birch. I walked two or three hours at a "stretch," and then, when I could find a dry, shady bank, I would rest for half an hour and finish some hastily-sketched landscape, or lay at full length, with my head on my knapsack, and peruse the countenances of those passing by. The observation which every traveller excites, soon ceases to be embarrassing. It was at first extremely unpleasant; but I am now so hardened, that the strange, magnetic influence of the human eye, which we cannot avoid feeling, passes by me as harmlessly as if turned aside by invisible mail.

During the day several showers came by, but as none of them penetrated further than my blouse, I kept on, and reached about sunset a little village in the valley. I chose a small inn, which had an air of neatness about it, and on going in, the tidy landlady's "be you welcome," as she brought a pair of slippers for my swollen feet, made me feel quite at home. After being furnished with eggs, milk, butter and bread, for supper, which I ate while listening to an animated discussion between the village schoolmaster and some farmers, I was ushered into a clean, sanded bedroom, and soon forgot all fatigue. For this, with breakfast in the morning, the bill was six and a half groschen—about sixteen cents! The air was freshened by the rain and I journeyed over the hills at a rapid rate. Stopping for dinner at the large village of Wabern, a boy at the inn asked me if I was going to America? I said no, I came from there. He then asked me many silly questions, after which he ran out and told the people of the village. When I set out again, the children pointed at me and cried: "See there! he is from America!" and the men took off their hats and bowed!

The sky was stormy, which, added to the gloom of the hills around, though some of the distant ranges lay in mingled light and shade — the softest alternation of, purple and brown. There were many isolated, rocky hills, two of which interested me, through their attendant legends. One is said to have been the scene of a battle between the Romans and Germans, where, after a long conflict the rock opened and swallowed up the former. The other, which is crowned with a rocky wall, so like a ruined fortress, as at a distance to be universally mistaken for one, tradition says is the death-place of Charlemagne, who still walks around its summit every night, clad in complete armor.

On ascending a hill late in the afternoon, I saw at a great distance the statue of Hercules, which stands on the Wilhelmshohe, near Cassel. Night set in with a dreary rain, and I stopped at an inn about five miles short of the city. While tea was preparing a company of students came in and asked for a separate room. Seeing I was alone, they invited me up with them. They seemed much interested in America, and leaving the table gradually, formed a ring around me, where I had enough to do to talk with them all at once. When the omnibus came along, the most of them went with it to Cassel; but five remained and persuaded me to set out with them on foot. They insisted on carrying my knapsack the whole way, through the rain and darkness, and when I had passed the city gate with them, unchallenged, conducted me to the comfortable hotel, *"Zur Krone."*

It is a pleasant thing to wake up in the morning in a strange city. Everything is new; you walk around it for the first time in the full enjoyment of the novelty, or the not less agreeable feeling of surprise, if it is different from your anticipations. Two of my friends of the previous night called for me in the morning, to show me around the city, and the first impression, made in such agreeable company, prepossessed me very favorably. I shall not, however, take up time in describing its many sights, particularly the Frederick's Platz, where the statue of Frederick the Second, who sold ten thousand of his subjects to England, has been re-erected, after having lain for years in a stable where it was thrown by the French.

I was much interested in young Carl K ——, one of my new acquaintances. His generous and unceasing kindness first won my esteem, and I found on nearer acquaintance, the qualities of his mind equal those of his heart. I saw many beautiful poems of his which were of remarkable merit, considering his youth, and thought I could read in his dark, dreamy eye, the unconscious presentiment of a power he does not yet possess. He seemed as one I had known for years.

He, with a brother student, accompanied me in the afternoon, to Wilhelmshohe, the summer residence of the Prince, on the side of a range of mountains three miles west of the city. The road leads in a direct line to the summit of the mountain, which is thirteen hundred feet in height, surmounted by a great structure, called the Giant's Castle, on the summit of which is a pyramid ninety-six feet high, supporting a statue of Hercules, copied after the Farnese, and thirty-one feet in height. By a gradual ascent through beautiful woods, we reached the princely residence, a magnificent mansion standing on a natural terrace of the mountain. Near it is a little theatre built by Jerome Buonaparte, in which he himself used to play. We looked into the green house in passing, where the floral splendor of every zone was combined. There were lofty halls, with glass roofs, where the orange grew to a great tree, and one could sit in myrtle bowers, with the brilliant bloom of the tropics around him. It was the only thing there I was guilty of coveting.

The greatest curiosity is the water-works, which are perhaps unequalled in the, world. The Giant's Castle on the summit contains an immense tank in which water is kept for the purpose; but unfortunately, at the time I was there, the pipes, which had been frozen through the winter, were not in condition to play. From the summit an inclined plane of masonry descends the mountain nine hundred feet, broken every one hundred and fifty feet by perpendicular descents. These are the Cascades, down which the water first rushes from the tank. After being again collected in a great basin at the bottom, it passes into an aqueduct, built like a Roman ruin, and goes over beautiful arches through the forest, where it falls in one sheet down a deep precipice. When it has descended several other beautiful falls, made in exact imitation of nature, it is finally collected and forms the great fountain, which rises twelve inches in diameter from the middle of a lake to the height of one hundred and ninety feet! We descended by lovely walks through the forest to the Löwenburg, built as the ruin of a knightly castle, and fitted out in every respect to correspond with descriptions of a fortress in the olden time, with moat, drawbridge, chapel and garden of pyramidal trees. Farther below, are a few small houses, inhabited by the descendants of the Hessians who fell in America, supported here at the Prince's expense!

Chapter XVII
ADVENTURES AMONG THE HARTZ

On taking leave of Carl at the gate over the Göttingen road, I felt tempted to bestow a malediction upon traveling, from its merciless breaking of all links, as soon as formed. It was painful to think we should meet no more. The tears started into his eyes, and feeling a mist gathering over mine, I gave his hand a parting pressure, turned my back upon Cassel and started up the long mountain, at a desperate rate. On the summit I passed out of Hesse into Hanover, and began to descend the remaining six miles. The road went down by many windings, but I shortened the way considerably by a footpath through a mossy old forest. The hills bordering the Weser are covered with wood, through which I saw the little red-roofed city of Münden, at the bottom. I stopped there for the night, and next morning walked around the place. It is one of the old German cities that have not yet felt the effect of the changing spirit of the age. It is still walled, though the towers are falling to ruin. The streets are narrow, crooked, and full of ugly old houses, and to stand in the little square before the public buildings, one would think himself born in the sixteenth century. Just below the city the Werra and Fulda unite and form the Weser. The triangular point has been made into a public walk, and the little steamboat was lying at anchor near, waiting to start for Bremen.

In the afternoon I got into the omnibus for Göttingen. The ride over the wild, dreary, monotonous hills was not at all interesting. There were two other passengers inside, one of whom, a grave, elderly man, took a great interest in America, but the conversation was principally on his side, for I had been taken with a fever in Münden. I lay crouched up in the corner of the vehicle, trying to keep off the chills which constantly came over me, and wishing only for Göttingen, that I might obtain medicine and a bed. We reached it at last, and I got out with my knapsack and walked wearily through half a dozen streets till I saw an inn. But on entering, I found it so dark and dirty and unfriendly, that I immediately went out again and hired the first pleasant looking boy I met, to take me to a good hotel. He conducted me to the first one in the city. I felt a trepidation of pocket, but my throbbing head urged more powerfully, so I ordered a comfortable room and a physician. The host, Herr Wilhelm, sent for Professor Trefurt, of the University, who told me I had over-exerted myself in walking. He made a second call the next day, when, as he was retiring, I inquired the amount of his fee. He begged to be excused and politely bowed himself out. I inquired the meaning of this of Herr Wilhelm, who said it was customary for travellers to leave what they chose for the physician, as there was no regular fee. He added, moreover, that twenty groschen, or about sixty cents, was sufficient for the two visits!

I stayed in Göttingen two dull, dreary, miserable days, without getting much better. I took but one short walk through the city, in which I saw the outsides of a few old churches and got a hard fall on the pavement. Thinking that the *cause* of my illness might perhaps become its *cure,* I resolved to go on rather than remain in the melancholy—in spite of its black-eyed maidens, melancholy— Göttingen. On the afternoon of the second day, I took the post to Nordheim, about twelve miles distant. The Gottingen valley, down which we drove, is green and beautiful, and the trees seem to have come out all at once. We were not within sight of the Hartz, but the mountains along the Weser were visible on the left. The roads were extremely muddy from the late rains, so that I proceeded but slowly.

A blue range along the horizon told me of the Hartz, as I passed; although there were some fine side-glimpses through the hills, I did not see much of them till I reached Osterode, about twelve miles further. Here the country begins to assume a different aspect. The city lies in a narrow valley, and as the road goes clown a steep hill towards it, one sees on each side many quarries of gypsum, and in front the gloomy pine mountains are piled one above another in real Alpine style. But alas! the city, though it looks exceedingly romantic from above, is one of the dirtiest I ever saw. I stopped at Herzberg, six miles farther, for the night. The scenery was very striking; and its effect was much heightened by a sky full of black clouds, which sent down a hail-storm as they passed over. The hills are covered with pine, fir and larch. The latter tree, in its first foliage, is most delicate and beautiful. Every bough is like a long ostrich plume, and when one of them stands among the dark pines, it seems so light and airy that the wind might carry it away. Just opposite Herzberg, the Hartz stands in its gloomy and mysterious grandeur, and I went to sleep with the pleasant thought that an hour's walk on the morrow would shut me up in its deep recesses.

The next morning I entered them. The road led up a narrow mountain valley, down which a stream was rushing—on all sides were magnificent forests of pine. It was glorious to look down their long aisles, dim and silent, with a floor of thick green moss. There was just room enough for the road and the wild stream which wound its way zigzag between the hills, affording the most beautiful mountain-view along the whole route. As I ascended, the mountains became rougher and wilder, and in the shady hollows were still drifts of snow. Enjoying everything very much, I walked on without taking notice of the road, and on reaching a wild, rocky chasm called the "Schlucht," was obliged to turn aside and take a footpath over a high mountain to Andreasberg, a town built on a summit two thousand feet above the sea. It is inhabited almost entirely by the workmen in the mines.

The way from Andreasberg to the Brocken leads along the Rehberger Graben, which carry water about six miles for the ore-works. After going through a thick pine wood, I came out on the mountain-side, where rough crags overhung the way above, and through the tops of the trees I had glimpses into the gorge below. It was scenery of the wildest character. Directly opposite rose a mountain wall, dark and stern through the gloomy sky; far below the little stream of the Oder foamed over the rocks with a continual roar, and one or two white cloud-wreaths were curling up from the forests.

I followed the water-ditch around every projection of the mountain, still ascending higher amid the same wild scenery, till at length I reached the Oderteich, a great dam, in a kind of valley formed by some mountain peaks on the side of the Brocken. It has a breastwork of granite, very firm, and furnishes a continual supply of water for the works. It began to rain soon, and I took a footpath which went winding up through the pine wood. The storm still increased, till everything was cloud and rain, so I was obliged to stop about five o'clock at Oderbruch, a toll-house and tavern on the side of the Brocken, on the boundary between Brunswick and Hanover—the second highest inhabited house in the Hartz. The Brocken was invisible through the storm and the weather forboded a difficult ascent. The night was cold, but by a warm fire I let the winds howl and the rain beat. When I awoke the next morning, we were in clouds. They were thick on every side, hiding what little view there was through the openings of the forest. After breakfast, however, they were somewhat thinner, and I concluded to start for the Brocken. It is not the usual way for travellers who ascend, being not only a bad road but difficult to find, as I soon discovered. The clouds gathered around again after I set out, and I was obliged to walk in a storm of mingled rain and snow. The snow lay several feet deep in the forests, and the path was, in many places, quite drifted over. The white cloud-masses were whirled past by the wind, continually enveloping me and shutting out every view. During the winter the path had become, in many places, the bed of a mountain torrent, so that I was obliged sometimes to wade knee-deep in snow, and sometimes to walk over the wet, spongy moss, crawling under the long, dripping branches of the stunted pines. After a long time of such dreary travelling, I came to two rocks called the Stag Horns, standing on a little peak. The storm, now all snow, blew more violently than ever, and the path became lost under the deep drifts.

Comforting myself with the assurance that if I could not find it, I could at least make my way back, I began searching, and after some time, came upon it again. Here the forest ceased; the way led on large stones over a marshy ascending plain, but what was above, or on either side, I could not see. It was solitude of the most awful kind. There was nothing but the storm, which had already wet me through, and the bleak gray waste of Locks. It grew steeper and steeper; I could barely trace the path by the rocks which were worn, and the snow threatened soon to cover these. Added to this, although the walking and fresh mountain air had removed my illness, I was still weak from the effects of it, and the consequences of a much longer exposure to the storm were greatly to be feared. I was wondering if the wind increased at the same rate, how much longer it would be before I should be carried off when suddenly something loomed up above me through the storm. A few steps more and I stood beside the Brocken House, on the very summit of the mountain! The mariner, who has been floating for days on a wreck at sea, could scarcely be more rejoiced at a friendly sail, than I was on entering the low building. Two large Alpine dogs in the passage, as I walked in, dripping with wet, gave notice to the inmates, and I was soon ushered into a warm room, where I changed my soaked garments for dry ones, and sat down by the fire with feelings of comfort not easily imagined. The old landlord was quite surprised, on hearing the path by which I came, that I found the way at all. The summit was wrapped in the thickest cloud, and he gave me no hope for several hours of any prospect at all, so I sat down and looked over the Stranger's Album.

I saw but two names from the United States—B. F. Atkins, of Boston, and C. A. Hay, from York, Pa. There were a great many long-winded German poems among them, one by Schelling, the philosopher. Some of them spoke of having seen the "Spectre of the

Brocken." I inquired of the landlord about the phenomenon; he says
in winter it is frequently seen, in summer more seldom. The cause
is very simple. It is always seen at sunrise, when the eastern side of
the Brocken is free from clouds, and at the same time, the mist rises
from the valley on the opposite side. The shadow of everything on
the Brocken is then thrown in grand proportions upon the mist, and
is seen surrounded with a luminous halo. It is somewhat singular
that such a spectacle can be seen upon the Brocken alone, but this
is probably accounted for by the formation of the mountain, which
collects the mist at just such a distance from the summit as to render
the shadow visible.

Soon after dinner the storm subsided and the clouds separated
a little. I could see down through the rifts on the plains of Brunswick,
and sometimes, when they opened a little more, the mountains below us to the east and the adjoining plains, as far as Magdeburg. It
was like looking on the earth from another planet, or from some
point in the air which had no connection with it; our station was
completely surrounded by clouds, rolling in great masses around
us, now and then giving glimpses through their openings of the blue
plains, dotted with cities and villages, far below. At one time when
they were tolerably well separated, I ascended the tower, fifty feet
high, standing near the Brocken House. The view on three sides was
quite clear, and I can easily imagine what a magnificent prospect it
must be in fine weather. The Brocken is only about four thousand
feet high, nearly the same as the loftiest peak of the Catskill, but
being the highest mountain in Northern Germany, it commands a
more extensive prospect. Imagine a circle described with a radius
of a hundred miles, comprising thirty cities, two or three hundred
villages and one whole mountain district! We could see Brunswick
and Magdeburg, and beyond them the great plain which extends to
the North Sea in one direction and to Berlin in the other, while
directly below us lay the dark mountains of the Hartz, with little villages in their sequestered valleys. It was but a few moments I could

look on this scene—in an instant the clouds swept together again and completely hid it. In accordance with a custom of the mountain, one of the girls made me a "Brocken nosegay," of heather, lichens and moss. I gave her a few pfennings and stowed it away carefully in a corner of my knapsack.

I now began descending the east side, by a good road over fields of bare rock and through largo forests of pine. Two or three bare brown peaks rose opposite with an air of the wildest sublimity, and in many places through the forest towered lofty crags. This is the way by which Goethe brings Faust up the Brocken, and the scenery is graphically described in that part of the poem. At the foot of the mountain is the little village of Schiercke, the highest in the Hartz. Here I took a narrow path through the woods, and after following a tediously long road over the hills, reached Elbingerode, where I spent the night, and left the next morning for Blankenburg. I happened to take the wrong road, however, and went through Rübeland, a little village in the valley of the Bode. There are many iron works here, and two celebrated caves, called "Baumann's Höhle," and "Biel's Höhle." I kept on through the gray, rocky hills to Huttenrode, where I inquired the way to the Rosstrappe, but was directed wrong, and after walking nearly two hours in a heavy rain, arrived at Ludwigshütte, on the Bode, in one of the wildest and loneliest corners of the Hartz. I dried my wet clothes at a little inn, ate a dinner of bread and milk, and learning that I was just as far from the Rosstrappe as ever, and that the way was impossible to find alone, I hunted up a guide.

We went over the mountains through a fine old forest, for about two hours, and came out on the brow of a hill near the end of the Hartz, with a beautiful view of the country below and around. Passing the little inn, the path led through thick bushes along the summit, over a narrow ledge of rocks that seemed to stretch out into the air, for on either side the foot of the precipice vanished into the depth below.

Arrived at last at the end, I looked around me. What a spectacle! I was standing on the end of a line of precipice which ran out from the mountain like a wall for several hundred feet—the hills around rising up perpendicularly from the gorge below, where the Bode pressed into a narrow channel foamed its way through. Sharp masses of gray rock rose up in many places from the main body like pillars, with trees clinging to the clefts, and although the passage was near seven hundred feet deep, the summits, in one place, were very near to one another. Near the point at which I stood, which was secured by a railing, was an impression in the rock like the hoof of a giant horse, from which the place takes its name. It is very distinct and perfect, and nearly two feet in length.

I went back to the little inn and sat down to rest and chat awhile with the talkative landlady. Notwithstanding her horrible Prussian dialect, I was much amused with the budget of wonders, which she keeps for the information of travelers. Among other things, she related to me the legend of the Rosstrappe, which I give in her own words: "A great many hundred years ago, when there were plenty of giants through the world, there was a certain beautiful princess, who was very much loved by one of them. Now, although the parents of this princess were afraid of the giant, and wanted her to marry him, she herself hated him, because she was in love with a brave knight. But, you see, the brave knight could do nothing against the great giant, and so a day was appointed for the wedding of the princess. When they were married, the giant had a great feast and he and all his servants got drunk. So the princess mounted his black horse and rode away over the mountains, till she reached this valley. She stood on that square rock which you see there opposite to us, and when she saw her knight on this side, where we are, she danced for joy, and the rock is called the *Tanzplatz,* to this very day. But when the giant found she had gone, he followed her as fast as he might; then a holy bishop, who saw the princess, blessed the feet of her horse, and she jumped on it across to this side, where his fore feet made two marks in the rock, though there is only one left now. You should not laugh at this, for if there were giants then, there must have been very big horses too, as one can see from the hoofmark, and the valley was narrower then than it is now. My dear man, who is very old now, (you see him through the bushes, there, digging,) says it was so when he was a child, and that the old people living then, told him there were once four just such hoof-tracks, on the *Tanzplatz,* where the horse stood before he jumped over. And we cannot doubt the words of the good old people, for there were many strange things then, we all know, which the dear Lord does not let happen now. But I must tell you, lieber Herr, that the giant tried to jump after her and fell away down into the valley, where they say he lives yet in the shape of a big black dog, guarding the crown of the princess, which fell off as she was going over. But this part of the story is perhaps not true, as nobody, that I ever heard of, has seen either the black dog or the crown!"

After listening to similar gossip for a while, I descended the mountain-side, a short distance to the Bülowshöhe. This is a rocky shaft that shoots upward from the mountain, having from its top a glorious view through the door which the Bode makes in passing out of the Hartz. I could see at a great distance the towers of Magdeburg, and further, the vast plain stretching away like a sea towards Berlin. From Thale, the village below, where the air was warmer than in the Hartz and the fruit-trees already in blossom, it was four hours' walk to Halberstadt, by a most tiresome road over long ranges of hills, all ploughed and planted, and extending as far as the eye could reach, without a single fence or hedge. It is pleasant to look over scenes where nature is so free and unshackled; but the people, alas! wear the fetters. The setting sun, which lighted up the old Brocken and his snowy top, showed me also Halberstadt, the end of my Hartz journey; but its deceitful towers fled as I approached, and I was half dead with fatigue on arriving there.

The ghostly, dark and echoing castle of an inn (the Black Eagle) where I stopped, was enough to inspire a lonely traveller, like myself, with unpleasant fancies. It looked heavy and massive enough to have been a stout baron's stronghold in some former century; the taciturn landlord and his wife, who, with a solemn servant girl, were the only tenants, had grown into perfect keeping with its gloomy character. When I groped my way under the heavy, arched portal into the guests' room—a large, lofty, cheerless hall—all was dark, and I could barely perceive, by the little light which came through two deep-set windows, the inmates of the house, sitting on opposite sides of the room. After some delay, the hostess brought a light. I entreated her to bring me something instantly for supper, and in half an hour she placed a mixture on the table, the like of which I never wish to taste again. She called it *beer-soup!* I found, on examination, it was beer, boiled with meat, and seasoned strongly with pepper and salt! My hunger disappeared, and pleading fatigue as an excuse for want of appetite, I left the table. When I was ready to retire, the landlady, who had been sitting silently in a dark corner, called the solemn servant girl, who took up a dim lamp, and bade me follow her to the "sleeping chamber." Taking up my knapsack and staff, I stumbled down the steps into the arched gateway; before me was a long, damp, deserted courtyard, across which the girl took her way. I followed her with some astonishment, imagining where the sleeping chamber could be, when she stopped at a small, one-story building, standing alone in the yard. Opening the door with a rusty key, she led me into a bare room, a few feet square, opening into another, equally bare, with the exception of a rough bed. "Certainly," said I, "I am not to sleep here!" "Yes," she answered, "this is the sleeping chamber," at the same time setting down the light and disappearing. I examined the place—it smelt mouldy, and the walls were cold and damp; there had been a window at the head of the bed, but it was walled up, and that at the foot was also closed to within a few inches of the top. The bed was coarse and dirty; and on turning down the ragged covers, I saw with horror, a dark brown stain near the pillow, like that of blood! For a moment I hesitated whether to steal out of the inn, and seek another lodging, late as it was; at last, overcoming my fears, I threw my clothes into a heap, and lay down, placing my heavy staff at the head of the bed. Persons passed up and down the courtyard several times, the light of their lamps streaming through the narrow aperture up against the ceiling, and I distinctly heard voices, which seemed to be near the door.

Twice did I sit up in bed, breathless, with my hand on the cane, in the most intense anxiety; but fatigue finally overcame suspicion, and I sank into a deep sleep, from which I was gladly awakened by daylight. In reality, there may have been no cause for my fears — I may have wronged the lonely innkeepers by them; but certainly no place or circumstances ever seemed to me more appropriate to a deed of robbery or crime. I left immediately, and when a turn in the street hid the ill-omened front of the inn, I began to breathe with my usual freedom.

Chapter XVIII
NOTES IN LEIPSIC AND DRESDEN

Leipsic, May 8. — I have now been nearly two days in this wide-famed city, and the more I see of it the better I like it. It is a pleasant, friendly town, old enough to be interesting, and new enough to be comfortable. There is much active business life, through which it is fast increasing in size and beauty. Its publishing establishments are the largest in the world, and its annual fairs attended by people from all parts of Europe. This is much for a city to accomplish, situated alone in the middle of a great plain, with no natural charms of scenery or treasures of art to attract strangers. The energy and enterprise of its merchants have accomplished all this, and it now stands, in importance, among the first cities of Europe.

The bad weather obliged me to take the railroad at Halberstadt, to keep the appointment with my friend, in this city. I left at six for Magdeburg, and after two hours' ride over a dull, tiresome plain, rode along under the mounds and fortifications by the side of the Elbe, and entered the old town. It was *very* cold, and the streets were muddy, so I contented myself with looking at the Broadway, *(der breite Weg)* the Cathedral and one or two curious old churches, and in walking along the parapet leading to the fortress, which has a view of the winding Elbe. The Citadel was interesting from having been the prison in which Baron Trenck was confined, whose narrative I read years ago when quite a child.

We were soon on the road to Leipsic. The way was over one great, uninterrupted plain — a more monotonous country, even, than Belgium. Two of the passengers in the car with me were much annoyed at being taken by the railway agents for Poles. Their movements were strictly watched by the gens d'arme at every station we passed, and they were not even allowed to sit together! At Kothen a branch track went off to Berlin. We passed by Halle without being able to see anything of it or its University, and arrived here in four hours after leaving Magdeburg.

On my first walk around the city, yesterday morning, I passed the *Augustus Platz*—a broad green lawn, on which front the University and several other public buildings. A chain of beautiful promenades encircles the city, on the site of its old fortifications. Following their course through walks shaded by large trees and bordered with flowering shrubs, I passed a small but chaste monument to Sebastian Bach, the composer, which was erected almost entirely at the private cost of Mendelssohn, and stands opposite the building in which Bach once directed the choirs. As I was standing beside it, a glorious choral, swelled by a hundred voices, came through the open windows, like a tribute to the genius of the great master.

Having found my friend we went together to the *Stern Warte,* or Observatory, which gives a fine view of the country around the city, and in particular the battlefield. The Castellan who is stationed there, is well acquainted with the localities, and pointed out the position of the hostile armies. It was one of the most bloody and hard-fought battles which history records. The army of Napoleon stretched like a semicircle around the southern and eastern sides of the city, and the plain beyond was occupied by the allies, whose forces met together here. Schwarzenberg, with his Austrians, came from Dresden; Blucher, from Halle, with the Emperor Alexander. Their forces amounted to three hundred thousand, while those of Napoleon ranked at one hundred and ninety-two thousand men. It must have been a terrific scene. Four days raged the battle, and the meeting of half a million of men in deadly conflict was accompanied by the thunder of sixteen hundred cannon. The small rivers which flow through Leipsic were swollen with blood, and the vast plain was strewed with more than fifty thousand dead. It is difficult to conceive of such slaughter, while looking at the quiet and tranquil landscape below. It seemed more like a legend of past ages, when ignorance and passion led men to murder and destroy, than an event which the last half century witnessed. For the sake of humanity it is to be hoped that the world will never see such another.

There are some lovely walks around Leipsic. We went yesterday afternoon with a few friends to the Rosenthal, a beautiful meadow, bordered by forests of the German oak, very few of whose Druid trunks have been left standing. There are Swiss cottages embowered in the foliage, where every afternoon the social citizens assemble to drink their coffee and enjoy a few hours' escape from the noisy and dusty streets. One can walk for miles along these lovely paths by the side of the velvet meadows, or the banks of some shaded stream. We visited the little village of Golis, a short distance off, where, in the second story of a little white house, hangs the sign: "Schiller's Room." Some of the Leipsic literati have built a stone arch over the entrance, with the inscription above: "Here dwelt Schiller in 1795, and wrote his *Hymn to Joy*." Everywhere through Germany the remembrances of Schiller are sacred. In every city where he lived, they show his dwelling. They know and reverence the mighty spirit who has been among them. The little room where he conceived that sublime poem is hallowed as if by the presence of unseen spirits.

I was anxious to see the spot where Poniatowsky fell. We returned over the plain to the city and passed in at the gate by which the Cossacks entered, pursuing the flying French. Crossing the lower part, we came to the little river Elster, in whose waves the gallant prince sank. The stone bridge by which we crossed was blown up by the French, to cut off pursuit. Napoleon had given orders that it should not be blown up till the Poles had all passed over, as the river, though narrow, is quite deep, and the banks are steep. Nevertheless, his officers did not wait, and the Poles, thus exposed to the fire of the enemy, were obliged to plunge into the stream to join the French army, which had begun the retreat towards Frankfort. Poniatowsky, severely wounded, made his way through a garden near and escaped on horseback into the water. He became entangled among the fugitives and sank. By walking a little distance along the road towards Frankfort, we could see the spot where his body was taken out of the river; it is now marked by a square stone, covered with the names of his countrymen who have visited it. We returned through the narrow arched way, by which Napoleon fled when the battle was lost.

Another interesting place in Leipsic is Auerback's Cellar, which, it is said, contains an old manuscript history of Faust, from which Goethe derived the first idea of his poem. He used to frequent this cellar, and one of his scenes in "Faust" is laid in it. We looked down the arched passage; not wishing to purchase any wine, we could find no pretence for entering. The streets are full of book stores and one half the business of the inhabitants appears to consist in printing, paper-making and binding. The publishers have a handsome Exchange of their own, and during the Fairs, the amount of business transacted is enormous. The establishment of Brockhaus is contained in an immense building, adjoining which stands his dwelling, in the midst of magnificent gardens. That of Tauchnitz is not less celebrated. His edition of the classics, in particular, are the best that have ever been made; and he has lately commenced publishing a number of English works, in a cheap form. Otto Wigand, who has also a large establishment, has begun to issue translations of American works. He has already published Prescott and Bancroft, and I believe intends giving out shortly, translations from some of our poets and novelists. I became acquainted at the Museum, with a young German author who had been some time in America, and was well versed in our literature. He is now engaged in translating American works, one of which—Hoffman's "Wild Scenes of the Forest and Prairie"— will soon appear. In no place in Germany have I found more knowledge of our country, her men and her institutions, than in Leipsic, and as yet I have seen few that would be preferable as a place of residence. Its attractions lie not in its scenery, but in the social and intellectual character of its inhabitants.

May 11.—At last in this "Florence of the Elbe," as the Saxons have christened it. Exclusive of its glorious galleries of art, which are scarcely surpassed by any in Europe, Dresden charms one by the natural beauty of its environs. It stands in a curve of the Elbe, in the midst of green meadows, gardens and fine old woods, with the hills of Saxony sweeping around like an amphitheatre, and the craggy peaks of the Highlands looking at it from afar. The domes and spires at a distance give it a rich Italian look, which is heightened by the white villas, embowered in trees, gleaming on the hills around. In the streets there is no bustle of business — nothing of the din and confusion of traffic which mark most cities; it seems like a place for study and quiet enjoyment.

The railroad brought us in three hours from Leipsic, over the eighty miles of plain that intervene. We came from the station through the *Neustadt,* passing the Japanese Palace and the equestrian statue of Augustus the Strong. The magnificent bridge over the Elbe was so much damaged by the late inundation as to be quite impassable; we were obliged to go some distance up the river bank and cross on a bridge of boats. Next morning my first search was for the picture gallery. We set off at random, and after passing the Church of Our Lady, with its lofty dome of solid stone, which withstood the heaviest bombs during the war with Frederick the Great, came to an open square, one side of which was occupied by an old, brown, red-roofed building, which I at once recognized, from pictures, as the object of our search.

I have just taken a last look at the gallery this morning, and left it with real regret; for, during the two visits, Raphael's heavenly picture of the Madonna and child had so grown into my love and admiration, that it was painful to think I should never see it again. There are many more which clung so strongly to my imagination, gratifying in the highest degree the love for the Beautiful, that I left them with sadness, and the thought that I would now only have the memory. I can see the inspired eye and god-like brow of the Jesus-child, as if I were still standing before the picture, and the sweet, holy countenance of the Madonna still looks upon me. Yet, though this picture is a miracle of art, the first glance filled me with disappointment. It has somewhat faded, during the three hundred years that have rolled away since the hand of Raphael worked on the canvas, and the glass with which it is covered for better preservation, injures the effect. After I had gazed on it awhile, every thought of this vanished. The figure of the virgin seemed to soar in the air, and it was difficult to think the clouds were not in motion. An aerial lightness clothes her form, and it is perfectly natural for such a figure to stand among the clouds. Two divine cherubs look up from below, and in her arms sits the sacred child. Those two faces beam from the picture like those of angels. The wild, prophetic eye and lofty brow of the young Jesus chains one like a spell. There is something more than mortal in its expression—something in the infant face which indicates a power mightier than the proudest manhood. There is no glory around the head; but the spirit which shines from those features, marks his divinity. In the sweet face of the mother there speaks a sorrowful foreboding mixed with its tenderness, as if she knew the world into which the Saviour was born, and foresaw the path in which he was to tread. It is a picture which one can scarce look upon without tears.

There are in the same room six pictures by Correggio, which are said to be among his best works; one of them his celebrated Magdalen. There is also Correggio's "Holy Night," or the virgin with the shepherds in the manger, in which all the light comes from the body of the child. The surprise of the shepherds is most beautifully expressed. In one of the halls there is a picture by Van der Werff, in which the touching story of Hagar is told more feelingly than words could do it. The young Ishmael is represented full of grief at parting with Isaac, who, in childish unconsciousness of what has taken place, draws in sport the corner of his mother's mantle around him, and smiles at the tears of his lost playmate. Nothing can come nearer real flesh and blood than the two portraits of Raphael Mengs, painted by himself when quite young. You almost think the artist has, in sport, crept up behind the frame, and wishes to make you believe he is a picture. It would be impossible to speak of half the gems of art contained in this unrivalled collection. There are twelve large halls, containing in all nearly two thousand pictures.

The plain, south of Dresden, was the scene of the hard-fought battle between Napoleon and the allied armies, in 1813. On the heights above the little village of Racknitz, Moreau was shot on the second day of the battle. We took a footpath through the meadows, shaded by cherry trees in bloom, and reached the spot after an hour's walk. The monument is simple—a square block of granite, surmounted by a helmet and sword, with the inscription: *"The hero Moreau fell here by the side of Alexander, August 17th, 1813."* I gathered, as a memorial, a few leaves of the oak which shades it.

By applying an hour before the appointed time, we obtained admission to the Royal Library. It contains three hundred thousand volumes—among them the most complete collection of historical works in existence. Each hall is devoted to a history of a separate country, and one large room is filled with that of Saxony alone. There is a large number of rare and curious manuscripts, among which are old Greek works of the seventh and eighth centuries; a Koran which once belonged to the Sultan Bajazet; the handwriting of Luther and Melancthon; a manuscript volume with pen and ink sketches, by Albert Durer, and the earliest works after the invention of printing. Among these latter was a book published by Faust and Schaeffer, at Mayence, in 1457. There were also Mexican manuscripts, written on the aloe leaf, and many illuminated volumes created by the monks of the Middle Ages.

We were fortunate in seeing the *Grüne Gewölbe,* or Green Gallery, a collection of jewels and costly articles, unsurpassed in Europe. The entrance is only granted to six persons at a time, who pay a fee of two thalers. The customary way is to employ a *Lohnbedienter,* who goes around from one hotel to another, till he has collected the number, when he brings them together and conducts them to the person in the palace, who has charge of the treasures. As our visit happened to be during the Pentecost holidays, when everybody in Dresden goes to the mountains, there was some difficulty in effecting this, but after two mornings spent in hunting up curious travelers, the servant finally conducted us in triumph to the palace. The first hall into which we were ushered, contained works in bronze. They were all small, and chosen with regard to their artistical value. Some by John of Bologna were exceedingly fine, as was also a group in iron, cut out of a single block; perhaps the only successful attempt in this branch. The next room contained statues, and vases covered with reliefs, in ivory. The most remarkable work was the fall of Lucifer and his angels, containing ninety-two figures in all, carved out of a single piece of ivory sixteen inches high! It was the work of an Italian monk, and cost him many years of hard labor. There were two tables of mosaic-work, that would not be out of place in the fabled halls of the eastern genii, so much did they exceed my former ideas of human skill. The tops were of jasper, and each had a border of fruit and flowers, in which every color was represented by some precious stone, all with the utmost delicacy and truth to nature! It is impossible to conceive the splendid effect it produced. Besides some fine pictures on gold by Raphael Mengs, there was a Madonna, the largest specimen of enamel painting in existence.

However costly the contents of these halls, they were only an introduction to those which followed. Each one exceeded the other in splendor and costliness. The walls were covered to the ceiling with rows of goblets, vases, &c., of polished jasper, agate and lapiz lazuli. Splendid mosaic tables stood around, with caskets of the most exquisite silver and gold work upon them, and vessels of solid silver, some of them weighing six hundred pounds were placed at the foot of the columns. We were shown two goblets, each prized at six thousand thalers, made of gold and precious stones; also the great pearl called the Spanish Dwarf, nearly as large as a pullet's egg; globes and vases cut entirely out of the mountain crystal; magnificent Nuremberg watches aid clocks, and a great number of figures, made ingeniously of rough pearls and diamonds. The officer showed us a hen's egg of silver. There was apparently nothing remarkable about it, but by unscrewing, it came apart, and disclosed the yolk of gold. This again opened and a golden chicken was seen; by touching a spring, a little diamond crown came from the inside, and the crown being again taken apart, out dropped a valuable diamond ring! The seventh hall contains the coronation robes of Augustus II., of Poland, and many costly specimens of carving in wood. A cherry-stone is shown in a glass case, which has one hundred and twenty-five faces, all perfectly finished, carved upon it! The next room we entered sent back a glare of splendor that perfectly dazzled us. It was all gold, diamond, ruby and sapphire! Every case sent out such a glow and glitter that it seemed like a cage of imprisoned lightnings. Wherever the eye turned it was met by a blaze of broken rainbows. They were there by hundreds, and every gem was a fortune. Whole cases of swords, with hilts and scabbards of solid gold, studded with gems; the great two-handed coronation sword of the German emperors; daggers covered with brilliants and rubies; diamond buttons, chains and orders, necklaces and bracelets of pearl and emerald, and the order of the Golden Fleece made in gems of every kind. We were also shown the largest known onyx, nearly seven inches long and four inches broad! One of the most remarkable works is the throne and court of Aurungzebe, the Indian king, by Dinglinger, a celebrated goldsmith of the last century. It contains one hundred and thirty-two figures, all of enamelled gold, and each one most perfectly and elaborately finished. It was purchased by Prince Augustus for fifty-eight thousand thalers (a Prussian or Saxon thaler is about 70 cts.), which was not a high sum, considering that the making of it occupied Dinglinger and thirteen workmen for seven years!

It is almost impossible to estimate the value of the treasures these halls contain. That of the gold and jewels alone must be many millions of dollars, and the amount of labor expended on these toys of royalty is incredible. As monuments of patient and untiring toil, they are interesting; but it is sad to think how much labor and skill and energy have been wasted, in producing things which are useless to the world, and only of secondary importance as works of art. Perhaps, however, if men could be diverted by such playthings from more dangerous games, it would be all the better.

Chapter XIX
RAMBLES IN THE SAXON SWITZERLAND

After four days' sojourn in Dresden we shouldered our knapsacks, not to be laid down again till we reached Prague. We were elated with the prospect of getting among the hills again, and we heeded not the frequent showers which had dampened the enjoyment of the Pentecost holidays, to the good citizens of Dresden, and might spoil our own. So we trudged gaily along the road to Pillnitz and waved an adieu to the domes behind us as the forest shut them out from view. After two hours' walk the road led down to the Elbe, where we crossed in a ferry-boat to Pillnitz, the seat of a handsome palace and gardens, belonging to the King of Saxony. He happened to be there at the time, on an afternoon excursion from Dresden; as we had seen him before, in the latter place, we passed directly on, only pausing to admire the flower-beds in the palace court. The King is a tall, benevolent looking man, and is apparently much liked by his people. As far as I have yet seen, Saxony is a prosperous and happy country. The people are noted all over Germany for their honest, social character, which is written on their cheerful, open countenances. On our entrance into the Saxon Switzerland, at Pillnitz, we were delighted with the neatness and home-like appearance of everything. Everybody greeted us; if we asked for information, they gave it cheerfully. The villages were all pleasant and clean and the meadows fresh and blooming. I felt half tempted to say, in the words of an old ballad, which I believe Longfellow has translated:

"The fairest kingdom on this earth,
  It is the Saxon land!"

Going along the left bank of the Elbe, we passed over meadows purple with the tri-colored violet, which we have at home in gardens, and every little bank was bright with cowslips. At length the path led down into a cleft or ravine filled with trees, whose tops were on a level with the country around. This is a peculiar feature of Saxon scenery. The country contains many of these clefts, some of which are several hundred feet deep, having walls of perpendicular rock, in whose crevices the mountain pine roots itself and grows to a tolerable height without any apparent soil to keep it alive. We descended by a footpath into this ravine, called the Liebethaler Grund. It is wider than many of the others, having room enough for a considerable stream and several mills. The sides are of sandstone rock, quite perpendicular. As we proceeded, it grew narrower and deeper, while the trees covering its sides and edges nearly shut out the sky. An hour's walk brought us to the end, where we ascended gradually to the upper level again.

After passing the night at the little village of Uttewalde, a short distance further, we set out early in the morning for the Bastei, a lofty precipice on the Elbe. The way led us directly through the Uttewalder Grund, the most remarkable of all these chasms. We went down by steps into its depths, which in the early morning were very cold. Water dripped from the rocks, which but a few feet apart, rose far above us, and a little stream made its way along the bottom, into which the sun has never shone. Heavy masses of rock, which had tumbled down from the sides lay in the way, and tall pine trees sprung from every cleft. In one place the passage is only four feet wide, and a large mass of rock, fallen from above, has lodged near tine bottom, making an arch across, under which the traveller has to creep. After going under two or three arches of this kind, the passage widened and an arrow cut upon a rock directed us to a side path, which branched off from this into a mountain. Here the stone masses immediately assumed another form. They projected out like shelves sometimes as much as twenty feet from the straight side, and hung over the way, looking as if they might break off every moment.

I felt glad when we had passed under them. Then as we ascended higher, we saw pillars of rock separated entirely from the side and rising a hundred feet in height, with trees growing on their summits. They stood there gray and timeworn, like the ruins of a Titan temple.

The path finally led us out into the forest and through the clustering pine trees, to the summit of the Bastei. An inn has been erected in the woods and an iron balustrade placed around the rock. Protected by this, we advanced to the end of the precipice and looked down to the swift Elbe, more than seven hundred feet below! Opposite through the blue mists of morning, rose Konigstein, crowned with an impregnable fortress, and the crags of Lilienstein, with a fine forest around their base, frowned from the left bank. On both sides were horrible precipices of gray rock, with rugged trees hanging from the crevices. A hill rising up from one side of the Bastei, terminates suddenly a short distance from it, in an abrupt precipice. In the intervening space stand three or four of those rock-columns, several hundred feet high, with their tops nearly on a level with the Bastei. A wooden bridge has been made across from one to the other, over which the traveller passes, looking on the trees and rocks far below him, to the mountain, where a steep zigzag path takes him to the Elbe below.

We crossed the Elbe for the fourth time at the foot of the Bastei, and walked along its right bank towards Konigstein. The injury caused by the inundation was everywhere apparent. The receding flood had left a deposit of sand, in many places several feet deep on the rich meadows, so that the labor of years will be requisite to remove it and restore the land to an arable condition. Even the farmhouses on the hillside, some distance from the river, had been reached, and the long grass hung in the highest branches of the fruit trees. The people were at work trying to repair their injuries, but it will fall heavily upon the poorer classes.

The mountain of Königstein is twelve hundred feet high. A precipice, varying from one to three hundred feet in height, runs entirely

around the summit, which is flat, and a mile and a half in circumference. This has been turned into a fortress, whose natural advantages
make it entirely impregnable. During the Thirty Years' War and the
late war with Napoleon, it was the only place in Saxony unoccupied
by the enemy. Hence is it used as a depository for the archives and
royal treasures, in times of danger. By giving up our passports at the
door, we received permission to enter; the officer called a guide to
take us around the battlements. There is quite a little village on the
summit, with gardens, fields, and a wood of considerable size. The
only entrance is by a road cut through the rock, which is strongly
guarded. A well seven hundred feet deep supplies the fortress with
water, and there are storehouses sufficient to hold supplies for many
years. The view from the ramparts is glorious—it takes in the whole
of the Saxon Highlands, as far as the lofty Schneeberg in Bohemia.
On the other side the eye follows the windings of the Elbe, as far as
the spires of Dresden. Lilienstein, a mountain of exactly similar
formation, but somewhat higher, stands directly opposite. On walking around, the guide pointed out a little square tower standing on
the brink of a precipice, with a ledge, about two feet wide, running
around it, just below the windows. He said during the reign of
Augustus the Strong, a baron attached to his court, rose in his sleep
after a night of revelry, and Stepping out the window, stretched
himself at full length along the ledge. A guard fortunately observed
his situation and informed Augustus of it, who had him bound and
secured with cords, and then awakened by music. It was a good
lesson, and one which no doubt sobered him for the future.

Passing through the little city of Königstein, we walked on to
Schandau, the capital of the Saxon Switzerland, situated on the left
bank. It had sustained great damage from the flood, the whole place
having been literally under water. Here we turned up a narrow valley
which led to the Kuhstall, some eight miles distant. The sides, as
usual, were of steep gray rock, but wide enough apart to give room
to some lovely meadows, with here and there a rustic cottage. The

mountain maidens, in their bright red dresses, with a fanciful scarf bound around the head, made a romantic addition to the scene. There were some quiet secluded nooks, where the light of day stole in dimly through the thick foliage above and the wild stream rushed less boisterously over the rocks. We sat down to rest in one of these cool retreats, and made the glen ring with a loud cheer for America. The echoes repeated the name as if they had heard it for the first time, and I gave them a strict injunction to give it back to the next countryman who should pass by.

As we advanced further into the hills the way became darker and wilder. We heard the sound of falling water in a little dell on one side, and going nearer, saw a picturesque fall of about fifteen feet. Great masses of black rock were piled together, over which the mountain-stream fell in a snowy sheet. The pines above and around grew so thick and close, that not a sunbeam could enter, and a kind of mysterious twilight pervaded the spot. In Greece it would have been chosen for an oracle. I have seen, somewhere, a picture of the Spirit of Poetry, sitting beside just such a cataract, and truly the nymph could choose no more appropriate dwelling. But alas for sentiment! while we were admiring its picturesque beauty, we did not notice a man who came from a hut near by and went up behind the rocks. All at once there was a roar of water, and a real torrent came pouring down. I looked up, and lo! there he stood, with a gate in his hand which had held the water imprisoned, looking down at us to observe the effect. I motioned him to shut it up again, and he ran down to us, lest he should lose his fee for the "sight!"

Our road now left the valley and ascended through a forest to the Kuhstall, which we came upon at once. It is a remarkable natural arch, through a rocky wall or rampart, one hundred and fifty feet thick. Going through, we came at the other end to the edge of a very deep precipice, while the rock towered precipitously far above. Below lay a deep circular valley, two miles in diameter, and surrounded on every side by ranges of crags, such as we saw on the

Bastei. It was entirely covered with a pine forest, and there only appeared to be two or three narrow passages which gave it a communication with the world. The top of the Kuhstall can be reached by a path which runs up through a split in the rock, directly to the summit. It is just wide enough for one person to squeeze himself through; pieces of wood have been fastened in as steps, and the rocks in many places close completely above. The place derives its name from having been used by the mountaineers as a hiding-place for their cattle in time of war.

Next morning we descended by another crevice in the rock to the lonely valley, which we crossed, and climbed the Little Winterberg on the opposite side. There is a wide and rugged view from a little tower on a precipitous rock near the summit, erected to commemorate the escape of Prince Augustus of Saxony, who, being pursued by a mad stag, rescued himself on the very brink, by a lucky blow. Among the many wild valleys that lay between the hills, we saw scarcely one without the peculiar rocky formation which gives to Saxon scenery its most interesting character. They resemble the remains of some mighty work of art, rather than one of the thousand varied forms in which Nature delights to clothe herself.

The Great Winterberg, which is reached by another hour's walk along an elevated ridge, is the highest of the mountains, celebrated for the grand view from its summit. We found the handsome Swiss hotel recently built there, full of tourists who had come to enjoy the scene, but the morning clouds hid everything. We ascended the tower, and looking between them as they rolled by, caught glimpses of the broad landscape below. The Giant's Mountains in Silesia were hidden by the mist, but sometimes when the wind freshened, we could see beyond the Elbe into Bohemian Switzerland, where the long Schneeberg rose conspicuous above the smaller mountains. Leaving the other travellers to wait at their leisure for clearer weather, we set off for the Prebischthor, in company with two or three students from the Polytechnic School in Dresden. An hour's walk over high hills, whose forest clothing had been swept off by fire a few years before, brought us to it.

The Prebischthor is a natural arch, ninety feet high, in a wall of rock which projects at right angles from the precipitous side of the mountain. A narrow path leads over the top of the arch to the end of the rock, where, protected by a railing, the traveller seems to hang in the air. The valley is far below him—mountains rise up on either side—and only the narrow bridge connects him with the earth. We descended by a wooden staircase to the bottom of the arch, near which a rustic inn is built against the rock, and thence into the valley below, which we followed through rude and lonely scenery, to Hirnischkretschen on the Elbe.

Crossing the river again for the sixth and last time, we followed the right bank to Neidergrund, the first Austrian village. Here our passports were viséd for Prague, and we were allowed to proceed without any examination of baggage. I noticed a manifest change in our fellow travelers the moment we crossed the border. They appeared anxious and careful; if we happened to speak of the state of the country, they always looked around to see if anybody was near, and if we even passed a workman on the road, quickly changed to some other subject. They spoke much of the jealous strictness of the government, and from what I heard from Austrians themselves, there may have been ground for their cautiousness.

We walked seven or eight miles along the bank of the Elbe, to Tetschen, there left our companions and took the road to Teplitz. The scenery was very picturesque; it must be delightful to float down the swift current in a boat, as we saw several merry companies do. The river is just small enough and the banks near enough together, to render such a mode of travelling delightful, and the strength of the current would carry one to Dresden in a day.

I was pleasantly disappointed on entering Bohemia. Instead of a dull, uninteresting country, as I expected, it is a land full of the most lovely scenery. There is everything which can gratify the eye—high blue mountains, valleys of the sweetest pastoral look and romantic old ruins. The very name of Bohemia is associated with wild and wonderful legends, of the rude barbaric ages. Even the chivalric tales of the feudal times of Germany grow tame beside these earlier and darker histories. The fallen fortresses of the Rhine, or the robber-castles of the Odenwald had not for me so exciting an interest as the shapeless ruins cumbering these lonely mountains. The civilized Saxon race was left behind; I saw around me the features and heard the language of one of those ancient Sclavonic tribes, whose original home was on the vast steppes of Central Asia. I have rarely enjoyed traveling more than our first two days' journey towards Prague. The range of the Erzgebirge ran along on our right; the snow still lay in patches upon it, but the valleys between, with their little clusters of white cottages, were green and beautiful. About six miles before reaching Teplitz, we passed Kulm, the great battlefield, which in a measure decided the fate of Napoleon. He sent Vandamme with 40,000 men to attack the allies before they could unite their forces, and thus effect their complete destruction. Only the almost despairing bravery of the Russian guards under Ostermann, who held him in check till the allied troops united, prevented Napoleon's design. At the junction of the roads, where the fighting was hottest, the Austrians have erected a monument to one of their generals. Not far from it is that of Prussia, simple and tasteful. A woody hill near, with the little village of Kulm at its foot, was the station occupied by Vandamme at the commencement of the battle. There is now a beautiful chapel on its summit, which can be seen far and wide. A little distance further, the Emperor of Russia has erected a third monument to the memory of the Russians who fell. Four lions rest on the pedestal base; on the top of the shaft, forty-five feet high, Victory is represented as engraving the date, "Aug. 30, 1813," on a shield. The dark, pine-covered mountains on the right, overlook the whole field and the valley of Teplitz; Napoleon rode along their crests several days after the battle, to witness the scene of his defeat.

Teplitz lies in a lovely valley, several miles wide, bounded by the Bohemian mountains on one side, and the Erzgebirge on the other. One straggling peak near is crowned with a picturesque ruin, at whose foot the spacious bath-buildings lie half hidden in foliage. As we went down the principal street, I noticed nearly every house was a hotel; we learned afterwards that in summer the usual average of visitors is five thousand. The waters resemble those of the celebrated Carlsbad; they are warm ana particularly efficacious in rheumatism and diseases of like character. After leaving Teplitz, the road turned to the east, towards a lofty mountain, which we had seen the morning before. The peasants as they passed by, saluted us with "Christ greet you!"

We stopped for the night at the foot of the peak called the Milleschauer, and must have ascended nearly 2,000 feet, for we had a wide view the next morning, although the mists and clouds hid the half of it. The weather being so unfavorable, we concluded not to ascend, and taking leave of the Jena student who came there for that purpose, descended through green fields and orchards snowy with blossoms, to Lobositz, on the Elbe. Here we reached the plains again, where everything wore the luxuriance of summer; it was a pleasant change from the dark and rough scenery we left. The road passed through Theresienstadt, the fortress of Northern Bohemia. The little city is surrounded by a double wall and moat, which can be filled with water, rendering it almost impossible to be taken. In the morning we were ferried over the Moldau, and after journeying nearly all day across barren, elevated plains, saw late in the afternoon the sixty-seven spires of Prague below us! The dark clouds which hung over the hills, gave us little time to look upon the singular scene; and we were soon comfortably settled in the half-barbaric, half-Asiatic city, with a pleasant prospect of seeing its wonders on the morrow.

Chapter XX
SCENES IN PRAGUE

Prague. —I feel as if out of the world, in this strange, fantastic, yet beautiful old city. We have been rambling all morning through its winding streets, stopping sometimes at a church to see the dusty tombs and shrines, or to hear the fine music which accompanies the morning mass. I have seen no city yet that so forcibly reminds one of the past, and makes him forget everything but the associations connected with the scenes around him. The language adds to the illusion. Three-fourths of the people in the streets speak Bohemian and many of the signs are written in the same tongue, which is not at all like German. The palace of the Bohemian kings still looks down on the city from the western heights, and their tombs stand in the Cathedral of the holy Johannes. When one has climbed up the stone steps leading to the fortress, there is a glorious prospect before him. Prague, with its spires and towers, lies in the valley below, through which curves the Moldau with its green islands, disappearing among the hills which enclose the city on every side. The fantastic Byzantine architecture of many of the churches and towers, gives the city a peculiar oriental appearance; it seems to have been transported from the hills of Syria. Its streets are full of palaces, fallen and dwelt in now by the poorer classes. Its famous University, which once boasted forty thousand students, has long since ceased to exist. In a word, it is, like Venice, *a fallen city*; though as in Venice, the improving spirit of the age is beginning to give it a little life, and to send a quicker stream through its narrow and winding arteries. The railroad, which, joining that to Brünn, shall bring it in connection with Vienna, will be finished this year; in anticipation of the increased business which will arise from this, speculators are building enormous hotels in the suburbs and tearing down the old buildings to give place to more splendid edifices. These operations, and the chain bridge which spans the Moldau towards the southern end of the city, are the only things which look modern—everything else is old, strange and solemn.

Having found out first a few of the locations, we hunted our way with difficulty through its labyrinths, seeking out every place of note or interest. Reaching the bridge at last, we concluded to cross over and ascend to the Hradschin—the palace of the Bohemian kings. The bridge was commenced in 1357, and was one hundred and fifty years in building. That was the way the old Germans did their work, and they made a structure which will last a thousand years longer. Every pier is surmounted with groups of saints and martyrs, all so worn and time-beaten, that there is little left of their beauty, if they ever had any. The most important of them, at least to Bohemians, is that of the holy "Johannes of Nepomuck," now considered as the patron-saint of the land. He was a priest many centuries ago, whom one of the kings threw from the bridge into the Moldau, because he refused to reveal to him what the queen confessed. The legend says the body swam for some time on the river, with five stars around its head. The 16th of May, the day before we arrived, was that set apart for his particular honor; the statue on the bridge was covered with an arch of green boughs and flowers, and the shrine lighted with burning tapers. A railing was erected around it, near which numbers of the believers were kneeling, and a priest stood in the inside. The bridge was covered with passers-by, who all took their hats off till they had passed. Had it been a place of public worship, the act would have been natural and appropriate, but to uncover before a statue seemed to us too much like idolatry, and we ventured over without doing it. A few years ago it might have been dangerous, but now we only met with scowling looks. There are many such shrines and statues through the city, and I noticed that the people always took off their hats and crossed themselves in passing. On the hill above the western end of the city, stands a chapel on the spot where the Bavarians put an end to Protestantism in Bohemia by the sword, and the deluded peasantry of the land make pilgrimages to this spot, as if it were rendered holy by an act over which religion weeps!

Ascending the broad flight of steps to the Hradschin, I paused a moment to look at the scene below. A slight blue haze hung over the clustering towers, and the city looked dim through it, like a city seen in a dream. It was well that it should so appear, for not less dim and misty are the memories that haunt its walls. There was no need of a magician's wand to bid that light cloud shadow forth the forms of other times. They came uncalled for, even by fancy. Far, far back in the past, I saw the warrior-princess who founded the kingly city— the renowned Libussa, whose prowess and talent inspired the women of Bohemia to rise at her death and storm the land that their sex might rule where it obeyed before. On the mountain opposite once stood the palace of the bloody Wlaska, who reigned with her Amazon band for seven years over half Bohemia. Those streets below had echoed with the fiery words of Huss, and the castle of his follower—the blind Ziska, who met and defeated the armies of the German Empire—moulders on the mountain above. Many a year of war and tempest has passed over the scene. The hills around have borne the armies of Wallenstein and Frederic the Great; the war-cry of Bavaria, Sweden and Poland has echoed in the valley, and the red glare of the midnight cannon or the flames of burning palaces have often gleamed along the "blood-dyed waters" of the Moldau!

But this was a daydream. The throng of people coming up the steps waked me out of it. We turned and followed them through several spacious courts, till we arrived at the Cathedral, which is magnificent in the extreme. The dark Gothic pillars, whose arches unite high above, are surrounded with gilded monuments and shrines, and the side chapels are rich in elaborate decorations. A priest was speaking from a pulpit in the centre, in the Bohemian language, which not being the most intelligible, I went to the other end to see the shrine of the holy Johannes of Nepomuck. It stands at the end of one of the side aisles and is composed of a mass of gorgeous silver ornaments. At a little distance, on each side, hang four massive lamps of silver, constantly burning. The pyramid of statues, of the same precious metal, has at each corner a richly carved urn, three feet high, with a crimson lamp burning at the top. Above, four silver angels, the size of life, are suspended in the air, holding up the corners of a splendid drapery of crimson and gold. If these figures were melted down and distributed among the poor and miserable people who inhabit Bohemia, they would then be angels indeed, bringing happiness and blessing to many a ruined home-altar.

In the same chapel is the splendid burial-place of the Bohemian kings, of gilded marble and alabaster. Numberless tombs, covered with elaborate ornamental work, fill the edifice. It gives one a singular feeling to stand at one end and look down the lofty hall, dim with incense smoke and dark with the weight of many centuries.

On the way down again, we stepped into the St. Nicholas Church, which was built by the Jesuits. The interior has a rich effect, being all of brown and gold. The massive pillars are made to resemble reddish-brown marble, with gilded capitals, and the statues at the base are profusely ornamented in the same style. The music chained me there a long time. There was a grand organ, assisted by a full orchestra and large choir of singers. It was placed above, and at every sound of the priest's bell, the flourish of trumpets and deep roll of the drums filled the dome with a burst of quivering sound, while the giant pipes of the organ breathed out their full harmony and the very air shook under the peal. It was like a triumphal strain; the soul became filled with thoughts of power and glory — every sense was changed into one dim, indistinct emotion of rapture, which held the spirit as if spellbound. I could almost forgive the Jesuits the superstition and bigotry they have planted in the minds of men, for the indescribable enjoyment that music gave. When it ceased, we went out to the world again, and the recollection of it seems now like a dream—but a dream whose influence will last longer than many a more palpable reality.

Not far from this place is the palace of Wallenstein, in the same condition as when he inhabited it, and still in the possession of his descendants. It is a plain; large building, having beautiful gardens attached to it, which are open to the public. We went through the courtyard, threaded a passage with a roof of rough stalactitic rock, and entered the garden where a revolving fountain was casting up its glittering arches. Among the flowers at the other end of the garden there is a remarkable fountain. It is but a single jet of water which rises from the middle of a broad basin of woven wire, but by some means it sustains a hollow gilded ball, sometimes for many minutes at a time. When the ball drops, the sloping sides of the basin convey it directly to the fountain again, and it is carried up to dance a while longer on the top of the jet. I watched it once, thus supported on the water, for full fifteen minutes.

There is another part of Prague which is not less interesting, though much less poetical—the Jews' City. In our rambles we got into it before we were aware, but hurried immediately out of it again, perfectly satisfied with one visit. We came first into a dark, narrow street, whose sides were lined with booths of old clothes and second-hand articles. A sharp featured old woman thrust a coat before my face, exclaiming, "Herr, buy a fine coat!" Instantly a man assailed me on the ether side, "Here are vests! pantaloons! shirts!" I broke loose from them and ran on, but it only became worse. One seized me by the arm, crying, "*Lieber* Herr, buy some stockings!" and another grasped my coat: "Hats, Herr! hats! *buy something, or sell me something!*" I rushed desperately on, shouting "no! no!" with all my might, and finally got safe through. My friend having escaped their clutches also, we hunted the way to the old Jewish cemetery. This stands in the middle of the city, and has not been used for a hundred years. We could find no entrance, but by climbing upon the ruins of an old house near, I could look over the wall. A cold shudder crept over me, to think that warm, joyous Life, as I then felt it, should grow chill and pass back to clay in such a foul charnel-house. Large mounds of earth, covered with black, decaying grave-stones, which were almost hidden under the weeds and rank grass, filled the inclosure. A few dark, crooked alder-trees grew among the crumbling tombs, and gave the scene an air of gloom and desolation, almost fearful. The dust of many a generation lies under these mouldering stones; they now scarcely occupy a thought in the minds of the living; and yet the present race toils and seeks for wealth alone, that it may pass away and leave nothing behind—not even a memory for that which will follow it!

Chapter XXI
JOURNEY THROUGH EASTERN BOHEMIA AND MORAVIA TO THE
DANUBE

Our road the first two days after leaving Prague led across broad, elevated plains, across which a cold wind came direct from the summits of the Riesengebirge, far to our left. Were it not for the pleasant view we had of the rich valley of the Upper Elbe, which afforded a delightful relief to the monotony of the hills around us, the journey would have been exceedingly tiresome. The snow still glistened on the distant mountains; but when the sun shone out, the broad valley below, clad in the luxuriance of summer, and extending for at least fifty miles with its woods, meadows and white villages, looked like a real Paradise. The long ridges over which we travelled extend for nearly a hundred and fifty miles—from the Elbe almost to the Danube. The soil is not fertile, the inhabitants are exceedingly poor, and from our own experience, the climate must be unhealthy.

In winter the country is exposed to the full sweep of the northern winds, and in summer the sun shines down on it with unbroken force. There are few streams running through it, and the highest part, which divides the waters of the Baltic from those of the Black Sea, is filled for a long distance with marshes and standing pools, whose exhalations must inevitably subject the inhabitants to disease. This was perceptible in their sallow, sickly countenances; many of the women are afflicted with the *goitre,* or swelling of the throat; I noticed that towards evening they always carefully muffled up their faces. According to their own statements, the people suffer much from the cold in winter, as the few forests the country affords are in possession of the noblemen to whom the land belongs, and they are not willing to let them be cut down. The dominions of these petty despots are marked along the road with as much precision as the boundaries of an empire; we saw sometimes their stately castles at a distance, forming quite a contrast to the poor scattering villages of the peasants.

At Kollin, the road, which had been running eastward in the direction of Olmutz, turned to the south, and we took leave of the Elbe, after tracing back his course from Magdeburg nearly to his home in the mountains of Silesia. The country was barren and monotonous, but a bright sunshine made it look somewhat cheerful. We passed, every few paces, some shrine or statue by the roadside. This had struck me, immediately on crossing the border, in the Saxon Switzerland — it seemed as if the boundary of Saxony was that of Protestantism. But here in the heart of Bohemia, the extent to which this image worship is carried, exceeds anything I had imagined. There is something pleasing as well as poetical in the idea of a shrine by the wayside, where the weary traveller can rest, and raise his heart in thankfulness to the Power that protects him; it was no doubt a pious spirit that placed them there; but the people appear to pay the reverence to the picture which they should give to its spiritual image, and the pictures themselves are so shocking and ghastly, they seem better calculated to excite horror than reverence. It was really repulsive to look on images of the Saviour covered with blood, and generally with swords sticking in different parts of the body. The

Almighty is represented as an old man, wearing a Bishop's mitre, and the image of the Virgin is always dressed in a gay silk robe, with beads and other ornaments. From the miserable painting, the faces often had an expression that would have been exceedingly ludicrous, if the shock given to our feelings of reverence were not predominant. The poor, degraded peasants always uncovered or crossed themselves when passing by these shrines, but it appeared to be rather the effect of habit than any good impulse, for the Bohemians are noted all over Germany for their dishonesty; we learned by experience they deserve it. It is not to be wondered at either; for a people so poor and miserable and oppressed will soon learn to take advantage of all who appear better off than themselves. They had one custom which was touching and beautiful. At the sound of the church bell, as it rung the morning, noon and evening chimes, every one uncovered, and repeated to himself a prayer. Often, as we rested at noon on a bank by the roadside, that voice spoke out from the house of worship and everyone heeded its tone. Would that to this innate spirit of reverence were added the light of Knowledge, which a tyrannical government denies them!

The third night of our journey we stopped at the little village of Stecken, and the next morning, after three hours' walk over the ridgy heights, reached the old Moravian city of Iglau, built on a hill. It happened to be *Corpus Christi* day, and the peasants of the neighborhood were hastening there in their gayest dresses. The young women wore a crimson scarf around the head, with long fringed and embroidered ends hanging over the shoulders, or falling in one smooth fold from the back of the head. They were attired in black velvet vests, with full white sleeves and skirts of some gay color, which were short enough to show to advantage their red stockings and polished shoe-buckles. Many of them were not deficient in personal beauty — there was a gypsy-like wildness in their eyes, that combined with their rich hair and graceful costume, reminded me of the Italian maidens. The towns too, with their open squares and arched passages, have quite a southern look; but the damp, gloomy weather was enough to dispel any illusion of this kind.

In the neighborhood of Iglau, and, in fact, through the whole of Bohemia, we saw some of the strangest teams that could well be imagined. I thought the Frankfort milkwomen with their donkeys and hearse-like carts, were comical objects enough, but they bear no comparison with these Bohemian turn-outs. Dogs — for economy's sake, perhaps—generally supply the place of oxen or horses, and it is no uncommon thing to see three large mastiffs abreast, harnessed to a country-cart. A donkey and a cow together, are sometimes met with, and one man, going to the festival at Iglau, had his wife and children in a little wagon, drawn by a dog and a donkey. These two, however, did not work well together; the dog would bite his lazy companion, and the man's time was constantly employed in whipping him off the donkey, and in whipping the donkey away from the side of the road. Once I saw a wagon drawn by a dog, with a woman pushing behind, while a man, doubtless her lord and master, sat comfortably within, smoking his pipe with the greatest complacency! The very climax of all was a woman and a dog harnessed together, taking a load of country produce to market! I hope, for the honor of the country, it was not emblematic of woman's condition there. But as we saw hundreds of them breaking stone along the road, and occupied at other laborious and not less menial labor, there is too much reason to fear that it is so.

As we approached Iglau, we heard cannon firing; the crowd increased, and following the road, we came to an open square, where a large number were already assembled; shrines were erected around it, hung with pictures and pine boughs, and a long procession of children was passing down the side as we entered. We went towards the middle, where Neptune and his Tritons poured the water from their urns into two fountains, and stopped to observe the scene. The procession came on, headed by a large body of priests, in white robes, with banners and crosses. They stopped before the principal shrine, in front of the Rathhaus, and began a solemn religious ceremony. The whole crowd of not less than ten thousand persons, stood silent and uncovered, and the deep voice of the officiating priest was heard over the whole square. At times the multitude sang responses, and I could mark the sound, swelling and rolling up like a mighty wave, till it broke and slowly sank down again to the deepest stillness. The effect was marred by the rough voice of the officers commanding the soldiery, and the volleys of musquetry which were occasionally discharged. It degraded the solemnity of the pageant to the level of a military parade.

In the afternoon we were overtaken by a travelling *handwerker,* on his way to Vienna, who joined company with us. We walked several miles together, talking on various matters, without his having the least suspicion we were not Germans. He had been at Trieste, and at length began speaking of the great beauty of the American vessels there. "Yes," said I, "our vessels are admired all over the world." He stared at me with out comprehending;—"*your* vessels?" "Our country's," I replied; "we are Americans!" I can see still his look of incredulous astonishment and hear the amazed tone with which he cried: "You Americans — it is impossible!" We convinced him nevertheless, to his great joy, for all through Germany there is a curiosity to see our countrymen and a kindly feeling towards them. "I shall write down in my book," said he, "so that I shall never forget it, that I once travelled with two Americans!" We stopped together for the night at the only inn in a large, beggarly village, where we obtained a frugal supper with difficulty, for a regiment of Polish lancers was quartered there for the night, and the pretty *Kellnerin* was so busy in waiting on the officers that she had no eye for wandering journeymen, as she took us to be. She even told us the beds were all occupied and we must sleep on the floor. Just then the landlord came by. "Is it possible, Herr Landlord," asked our new companion, "that there is no bed here for us? Have the goodness to look again, for we are not in the habit of sleeping on the floor, like dogs!" This speech had its effect, for the *Kellnerin* was commanded to find us beds. She came back unwillingly after a time and reported that two, only, were vacant. As a German bed is only a yard wide, we pushed these two together, but they were still too small for three persons, and I had a severe cold in the morning, from sleeping crouched up against the damp wall.

The next day we passed the dividing ridge which separates the waters of the Elbe from the Danube, and in the evening arrived at Znaim, the capital of Moravia. It is built on a steep hill looking down on the valley of the Thaya, whose waters mingle with the Danube near Pressburg. The old castle on the height near, was formerly the residence of the Moravian monarchs, and traces of the ancient walls and battlements of the city are still to be seen. The handwerker took us to the inn frequented by his craft—the leather-curriers—and we conversed together till bedtime. While telling me of the oppressive laws of Austria, the degrading vassalage of the peasants and the hor-rors of the conscription system, he paused as in deep thought, and looking at me with a suppressed sigh, said: "Is it not true, America is free?" I told him of our country and her institutions, adding that though we were not yet as free as we hoped and wished to be, we enjoyed far more liberty than any country in the world. "Ah!" said he, "it is hard to leave one's fatherland oppressed as it is, but I wish I could go to America!"

We left next morning at eight o'clock, after having done full justice to the beds of the "Golden Stag," and taken leave of Florian Francke, the honest and hearty old landlord. Znaim appears to great advan-tage from the Vienna road; the wind which blew with fury against our backs, would not permit us to look long at it, but pushed us on towards the Austrian border. In the course of three hours we were obliged to stop at a little village; it blew a perfect hurricane and the rain began to soak through our garments. Here we stayed three hours among the wagoners who stopped on account of the weather. One miserable, drunken wretch, whom one would not wish to look at more than once, distinguished himself by insulting those around him, and devouring like a beast, large quantities of food. When the reckoning was given him, he declared he had already paid, and the waiter denying it, he said, "Stop, I will show you something!" pulled out his passport and pointed to the name—"Baron von Reitzen- stein." It availed nothing; he had fallen so low that his title inspired no respect, and when we left the inn they were still endeavoring to get their money and threatening him with a summary proceeding if the demand was not complied with.

Next morning the sky was clear and a glorious day opened before us. The country became more beautiful as we approached the Dan- ube; the hills were covered with vineyards, just in the tender green of their first leaves, and the rich valleys lay in Sabbath stillness in the warm sunshine. Sometimes from an eminence we could see far and wide over the garden-like slopes, where little white villages shone among the blossoming fruit-trees. A chain of blue hills rose in front, which I knew almost instinctively stood by the Danube; when we climbed to the last height and began to descend to the valley, where the river was still hidden by luxuriant groves, I saw far to the south- west, a range of faint, silvery summits, rising through the dim ether like an airy vision. There was no mistaking those snowy mountains. My heart bounded with a sudden thrill of rapturous excitement at this first view of the Alps! They were at a great distance, and their outline was almost blended with the blue drapery of air which clothed them. I gazed till my vision became dim and I could no longer trace their airy lines. They called up images blended with the grandest events in the world's history. I thought of the glorious spirits who have looked upon them and trodden their rugged sides — of the storms in which they veil their countenances, and the ava- lanches they hurl thundering to the valleys — of the voices of great deeds, which have echoed from their crags over the wide earth — and of the ages which have broken, like the waves of a mighty sea, upon their everlasting summits.

As we descended, the hills and forests shut out this sublime vision, and I looked to the wood-clothed mountains opposite and tried to catch a glimpse of the current that rolled at their feet. We here entered upon a rich plain, about ten miles in diameter, which lay between a backward sweep of the hills and a curve of the Danube. It was covered with the richest grain; everything wore the luxuriance of summer, and we seemed to have changed seasons since leaving the dreary hills of Bohemia. Continuing over the plain, we had on our left the fields of Wagram and Essling, the scene of two of Napoleon's blood-bought victories. The outposts of the Carpathians skirted the horizon—that great mountain range which stretches through Hungary to the borders of Russia.

At length the road came to the river's side, and we crossed on wooden bridges over two or three arms of the Danube, all of which together were little wider than the Schuylkill at Philadelphia. When we crossed the last bridge, we came to a kind of island covered with groves of the silver ash. Crowds of people filled the cool walks; booths of refreshment stood by the roadside, and music was everywhere heard. The road finally terminated in a circle, where beautiful alleys radiated into the groves; from the opposite side a broad street lined with stately buildings extended into the heart of the city, and through this avenue, filled with crowds of carriages and people on their way to those delightful walks, we entered Vienna!

Chapter XXII
VIENNA

May 31. — I have at last seen the thousand wonders of this great capital—this German Paris—this connecting link between the civilization of Europe and the barbaric magnificence of the East. It looks familiar to be in a city again, whose streets are thronged with people, and resound with the din and bustle of business. It reminds me of the never-ending crowds of London, or the life and tumult of our scarcely less active New York. Although the end may be sordid for which so many are laboring, yet the very sight of so much activity is gratifying. It is peculiarly so to an American. After residing in a foreign land for some time, the peculiarities of our nation are more easily noticed; I find in my countrymen abroad a vein of restless energy — a love for exciting action — which to many of our good German friends is perfectly incomprehensible. It might have been this which gave at once a favorable impression of Vienna.

The morning of our arrival we sallied out from our lodgings in the Leopoldstadt, to explore the world before us. Entering the broad Praterstrasse, we passed down to the little arm of the Danube, which separates this part of the new city from the old. A row of magnificent coffee-houses occupy the bank, and numbers of persons were taking their breakfasts in the shady porticoes. The Ferdinand's Bridge, which crosses the stream, was filled with people; in the motley crowd we saw the dark-eyed Greek, and Turks in their turbans and flowing robes. Little brown Hungarian boys were going around, selling bunches of lilies, and Italians with baskets of oranges stood by the side-walk. The throng became greater as we penetrated into the old city. The streets were filled with carts and carriages, and as there are no side-pavements, it required constant attention to keep out of their way. Splendid shops, fitted up with great taste, occupied the whole of the lower stories, and goods of all kinds hung beneath the canvas awnings in front of them. Almost every store or shop was dedicated to some particular person or place, which was represented on a large panel by the door. The number of these paintings added much to the splendor of the scene; I was gratified to find, among the images of kings and dukes, one dedicated "to the American," with an Indian chief in full costume.

The *Altstadt,* or old city, which contains about sixty thousand inhabitants, is completely separated from the suburbs, whose population, taking the whole extent within the outer barrier, numbers nearly half a million. It is situated on a small arm of the Danube, and encompassed by a series of public promenades, gardens and walks, varying from a quarter to half a mile in length, called the Glacis. This formerly belonged to the fortifications of the city, but as the suburbs grew up so rapidly on all sides, it was changed appropriately to a public walk. The city is still surrounded with a massive wall and a deep wide moat; but since it was taken by Napoleon in 1809, the moat has been changed into a garden, with a beautiful carriage road along the bottom, around the whole city. It is a beautiful sight, to stand on the summit of the wall and look over the broad Glacis, with its shady roads branching in every direction, and filled with inexhaustible streams of people. The Vorstaedte, or new cities, stretch in a circle around, beyond this; all the finest buildings front on the Glacis, among which the splendid Vienna Theatre and the church of San Carlo Borromeo are conspicuous. The mountains of the Vienna Forest bound the view, with here and there a stately castle on their woody summits. I was reminded of London as seen from Regent's Park, and truly this part of Vienna can well compare with it. On penetrating into the suburbs, the resemblance is at an end. Many of the public thoroughfares are still unpaved, and in dry weather one is almost choked by the clouds of fine dust. A furious wind blows from the mountains, sweeping the streets almost constantly and filling the eyes and ears with it, making the city an unhealthy residence for strangers.

There is no lack of places for pleasure or amusement. Beside the numberless walks of the Glacis, there are the Imperial Gardens, with their cool shades and flowers and fountains; the Augarten, laid out and opened to the public by the Emperor Joseph and the Prater, the largest and most beautiful of all. It lies on an island formed by the arms of the Danube, and is between two and three miles square. From the circle at the end of the Praterstrasse, broad carriage-ways extend through its forests of oak and silver ash, and over its verdant lawns to the principal stream, which bounds it on the north. These roads are lined with stately horse chestnuts, whose branches unite and form a dense canopy, completely shutting out the sun. Every afternoon the beauty and nobility of Vienna whirl through the cool groves in their gay equipages, while the sidewalks are thronged with pedestrians, and the numberless tables and seats with which every house of refreshment is surrounded, are filled with merry guests. Here, on Sundays and holidays, the people repair in thousands. The woods are full of tame deer, which run perfectly free over the whole Prater. I saw several in one of the lawns, lying down in the grass, with a number of children playing around or sitting beside them. It is delightful to walk there in the cool of the evening, when the paths are crowded, and everybody is enjoying the release from the dusty city. It is this free, social life which renders Vienna so attractive to foreigners and draws yearly thousands of visitors from all parts of Europe.

St. Stephen's Cathedral, in the centre of the old city, is one of the finest specimens of Gothic architecture in Germany. Its unrivalled tower, which rises to the height of four hundred and twenty-eight feet, is visible from every part of Vienna. It is entirely of stone, most elaborately ornamented, and is supposed to be the strongest in Europe. If the tower was finished, it might rival any church in Europe in richness and brilliancy of appearance. The inside is solemn and grand; but the effect is injured by the number of small chapels and shrines. In one of these rests the remains of Prince Eugene of Savoy, *"der edle Ritter,"* known in a ballad to every man, woman and child in Germany.

The Belvidere Gallery fills thirty-five halls, and contains three thousand pictures! It is absolutely bewildering to walk through such vast collections; you can do no more than glance at each painting, and hurry by face after face, and figure after figure, on which you would willingly gaze for hours and inhale the atmosphere of beauty that surrounds them. Then after you leave, the brain is filled with their forms — radiant spirit-faces look upon you, and you see constantly, in fancy, the calm brow of a Madonna, the sweet young face of a child, or the blending of divine with mortal beauty in an angel's countenance. I endeavor, if possible, always to make several visits—to study those pictures which cling first to the memory, and pass over those which make little or no impression. It is better to have a few images fresh and enduring, than a confused and indistinct memory of many.

From the number of Madonnas in every European gallery, it would almost seem that the old artists painted nothing else. The subject is one which requires the highest genius to do it justice, and it is therefore unpleasant to see so many still, inexpressive faces of the virgin and child, particularly by the Dutch artists, who clothe their figures sometimes in the stiff costume of their own time. Raphael and Murillo appear to me to be almost the only painters who have expressed what, perhaps, was above the power of other masters —the combined love and reverence of the mother, and the divine expression in the face of the child, prophetic of his mission and godlike power.

There were many glorious old paintings in the second story, which is entirely taken up with pictures; two or three of the halls were devoted to selected works from modern artists. Two of these I would give everything I have to possess.

One of them is a winter scene, representing the portico of an old Gothic church. At the base of one of the pillars a woman is seated in the snow, half-benumbed, clasping an infant to her breast, while immediately in front stands a boy of perhaps seven or eight years, his little hands folded in prayer, while the chill wind tosses the long curls from his forehead. There is something so pure and holy in the expression of his childish countenance, so much feeling in the lip and sorrowful eye, that it moves one almost to tears to look upon it. I turned back half a dozen times from the other pictures to view it again, and blessed the artist in my heart for the lesson he gave. The other is by a young Italian painter, whose name I have forgotten, but who, if he never painted anything else, is worthy a high place among the artists of his country. It represents some scene from the history of Venice. On an open piazza, a noble prisoner, wasted and pale from long confinement, has just had an interview with his children. He reaches his arm toward them as if for the last time, while a savage keeper drags him away. A lovely little girl kneels at the feet of the Doge, but there is no compassion in his stern features, and it is easy to see that her father is doomed.

The Lower Belvidere, separated from the Upper by a large garden, laid out in the style of that at Versailles, contains the celebrated *Ambraser Sammlung,* a collection of armor. In the first hall I noticed the complete armor of the Emperor Maximilian, for man and horse — the armor of Charles V., and Prince Moritz of Saxony, while the walls were filled with figures of German nobles and knights, in the suits they wore in life. There is also the armor of the great "Bayer of Trient," trabant of the Archduke Ferdinand. He was nearly nine feet in stature, and his spear, though not equal to Satan's, in Paradise Lost, would still make a tree of tolerable dimensions.

In the second hall we saw weapons taken from the Turkish army who besieged Vienna, with the horse-tail standards of the Grand Vizier, Kara Mustapha. The most interesting article was the battle-axe of the unfortunate Montezuma, which was probably given to the Emperor Charles V., by Cortez. It is a plain instrument of dark colored stone, about three feet long.

We also visited the *Bürgerliche Zeughaus,* a collection of arms and weapons, belonging to the citizens of Vienna. It contains sixteen thousand weapons and suits of armor, including those plundered from the Turks, when John Sobieski conquered them and relieved Vienna from the siege. Besides a great number of sabres, lances and horsetails, there is the blood-red harrier of the Grand Vizier, as well as his skull and shroud, which is covered with sentences from the Koran. On his return to Belgrade, after the defeat at Vienna, the Sultan sent him a bow-string, and he was accordingly strangled. The

Austrians having taken Belgrade some time after, they opened his grave and carried off his skull and shroud, as well as the bow-string, as relics. Another large and richly embroidered banner, which hung in a broad sheet from the ceiling, was far more interesting to me. It had once waved from the vessels of the Knights of Malta, and had, perhaps, on the prow of the Grand Master's ship, led that romantic band to battle against the Infidel.

A large number of peasants and common soldiers were admitted to view the armory at the same time. The grave *custode* who showed us the curiosities, explaining everything in phrases known by heart for years and making the same starts of admiration whenever he came to any thing peculiarly remarkable, singled us out as the two persons most worthy of attention. Accordingly his remarks were directed entirely to us, and his humble countrymen might as well have been invisible, for the notice he took of them. On passing out, we gave him a coin worth about fifteen cents, which happened to be so much more than the others gave him, that, bowing graciously, he invited us to write our names in the album for strangers. While we were doing this, a poor handwerker lingered behind, apparently for the same object, whom he scornfully dismissed, shaking the fifteen cent piece in his hand, and saying: "The album is not for such as you—it is for noble gentlemen!"

On our way through the city, we often noticed a house on the southern side of St. Stephen's Platz, dedicated to "the Iron Stick." In a niche by the window, stood what appeared to be the limb of a tree, completely filled with nails, which were driven in so thick that no part of the original wood is visible. We learned afterwards the legend concerning it. The Vienna Forest is said to have extended, several hundred years ago, to this place. A locksmith's apprentice was enabled, by the devil's help, to make the iron bars and padlock which confine the limb in its place; every locksmith's apprentice who came to Vienna after that, drove a nail into it, till finally there was room for no more. It is a singular legend, and whoever may have placed the limb there originally, there it has remained for two or three hundred years at least.

We spent two or three hours delightfully one evening in listening to Strauss's band. We went about sunset to the Odeon, a new building in the Leopoldstadt. It has a refreshment hall nearly five hundred feet long, with a handsome fresco ceiling and glass doors opening into a garden walk of the same length. Both the hall and garden were filled with tables, where the people seated themselves as they came, and conversed sociably over their coffee and wine. The orchestra was placed in a little ornamental temple in the garden, in front of which I stationed myself; for I was anxious to see the world's waltz-king, whose magic tones can set the heels of half Christendom in motion. After the band had finished tuning their instruments, a middle-sized, handsome man stepped forward with long strides, with a violin in one hand and bow in the other, and began waving the latter up and down, like a magician summoning his spirits. As if he had waved the sound out of his bow, the tones leaped forth from the instruments, and guided by his eye and hand, fell into a merry measure. The accuracy with which every instrument performed its part, was truly marvellous. He could not have struck the measure or the harmony more certainly from the keys of his own piano, than from that large band. The sounds struggled forth, so perfect and distinct, that one almost expected to see them embodied, whirling in wild dance around him. Sometimes the air was so exquisitely light and bounding, the feet could scarcely keep on the earth; then it sank into a mournful lament, with a sobbing tremulousness, and died away in a long-breathed sigh. Strauss seemed to feel the music in every limb. He would wave his fiddle-bow awhile, then commence playing with desperate energy, moving his whole body to the measure, till the sweat rolled from his brow. A book was lying on the stand before him, but he made no use of it. He often glanced around with a kind of half-triumphant smile at the restless crowd, whose feet could scarcely be restrained from bounding to the magic measure. It was the horn of Oberon realized. The composition of the music displayed great talent, but its charm consisted more in the exquisite combination of the different instruments, and the perfect, the wonderful exactness with which each performed its part—a piece of art of the most elaborate and refined character.

The company, which consisted of several hundred, appeared to be full of enjoyment. They sat under the trees in the calm, cool twilight, with the stars twinkling above, and talked and laughed sociably together between the pauses of the music, or strolled up and down the lighted alleys. We walked up and down with them, and thought how much we should enjoy such a scene at home, where the faces around us would be those of friends, and the language our mother tongue.

We went a long way through the suburbs one bright afternoon, to a little cemetery about a mile from the city, to find the grave of Beethoven. On ringing at the gate a girl admitted us into the grounds, in which are many monuments of noble families who have vaults there. I passed up the narrow walk, reading the inscriptions, till I came to the tomb of Franz Clement, a young composer, who died two or three years ago. On turning again, my eye fell instantly on the word "BEETHOVEN," in golden letters, on a tombstone of gray marble. A simple gilded lyre decorated the pedestal, above which was a serpent encircling a butterfly—the emblem of resurrection to eternal life. Here then, mouldered the remains of that restless spirit, who seemed to have strayed to earth from another clime, from such a height did he draw his glorious conceptions. The perfection he sought for here in vain, he has now attained in a world where the soul is freed from the bars which bind it in this. There were no flowers planted around the tomb by those who revered his genius; only one wreath, withered and dead, lay among the grass, as if left long ago by some solitary pilgrim, and a few wild buttercups hung with their bright blossoms over the slab. It might have been wrong, but I could not resist the temptation to steal one or two, while the old grave-digger was busy preparing a new tenement. I thought that other buds would open in a few days, but those I took would be treasured many a year as sacred relics. A few paces off is the grave of Schubert, the composer, whose beautiful songs are heard all over Germany.

It would employ one a week to visit all the rich collections of art in Vienna. They are all open to the public on certain days of the week, and we have been kept constantly in motion, running from one part of the city to another, in order to arrive at some gallery at the appointed time. Tickets, which have to be procured often in quite different parts of the city, are necessary for admittance to many; on applying after much trouble and search, we frequently came at the wrong hour, and must leave without effecting our object. We employed no guide, but preferred finding everything ourselves. We made a list every morning, of the collections open during the day, and employed the rest of the time in visiting the churches and public gardens, or rambling through the extensive suburbs.

We visited the Imperial Library a day or two ago. The hall is 245 feet long, with a magnificent dome in the centre, under which stands the statue of Charles V., of Carrara marble, surrounded by twelve other monarchs of the house of Hapsburg. The walls are of variegated marble, richly ornamented with gold, and the ceiling and dome are covered with brilliant fresco paintings. The library numbers 300,000 volumes, and 16,000 manuscripts, which are kept in walnut cases, gilded and adorned with medallions. The rich and harmonious effect of the whole cannot easily be imagined. It is exceedingly appropriate that a hall of such splendor, should be used to hold a library. The pomp of a palace may seem hollow and vain, for it is but the dwelling of a man; but no building can be too magnificent for the hundreds of great and immortal spirits to dwell in, who have visited earth during thirty centuries.

Among other curiosities preserved in the collection, we were shown a brass plate, containing one of the records of the Roman

Senate, made 180 years before Christ, Greek manuscripts of the fifth and sixth centuries, and a volume of Psalms, printed on parchment, in the year 1457, by Faust and Schaeffer, the inventors of printing. There were also Mexican manuscripts, presented by Cortez; the prayer-book of Hildegard, wife of Charlemagne, in letters of gold; the signature of San Carlo Borromeo, and a Greek testament of the thirteenth century, which had been used by Erasmus in making his translation and contains notes in his own hand. The most interesting article was the "Jerusalem Delivered" of Tasso, in the poet's own hand, with his erasions and corrections.

We also visited the Cabinet of Natural History, which is open twice a week "to all respectably dressed persons," as the notice at the door says. But Heaven forbid that I should attempt to describe what we saw there. The Mineral Cabinet had a greater interest to me, inasmuch as it called up the recollections of many a school-boy ramble over the hills and into all kinds of quarries, far and near. It is said to be the most perfect collection in existence. I was pleased to find many old acquaintances there, from the mines of Pennsylvania; Massachusetts and New York were also very well represented. I had no idea before, that the mineral wealth of Austria was so great. Besides the iron and lead mines among the hills of Styria and the quicksilver of Idria, there is no small amount of gold and silver found, and the Carpathian mountains are rich in jasper, opal and lapiz lazuli. The largest opal ever found, was in this collection. It weighs thirty-four ounces and looks like a condensed rainbow.

In passing the palace, we saw several persons entering the basement story under the Library, and had the curiosity to follow them. By so doing, we saw the splendid equipages of the house of Austria. There must have been near a hundred carriages and sleds, of every shape and style, from the heavy, square vehicle of the last century to the most light and elegant conveyance of the present day. One clumsy, but magnificent machine, of crimson and gold, was pointed out as being a hundred and fifty years old. The misery we witnessed in starving Bohemia, formed a striking contrast to all this splendor.

Beside the Imperial Picture Gallery, there are several belonging to princes and noblemen in Vienna, which are scarcely less valuable. The most important of these is that of Prince Liechtenstein, which we visited yesterday. We applied to the porter's lodge for admittance to the gallery, but he refused to open it for two persons; as we did not wish a long walk for nothing, we concluded to wait for other visitors. Presently a gentleman and lady came and inquired if the gallery was open. We told him it would probably be opened now, although the porter required a larger number, and he went to ask. After a short time he returned, saying: "He will come immediately; I thought best to put the number a little higher, and so I told him there were six of us!" Having little artistic knowledge of paintings, I judge of them according to the effect they produce upon me —in proportion as they gratify the innate love for the beautiful and the true. I have been therefore disappointed in some painters whose names are widely known, and surprised again to find works of great beauty by others of smaller fame. Judging by such a standard, I should say that "Cupid sleeping in the lap of Venus," by Correggio, is the glory of this collection. The beautiful limbs of the boy-god droop in the repose of slumber, as his head rests on his mother's knee, and there is a smile lingering around his half-parted lips, as if he was dreaming new triumphs. The face is not that of the wicked, mischief-loving child, but rather a sweet cherub, bringing a blessing to all he visits. The figure of the goddess is exquisite. Her countenance, unearthly in its loveliness, expresses the tenderness of a young mother, as she sits with one finger pressed on her rosy lip, watching his slumber. It is a picture which "stings the brain with beauty."

The chapel of St. Augustine contains one of the best works of Canova—the monument of the Grand Duchess, Maria Christina, of Sachsen-Teschen. It is a pyramid of gray marble, twenty-eight feet high, with an opening in the side, representing the entrance to a sepulchre. A female figure personating Virtue bears in an urn to the grave, the ashes of the departed, attended by two children with torches. The figure of Compassion follows, leading an aged beggar to the tomb of his benefactor, and a little child with its hands folded. On the lower step rests a mourning Genius beside a sleeping lion, and a bas-relief on the pyramid above represents an angel carrying Christina's image, surrounded with the emblem of eternity, to Heaven. A spirit of deep sorrow, which is touchingly portrayed in the countenance of the old man, pervades the whole group. While we looked at it, the organ breathed out a slow, mournful strain, which harmonized so fully with the expression of the figures, that we seemed to be listening to the requiem of the one they mourned. The combined effect of music and sculpture, thus united in their deep pathos, was such, that I could have sat down and wept. It was not from sadness at the death of a benevolent though unknown individual,—but the feeling of grief, of perfect, unmingled sorrow, so powerfully represented, came to the heart like an echo of its own emotion, and carried it away with irresistible influence. Travellers have described the same feeling while listening to the Miserere in the Sistine Chapel, at Rome. Canova could not have chiseled the monument without tears.

One of the most interesting objects in Vienna, is the Imperial Armory. We were admitted through tickets previously procured from the Armory Direction; as there was already one large company within, we were told to wait in the court till our turn came. Around the wall on the inside, is suspended the enormous chain which the Turks stretched across the Danube at Buda, in the year 1529, to obstruct the navigation. It has eight thousand links and is nearly a mile in length. The court is filled with cannon of all shapes and sizes, many of which were conquered from other nations. I saw a great many which were cast during the French Revolution, with the words "Liberté! Égalité!" upon them, and a number of others bearing the simple letter "N."

Finally the first company came down and the forty or fifty persons who had collected during the interval, were admitted. The Armory runs around a hollow square, and must be at least a quarter of a mile in length. We were all taken into a circular hall, made entirely of weapons, to represent the four quarters of the globe. Here the crusty old guide who admitted us, rapped with his stick on the shield of an old knight who stood near, to keep silence, and then addressed us: "When I speak everyone must be silent. No one can write or draw anything. No one shall touch anything, or go to look at anything else, before I have done speaking. Otherwise, they shall be taken immediately into the street again!" Thus in every hall he rapped and scolded, driving the women to one side with his stick and the men to the other, till we were nearly through, when the thought of the coming fee made him a little more polite. He had a regular set of descriptions by heart, which he went through with a great flourish, pointing particularly to the common military caps of the late Emperors of Prussia and Austria, as "treasures beyond all price to the nation!" Whereupon, the crowd of common people gazed reverently on the shabby beavers, and I verily believe, would have devoutly kissed them, had the glass covering been removed. I happened to be next to a tall, dignified young man, who looked on all this with a displeasure almost amounting to contempt. Seeing I was a foreigner, he spoke, in a low tone, bitterly of the Austrian government. "You are not then an Austrian?" I asked. "No, thank God!" was the reply: "but I have seen enough of Austrian tyranny. I am a Pole."

The first wing contains banners used in the French Revolution, and liberty trees with the red cap; the armor of Rudolph of Hapsburg, Maximilian I., the Emperor Charles V., and the hat, sword and order of Marshal Schwarzenberg. Some of the halls represent a fortification, with walls, ditches and embankments, made of muskets and swords. A long room in the second wing contains an encampment, in which twelve or fifteen large tents are formed in like manner. Along the sides are grouped old Austrian banners, standards taken from the French, and horsetails and flags captured from the Turks. "They make a great boast," said the Pole, "of a half dozen French colors, but let them go to the Hospital des Invalides, in Paris, and they will find hundreds of the best banners of Austria!" They also exhibited the armor of a dwarf king of Bohemia and Hungary, who died, a gray-headed old man, in his twentieth year; the sword of Marlborough; the coat of Gustavus Adolphus, pierced in the breast and back with the bullet which killed him at Lützen; the armor of the old Bohemian princess Libussa, and that of the amazon Wlaska, with a steel visor made to fit the features of her face. The last wing was the most remarkable. Here we saw the helm and breastplate of Attila, king of the Huns, which once glanced at the head of his myriads of wild hordes, before the walls of Rome; the armor of Count Stahremberg, who commanded Vienna during the Turkish siege in 1529, and the holy banner of Mahomet, taken at that time from the Grand Vizier, together with the steel harness of John Sobieski of Poland, who rescued Vienna from the Turkish troops under Kara Mustapha; the hat, sword and breastplate of Godfrey of Bouillon, the Crusader-king of Jerusalem, with the banners of the cross the Crusaders had borne to Palestine, and the standard they captured from the Turks on the walls of the Holy City! I felt all my boyish enthusiasm for the romantic age of the Crusaders revive, as I looked on the torn and mouldering banners which once waved on the hills of Judea, or perhaps followed the sword of the Lion Heart through the fight on the field of Ascalon! What tales could they not tell, those old standards, cut and shivered by spear and lance! What brave hands have carried them through the storm of battle, what dying eyes have looked upwards to the cross on their folds, as the last prayer was breathed for the rescue of the Holy Sepulchre!

I must now close the catalogue. This morning we shall look upon Vienna for the last time. Our knapsacks are repacked, and the passports (precious documents!) viséd for Munich. The getting of this visé, however, caused a comical scene at the Police Office, yesterday.

We entered the Inspector's Hall and took our stand quietly among the crowd of persons who were gathered around a railing which separated them from the main office. One of the clerks came up, scowling at us, and asked in a rough tone, "What do you want here?" We handed him our tickets of sojourn (for when a traveler spends more than twenty-four hours in a German city, he must take out a permission and pay for it) with the request that he would give us our passports. He glanced over the tickets, came back and with constrained politeness asked us to step within the railing. Here we were introduced to the Chief Inspector. "I desire Herr —— to come here," said he to a servant; then turning to us, "I am happy to see the gentlemen in Vienna." An officer immediately came up, who addressed us in fluent English. "You may speak in your native tongue," said the Inspector, "excuse our neglect; from the facility with which you speak German, we supposed you were natives of Austria!" Our passports were signed at once and given us with a gracious bow, accompanied by the hope that we would visit Vienna again before long. All this, of course, was perfectly unintelligible to the wondering crowd outside the railing. Seeing however, the honors we were receiving, they crowded back and respectfully made room for us to pass out. I kept a grave face till we reached the bottom of the stairs, when I gave way to restrained laughter in a manner that shocked the dignity of the guard, who looked savagely at me over his forest of moustache. I would nevertheless have felt grateful for the attention we received as Americans, were it not for our uncourteous reception as suspected Austrians.

We have just been exercising the risible muscles again,—though from a very different cause, and one which, according to common custom, ought to draw forth symptoms of a lachrymose nature. This morning B —— suggested an examination of our funds, for we had neglected keeping a strict account, and what with being cheated in Bohemia and tempted by the amusements of Vienna, there was an apparent dwindling away. So we emptied our pockets and purses, counted up the contents, and found we had just ten florins, or four dollars apiece. The thought of our situation, away in the heart of Austria, five hundred miles from our Frankfort home, seems irresistibly laughable. By allowing twenty days for the journey, we shall have half a florin a day, to travel on. This is a homeopathic allowance, indeed, but we have concluded to try it. So now adieu, Vienna! In two hours we shall be among the hills again.

Chapter XXIII
UP THE DANUBE

We passed out of Vienna in the face of one of the strongest winds it was ever my lot to encounter. It swept across the plain with such force that it was almost impossible to advance till we got under the lee of a range of hills. About two miles from the barrier we passed Schoenbrunn, the Austrian Versailles. It was built by the Empress Maria Theresa, and was the residence of Napoleon in 1809, when Vienna was in the hands of the French. Later, in 1832, the Duke of Reichstadt died in the same room which his father once occupied. Behind the palace is a magnificent garden, at the foot of a hill covered with rich forests and crowned with an open pillared hall, 300 feet long, called the *Gloriette.* The colossal eagle which surmounts it, can be seen a great distance.

The lovely valley in which Schoenbrunn lies, follows the course of the little river Vienna into the heart of that mountain region lying between the Styrian Alps and the Danube, and called the Vienna Forest. Into this our road led, between hills covered with wood, with here and there a lovely green meadow, where herds of cattle were grazing. The third day we came to the Danube again at Melk, a little city built under the edge of a steep hill, on whose summit stands the palace-like abbey of the Benedictine Monks. The old friars must have had a merry life of it, for the wine-cellar of the abbey furnished the French army 50,000 measures for several days in succession. The shores of the Danube here are extremely beautiful. The valley where it spreads out, is filled with groves, but where the hills approach the stream, its banks are rocky and precipitous, like the Rhine. Although not so picturesque as the latter river, the scenery of the Danube is on a grander scale. On the south side, the mountains sloped down to it with a majestic sweep, and there must be delightful glances into the valleys that lie between, in passing down the current.

But we soon left the river, and journeyed on through the enchanting inland vales. To give an idea of the glorious enjoyment of traveling through such scenes, let me copy a leaf out of my journal, written as we rested at noon on the top of a lofty hill: — "Here, while the delightful mountain breeze that comes fresh from the Alps cools my forehead, and the pines around are sighing their eternal anthem, I seize a few moments to tell what a paradise is around me. I have felt an elevation of mind and spirit, a perfect rapture from morning till night, since we left Vienna. It is the brightest and balmiest June weather; an ever fresh breeze sings through the trees and waves the ripening grain on the verdant meadows and hill-slopes. The air is filled with bird-music. The larks sing above us out of sight, the bullfinch wakes his notes in the grove, and at eve the nightingale pours forth her thrilling strain. The meadows are literally covered with flowers — beautiful purple salvias, pinks such as we have at home in our gardens and glowing buttercups, color the banks of every stream. I never saw richer or more luxuriant foliage. Magnificent forests clothe the hills, and the villages are imbedded in fruit trees, shrubbery and flowers. Sometimes we go for miles through some enchanting valley, lying like a paradise between the mountains, while the distant, white Alps look on it from afar; sometimes over swelling ranges of hills, where we can see to the right the valley of the Danube, threaded by his silver current and dotted with many white cottages and glittering spires, and farther beyond, the blue mountains of the Bohemian Forest. To the left, the range of the Styrian Alps stretches along the sky, summit above summit, the farther ones robed in perpetual snow. I could never tire gazing on those glorious hills. They fill the soul with a conception of sublimity, such as one feels when listening to triumphal music. They seem like the marble domes of a mighty range of temples, where earth worships her Maker with an organ-anthem of storms!

"There is a luxury in traveling here. We walk all day through such scenes, resting often in the shade of the fruit trees which line the road, or on a mossy bank by the side of some cool forest. Sometimes for enjoyment as well as variety, we make our dining place by a clear spring instead of within a smoky tavern; and our simple meals have a relish an epicure could never attain. Away with your railroads and steamboats and mail-coaches, or keep them for those who have no eye but for the sordid interests of life! With my knapsack and pilgrim-staff, I ask not their aid. If a mind and soul full of rapture with beauty, a frame in glowing and vigorous health, and slumbers unbroken even by dreams, are blessings anyone would attain, let him pedestrianize it through Lower Austria!"

I have never been so strongly and constantly reminded of America, as during this journey. Perhaps the balmy season, the same in which I last looked upon the dear scenes of home, may have its effect; but there is besides a richness in the forests and waving fields of grain, a wild luxuriance over every landscape, which I have seen nowhere else in Europe. The large farm houses, buried in orchards, scattered over the valleys, add to the effect. Everything seems to speak of happiness and prosperity.

We were met one morning by a band of wandering Bohemian gypsies — the first of the kind I ever saw. A young woman with a small child in her arms came directly up to me, and looking full in my face with her wild black eyes, said, without any preface: "Yes, he too has met with sorrow and trouble already, and will still have more. But he is not false—he is true and sincere, and will also meet with good luck!" She said she could tell me three numbers with which I should buy a lottery ticket and win a great prize. I told her I would have nothing to do with the lottery, and would buy no ticket, but she persisted, saying: "Has he a twenty kreutzer piece?—will he give it? Lay it in his hand and make a cross over it, and I will reveal the numbers!" On my refusal, she became angry, and left me, saying: "Let him take care—the third day something will happen to him!" An old, wrinkled hag made the same proposition to my companion with no better success. They reminded me strikingly of our Indians; their complexion is a dark brown, and their eyes and hair are black as night. These belonged to a small tribe who wander through the forests of Bohemia, and support themselves by cheating and stealing.

We stopped the fourth night at Enns, a small city on the river of the same name, which divides Upper from Lower Austria. After leaving the beautiful little village where we passed the night before, the road ascended one of those long ranges of hills, which stretch off from the Danube towards the Alps. We walked for miles over the broad and uneven summit, enjoying the enchanting view which opened on both sides. If we looked to the right, we could trace the windings of the Danube for twenty miles, his current filled with green, wooded islands; white cities lie at the foot of the hills, which, covered to the summit with grain-fields and vineyards, extended back one behind another, till the farthest were lost in the distance. I was glad we had taken the way from Vienna to Linz by land, for from the heights we had a view of the whole course of the Danube, enjoying besides, the beauty of the inland vales and the far-off Styrian Alps. From the hills we passed over we could see the snowy range as far as the Alps of Salzburg—some of them seemed robed to the very base in their white mantles. In the morning the glaciers on their summit glittered like stars; it was the first time I saw the sun reflected at a hundred miles' distance!

On descending we came into a garden-like plain, over which rose the towers of Enns, built by the ransom money paid to Austria for the deliverance of the Lion-Hearted Richard. The country legends say that St. Florian was thrown into the river by the Romans in the third century, with a millstone around his neck, which, however, held him above the water like cork, until he had finished preaching them a sermon. In the villages we often saw his image painted on the houses, in the act of pouring a pail of water on a burning building, with the inscription beneath — "Oh, holy Florian, pray for us!" This was supposed to be a charm against fire. In Upper Austria, it is customary to erect a shrine on the road, wherever an accident has happened, with a painting and description of it, and an admonition to all passers-by to pray for the soul of the unfortunate person. On one of them, for instance, was a cart with a wild ox, which a man was holding by the horns; a woman kneeling by the wheels appeared to be drawing a little girl by the feet from under it, and the inscription stated: "By calling on Jesus, Mary and Joseph, the girl was happily rescued." Many of the shrines had images which the people no doubt, in their ignorance and simplicity, considered holy, but they were to us impious and almost blasphemous.

From Enns a morning's walk brought us to Linz. The peasant girls in their broad straw hats were weeding the young wheat, looking as cheerful and contented as the larks that sung above them. A mile or two from Linz we passed one or two of the round towers belonging to the new fortifications of the city. As walls have grown out of fashion, Duke Maximilian substituted an invention of his own. The city is surrounded by thirty-two towers, one to three miles distant from it, and so placed that they form a complete line of communication and defence. They are sunk in the earth, surrounded with a ditch and embankments, and each is capable of containing ten cannon and three hundred men. The pointed roofs of these towers are seen on all the hills around. We were obliged to give up our passports at the barrier, the officer telling us to call for them in three hours at the City Police Office; we spent the intervening time very agreeably in rambling through this gay, cheerful-looking town. With its gilded spires and ornamented houses, with their green lattice-blinds, it reminds one strongly of Italy, or at least of what Italy is said to be. It has now quite an active and business-like aspect, occasioned by the steamboat and railroad lines which connect it with Vienna, Prague, Ratisbon and Salzburg. Although we had not exceeded our daily allowance by more than a few kreutzers, we found that twenty days would be hardly sufficient to accomplish the journey, and our funds must therefore be replenished. Accordingly I wrote from Linz to Frankfort, directing a small sum to be forwarded to Munich, which city we hoped to reach in eight days.

We took the horse cars at Linz for Lambach, seventeen miles on the way towards Gmunden. The mountains were covered with clouds as we approached them, and the storms they had been brewing for two or three days began to march down on the plain. They had nearly reached us, when we crossed the Traun and arrived at Lambach, a small city built upon a hill. We left the next day at noon, and on ascending the hill after crossing the Traun, had an opportunity of seeing the portrait on the Traunstein, of which the old landlord told us. I saw it at the first glance—certainly it is a most remarkable freak of nature. The rough back of the mountain forms the exact profile of the human countenance, as if regularly hewn out of the rock. What is still more singular, it is said to be a correct portrait of the unfortunate Louis XVI. The landlord said it was immediately recognized by all Frenchmen. The road followed the course of the Traun, whose green waters roared at the bottom of the glen below us; we walked for several miles through a fine forest, through whose openings we caught glimpses of the mountains we longed to reach.

The river roared at last somewhat louder, and on looking down the bank, I saw rocks and rapids, and a few houses built on the edge of the stream. Thinking it must be near the fall, we went down the path, and on crossing a little wooden bridge, the whole affair burst in sight! Judge of our surprise at finding a fall of fifteen feet, after we had been led to expect a tremendous leap of forty or fifty, with all the accompaniment of rocks and precipices. Of course, the whole descent of the river at the place was much greater, and there were some romantic cascades over the rocks which blocked its course. Its greatest beauty consisted in the color of the water — the brilliant green of the waves being broken into foam of the most dazzling white — and the great force with which it is thrown below.

The Traunstein grew higher as we approached, presenting the same profile till we had nearly reached Gmunden. From the green upland meadows above the town, the view of the mountain range was glorious, and I could easily conceive the effect of the Unknown Student's appeal to the people to fight for those free hills. I think it is Hewitt who relates the incident — one of the most romantic in German history. Count Pappenheim led his forces here in the year 1626, to suppress a revolution of the people of the whole Salzburg region, who had risen against an invasion of their rights by the Austrian government. The battle which took place on these meadows was about being decided in favor of the oppressors, when a young man, clad as a student, suddenly appeared and addressed the people, pointing to the Alps above them and the sweet lake below, and asking if that land should not be free. The effect was electrical; they returned to the charge and drove back the troops of Pappenheim, who were about taking to flight, when the unknown leader fell, mortally wounded. This struck a sudden panic through his followers, and the Austrians turning again, gained a complete victory. But the name of the brave student is unknown, his deed unsung by his country's bards, and almost forgotten.

Chapter XXIV
THE UNKNOWN STUDENT

Ha! spears on Gmunden's meadows green,
   And banners on the wood-crowned height!
Rank after rank, their helmets' sheen
   Sends back the morning light!
Where late the mountain maiden sang,
The battle-trumpet's brazen clang
   Vibrates along the air;
And wild dragoons wheel o'er the plain,
Trampling to earth the yellow grain,
From which no more the merry swain
   His harvest sheaves shall bear.

The eagle, in his sweep at morn,
   To meet the monarch-sun on high,
Heard the unwonted warrior's horn
   Peal faintly up the sky!
He saw the foemen, moving slow
In serried legions, far below,
   Against that peasant-band,
Who dared to break the tyrant's thrall
And by the sword of Austria fall,
Or keep the ancient Right of all,
   Held by their mountain-land!

They came to meet that mail clad host
   From glen and wood and ripening field;
A brave, stout arm, each man could boast —
   A soul, unused to yield!

They met a shout, prolonged and loud,
Went hovering upward with the cloud
    That closed around them dun;
Blade upon blade unceasing clashed,
Spears in the onset shivering crashed,
And the red glare of cannon flashed
    Athwart the smoky sun!

The mountain warriors wavered back,
    Borne down by myriaads of the foe,
Like pines before the torrent's track
    When spring has warmed the snow.
Shall Faith and Freedom vainly call,
And Gmunden's warrior-herdsmen fall
    On the red field in vain?
No! from the throng that back retired,
A student boy sprang forth inspired,
And while his words their bosoms fired,
    Led on the charge again!

"And thus your free arms would ye give
    So tamely to a tyrant's band,
And with the hearts of vassals live
    In this, your chainless land?
The emerald lake is spread below,
And tower above, the hills of snow
    Here, field and forest lie;
This land, so glorious and so free
Say, shall it crushed and trodden be?
Say, would ye rather bend the knee
    Than for its freedom die?

"Look! yonder stand in midday's glare

The everlasting Alps of snow,
And from their peaks a purer air
    Breathes o'er the vales below!
The Traunstein's brow is bent in pride
He brooks no craven on his side
    Would ye be fettered then?
There lifts the Sonnenstein his head,
There chafes the Traun his rocky bed
And Aurach's lovely vale is spread
    Look on them and be men!

"Let, like a trumpet's sound of fire,
    These stir your souls to manhood's pan
The glory of the Alps inspire
    Each yet unconquered heart!
For, through their unpolluted air
Soars fresher up the grateful prayer
    From freemen, unto God;
A blessing on those mountains old!
On to the combat, brethren bold!
Strike, that ye free the valleys hold,
    Where free your fathers trod!"

And like a mighty storm that tears
    The icy avalanche from its bed,
They rushed against th' opposing spears
    The student at their head
The bands of Austria fought in vain;
A bloodier harvest heaped the plain
    At every charge they made;
Each herdsman was a hero then —
The mountain hunters stood like men,
And echoed from the farthest glen

The clash of blade on blade!

The banner in the student's hand
   Waved triumph from the fight before;
What terror seized the conq'ring band?
   It fell, to rise no more!
And with it died the lefty flame,
That from his lips in lightning came
   And burned upon their own;
Dread Pappenheim led back the foe,
The mountain peasants yielded slow,
And plain above and lake below
   Were red when evening shone!

Now many a year has passed away
   Since battle's blast rolled o'er the plain,
The Alps are bright in morning's ray
   The Traunstein smiles again.
But underneath the flowery sod,
By happy peasant children trod,
   A hero's ashes lay.
O'er him no grateful nation wept,
Fame, of his deed no record kept,
And dull Forgetfulness hath swept
   His very name away!

To many a grave, by poets sung,
   There falls to dust a lofty brow,
But he alone, the brave and young,
   Sleeps there forgotten now.
The Alps upon that field look down,
Which won his bright and brief renown,
   Beside the lake's green shore;

Still wears the land a tyrant's chain
Still bondmen tread the battle-plain,
Called by his glorious soul in vain
   To win their rights of yore.

Chapter XXV
THE AUSTRIAN ALPS

It was nearly dark when we came to the end of the plain and looked on the city at our feet and the lovely lake that lost itself in the mountains before us. We were early on board the steamboat next morning, with a cloudless sky above us and a snow-crested Alp beckoning on from the end of the lake. The water was of the most beautiful green hue, the morning light colored the peaks around with purple, and a misty veil rolled up the rocks of the Traunstein. We stood on the prow and enjoyed to the fullest extent the enchanting scenery. The white houses of Gmunden sank down to the water's edge like a flock of ducks; half-way we passed castle Ort, on a rock in the lake, whose summit is covered with trees.

As we neared the other extremity, the mountains became steeper and loftier; there was no path along their wild sides, nor even a fisher's hut nestled at their feet, and the snow filled the ravines more than half-way from the summit. An hour and a quarter brought us to Ebensee, at the head of the lake, where we landed and plodded on towards Ischl, following the Traun up a narrow valley, whose mountain-walls shut out more than half the sky. They are covered with forests, and the country is inhabited entirely by the woodmen who fell the mountain pines and float the timber rafts down to the Danube. The steeps are marked with white lines, where the trees have been rolled, or rather thrown from the summit. Often they descend several miles over rocks and precipices, where the least deviation from the track would dash them in a thousand pieces. This generally takes place in the winter when the sides are covered with snow and ice. It must be a dangerous business, for there are many crosses by the way-side where the pictures represent persons accidentally killed by the trees; an additional painting represents them as burning in the flames of purgatory, and the pious traveler is requested to pray an Ave or a Paternoster for the repose of their souls.

On we went, up the valley of the Traun, between mountains five and six thousand feet high, through scenes constantly changing and constantly grand, for three or four hours. Finally the hills opened, disclosing a little triangular valley, whose base was formed by a mighty mountain covered with clouds. Through the two side-angles came the Traun and his tributary the Ischl, while the little town of Ischl lay in the centre. Within a few years this has become a very fashionable bathing-place, and the influx of rich visitors, which in the summer sometimes amounts to two thousand, has entirely destroyed the primitive simplicity the inhabitants originally possessed. From Ischl we took a road through the forests to St. Wolfgang, on the lake of the same name. The last part of the way led along the banks of the lake, disclosing some delicious views. These Alpine lakes surpass any scenery I have yet seen. The water is of the most beautiful green, like a sheet of molten beryl, and the cloud-piercing mountains that encompass them shut out the sun for nearly half the day. St. Wolfgang is a lovely village in a cool and quiet nook at the foot of the Schafberg. The houses are built in the picturesque Swiss style, with flat, projecting roofs and ornamented balconies, and the people are the very picture of neatness and cheerfulness.

We started next morning to ascend the Schafberg, which is called the Righi of the Austrian Switzerland. It is somewhat higher than its Swiss namesake, and commands a prospect scarcely less extensive or grand. We followed a footpath through the thick forest by the side of a roaring torrent. The morning mist still covered the lake, but the white summits of the Salzburg and Noric Alps opposite us, rose above it and stood pure and bright in the upper air. We passed a little mill and one or two cottages, and then wound round one of the lesser heights into a deep ravine, down in whose dark shadow we sometimes heard the axe and saw of the mountain woodmen. Finally the path disappeared altogether under a mass of logs and rocks, which appeared to have been whirled together by a sudden flood. We deliberated what to do; the summit rose several thousand feet above us, almost precipitously steep, but we did not like to turn back, and there was still a hope of meeting with the path again. Clambering over the ruins and rubbish we pulled ourselves by the limbs of trees up a steep ascent and descended again to the stream. We here saw the ravine was closed by a wall of rock and our only chance was to cross to the west side of the mountain, where the ascent seemed somewhat easier. A couple of mountain maidens whom we fortunately met, carrying home grass for their goats, told us the mountain could be ascended on that side, by one who could climb well—laying a strong emphasis on the word. The very doubt implied in this expression was enough to decide us; so we began the work. And work it was, too! The side was very steep, the trees all leaned downwards, and we slipped at every step on the dry leaves and grass. After making a short distance this way with the greatest labor, we came to the track of an avalanche, which had swept away the trees and earth. Here the rock had been worn rough by torrents, but by using both hands and feet, we climbed directly up the side of the mountain, sometimes dragging ourselves up by the branches of trees where the rocks were smooth. After half an hour of such work we came above the forests, on the bare side of the mountain. The summit was far above us and so steep that our limbs involuntarily shrunk from the task of climbing. The side ran up at an angle of nearly sixty degrees, and the least slip threw us flat on our faces. We had to use both hand and foot, and were obliged to rest every few minutes to recover breath. Crimson-flowered moss and bright blue gentians covered the rocks, and I filled my books with blossoms for friends at home.

Up and up, for what seemed an age, we clambered. So steep was it, that the least rocky projection hid my friend from sight, as he was coming up below me. I let stones roll sometimes, which went down, down, almost like a cannon-ball, till I could see them no more. At length we reached the region of dwarf pines, which was even more difficult to pass through. Although the mountain was not so steep, this forest, centuries old, reached no higher than our breasts, and the trees leaned downwards, so that we were obliged to take hold of the tops of those above us, and drag ourselves up through the others. Here and there lay large patches of snow; we sat down in the glowing June sun, and bathed our hands and faces in it. Finally the sky became bluer and broader, the clouds seemed nearer, and a few more steps through the bushes brought us to the summit of the mountain, on the edge of a precipice a thousand feet deep, whose bottom stood in a vast field of snow

We lay down on the heather, exhausted by five hours' incessant toil, and drank in like a refreshing draught, the sublimity of the scene. The green lakes of the Salzburg Alps lay far below us, and the whole southern horizon was filled with the mighty range of the Styr-ian and Noric Alps, their summits of never-melting snow mingling and blending with the clouds. On the other side the mountains of Salzburg lifted their ridgy backs from the plains of Bavaria and the Chiem lake lay spread out in the blue distance. A line of mist far to the north betrayed the path of the Danube, and beyond it we could barely trace the outline of the Bohemian mountains. With a glass the spires of Munich, one hundred and twenty miles distant, can be seen. It was a view whose grandeur I can never forget. In that dome of the cloud we seemed to breathe a purer air than that of earth.

After an hour or two, we began to think of descending, as the path was yet to be found. The summit, which was a mile or more in length, extended farther westward, and by climbing over the dwarf pines for some time, we saw a little wooden house above us. It stood near the highest part of the peak, and two or three men were engaged in repairing it, as a shelter for travelers. They pointed out the path which went down on the side toward St. Gilgen, and we began descending. The mountain on this side is much less steep, but the descent is fatiguing enough. The path led along the side of a glen where mountain goats were grazing, and further down we saw cattle feeding on the little spots of verdure which lay in the forest. My knees became so weak from this continued descent, that they would scarcely support me; but we were three hours, partly walking and partly running down, before we reached the bottom. Half an hour's walk around the head of the St. Wolfgang See, brought us to the little village of St. Gilgen.

The valley of St. Gilgen lies like a little paradise between the mountains. Lovely green fields and woods slope gradually from the mountain behind, to the still greener lake spread out before it, in whose bosom the white Alps are mirrored. Its picturesque cottages cluster around the neat church with its lofty spire, and the simple inhabitants have countenances as bright and cheerful as the blue sky above them. We breathed an air of poetry. The Arcadian simplicity of the people, the pastoral beauty of the fields around and the grandeur of the mountains which shut it out from the world, realized my ideas of a dwelling-place, where, with a few kindred spirits, the bliss of Eden might almost be restored.

We stopped there two or three hours to relieve our hunger and fatigue. My boots had suffered severely in our mountain adventure, and I called at a shoemaker's cottage to get them repaired. I sat down and talked for half an hour with the family. The man and his wife spoke of the delightful scenery around them, and expressed themselves with correctness and even elegance. They were much pleased that I admired their village so greatly, and related everything which they supposed could interest me. As I rose to go, my head nearly touched the ceiling, which was very low. The man exclaimed: "Ach Gott! how tall!" I told him the people were all tall in our country; he then asked where I came from, and I had no sooner said

America, than he threw up his hands and uttered an ejaculation of the greatest surprise. His wife observed that "it was wonderful how far man was permitted to travel." They wished me a prosperous journey and a safe return home.

St. Gilgen was also interesting to me from that beautiful chapter in "Hyperion"—"Footsteps of Angels,"— and on passing the church on my way back to the inn, I entered the grave-yard mentioned in it. The green turf grows thickly over the rows of mounds, with here and there a rose planted by the hand of affection, and the white crosses were hung with wreaths, some of which had been freshly laid on. Behind the church, under the shade of a tree, stood a small chapel,—I opened the unfastened door, and entered. The afternoon sun shone through the side window, and all was still around. A little shrine, adorned with flowers, stood at the other end, and there were two tablets on the wall, to persons who slumbered beneath. I approached these and read on one of them with feelings not easily described: "Look not mournfully into the past—it comes not again; wisely improve the present—it is thine; and go forward to meet the shadowy future, without fear, and with a manly heart!" This then was the spot where Paul Flemming came in loneliness and sorrow to muse over what he had lost, and these were the words whose truth and eloquence strengthened and consoled him, "as if the unknown tenant of the grave had opened his lips of dust and spoken those words of consolation his soul needed." I sat down and mused a long time, for there was something in the silent holiness of the spot, that impressed me more than I could well describe.

We reached a little village on the Fuschel See, the same evening, and set off the next morning for Salzburg. The day was hot and we walked slowly, so that it was not till two o'clock that we saw the castellated rocks on the side of the Gaissberg, guarding the entrance to the valley of Salzburg. A short distance further, the whole glorious panorama was spread out below us. From the height on which we stood, we looked directly on the summit of the Capuchin Mountain, which hid part of the city from sight; the double peak of the Staufen rose opposite, and a heavy storm was raging along the Alpine heights around it, while the lovely valley lay in sunshine below, threaded by the bright current of the Salza. As we descended and passed around the foot of the hill, the Untersberg came in sight, whose broad summits lift themselves seven thousand feet above the plain. The legend says that Charlemagne and his warriors sit in its subterraneous caverns in complete armor, and that they will arise and come forth again, when Germany recovers her former power and glory.

I wish I could convey in words some idea of the elevation of spirit experienced while looking on these eternal mountains. They fill the soul with a sensation of power and grandeur which frees it awhile from the cramps and fetters of common life. It rises and expands to the level of their sublimity, till its thoughts stand solemnly aloft, like their summits, piercing the free heaven. Their dazzling and imperishable beauty is to the mind an image of its own enduring existence. When I stand upon some snowy summit—the invisible apex of that mighty pyramid — there seems a majesty in my weak will which might defy the elements. This sense of power, inspired by a silent sympathy with the forms of nature, is beautifully described— as shown in the free, unconscious instincts of childhood — by the poet Uhland, in his ballad of the "Mountain Boy." I have attempted a translation.

THE MOUNTAIN BOY

A herd-boy on the mountain's brow,
I see the castles all below.
The sunbeam here is earliest cast
And by my side it lingers last
   I am the boy of the mountain!

The mother-house of streams is here
I drink them in their cradles clear;
From out the rock they foam below,
I spring to catch them as they go!
    I am the boy of the mountain!

To me belongs the mountain's bound,
Where gathering tempests march around;
But though from north and south they shout,
Above them still my song rings out
    "I am the boy of the mountain!"

Below me clouds and thunders move;
I stand amid the blue above.
I shout to them with fearless breast
"Go, leave my father's house in rest!"
    I am the boy of the mountain!

And when the loud bell shakes the spires
And flame aloft the signal-fires,
I go below and join the throng
And swing my sword and sing my song:
    "I am the boy of the mountain!"

Salzburg lies on both sides of the Salza, hemmed in on either
hand by precipitous mountains. A large fortress overlooks it on the
south, from the summit of a perpendicular rock, against which the
houses in that part of the city are built. The streets are narrow and
crooked, but the newer part contains many open squares, adorned
with handsome fountains. The variety of costume among the people,
is very interesting. The inhabitants of the salt district have a peculiar
dress; the women wear round fur caps, with little wings of gauze at
the side. I saw other women with head-dresses of gold or silver fila-

gree, something in shape like a Roman helmet, with a projection at the back of the head, a foot long. The most interesting objects in Salzburg to us, were the house of Mozart, in which the composer was born, and the monument lately erected to him. The St. Peter's Church, near by, contains the tomb of Haydn, the great composer, and the Church of St. Sebastian, that of the renowned Paracelsus, who was also a native of Salzburg.

Two or three hours sufficed to see everything of interest in the city. We had intended to go further through the Alps, to the beautiful vales of the Tyrol, but our time was getting short, our boots, which are the pedestrian's sole dependence, began to show symptoms of wearing out, and our expenses among the lakes and mountains of Upper Austria, left us but two florins apiece, so we reluctantly turned our backs upon the snowy hills and set out for Munich, ninety miles distant. After passing the night at Saalbruck, on the banks of the stream which separates the two kingdoms, we entered Bavaria next morning. I could not help feeling glad to leave Austria, although within her bounds I had passed scenes whose beauty will long haunt me, and met with many honest friendly hearts among her people. We noticed a change as soon as we had crossed the border. The roads were neater and handsomer, and the country people greeted us in going by, with a friendly cheerfulness that made us feel half at home. The houses are built in the picturesque Swiss fashion, their balconies often ornamented with curious figures, carved in wood. Many of them, where they are situated remote from a church, have a little bell on the roof which they ring for morning and evening prayers; we often heard these simple monitors sounding from the cottages as we passed by.

The next night we stopped at the little village of Stein, famous in former times for its robber-knight, Hans von Stein. The ruins of his castle stand on the rock above, and the caverns hewn in the sides of the precipice, where he used to confine his prisoners, are still visible. Walking on through a pleasant, well-cultivated country, we came to Wasserburg, on the Inn. The situation of the city is peculiar. The Inn has gradually worn his channel deeper in the sandy soil, so that he now flows at the bottom of a glen, a hundred feet below the plains around. Wasserburg lies in a basin, formed by the change of the current, which flows around it like a horse-shoe, leaving only a narrow neck of land which connects it with the country above.

We left the little village where we were quartered for the night and took a footpath which led across the country to the field of Hohenlinden, about six miles distant. The name had been familiar to me from childhood, and my love for Campbell, with the recollection of the school-exhibitions where "On Linden when the sun was low" had been so often declaimed, induced me to make the excursion to it. We traversed a large forest, belonging to the King of Bavaria, and came out on a plain covered with grain-fields and bounded on the right by a semicircle of low hills. Over the fields, about two miles distant, a tall, minaret-like spire rose from a small cluster of houses, and this was Hohenlinden!

To tell the truth, I had been expecting something more. The "hills of blood-stained snow" are very small hills indeed, and the "Isar, rolling rapidly," is several miles off; it was the spot, however, and we recited Campbell's poem, of course, and brought away a few wild flowers as memorials. There is no monument or any other token of the battle, and the people seem to endeavor to forgot the scene of Moreau's victory and their defeat.

From a hill twelve miles off we had our first view of the spires of Munich, looking like distant ships over the sea-like plain. They kept in sight till we arrived at eight o'clock in the evening, after a walk of more than thirty miles. We crossed the rapid Isar on three bridges, entered the magnificent Isar Gate, and were soon comfortably quartered in the heart of Munich.

Entering the city without knowing a single soul within it, we made within a few minutes an agreeable acquaintance. After we passed the Isar Gate, we began looking for a decent inn, for the day's walk was very fatiguing. Presently a young man, who had been watching us for some time, came up and said, if we would allow him, he would conduct us to a good lodging-place. Finding we were strangers, he expressed the greatest regret that he had not time to go with us everyday around the city. Our surprise and delight at the splendor of Munich, he said, would more than repay him for the trouble. In his anxiety to show us something, he took us some distance out of the way, (although it was growing dark and we were very tired,) to see the Palace and the Theatre, with its front of rich frescoes.

Chapter XXVI
MUNICH

June 14.—I thought I had seen everything in Vienna that could excite admiration or gratify fancy; here I have my former sensations to live over again, in an augmented degree. It is well I was at first somewhat prepared by our previous travel, otherwise the glare and splendor of wealth and art in this German Athens might possibly blind me to the beauties of the cities we shall yet visit. I have been walking in a dream where the fairy tales of boyhood were realized, and the golden and jeweled halls of the Eastern genii rose glittering around me —"a vision of the brain no more." All I had conceived of oriental magnificence, all descriptions of the splendor of kingly halls and palaces, fall far short of what I here see. Where shall I begin to describe the crowd of splendid edifices that line its streets, or how give an idea of the profusion of paintings and statues—of marble, jasper and gold?

Art has done everything for Munich. It lies on a large, flat plain, sixteen hundred feet above the sea, and continually exposed to the cold winds from the Alps. At the beginning of the present century it was but a third-rate city, and was rarely visited by foreigners. Since that time its population and limits have been doubled, and many magnificent edifices in every style of architecture erected, rendering it scarcely secondary in this respect to any capital in Europe. Every art that wealth or taste could devise, seems to have been spent in its decoration. Broad, spacious streets and squares have been laid out, churches, halls and colleges erected, and schools of painting and sculpture established, which draw artists from all parts of the world. All this was principally brought about by the taste of the present king, Ludwig I., who began twenty or thirty years ago, when he was Crown Prince, to collect the best German artists around him and form plans for the execution of his grand design. He can boast of having done more for the arts than any other living monarch, and if he had accomplished it all without oppressing his people, he would deserve an immortality of fame.

Now, if you have nothing else to do, let us take a stroll down the Ludwigstrasse. As we pass the Theatiner Church, with its dome and towers, the broad street opens before us, stretching away to the north, between rows of magnificent buildings. Just at this southern end, is the *Schlusshalle,* an open temple of white marble terminating the avenue. To the right of us extend the arcades, with the trees of the Royal Garden peeping above them; on the left is the spacious concert building of the Odeon, and the palace of the Duke of Leuchtenberg, son of Eugene Beauharnois. Passing through a row of palace-like private buildings, we come to the Army Department, on the right — a neat and tasteful building of white sandstone. Beside it stands the Library, which possesses the first special claim on our admiration. With its splendid front of five hundred and eighteen feet, the yellowish brown cement with which the body is covered, making an agreeable contrast with the dark red window-arches and cornices, and the statues of Homer, Hippocrates, Thucydides and Aristotle guarding the portal, is it not a worthy receptacle for the treasures of ancient and modern lore which its halls contain?

Nearly opposite stands the Institute for the Blind, a plain but large building of dark red brick, covered with cement, and further, the

Ludwig's Kirche, or Church of St. Louis. How lightly the two square towers of gray marble lift their network of sculpture! And what a novel and beautiful effect is produced by uniting the Byzantine style of architecture to the form of the Latin cross! Over the arched portal stand marble statues by Schwanthaler, and the roof of brilliant tiles worked into mosaic, looks like a rich Turkey carpet covering the whole. We must enter to get an idea of the splendor of this church. Instead of the pointed arch which one would expect to see meeting above his head, the lofty pillars on each side bear an unbroken semi-circular vault, which is painted a brilliant blue, and spangled with silver mars. These pillars, and the little arches above, which spring from them, are painted in an arabesque style with gold and brilliant colors, and each side-chapel is a perfect casket of richness and elegance. The windows are of silvered glass, through which the light glimmers softly on the splendor within. The whole end of the church behind the high altar, is taken up with Cornelius's celebrated fresco painting of the "Last Judgment,"—the largest painting in the world —and the circular dome in the centre of the cross contains groups of martyrs, prophets, saints and kings, painted in fresco on a ground of gold. The work of Cornelius has been greatly praised for sublimity of design and beauty of execution, by many acknowledged judges; I was disappointed in it, but the fault lay most probably in me and not in the painting. The richness and elegance of the church took me all "aback;" it was so entirely different from anything I had seen, that it was difficult to decide whether I was most charmed by its novelty or its beauty. Still, as a building designed to excite feelings of worship, it seems to me inappropriate. A vast, dim Cathedral would be far preferable; the devout, humble heart cannot feel at home amid such glare and brightness.

As we leave the church and walk further on, the street expands suddenly into a broad square. One side is formed by the new University building and the other by the Royal Seminary, both displaying in their architecture new forms of the graceful Byzantine school, which the architects of Munich have adapted in a striking manner to so many varied purposes. On each side stands a splendid colossal fountain of bronze, throwing up a great mass of water, which falls in a triple cataract to the marble basin below. A short distance beyond this square the Ludwigstrasse terminates. It is said the end will be closed by a magnificent gate, on a style to correspond with the unequalled avenue to which it will give entrance. To one standing at the southern end, it would form a proper termination to the grand vista. Before we leave, turn around and glance back, down this street, which extends for half a mile between such buildings as we have just viewed, and tell me if it is not something of which a city and a king may boast, to have created all this within less than twenty years.

We went one morning to see the collection of paintings formerly belonging to Eugene Beauharnois, who was brother-in-law to the present king of Bavaria, in the palace of his son, the Duke of Leuchtenberg. The first hall contains works principally by French artists, among which are two by Gerard—a beautiful portrait of Josephine, and the blind Belisarius carrying his dead companion. The boy's head lies on the old man's shoulder; but for the livid paleness of his limbs, he would seem to be only asleep, while a deep and settled sorrow marks the venerable features of the unfortunate Emperor. In the middle of the room are six pieces of statuary, among which Canova's world-renowned group of the Graces at once attracts the eye. There is also a kneeling Magdalen, lovely in her woe, by the same sculptor, and a very touching work of Schadow, representing a shepherd boy tenderly binding his sash around a lamb which he has accidentally wounded with his arrow.

We have since seen in the St. Michael's Church, the monument to Eugene Beauharnois, from the chisel of Bertel Thorwaldsen. The noble, manly figure of the son of Josephine is represented in the Roman mantle, with his helmet and sword lying on the ground by him. On one side sits History, writing on a tablet; on the other, stand the two brother-angels, Death and Immortality. They lean lovingly together, with arms around each other, but the sweet countenance of Death has a cast of sorrow, as he stands with inverted torch and a wreath of poppies among his clustering locks. Immortality, crowned with never-fading flowers, looks upwards with a smile of triumph, and holds in one hand his blazing torch. It is a beautiful idea, and Thorwaldsen has made the marble eloquent with feeling.

The inside of the square formed by the Arcades and the New Residence, is filled with noble old trees, which in summer make a leafy roof over the pleasant walks. In the middle, stands a grotto, ornamented with rough pebbles and shells, and only needing a fountain to make it a perfect hall of Neptune. Passing through the northern Arcade, one comes into the, magnificent park, called the English Garden, which extends more than four miles along the bank of the Isar, several branches of whose milky current wander through it, and form one or two pretty cascades. It is a beautiful alternation of forest and meadow, and has all the richness and garden-like luxuriance of English scenery. Winding walks lead along the Isar, or through the wood of venerable oaks, and sometimes a lawn of half a mile in length, with a picturesque temple at its farther end, comes in sight through the trees. I was better pleased with this park than with the Prater in Vienna. Its paths are always filled with persons enjoying the change from the dusty streets to its quiet and cool retirement.

The New Residence is not only one of the wonders of Munich, but of the world. Although commenced in 1826 and carried on constantly since that time by a number of architects, sculptors and painters, it is not yet finished; if art were not inexhaustible it would be difficult to imagine what more could be added. The north side of the Max Joseph Platz is taken up by its front of four hundred and thirty feet, which was nine years in building, under the direction of the architect Klenze. The exterior is copied after the Palazzo Pitti, in Florence. The building is of light brown sandstone, and combines an elegance and even splendor, with the most chaste and classic style. The northern front, which faces on the Royal Garden, is now nearly finished. It has the enormous length of eight hundred feet; in the middle is a portico of ten Ionic columns; instead of supporting a triangular façade, each pillar stands separate and bears a marble statue from the chisel of Schwanthaler.

The interior of the building does not disappoint the promise of the outside. It is open every afternoon in the absence of the king, for the inspection of visitors; fortunately for us, his majesty is at present on a journey through his provinces on the Rhine. We went early to the waiting hall, where several travelers were already assembled, and at four o'clock, were admitted into the newer part of the palace, containing the throne hall, ballroom, etc. On entering the first hall, designed for the lackeys and royal servants, we were all obliged to thrust our feet into cloth slippers to walk over the polished mosaic floor. The walls are of scagliola marble and the ceilings ornamented brilliantly in fresco. The second hall, also for servants, gives tokens of increasing splendor in the richer decorations of the walls and the more elaborate mosaic of the floor. We next entered the receiving saloon, in which the Court Marshal receives the guests. The ceiling is of arabesque, sculpture, profusely painted and gilded. Passing through a little cabinet, we entered the great dancing saloon. Its floor is the richest mosaic of wood of different colors, the sides are of polished scagliola marble, and the ceiling a dazzling mixture of sculpture, painting and gold. At one end is a gallery for the orchestra, supported by six columns of variegated marble, above which are six dancing nymphs, painted so beautifully that they appear like living creatures. Every decoration which could be devised has been used to heighten its splendor, and the artists appear to have made free use of the Arabian Nights in forming the plan.

We entered next two smaller rooms containing the portraits of beautiful women, principally from the German nobility. I gave the preference to the daughter of Marco Bozzaris, now maid of honor to the Queen of Greece. She had a wild dark eye, a beautiful proud lip, and her rich black hair rolled in glossy waves down her neck from under the red Grecian cap stuck jauntily on the side of her head. She wore a scarf and close-fitting vest embroidered with gold, and there was a free, lofty spirit in her countenance worthy the name she bore. These pictures form a gallery of beauty, whose equal cannot easily be found.

Returning to the dancing hall, we entered the dining saloon, also called the Hall of Charlemagne. Each wall has two magnificent fresco paintings of very large size, representing some event in the life of the great emperor, beginning with his anointing at St. Deny's as a boy of twelve years, and ending with his coronation by Leo III.

A second dining saloon, the Hall of Barbarossa, adjoins the first. It has also eight frescoes as the former, representing the principal events in the life of Frederic Barbarossa. Then comes a third, called the Hapsburg Hall, with four grand paintings from the life of Rudolph of Hapsburg, and a triumphal procession along the frieze, showing the improvement in the arts and sciences which was accomplished under his reign. The drawing, composition and rich tone of coloring of these glorious frescoes, are scarcely excelled by any in existence.

Finally we entered the Hall of the Throne. Here the encaustic decoration, so plentifully employed in the other rooms, is dropped, and an effect even more brilliant obtained by the united use of marble and gold. Picture a long hall with a floor of polished marble, on each side twelve columns of white marble with gilded capitals, between which stand colossal statues of gold. At the other end is the throne of gold and crimson, with gorgeous hangings of crimson velvet. The twelve statues in the hall are called the "Wittlesbach Ancestors," and represent renowned members of the house of Wittlesbach from which the present family of Bavaria is descended. They were cast in bronze by Stiglmaier, after the models of Schwanthaler, and then completely covered with a coating of gold, so that they resemble solid golden statues. The value of the precious metal on each one is about $3,000, as they are nine feet in height! What would the politicians who made such an outcry about the new papering of the President's House, say to such a palace as this?

Going back to the starting point, we went to the other wing of the edifice and joined the party who came to visit the apartments of the king. Here we were led through two or three rooms, appropriated to the servants, with all the splendor of marble doors, floors of mosaic, and frescoed ceilings. From these we entered the king's dwelling. The entrance halls are decorated with paintings of the Argonauts and illustrations of the Hymns of Hesiod, after drawings by Schwanthaler. Then came the Service Hall, containing frescoes illustrating Homer, by Schnorr, and the Throne Hall, with Schwanthaler's bas-reliefs of the songs of Pindar, on a ground of gold. The throne stands under a splendid crimson canopy. The Dining Room with its floor of polished wood is filled with illustrations of the songs of Anacreon. To these follow the Dressing Room, with twenty-seven illustrations of the Comedies of Aristophanes, and the sleeping chamber with frescoes after the poems of Theocritus, and two beautiful bas-reliefs representing angels bearing children to Heaven. It is no wonder the King writes poetry, when he breathes, eats, and even sleeps in an atmosphere of it.

We were shown the rooms for the private parties of the Court, the school-room, with scenes from the life of the Ancient Greeks, and then conducted down the marble staircases to the lower story, which is to contain Schnorr's magnificent frescoes of the Nibelungen Lied — the old German Iliad. Two halls are at present finished; the first has the figure of the author, Heinrich von Ofterdingen, and those of Chriemhilde, Brunhilde, Siegfried and the other personages of the poem; and the second, called the Marriage Hall, contains the marriage of Chriemhilde and Siegfried, and the triumphal entry of Siegfried into Worms.

Adjoining the new residence on the east, is the Royal Chapel, lately finished in the Byzantine style, under the direction of Klenze. To enter it, is like stepping into a casket of jewels. The sides are formed by a double range of arches, the windows being so far back as to be almost out of sight, so that the eye falls on nothing but painting and gold. The lower row of arches is of alternate green and purple marble, beautifully polished; but the upper, as well as the small chancel behind the high altar, is entirely covered with fresco paintings on a ground of gold! The richness and splendor of the whole church is absolutely incredible. Even after one has seen the Ludwig's Kirche and the Residence itself, it excites astonishment. I was surprised, however, to find at this age, a painting on the wall behind the altar, representing the Almighty. It seems as if man's presumption has no end. The simple altar of Athens, with its inscription *"to the Unknown God,"* was more truly reverent than this. As I sat down awhile under one of the arches, a poor woman came in, carrying a heavy basket, and going to the steps which led up to the altar, knelt down and prayed, spreading her arms out in the form of a cross. Then, after stooping and kissing the first step, she dragged herself with her knees upon it, and commenced praying again with outspread arms. This she continued till she had climbed them all, which occupied some time; then, as if she had fulfilled a vow she turned and departed. She was undoubtedly sincere in her piety, but it made me sad to look upon such deluded superstition.

We visited yesterday morning the Glyptothek, the finest collection of ancient sculpture except that in the British Museum, I have yet seen, and perhaps elsewhere unsurpassed, north of the Alps. The building which was finished by Klenze, in 1830, has an Ionic portico of white marble, with a group of allegorical figures, representing Sculpture and the kindred arts. On each side of the portico, there are three niches in the front, containing on one side, Pericles, Phidias and Vulcan; on the other, Hadrian, Prometheus and Dædalus. The whole building forms a hollow square, and is lighted entirely from the inner side. There are in all twelve halls, each containing the remains of a particular era in the art, and arranged according to time, so that, beginning with the clumsy productions of the ancient Egyptians, one passes through the different stages of Grecian art, afterwards that of Rome, and finally ends with the works of our own times—the almost Grecian perfection of Thorwaldsen and Canova. These halls are worthy to hold such treasures, and what more could be said of them? The floors are of marble mosaic, the sides of green or purple scagliola, and the vaulted ceilings covered with raised ornaments on a ground of gold. No two are alike in color and decoration, and yet there is a unity of taste and design in the whole, which renders the variety delightful.

From the Egyptian Hall, we enter one containing the oldest remains of Grecian sculpture, before the artists won power to mould the marble to their conceptions. Then follow the celebrated Egina marbles, frown the temple of Jupiter Panhellenius, on the island of Egina. They formerly stood in the two porticoes, the one group representing the fight for the body of Laomedon, the other the struggle for the dead Patroclus. The parts wanting have been admirably restored by Bertel Thorwaldsen. They form almost the only existing specimens of the Eginetan school. Passing through the Apollo Hall, we enter the large hall of Bacchus, in which the progress of the art is distinctly apparent. A satyr, lying asleep on a goat-skin which he has thrown over a rock, is believed to be the work of Praxiteles. The relaxation of the figure and perfect repose of every limb, is wonderful. The countenance has traits of individuality which led me to think it might have been a portrait, perhaps of some rude country swain.

In the Hall of Niobe, which follows, is one of the most perfect works that ever grew into life under a sculptor's chisel. Mutilated as it is, without head and arms, I never saw a more expressive figure. Ilioneus, the son of Niobe, is represented as kneeling, apparently in the moment in which Apollo raises his arrow, and there is an imploring supplication in his attitude which is touching in the highest degree. His beautiful young limbs seem to shrink involuntarily from the deadly shaft; there is an expression of prayer, almost of agony, in the position of his body. It should be left untouched. No head could be added, which would equal that one pictures to oneself, while gazing upon it.

The Pinacothek is a magnificent building of yellow sandstone, five hundred and thirty feet long, containing thirteen hundred pictures, selected with great care from the whole private collection of the king, which amounts to nine thousand. Above the cornice on the southern side, stand twenty-five colossal statues of celebrated paint-ers, by Schwanthaler. As we approached, the tall bronze door was opened by a servant in the Bavarian livery, whose size harmonized so well with the giant proportions of the building, that, until I stood beside him and could mark the contrast, I did not notice his enor-mous frame. I saw then that he must be near eight feet high, and stout in proportion. He reminded me of the great "Bayer of Trient," in Vienna. The Pinacothek contains the most complete collection of works by old German artists, anywhere to be found. There are in the hall of the Spanish masters, half a dozen of Murillo's inimitable beggar groups. It was a relief, after looking upon the distressingly stiff figures of the old German school, to view these fresh, natural countenances. One little black-eyed boy has just cut a slice out of a melon and turns with a full mouth to his companion, who is busy eating a bunch of grapes. The simple, contented expression on the faces of the beggars is admirable. I thought I detected in a beautiful child, with dark curly locks, the original of his celebrated Infant St. John. I was much interested in two small juvenile works of Raphael and his own portrait. The latter was taken most probably after he became known as a painter. The calm, serious smile which we see on his portrait as a boy, had vanished, and the thin features and sunken eye told of intense mental labor.

One of the most remarkable buildings now in the course of erec-tion is the Basilica, or Church of St. Bonifacius. It represents another form of the Byzantine style, a kind of double edifice, a little like a North River steamboat, with a two story cabin on deck. The inside is not yet finished, although the artists have been at work on it for six years, but we heard many accounts of its splendor, which is said to exceed anything that has been yet done in Munich. We visited today the atelier of Schwanthaler, which is always open to strangers. The sculptor himself was not there, but five or six of his scholars were at work in the rooms, building up clay statues after his models and working out bas-reliefs in frames. We saw here the original models of the statues on the Pinacothek, and the "Wittelsbach Ancestors" in the Throne Hall of the palace. I was glad also to find a miniature copy in plaster, of the Herrmannsschlacht, or combat of the old German hero, Herrmann, with the Romans, from the frieze of the Walhalla, at Ratisbon. It is one of Schwanthaler's best works. Herrmann, as the middle figure, is represented in fight with the Roman general; behind him the warriors are rushing on, and an old bard is striking the chords of his harp to inspire them, while women bind up the wounds of the fallen. The Roman soldiers on the other side are about turning in confusion to fly. It is a lofty and appropriate subject for the portico of a building containing the figures of the men who have labored for the glory and elevation of their Fatherland.

Our new-found friend came to visit us last evening and learn our impressions of Munich. In the course of conversation we surprised him by revealing the name of our country. His countenance brightened up and he asked us many questions about the state of society in America. In return, he told us something more about himself— his story was simple, but it interested me. His father was a merchant, who, having been ruined by unlucky transactions, died, leaving a numerous family without the means of support. His children were obliged to commence life alone and unaided, which, in a country where labor is so cheap, is difficult and disheartening. Our friend chose the profession of a machinist, which, after encountering great obstacles, he succeeded in learning, and now supports himself as a common laborer. But his position in this respect prevents him from occupying that station in society for which he is intellectually fitted. His own words, uttered with a simple pathos which I can never forget, will best describe how painful this must be to a sensitive spirit. "I tell you thus frankly my feelings," said he, "because I know you will understand me. I could not say this to any of my associates, for they would not comprehend it, and they would say I am proud, because I cannot bring my soul down to their level. I am poor and have but little to subsist upon; but the spirit has needs as well as the body, and I feel it a duty and a desire to satisfy them also. When I am with any of my common fellow-laborers, what do I gain from them? Their leisure hours are spent in drinking and idle amusement, and I cannot join them, for I have no sympathy with such things. To mingle with those above me, would be impossible. Therefore I am alone—I have no associate!"

I have gone into minute, and it may be, tiresome detail, in describing some of the edifices of Munich, because it seemed the only way in which I could give an idea of their wonderful beauty. It is true that in copying after the manner of the daguerreotype, there is danger of imitating its *dullness* also, but I trust to the glitter of gold and rich paintings, for a little brightness in the picture. We leave tomorrow morning, having received the gum written for, which, to our surprise, will be barely sufficient to enable us to reach Heidelberg.

Chapter XXVII
THROUGH WURTEMBERG TO HEIDELBERG

We left Munich in the morning train for Augsburg. Between the two cities extends a vast unbroken plain, exceedingly barren and monotonous. Here and there is a little scrubby woodland, and sometimes we passed over a muddy stream which came down from the Alps.

The land is not more than half-cultivated, and the villages are small and poor. We saw many of the peasants at their stations, in their gay Sunday dresses; the women wore short gowns with laced bodices, of gay colors, and little caps on the top of their heads, with streamers of ribbons three feet long. After two hours' ride, we saw the tall towers of Augsburg, and alighted on the outside of the wall. The deep moat which surrounds the city, is all grown over with velvet turf, the towers and bastions are empty and desolate, and we passed unchallenged under the gloomy archway. Immediately on entering the city, signs of its ancient splendor are apparent. The houses are old, many of them with quaint, elaborately carved ornaments, and often covered with fresco paintings. These generally represent some scene from the Bible history, encircled with arabesque borders, and pious maxims in illuminated scrolls. We went into the old *Rathhaus,* whose golden hall still speaks of the days of Augsburg's pride. I saw in the basement a bronze eagle, weighing sixteen tons, with an inscription on the pedestal stating that it was cast in 1606, and formerly stood on the top of an old public building, since torn down. In front of the Rathhaus is a fine bronze fountain, with a number of figures of angels and tritons.

The same afternoon, we left Augsburg for Ulm. Long, low ranges of hills, running from the Danube, stretched far across the country, and between them lay many rich, green valleys. We passed, occasionally, large villages, perhaps as old as the times of the crusaders, and looking quite pastoral and romantic from the outside; but we were always glad when we had gone through them and into the clean country again. The afternoon of the second day we came in sight of the fertile plain of the Danube; far, far to the right lay the field of Blenheim, where Marlborough and the Prince Eugene conquered the united French and Bavarian forces and decided the war of the Spanish succession.

We determined to reach Ulm the same evening, although a heavy storm was raging along the distant hills of Wurtemberg. The dark mass of the mighty Cathedral rose in the distance through the twilight, a perfect mountain in comparison with the little houses clustered around its base. We reached New Ulm, finally, and passed over the heavy wooden bridge into Wurtemberg, unchallenged for passport or baggage. I thought I could feel a difference in the atmosphere when I reached the other side — it breathed of the freer spirit that ruled through the land. The Danube is here a little muddy stream, hardly as large as my native Brandywine, and a traveler who sees it at Ulm for the first time would most probably be disappointed. It is not until below Vienna, where it receives the Drave and Save, that it becomes a river of more than ordinary magnitude.

We entered Ulm, as I have already said. It was after nine o'clock, nearly dark, and beginning to rain; we had walked thirty-three miles, and being of course tired, we entered the first inn we saw. But, to our consternation, it was impossible to get a place — the fair had just commenced, and the inn was full to the roof. We must hunt for another, and then another, and yet another, with like fate at each. It grew quite dark, the rain increased, and we were unacquainted with the city. I grew desperate, and at last, when we had stopped at the eighth inn in vain, I told the people we must have lodgings, for it was impossible we should walk around in the rain all night. Some of the guests interfering in our favor, the hostess finally sent a servant with us to the first hotel in the city. I told him on the way we were Americans, strangers in Ulm, and not accustomed to sleeping in the streets. "Well," said he, "I will go before, and recommend you to the landlord of the Golden Wheel." I knew not what magic he used, but in half an hour our weary limbs were stretched in delightful repose and we thanked Heaven more gratefully than ever before, for the blessing of a good bed.

Next morning we ran about through the booths of the fair, and gazed up from all sides at the vast Cathedral. The style is the simplest and grandest Gothic; but the tower, which, to harmonize with the body of the church, should be 520 feet high, was left unfinished at the height of 234 feet. I could not enough admire the grandeur of proportion in the great building. It seemed singular that the little race of animals who swarmed around its base, should have the power to conceive or execute such a gigantic work.

There is an immense fortification now in progress of erection behind Ulm. It leans on the side of the hill which rises from the Danube, and must be nearly a mile in length. Hundreds of laborers are at work, and from the appearance of the foundations, many years will be required to finish it. The lofty mountain-plain which we afterwards passed over, for eight or ten miles, divides the waters of the Danube from the Rhine. From the heights above Ulm, we bade adieu to the far, misty Alps, till we shall see them again in Switzerland. Late in the afternoon, we came to a lovely green valley, sunk as it were in the earth. Around us, on all sides, stretched the bare, lofty plains; but the valley lay below, its steep sides covered with the richest forest. At the bottom flowed the Fils. Our road led directly down the side; the glen spread out broader as we advanced, and smiling villages stood beside the stream. A short distance before reaching Esslingen, we came upon the banks of the Neckar, whom we hailed as an old acquaintance, although much smaller here in his mountain home than when he sweeps the walls of Heidelberg.

Delightful Wurtemberg! Shall I ever forget thy lovely green vales, watered by the classic current of the Neckar, or thy lofty hills covered with vineyards and waving forests, and crowned with heavy ruins, that tell many a tale of Barbarossa and Duke Ulric and Goetz with the Iron Hand! No—were even the Suabian hills less beautiful —were the Suabian people less faithful and kind and true, still I would love the land for the great spirits it has produced; still would the birthplace of Frederick Schiller, of Uhland and Hauff, be sacred. I do not wonder Wurtemberg can boast such glorious poets. Its lovely landscapes seem to have been made expressly for the cradle of genius; amid no other scenes could his infant mind catch a more benign inspiration. Even the common people are deeply imbued with a poetic feeling. We saw it in their friendly greetings and open, expressive countenances; it is shown in their love for their beautiful homes and the rapture and reverence with which they speak of their country's bards. No river in the world, equal to the Neckar in size, flows for its whole course through more a delightful scenery, or among kinder and happier people.

After leaving Esslingen, we followed its banks for some time, at the foot of an amphitheatre of hills, covered to the very summit, as far as the eye could reach, with vineyards. The morning was cloudy, and white mist-wreaths hung along the sides. We took a road that led over the top of a range, and on arriving at the summit, saw all at once the city of Stuttgard, lying beneath our feet. It lay in a basin encircled by mountains, with a narrow valley opening to the southeast, and running off between the hills to the Neckar. The situation of the city is one of wonderful beauty, and even after seeing Salzburg, I could not but be charmed with it.

We descended the mountain and entered it. I inquired immediately for the monument of Schiller, for there was little else in the city I cared to see. We had become tired of running about cities, hunting this or that old church or palace, which perhaps was nothing when found. Stuttgard has neither galleries, ruins, nor splendid buildings, to interest the traveler; but it has Bertel Thorwaldsen's statue of Schiller, calling up at the same time its shame and its glory. For the poet in his youth was obliged to fly from this very same city —from home and friends, to escape the persecution of the government on account of the free sentiments expressed in his early works. We found the statue, without much difficulty. It stands in the Schloss Platz, at the southern end of the city, in an unfavorable situation, surrounded by dark old buildings. It should rather be placed aloft on a mountain summit, in the pure, free air of heaven, braving the storm and the tempest. The figure is fourteen feet high and stands on a pedestal of bronze, with bas reliefs on the four sides. The head, crowned with a laurel wreath, is inclined as if in deep thought, and all the earnest soul is seen in the countenance. Thorwaldsen has copied so truly the expression of poetic reverie, that I waited half-expecting he would raise his head and look around him.

As we passed out the eastern gate, the workmen were busy near the city, making an embankment for the new railroad to Heilbroun, and we were obliged to wade through half a mile of mud. Finally the road turned to the left over a mountain, and we walked on in the rain, regardless of the touching entreaties of an omnibus-driver, who felt a great concern for our health, especially as he had two empty seats. There is a peculiarly agreeable sensation in walking in a storm, when the winds sweep by and the raindrops rattle through the trees, and the dark clouds roll past just above one's head. It gives a dash of sublimity to the most common scene. If the rain did not finally soak through the boots, and if one did not lose every romantic feeling in wet garments, I would prefer storm to sunshine, for visiting some kinds of scenery. You remember, we saw the North Coast of Ireland and the Giant's Causeway in stormy weather, at the expense of being completely drenched, it is true; but our recollections of that wild day's journey are as vivid as any event of our lives — and the name of the Giant's Causeway calls up a series of pictures as terribly sublime as any we would wish to behold.

The rain at last did come down, a little too hard for comfort, and we were quite willing to take shelter when we reached Ludwigsburg. This is here called a new city, having been laid out with broad streets and spacious squares, about a century ago, and is now about the size of our five-year old city of Milwaukie! It is the chief military station of Wurtemberg, and has a splendid castle and gardens, belonging to the king. A few miles to the eastward is the little village where Schiller was born. It is said the house where his parents lived is still standing.

It was not the weather alone, which prevented our making a pilgrimage to it, nor was it alone a peculiar fondness for rain which induced us to persist in walking in the storm. Our feeble pockets, if they could have raised an audible jingle, would have told another tale. Our scanty allowance was dwindling rapidly away, in spite of a desperate system of economy. We left Ulm with a florin and a half apiece—about sixty cents—to walk to Heidelberg, a distance of 110 miles. It was the evening of the third day, and this was almost exhausted. As soon therefore as he rain slackened a little, we started again, although the roads were very bad. At Betigheim, where we passed the night, the people told us of a much nearer and more beautiful road, passing through the Zabergau, a region famed for its fertility and pastoral beauty. At the inn we were charged higher than usual for a bed, so that we had but thirteen kreutzers to start with in the morning. Our fare that day was a little bread and water; we walked steadily on, but owing to the wet roads, made only thirty miles.

A more delightful region than the Zabergau I have seldom passed through. The fields were full of rich, heavy grain, and the trees had a luxuriance of foliage that reminded me of the vale of the Jed, in Scotland. Without a single hedge or fence, stood the long sweep of hills, covered with waving fields of grain, except where they were steep and rocky, and the vineyard terraces rose one above another. Sometimes a fine old forest grew along the summit, like a mane waving back from the curved neck of a steed, and white villages lay coiled in the valleys between. A line of blue mountains always closed the vista, on looking down one of these long valleys; occasionally a ruined castle with donjon tower, was seen on a mountain at the side, making the picture complete. As we lay sometimes on the hillside and looked on one of those sweet vales, we were astonished at its Arcadian beauty. The meadows were as smooth as a mirror, and there seemed to be scarcely a grass-blade out of place. The streams wound through ("snaked themselves through," is the German expression,) with a subdued ripple, as if they feared to displace a pebble, and the great ash trees which stood here and there, had lined each of their leaves as carefully with silver and turned them as gracefully to the wind, as if they were making their toilettes for the gala-day of nature.

That evening brought us into the dominions of Baden, within five hours' walk of Heidelberg. At the humblest inn in a humble village, we found a bed which we could barely pay for, leaving a kreutzer or two for breakfast. Soon after starting the next morning, the distant Kaiserstuhl suddenly emerged from the mist, with the high tower on its summit, where nearly ten months before, we sat and looked at the summits of the Vosges in France, with all the excitement one feels on entering a foreign land. Now, the scenery around that same Kaiserstuhl was nearly as familiar to us as that of our own homes. Entering the hills again, we knew by the blue mountains of the Odenwald, that we were approaching the Neckar. At length we reached the last height. The town of Neckargemünd lay before us on the steep hillside, and the mountains on either side were scarred with quarries of the rich red sandstone, so much used in building. The blocks are hewn out, high up on the mountain side, and then sent rolling and sliding down to the river, where they are laden in boats and floated down with the current to the distant cities of the Rhine.

We were rejoiced on turning around the corner of a mountain,, to see on the opposite side of the river, the road winding up through the forests, where last fall our Heidelberg friends accompanied us, as we set out to walk to Frankfort, through the Odenwald. Many causes combined to render it a glad scene to us. We were going to meet our comrade again, after a separation of months; we were bringing an eventful journey to its close; and finally, we were weak and worn out from fasting and the labor of walking in the rain. A little further we saw Kloster Neuburg, formerly an old convent, and remembered how we used to look at it everyday from the windows of our room on the Neckar; but we shouted aloud, when we saw at last the well-known bridge spanning the river, and the glorious old castle lifting its shattered towers from the side of the mountain above us. I always felt a strong attachment to this matchless ruin, and as I beheld it again, with the warm sunshine falling through each broken arch, the wild ivy draping its desolate chambers, it seemed to smile on me like the face of a friend, and I confessed I had seen many a grander scene, but few that would cling to the memory so familiarly.

While we were in Heidelberg, a student was buried by torchlight. This is done when particular honor is shown to the memory of the departed brother. They assembled at dark in the University Square, each with a blazing pine torch three feet long, and formed into a double line. Between the files walked at short distances an officer, who, with his sword, broad lace collar, and the black and white plumes in his cap, looked like a cavalier of the olden time. Persons with torches walked on each side of the hearse, and the band played a lament so deeply mournful, that the scene, notwithstanding its singularity, was very sad and touching. The thick smoke from the torches filled the air, and a lurid, red light was cast over the hushed crowds in the streets and streamed into the dark alleys. The Haupt-strasse was filled with two lines of flame, as the procession passed down it; when they reached the extremity of the city, the hearse went on, attended with torch-bearers, to the Cemetery, some distance further, and the students turned back, running and whirling their torches in mingled confusion. The music struck up a merry march, and in the smoke and red glare, they looked like a company of mad demons. The presence of death awed them to silence for awhile, but as soon as it had left them, they turned relieved to revel again and thought no more of the lesson. It gave me a painful feeling to see them rushing so wildly and disorderly back. They assembled again in the square, and tossing their torches up into the air cast them blazing into a pile; while the flame and black smoke rose in a column into the air, they sang in solemn chorus, the song *"Gaudeamus igitur,"* with which they close all public assemblies.

I shall neglect telling how we left Heidelberg, and walked along the Bergstrasse again, for the sixth time; how we passed the old Melibochus and on through the quiet city of Darmstadt; how we watched the blue summits of the Taunus rising higher and higher over the plain, as a new land rises from the sea, and finally, how we reached at last the old watch-tower and looked down on the valley of the Main, clothed in the bloom and verdure of summer, with the houses and spires of Frankfort in the middle of the well-known panorama. We again took possession of our old rooms, and having to wait for a remittance from America, as well as a more suitable season for visiting Italy, we sat down to a month's rest and study.

Chapter XXVIII
FREIBURG AND THE BLACK FOREST

Frankfort, July 29, 1843.—It would be ingratitude towards the old city in which I have passed so many pleasant and profitable hours, to leave it, perhaps forever, without a few words of farewell. How often will the old bridge, with its view up the Main, over the houses of Oberrad to the far mountains of the Odenwald, rise freshly and distinctly in memory, when I shall have been long absent from them! How often will I hear in fancy as I now do in reality, the heavy tread of passersby on the rough pavement below, and the deep bell of the Cathedral, chiming the swift hours, with a hollow tone that seems to warn me, rightly to employ them! Even this old room, with its bare walls, little table and chairs, which I have thought and studied in so long, that it seems diffiult to think and study anywhere else, will crowd out of memory images of many a loftier scene. May I but preserve for the future the hope and trust which have cheered and sustained me here, through the sorrow of absence and the anxiety of uncertain toil! It is growing towards midnight and I think of many a night when I sat here at this hour, answering the spirit-greeting which friends sent me at sunset over the sea. All this has now an end. I must begin a new wandering, and perhaps in ten days more I shall have a better place for thought, among the mountain-chambers of the everlasting Alps. I look forward to the journey with romantic, enthusiastic anticipation, for afar in the silvery distance, stand the Coliseum and St. Peter's, Vesuvius and the lovely Naples. Farewell, friends who have so long given us a home

Aug. 9.—The airy, basket-work tower of the Freiburg Minster rises before me over the black roofs of the houses, and behind stand the gloomy, pine-covered mountains of the Black Forest. Of our walk to Heidelberg over the oft-trodden Bergstrasse, I shall say nothing, nor how we climbed the Kaiserstuhl again, and danced around on the top of the tower for one hour, amid cloud and mist, while there was sunshine below in the valley of the Neckar. I left Heidelberg yesterday morning in the *stehwagen* for Carlsruhe. The engine whistled, the train started, and although I kept my eyes steadily fixed on the spire of the Hauptkirche, three minutes hid it, and all the rest of the city from sight. Carlsruhe, the capital of Baden, which we reached in an hour and a half, is unanimously pronounced by travelers to be a most dull and tiresome city. From a glance I had through one of the gates, I should think its reputation was not undeserved. Even its name, in German, signifies a place of repose.

I stopped at Kork, on the branch road leading to Strasbourg, to meet a German-American about to return to my home in Pennsylvania, where he had lived for some time. I inquired according to the direction he had sent me to Frankfort, but he was not there; however, an old man, finding who I was, said Herr Otto had directed him to go with me to Hesselhurst, a village four or five miles off, where he would meet me. So we set off immediately over the plain, and reached the village at dusk.

At the little inn, were several of the farmers of the neighborhood, who seemed to consider it as something extraordinary to see a real, live, native-born American. They overwhelmed me with questions about the state of our country, its government, etc. The hostess brought me a supper of fried eggs and *wurst,* while they gathered around the table and began a real category in the dialect of the country, which is difficult to understand. I gave them the best information I could about our mode of farming, the different kinds of produce raised, and the prices paid to laborers; one honest old man cried out, on my saying I had worked on a farm, "Ah! little brother, give me your hand!" which he shook most heartily. I told them also something about our government, and the militia system, so different from the conscription of Europe, when a farmer becoming quite warm in our favor, said to the others with an air of the greatest decision: "One American is better than twenty Germans!" What particularly amused me, was, that although I spoke German with them, they seemed to think I did not understand what they said among one another, and therefore commented very freely over my appearance. I suppose they had the idea that we were a rude, savage race, for I overheard one say: "One sees, nevertheless, that he has been educated!" Their honest, unsophisticated mode of expression was very interesting to me, and we talked together till a late hour.

My friend arrived at three o'clock the next morning, and after two or three hours' talk about home, and the friends whom he expected to see so much sooner than I, a young farmer drove me in his wagon to Offenburg, a small city at the foot of the Black Forest, where I took the cars for Freiburg. The scenery between the two places is grand. The broad mountains of the Black Forest rear their fronts on the east, and the blue lines of the French Vosges meet the clouds on the west. The night before, in walking over the plain, I saw distinctly the whole of the Strasbourg Minster, whose spire is the highest in Europe, being four hundred and ninety feet, or but twenty-five feet lower than the Pyramid of Cheops.

I visited the Minster of Freiburg yesterday morning. It is a grand, gloomy old pile, dating from the eleventh century—one of the few Gothic churches in Germany that have ever been completed. The tower of beautiful fretwork, rises to the height of three hundred and ninety-five feet, and the body of the church including the choir, is of the same length. The interior is solemn and majestic. Windows stained in colors that burn, let in a "dim, religious light" which accords very well with the dark old pillars and antique shrines. In two of the chapels there are some fine altar-pieces by Holbein and one of his scholars; and a very large crucifix of silver and ebony, which is kept with great care, is said to have been carried with the Crusaders to the Holy Land. This morning was the great market-day, and the peasantry of the Black Forest came down from the mountains to dispose of their produce. The square around the Minster was filled with them, and the singular costume of the women gave the scene quite a strange appearance. Many of them wore bright red headdresses and shawls, others had high-crowned hats of yellow oilcloth; the young girls wore their hair in long plaits, reaching nearly to their feet. They brought grain, butter and cheese and a great deal of fruit to sell—I bought some of the wild, aromatic plums of the country, at the rate of thirty for a cent.

The railroad has only been open to Freiburg within a few days, and is consequently an object of great curiosity to the peasants, many of whom never saw the like before. They throng around the station at the departure of the train and watch with great interest the operations of getting up the steam and starting. One of the scenes that grated most harshly on my feelings, was seeing yesterday a company of women employed on the unfinished part of the road. They were digging and shoveling away in the rain, nearly up to their knees in mud and clay.

I called at the Institute for the Blind, under the direction of Mr. Müller. He showed me some beautiful basket and woven work by his pupils; the accuracy and skill with which everything was made astonished me. They read with amazing facility from the raised type, and by means of frames are taught to write with ease and distinctness. In music, that great solace of the blind, they most excelled. They sang with an expression so true and touching, that it was a delight to listen. The system of instruction adopted appears to be most excellent, and gives to the blind nearly every advantage which their more fortunate brethren enjoy.

I am indebted to Mr. Müller, to whom I was introduced by an acquaintance with his friend, Dr. Rivinus, of West Chester, Pa., for many kind attentions. He went with us this afternoon to the Jäger-haus, on a mountain near, where we had a very fine view of the city and its great black Minster, with the plain of the Briesgau, broken only by the Kaiserstuhl, a long mountain near the Rhine, whose golden stream glittered off in the distance.

On climbing the Schlossberg, an eminence near the city, we met the Grand Duchess Stephanie, a natural daughter of Napoleon, as I have heard, and now generally believed to be the mother of Caspar Hauser. Through a work lately published, which has since been suppressed, the whole history has come to light. Caspar Hauser was the lineal descendant of the house of Baden, and heir to the throne. The guilt of his imprisonment and murder rests, therefore, upon the present reigning family.

A chapel on the Schönberg, the mountain opposite, was pointed out as the spot where Louis XV., if I mistake not, usually stood while his army besieged Freiburg. A German officer having sent a ball to this chapel which struck the wall just above the king's head, the latter sent word that if they did not cease firing he would point his cannons at the Minster. The citizens thought it best to spare the monarch and save the cathedral.

We attended a meeting of the *Walhalla,* or society of the students who visit the Freiburg University. They pleased me better than the enthusiastic but somewhat unrestrained Burschenschaft of Heidelberg. Here, they have abolished duelling; the greatest friendship prevails among the students, and they have not that contempt for everything *philister,* or unconnected with their studies, which prevails in other universities. Many respectable citizens attend their meetings; tonight there was a member of the Chamber of Deputies at Carlsruhe present, who delivered two speeches, in which every third word was "freedom!" An address was delivered also by a merchant of the city, in which he made a play upon the word *spear,* which signifies also in a cant sense, *citizen,* and seemed to indicate that both would do their work in the good cause. He was loudly applauded. Their song of union was by Charles Follen, and the students were much pleased when I told them how he was honored and esteemed in America.

After two days, delightfully spent, we shouldered our knapsacks and left Freiburg. The beautiful valley, at the mouth of which the city lies, runs like an avenue for seven miles directly into the mountains, and presents in its loveliness such a contrast to the horrid passage which follows, that it almost deserves the name which has been given to a little inn at its head — the "Kingdom of Heaven." The mountains of the Black Forest enclose it on each side like walls, covered to the summit with luxuriant woods, and in some places with those forests of gloomy pine which give this region its name. After traversing its whole length, just before plunging into the mountain-depths, the traveler rarely meets with a finer picture than that which, on looking back, he sees framed between the hills at the other end. Freiburg looks around the foot of one of the heights, with the spire of her cathedral peeping above the top, while the French Vosges grew dim in the far perspective.

The road now enters a wild, narrow valley, which grows smaller as we proceed. From Himmelreich, a large rude inn by the side of the green meadows, we enter the Hollenthal — that is, from the "Kingdom of Heaven" to the "Valley of Hell!" The latter place better deserves its appellation than the former. The road winds between precipices of black rock, above which the thick foliage shuts out the brightness of day and gives a sombre hue to the scene. A torrent foams down the chasm, and in one place two mighty pillars interpose to prevent all passage. The stream, however, has worn its way through, and the road is hewn in the rock by its side. This cleft is the only entrance to a valley three or four miles long, which lies in the very heart of the mountains. It is inhabited by a few woodmen and their families, and but for the road which passes through, would be as perfect a solitude as the Happy Valley of Rasselas. At the further end, a winding road called "The Ascent," loads up the steep mountain to an elevated region of country, thinly settled and covered with herds of cattle. The cherries which, in the Rhine-plain below, had long gone, were just ripe here. The people spoke a most barbarous dialect; they were social and friendly, for everybody greeted us, and sometimes, as we sat on a bank by the roadside, those who passed by would say "Rest thee!" or "Thrice rest!"

Passing by the Titi Lake, a small body of water which was spread out among the hills like a sheet of ink, so deep was its Stygian hue, we commenced ascending a mountain. The highest peak of the Schwarzwald, the Feldberg, rose not far off, and on arriving at the top of this mountain, we saw that a half hour's walk would bring us to its summit. This was too great a temptation for my love of climbing heights; so with a look at the descending sun to calculate how much time we could spare, we set out. There was no path, but we pressed directly up the steep side, through bushes and long grass, and in a short time reached the top, breathless from such exertion in the thin atmosphere. The pine woods shut out the view to the north and east, which is said to be magnificent, as the mountain is about five thousand feet high. The wild, black peaks of the Black Forest were spread below us, and the sun sank through golden mist towards the Alsatian hills. Afar to the south, through cloud and storm, we could just trace the white outline of the Swiss Alps. The wind swept through the pines around, and bent the long yellow grass among which we sat, with a strange, mournful sound, well suiting the gloomy and mysterious region. It soon grew cold, the golden clouds settled down towards us, and we made haste to descend to the village of Lenzkirch before dark.

Next morning we set out early, without waiting to see the trial of archery which was to take place among the mountain youths. Their booths and targets, gay with banners, stood on a green meadow beside the town. We walked through the Black Forest the whole forenoon. It might be owing to the many wild stories whose scenes are laid among these hills, but with me there was a peculiar feeling of solemnity pervading the whole region. The great pine woods are of the very darkest hue of green, and down their hoary, moss-floored aisles, daylight seems never to have shone. The air was pure and clear, and the sunshine bright, but it imparted no gaiety to the scenery except the little meadows of living emerald which lay occasionally in the lap of a dell, the landscape wore a solemn and serious air. In a storm, it must be sublime.

About noon, from the top of the last range of hills, we had a glorious view. The line of the distant Alps could be faintly traced high in the clouds, and all the heights between were plainly visible, from the Lake of Constance to the misty Jura, which flanked the Vosges of the west. From our lofty station we overlooked half Switzerland, and had the air been a little clearer, we could have seen Mont Blanc and the mountains of Savoy. I could not help envying the feelings of the Swiss, who, after long absence from their native land, first see the Alps from this road. If to the emotions with which I then looked on them were added the passionate love of home and country which a long absence creates, such excess of rapture would be almost too great to be borne.

In the afternoon we crossed the border, and took leave of Germany with regret, after near a year's residence within bounds. Still it was pleasant to know we were in a republic once more; the first step we took made us aware of the change. There was no policeman to call for our passports or search our baggage. It was just dark when we reached the hill overlooking the Rhine, on whose steep banks is perched the antique town of Schaffhausen. It is still walled in, with towers at regular intervals; the streets are wide and spacious, and the houses rendered extremely picturesque by the quaint projecting windows. The buildings are nearly all old, as we learned by the dates above the doors. At the inn, I met with one of the free troopers who marched against Luzerne. He was full of spirit, and ready to undertake another such journey. Indeed it is the universal opinion that the present condition of things cannot last much longer.

We took a walk before breakfast to the Falls of the Rhine, about a mile and a half from Schaffhausen. I confess I was somewhat disappointed in them, after the glowing descriptions of travelers. The river at, this place is little more than thirty yards wide, and the body of water, although issuing from the Lake of Constance, is not remarkably strong. For some distance above, the fall of the water is very rapid, and as it finally reaches the spot where, narrowed between rocks, it makes the grand plunge, it has acquired a great velocity. Three rocks stand in the middle of the current, which thunders against and around their bases, but cannot shake them down. These and the rocks in the bed of the stream, break the force of the fall, so that it descends to the bottom, about fifty feet below, not in one sheet, but shivered into a hundred leaps of snowy foam. The precipitous shores, and the tasteful little castle which is perched upon the steep just over the boiling spray, add much to its beauty, taken as a picture. As a specimen of the picturesque, the whole scene is perfect. I should think Trenton Falls, in New York, must excel these in wild, startling effect; but there is such a scarcity of waterfalls in this land, that the Germans go into raptures about them, and will hardly believe that Niagara itself possesses more sublimity.

Chapter XXIX
PEOPLE AND PLACES IN EASTERN SWITZERLAND

We left Schaffhausen for Zürich, in mist and rain, and walked for some time along the north bank of the Rhine. We could have enjoyed the scenery much better, had it not been for the rain, which not only hid the mountains from sight, but kept us constantly half soaked. We crossed the rapid Rhine at Eglisau, a curious antique village, and then continued our way through the forests of Canton Zürich, to Bülach, with its groves of lindens — "those tall and stately trees, with velvet down upon their shining leaves, and rustic benches placed beneath their overhanging eaves."

When we left the little village where the rain obliged us to stop for the night, it was clear and delightful. The farmers were out, busy at work, their long, straight scythes glancing through the wet grass, while the thick pines sparkled with thousands of dewy diamonds. The country was so beautiful and cheerful, that we half felt like being in America.

The farm-houses were scattered over the country in real American style, and the glorious valley of the Limmat, bordered on the west by a range of woody hills, reminded me of some scenes in my native Pennsylvania. The houses were neatly and tastefully built, with little gardens around them—and the countenances of the people spoke of intelligence and independence. There was the same air of peace and prosperity which delighted us in the valleys of Upper Austria, with a look of freedom which those had not. The faces of a people are the best index to their condition. I could read on their brows a lofty self-respect, a consciousness of the liberties they enjoy, which the Germans of the laboring class never show. It could not be imagination, for the recent occurrences in Switzerland, with the many statements I had heard in Germany, had prejudiced me somewhat against the land; and these marks of prosperity and freedom were as surprising as they were delightful.

As we approached Zürich, the noise of employment from mills, furnaces and factories, came to us like familiar sounds, reminding us of the bustle of our home cities. The situation of the city is lovely. It lies at the head of the lake, and on both sides of the little river Limmat, whose clear green waters carry the collected meltings of the Alps to the Rhine. Around the lake rise lofty green hills, which, sloping gently back, bear on their sides hundreds of pleasant country-houses and farms, and the snowy Alpine range extends along the southern sky. The Limmat is spanned by a number of bridges, and its swift waters turn many mills which are built above them. From these bridges one can look out over the blue lake and down the thronged streets of the city on each side, whose bright, cheerful houses remind him of Italy.

Zürich can boast of finer promenades than any other city in Switzerland. The old battlements are planted with trees and transformed into pleasant walks, which being elevated above the city, command views of its beautiful environs. A favorite place of resort is the Lindenhof, an elevated courtyard, shaded by immense trees. The fountains of water under them are always surrounded by washerwomen, and in the morning groups of merry school children may be seen tumbling over the grass. The teachers take them there in a body for exercise and recreation. The Swiss children are beautiful, bright-eyed creatures; there is scarcely one who does not exhibit the dawning of an active, energetic spirit. It may be partly attributed to the fresh, healthy climate of Switzerland, but I am partial enough to republics to believe that the influence of the Government under which they live, has also its share in producing the effect.

There is a handsome promenade on an elevated bastion which overlooks the city and lakes. While enjoying the cool morning breeze and listening to the stir of the streets below us, we were also made aware of the social and friendly politeness of the people. Those who passed by, on their walk around the rampart, greeted us, almost with the familiarity of an acquaintance. Simple as was the act, we felt grateful, for it had at least the seeming of a friendly interest and a sympathy with the loneliness which the stranger sometimes feels. A school-teacher leading her troop of merry children on their morning walk around the bastion, nodded to us pleasantly and forthwith the whole company of chubby-cheeked rogues, looking up at us with a pleasant archness, lisped a *"guten morgen"* that made the hearts glad within us. I know of nothing that has given me a more sweet and tender delight than the greeting of a little child, who, leaving his noisy playmates, ran across the street to me, and taking my hand, which he could barely clasp in both his soft little ones, looked up in my face with an expression so winning and affectionate, that I loved him at once. The happy, honest farmers, too, spoke to us cheerfully everywhere. We learned a lesson from all this — we felt that not a word of kindness is ever wasted, that a simple friendly glance may cheer the spirit and warm the lonely heart, and that the slightest deed, prompted by generous sympathy, becomes a living joy in the memory of the receiver, which blesses unceasingly him who bestowed it.

We left Zürich the same afternoon, to walk to Stafa, where we were told the poet Ferdinand Freiligrath resided. The road led along the bank of the lake, whose shores sloped gently up from the water, covered with gardens and farm-houses, which, with the bolder mountains that rose behind them, made a combination of the lovely and grand, on which the eye rested with rapture and delight. The sweetest cottages were embowered among the orchards, and the whole country bloomed like a garden. The waters of the lake are of a pale, transparent green, and so clear that we could see its bottom of white pebbles, for some distance. Here and there floated a quiet boat on its surface. The opposite hills were covered with a soft blue haze, and white villages sat along the shore, "like swans among the reeds." Behind, we saw the woody range of the Brünig Alp. The people bade us a pleasant good evening; there was a universal air of cheerfulness and content on their countenances.

Towards evening, the clouds which hung in the south the whole day, dispersed a little and we could see the Dodiberg and the Alps of Glarus. As sunset drew on, the broad summits of snow and the clouds which were rolled around them, assumed a soft rosy hue, which increased in brilliancy as the light of day faded. The rough, icy crags and snowy steeps were fused in the warm light and half blended with the bright clouds. This blaze, as it were, of the mountains at sunset, is called the Alp-glow, and exceeds all one's highest conceptions of Alpine grandeur. We watched the fading glory till it quite died away, and the summits wore a livid, ashy hue, like the mountains of a world wherein there was no life. In a few minutes more the dusk of twilight spread over the scene, the boatmen glided home over the still lake and the herdsmen drove their cattle back from pasture on the slopes and meadows.

On inquiring for Freiligrath at Stafa, we found he had removed to Rapperschwyl, some distance further. As it was already late, we waited for the steamboat which leaves Zürich every evening. It came along about eight o'clock, and a little boat carried us out through rain and darkness to meet it, as it came like a fiery-eyed monster over the water. We stepped on board the "Republican," and in half an hour were brought to the wharf at Rapperschwyl.

There are two small islands in the lake, one of which, with a little chapel rising from among its green trees, is Ufnau, the grave of Ulrich von Hutten, one of the fathers of the German Reformation. His fiery poems have been the source from which many a German bard has derived his inspiration, and Freiligrath who now lives in sight of his tomb, has published an indignant poem, because an inn with gaming tables has been established in the ruins of the castle near Creuznach, where Hutten found refuge from his enemies with Franz von Sickingen, brother-in-law of "Goetz with the Iron Hand." The monks of Einsiedeln, to whom Ufnau belongs, have carefully obliterated all traces of his grave, so that the exact spot is not known, in order that even a tombstone might be denied him who once strove to overturn their order. It matters little to that bold spirit whose motto was: *"The die is cast—I have dared it!"*—the whole island is his monument, if he need one.

I spent the whole of the morning with Freiligrath, the poet, who was lately banished from Germany on account of the liberal principles his last volume contains. He lives in a pleasant country-house on the Meyerberg, an eminence near Rapperschwyl overlooking a glorious prospect. On leaving Frankfort, R. S. Willis gave me a letter to him, and I was glad to meet with a man personally whom I admired so much through his writings, and whose boldness in speaking out against the tyranny which his country suffers, forms such a noble contrast to the cautious slowness of his countrymen. He received me kindly and conversed much upon American literature. He is a warm admirer of Bryant and Longfellow, and has translated many of their poems into German. He said he had received a warm invitation from a colony of Germans in Wisconsin, to join them and enjoy that freedom which his native land denies, but that his circumstances would not allow it at present. He is perhaps thirty-five years of age. His brow is high and noble, and his eyes, which are large and of a clear gray, beam with serious, saddened thought. His long chestnut hair, uniting with a handsome beard and moustache, gives a lion-like dignity to his energetic countenance. His talented wife, Ida Freiligrath, who shares his literary labors, and an amiable sister, are with him in exile, and he is happier in their faithfulness than when he enjoyed the favors of a corrupt king.

We crossed the long bridge from Rapperschwyl, and took the road over the mountain opposite, ascending for nearly two hours along the side, with glorious views of the Lake of Zürich and the mountains which enclose it. The upper and lower ends of the lake were completely hid by the storms, which, to our regret, veiled the Alps, but the part below lay spread out dim and grand, like a vast picture. It rained almost constantly, and we were obliged occasionally to take shelter in the pine forests, whenever a heavier cloud passed over. The road was lined with beggars, who dropped on their knees in the rain before us, or placed bars across the way, and then took them down again, for which they demanded money.

At length we reached the top of the pass. Many pilgrims to Einsiedeln had stopped at a little inn there, some of whom came a long distance to pay their vows, especially as the next day was the Ascension day of the Virgin, whose image there is noted for performing many miracles. Passing on, we crossed a wild torrent by an arch called the "Devil's Bridge." The lofty, elevated plains were covered with scanty patches of grain and potatoes, and the boys tended their goats on the grassy slopes, sometimes trilling or *yodling* an Alpine melody. An hour's walk brought us to Einsiedeln, a small town, whose only attraction is the Abbey—after Loretto, in Italy, the most celebrated resort for pilgrims in Europe.

We entered immediately into the great church. The gorgeous vaulted roof and long aisles were dim with the early evening; hundreds of worshippers sat around the sides, or kneeled in groups on the broad stone pavements, chanting over their Paternosters and Ave Marias in a shrill, monotonous tone, while the holy image near the entrance was surrounded by persons, many of whom came in the hope of being healed of some disorder under which they suffered. I could not distinctly make out the image, for it was placed back within the grating, and a strong crimson lamp behind it was made to throw the light around, in the form of a glory. Many of the pilgrims came a long distance. I saw some in the costume of the Black Forest, and others who appeared to be natives of the Italian Cantons; and a group of young women wearing conical fur caps, from the forests of Bregenz, on the Lake of Constance.

I was astonished at the splendor of this church, situated in a lonely and unproductive Alpine valley. The lofty arches of the ceiling, which are covered with superb fresco paintings, rest on enor-

mous pillars of granite, and every image and shrine is richly ornamented with gold. Some, of the chapels were filled with the remains
of martyrs, and these were always surrounded with throngs of believers. The choir was closed by a tall iron grating; a single lamp,
which swung from the roof, enabled me to see through the darkness,
that though more rich in ornaments than the body of the church, it
was less grand and impressive. The frescoes which cover the ceiling,
are said to be the finest paintings of the kind in Switzerland.

In the morning our starting was delayed by the rain, and we took
advantage of it to hear mass in the Abbey and enjoy the heavenly
music. The latter was of the loftiest kind; there was one voice among
the singers I shall not soon forget. It was like the warble of a bird
who sings out of very wantonness. On and on it sounded, making
its clear, radiant sweetness heard above the chant of the choir and
the thunder of the orchestra. Such a rich, varied and untiring strain
of melody I have rarely listened to.

When the service ceased, we took a small road leading to Schwytz.
We had now fairly entered the Alpine region, and our first task was
to cross a mountain. This having been done, we kept along the back
of the ridge which bounds the lake of Zug on the south, terminating
in the well known Rossberg. The scenery became wilder with every
step. The luxuriant fields of herbage on the mountains were spotted
with the picturesque *chalets* of the hunters and Alp-herds; cattle and
goats were browsing along the declivities, their bells tinkling most
musically, and the little streams fell in foam down the steeps. We
here began to realize our anticipations of Swiss scenery. Just on the
other side of the range, along which we traveled, lay the little lake
of Egeri and valley of Morgarten, where Tell and his followers overcame the army of the German Emperor; near the lake of Lowertz, we
found a chapel by the roadside, built on the spot where the house
of Werner Stauffacher, one of the "three men of Grütli," formerly
stood. It bears a poetical inscription in old German, and a rude
painting of the Battle of Morgarten.

As we wound around the lake of Lowertz, we saw the valley lying between the Rossberg and the Righi, which latter mountain stood full in view. To our regret, and that of all other travelers, the clouds hung low upon it, as they had done for a week at least, and there was no prospect of a change. The Rossberg, from which we descended, is about four thousand feet in height; a dark brown stripe from its very summit to the valley below, shows the track of the avalanche which, in 1806, overwhelmed Goldau, and laid waste the beautiful vale of Lowertz. We could trace the masses of rock and earth as far as the foot of the Righi. Four hundred and fifty persons perished by this catastrophe, which was so sudden that in five minutes the whole lovely valley was transformed into a desolate wilderness. The shock was so great that the lake of Lowertz overflowed its banks, and part of the village of Steinen at the upper end was destroyed by the waters.

An hour's walk through a blooming Alpine vale brought us to the little town of Schwytz, the capital of the Canton. It stands at the foot of a rock-mountain, in shape not unlike Gibraltar, but double its height. The bare and rugged summits seem to hang directly over the town, but the people dwell below without fear, although the warning ruins of Goldau are full in sight. A narrow blue line at the end of the valley which stretches westward, marks the lake of the Four Cantons. Down this valley we hurried, that we might not miss the boat which plies daily, from Luzerne to Fluelen. I regretted not being able to visit Luzerne, for I had a letter to the distinguished Swiss composer, Schnyder von Wartensee, who resides there at present. The place is said to present a most desolate appearance, being avoided by travelers, and even by artisans, so that business of all kinds has almost entirely ceased.

At the little town of Brunnen, on the lake, we awaited the coming of the steamboat. The scenery around it is exceedingly grand. Looking down towards Luzerne, we could see the dark mass of Mount Pilatus on one side, and on the other the graceful outline of the

Righi, still wearing his hood of clouds. We put off in a skiff to meet the boat, with two Capuchin friars in long brown mantles and cowls, carrying rosaries at their girdles.

Nearly opposite Brunnen is the meadow of Grütli, where the union of the Swiss patriots took place, and the bond was sealed that enabled them to cast off their chains. It is a little green slope on the side of the mountain, between the two Cantons of Uri and Unterwalden, surrounded on all sides by precipices. A little crystal spring in the centre is believed by the common people to have gushed up on the spot where the three "linked the hands that made them free." It is also a popular belief that they slumber in a rocky cavern near the spot, and that they will arise and come forth when the liberties of Switzerland are in danger. She stands at present greatly in need of a new triad to restore the ancient harmony.

We passed this glorious scene, almost the only green spot on the bleak mountain-side, and swept around the base of the Axenberg, at whose foot, in a rocky cave, stands the chapel of William Tell. This is built on the spot where he leaped from Gessler's boat during the storm. It sits at the base of the rock, on the water's edge, and can be seen far over the waves. The Alps, whose eternal snows are lifted dazzling to the sky, complete the grandeur of a scene so hallowed by the footsteps of freedom. The grand and lonely solemnity of the landscape impressed me with an awe, like that one feels when standing in a mighty cathedral, when the aisles are dim with twilight. And how full of interest to a citizen of young and free America is a shrine where the votaries of Liberty have turned to gather strength and courage, through the storms and convulsions of five hundred years!

We stopped at the village of Fluelen, at the head of the lake, and walked on to Altorf, a distance of half a league. Here, in the market-place, is a tower said to be built on the spot where the linden tree stood, under which the child of Tell was placed, while, about a hundred yards distant, is a fountain with Tell's statue, on the spot from whence he shot the apple. If these localities are correct, he must indeed have been master of the cross-bow. The tower is covered with rude paintings of the principal events in the history of Swiss liberty. I viewed these scenes with double interest from having read Schiller's "Wilhelm Tell," one of the most splendid tragedies ever written. The beautiful reply of his boy, when he described to him the condition of the "land where there are no mountains," was sounding in my ears during the whole day's journey:

> "Father, I'd feel oppressed in that broad land,
>   I'd rather dwell beneath the avalanche"

The little village of Burglen, whose spire we saw above the forest, in a glen near by, was the birthplace of Tell, and the place where his dwelling stood, is now marked by a small chapel. In the Schachen, a noisy mountain stream that comes down to join the Reuss, he was drowned, when an old man, in attempting to rescue a child who had fallen in— a death worthy of the hero! We bestowed a blessing on his memory in passing, and then followed the banks of the rapid Reuss. Twilight was gathering in the deep Alpine glen, and the mountains on each side, half-seen through the mist, looked like vast, awful phantoms. Soon they darkened to black, indistinct masses; all was silent except the deepened roar of the falling floods; dark clouds brooded above us like the outspread wings of night, and we were glad, when the little village of Amstegg was reached, and the parlor of the inn opened to us a more cheerful, if not so romantic scene.

Chapter XXX
PASSAGE OF THE ST. GOTHARD AND DESCENT INTO ITALY

Leaving Amstegg, I passed the whole day among snowy, skypiercing Alps, torrents, chasms and clouds! The clouds appeared to be breaking up as we set out, and the white top of the Reussberg was now and then visible in the sky. Just above the village are the remains of Zwing Uri, the castle begun by the tyrant Gessler, for the complete subjugation of the canton.

Following the Reuss up through a narrow valley, we passed the Bristenstock, which lifts its jagged crags nine thousand feet in the air, while on the other side stand the snowy summits which lean towards the Rhône Glacier and St. Gothard. From the deep glen where the Reuss foamed down towards the Lake of the Forest Cantons, the mountains rose with a majestic sweep so far into the sky that the brain grew almost dizzy in following their outlines. Woods, chalets and slopes of herbage covered their bases, where the mountain cattle and goats were browsing, while the herd-boys sang their native melodies or woke the ringing echoes with the loud, sweet sounds of their wooden horns; higher up, the sides were broken into crags and covered with stunted pines; then succeeded a belt of bare rock with a little snow lying in the crevices, and the summits of dazzling white looked out from the clouds nearly three-fourths the height of the zenith. Sometimes when the vale was filled with clouds, it was startling to see them parting around a solitary summit, apparently isolated in the air at an immense height, for the mountain to which it belonged was hidden to the very base!

The road passed from one side of the valley to the other, crossing the Reuss on bridges sometimes ninety feet high. After three or four hours walking, we reached a frightful pass called the Schollenen. So narrow is the passage that before reaching it, the road seemed to enter directly into the mountain. Precipices a thousand feet high tower above, and the stream roars and boils in the black depth below. The road is a wonder of art, it winds around the edge of horrible chasms or is carried on lofty arches across, with sometimes a hold apparently so frail that one involuntarily shudders. At a place called the Devil's Bridge, the Reuss leaps about seventy feet in three or four cascades, sending up continually a cloud of spray, while a wind created by the fall, blows and whirls around, with a force that nearly lifts one from his feet. Wordsworth has described the scene in the following lines:

> "Plunge with the Reuss embrowned by terror's breath,
>   Where danger roofs the narrow walks of Death;
>   By floods that, thundering from their dizzy height,
>   Swell more gigantic on the steadfast sight,
>   Black, drizzling crags, that, beaten by the din,
>   Vibrate, as if a voice complained within,
>   Loose hanging rocks, the Day's blessed eye that hide,
>   And crosses reared to Death on every side!"

Beyond the Devil's Bridge, the mountains which nearly touched before, interlock into each other, and a tunnel three hundred and seventy-five feet long leads through the rock into the vale of Urseren, surrounded by the Upper Alps. The little town of Andermatt lies in the middle of this valley, which with the peak around is covered with short, yellowish-brown grass. We met near Amstegg a little Italian boy walking home, from Germany, quite alone and without money, for we saw him give his last kreutzer to a blind beggar along the road. We therefore took him with us, as he was afraid to cross the St. Gothard alone.

After refreshing ourselves at Andermatt, we started, five in number, including a German student, for the St. Gothard. Behind the village of Hospiz, which stands at the bottom of the valley leading to Realp and the Furca pass, the way commences, winding backwards and forwards, higher and higher, through a valley covered with rocks, with the mighty summits of the Alps around, untenanted save by the chamois and mountain eagle. Not a tree was to be seen. The sides of the mountains were covered with loose rocks waiting for the next torrent to wash them down, and the tops were robed in eternal snow. A thick cloud rolled down over us as we went on, following the diminishing brooks to their snowy source in the peak of St. Gothard. We cut off the bends of the road by footpaths up the rocks, which we ascended in single file, one of the Americans going ahead and little Pietro with his staff and bundle bringing up the rear. The rarefied air we breathed, seven thousand feet above the sea, was like exhilarating gas. We felt no fatigue, but ran and shouted and threw snowballs, in the middle of August!

After three hours' walk we reached the two clear and silent lakes which send their waters to the Adriatic and the North Sea. Here, as we looked down the Italian side, the sky became clear; we saw the top of St. Gothard many thousand feet above, and stretching to the south, the summits of the mountains which guard the vales of the Ticino and the Adda. The former monastery has been turned into an inn; there is, however, a kind of church attached, attended by a single monk. It was so cold that although late, we determined to descend to the first village. The Italian side is very steep, and the road, called the Via Trimola, is like a thread dropped down and constantly doubling back upon itself. The deep chasms were filled with snow, although exposed to the full force of the sun, and for a long distance there was scarcely a sign of vegetation.

We thought as we went down, that every step was bringing us nearer to a sunnier land—that the glories of Italy, which had so long lain in the airy background of the future, would soon spread themselves before us in their real or imagined beauty. Reaching at dusk the last height above the vale of the Ticino, we saw the little village of Airolo with its musical name, lying in a hollow of the mountains.

A few minutes of leaping, sliding and rolling, took us down the grassy declivity, and we found we had descended from the top in an hour and a half although the distance by the road is nine miles! I need not say how glad we were to relieve our trembling knees and exhausted limbs.

I have endeavored several times to give some idea of the sublimity of the Alps, but words seem almost powerless to measure these mighty mountains. No effort of the imagination could possibly equal their real grandeur. I wish also to describe the feelings inspired by being among them,—feelings which can best be expressed through the warmer medium of poetry.

SONG OF THE ALP

I.

I sit aloft on my thunder throne,
And my voice of dread the nations own
   As I speak in storm below!
The valleys quake with a breathless fear,
When I hurl in wrath my icy spear
   And shake my locks of snow!
When the avalanche forth like a tiger leaps,
   How the vassal-mountains quiver!
And the storm that sweeps through the airy deeps
   Makes the hoary pine-wood shiver!
Above them all, in a brighter air,
I lift my forehead proud and bare,
And the lengthened sweep of my forest-robe
Trails down to, the low and captured globe,
Till its borders touch the dark green wave
In whose soundless depths my feet I lave.
The winds, unprisoned, around me blow,
And terrible tempests whirl the snow;
Rocks from their caverned beds are torn,

And the blasted forest to heaven is borne;
High through the din of the stormy band,
Like misty giants the mountains stand,
And their thunder-revel o'er-sounds the woe,
That cries from the desolate vales below!
I part the clouds with my lifted crown,
Till the sun-ray slants on the glaciers down,
And trembling men, in the valleys pale,
Rejoice at the gleam of my icy mail!

II.

I wear a crown of the sunbeams gold,
With glacier-gems on my forehead old
   A monarch crowned by God!
What son of the servile earth may dare
Such signs of a regal power to wear,
   While chained to her darkened sod?
I know of a nobler and grander lore
   Than Time records on his crumbling pages,
And the soul of my solitude teaches more
   Than the gathered deeds of perished ages!
For I have ruled since Time began
And wear no fetter made by man.
I scorn the coward and craven race
Who dwell around my mighty base,
For they leave the lessons I grandly gave
And bend to the yoke of the crouching slave.
I shout aloud to the chainless skies;
The stream through its falling foam replies,
And my voice, like the sound of the surging sea,
To the nations thunders: "I am free!"
I spoke to Tell when a tyrants hand
Lay heavy and hard on his native land,

And the spirit whose glory from mine he won
Blessed the Alpine dwellers with Freedom's sun!
The student-boy on the Gmunden-plain
Heard my solemn voice, but he fought in vain;
I called from the crags of the Passeir-glen,
When the despot stood in my realm again,
And Hofer sprang at the proud command
And roused the men of the Tyrol land!

III.

I struggle up to the dim blue heaven,
From the world, far down in whose breast are driven
    The props of my pillared throne;
And the rosy fires of morning glow
Like a glorious thought, on my brow of snow,
    While the vales are dark and lone!
Ere twilight summons the first faint star,
I seem to the nations who dwell afar
Like a shadowy cloud, whose every fold
The sunset dyes with its purest gold,
And the soul mounts up through that gateway fair
To try its wings in a loftier air
The finger of God on my brow is pressed—
His spirit beats in my giant breast,
And I breathe, as the endless ages roll,
His silent words to the eager soul!
I prompt the thoughts of the mighty mind,
Who leaves his century far behind
And speaks from the Future's sun-lit snow
To the Present, that sleeps in its gloom below!
I stand, unchanged, in creation's youth—
A glorious type of Eternal Truth,
That, free and pure, from its native skies

Shines through Oppression's veil of lies,
And lights the world's long-fettered sod
With thoughts of Freedom and of God!

When, at night, I looked out of my chamber-window, the silver moon of Italy, (for we fancied that her light was softer and that the skies were already bluer) hung trembling above the fields of snow that stretched in their wintry brilliance along the mountains around. I heard the roar of the Ticino and the deepened sound of filling cascades, and thought, if I were to take those waters for my guide, to what glorious places they would lead me!

We left Airolo early the next morning, to continue our journey down the valley of the Ticino. The mists and clouds of Switzerland were exchanged for a sky of the purest blue, and we felt, for the first time in ten days, uncomfortably warm. The mountains which flank the Alps on this side, are still giants — lofty and bare, and covered with snow in many places. The limit of the German dialect is on the summit of St. Gothard, and the peasants saluted us with a "*buon giorno,*" as they passed. This, with the clearness of the skies and the warmth of the air, made us feel that Italy was growing nearer.

The mountains are covered with forests of dark pine, and many beautiful cascades come tumbling over the rocks in their haste to join the Ticino. One of these was so strangely beautiful, that I cannot pass it without a particular description. We saw it soon after leaving Airolo, on the opposite side of the valley. A stream of considerable size comes down the mountain, leaping from crag to crag till within forty or fifty feet of the bottom, where it is caught in a hollow rock, and flung upwards into the air, forming a beautiful arch as it falls out into the valley. As it is whirled up thus, feathery curls of spray are constantly driven off and seem to wave round it like the fibres on an ostrich plume. The sun shining through, gave it a sparry brilliance which was perfectly magnificent. If I were an artist, I would give much for such a new form of beauty.

On our first day's journey we passed through two terrific mountain gorges, almost equalling in grandeur the passage of the "Devil's Bridge." The Ticino, in its course to Lago Maggiore has to make a descent of nearly three thousand feet, passing through three valleys, which lie like terraces, one below the other. In its course from one to the other, it has to force its way down in twenty cataracts through a cleft in the mountains. The road, constructed with the utmost labor, threads these dark chasms, sometimes carried in a tunnel through the rock, sometimes passing on arches above the boiling flood. The precipices of bare rock rise far above and render the way difficult and dangerous. I here noticed another very beautiful effect of the water, perhaps attributable to some mineral substance it contained. The spray and foam thrown up in the dashing of the vexed current, was of a light, delicate pink, although the stream itself was a soft blue; and the contrast of these two colors was very remarkable.

As we kept on, however, there was a very perceptible change in the scenery. The gloomy pines disappeared and the mountains were covered, in their stead, with picturesque chestnut trees, with leaves of a shining green. The grass and vegetation was much more luxuriant than on the other side of the Alps, and fields of maize and mulberry orchards covered the valley. We saw the people busy at work reeling silk in the villages. Every mile we advanced made a sensible change in the vegetation. The chestnuts were larger, the maize higher, the few straggling grape-vines increased into bowers and vineyards, while the gardens were filled with plum, pear and fig-trees, and the stands of delicious fruit which we saw in the villages, gave us promise of the luxuriance that was to come.

The vineyards are much more beautiful than the German fields of stakes. The vines are not trimmed, but grow from year to year over a frame higher than the head, supported through the whole field on stone pillars. They interlace and form a complete leafy screen, while the clusters hang below. The light came dimly through the green, transparent leaves, and nothing was wanting to make them real bowers of Arcadia. Although we were still in Switzerland, the people began to have that lazy, indolent look which characterizes the Italians; most of the occupations were carried on in the open air, and brown-robed, sandalled friars were going about from house to house, collecting money and provisions for their support.

We passed Faido and Giornico, near which last village are the remains of an old castle, supposed to have been built by the ancient Gauls, and stopped for the night at Cresciano, which being entirely Italian, we had an opportunity to put in practice the few words we had picked up from Pietro. The little fellow parted from us with regret a few hours before, at Biasco, where he had relations. The rustic landlord at Cresciano was an honest young fellow, who tried to serve us as well as he could, but we made some ludicrous mistakes through our ignorance of the language.

Three hours' walk brought us to Bellinzona, the capital of the canton. Before reaching it, our road joined that of the Splügen which comes down through the valley of Bernardino. From the bridge where the junction takes place we had a triple view, whose grandeur took me by surprise, even after coming from Switzerland. We stood at the union of three valleys — that leading to St. Gothard, terminated by the glaciers of the Bernese Oberland, that running off obliquely to the Splügen, and finally the broad vale of the Ticino, extending to Lago Maggiore, whose purple mountains closed the vista. Each valley was perhaps two miles broad and from twenty to thirty long, and the mountains that enclosed them from five to seven thousand feet in height, so you may perhaps form some idea what a view down three such avenues in this Alpine temple would be. Bellinzona is romantically situated, on a slight eminence, with three castles to defend it, with those square turreted towers and battlements, which remind one involuntarily of the days of the Goths and Vandals.

We left Bellinzona at about noon, and saw, soon after, from an eminence, the blue line of Lago Maggiore stretched across the bottom of the valley. We saw sunset fade away over the lake, but it was clouded, and did not realize my ideal of such a scene in Italy. A band of wild Italians paraded up and down the village, drawing one of their number in a hand-cart. They made a great noise with a drum and trumpet, and were received everywhere with shouts of laughter. A great jug of wine was not wanting, and the whole seemed to me a very characteristic scene.

We were early awakened at Magadino, at the head of Lago Maggiore, and after swallowing a hasty breakfast, went on board the steamboat "San Carlo," for Sesto Calende. We got under way at six o'clock, and were soon in motion over the crystal mirror. The water is of the most lovely green hue, and so transparent that we seemed to be floating in mid-air. Another heaven arched far below us; other chains of mountains joined their bases to those which surrounded the lake, and the mirrored cascades leaped upward to meet their originals at the surface. It may be because I have seen it more recently, that the water of Lago Maggiore appears to be the most beautiful in the world. I was delighted with the Scotch lakes, and enraptured with the Traunsee and "Zürich's waters," but this last exceeds them both. I am now incapable of any stronger feeling, until I see the Aegean from the Grecian Isles.

The morning was cloudy, and the white wreaths hung low on the mountains, whose rocky sides were covered everywhere with the rank and luxuriant growth of this climate. As we advanced further over this glorious mirror, the houses became more Italianlike; the lower stories rested on arched passages, and the windows were open, without glass, while in the gardens stood the solemn, graceful cypress, and vines, heavy with ripening grapes, hung from bough to bough through the mulberry orchards. Half-way down, in a broad bay, which receives the waters of a stream that comes down with the Simplon, are the celebrated Borromean Islands. They are four in number, and seem to float like fairy creations on the water, while the lofty hills form a background whose grandeur enhances by contrast their exquisite beauty. There was something there in the scene that reminded me of Claude Melnotte's description of his home, by Bulwer, and like the lady of Lyons, I answer readily, "I like the picture."

On passing by Isola Madre, we could see the roses in its terraced garden's and the broad-leaved aloes clinging to the rocks. Isola Bella, the loveliest of them all, as its name denotes, was farther off; it rose like a pyramid from the water, terrace above terrace to the summit, and its gardens of never fading foliage, with the glorious panorama around, might make it a paradise, if life were to be dreamed away. On the northern side of the bay lies a large town (I forget its name,) with a lofty Romanesque tower, and noble mountains sweep around as if to shut out the world from such a scene. The sea was perfectly calm, and groves and gardens slept mirrored in the dark green wave, while the Alps rose afar through the dim, cloudy air. Towards the other end the hills sink lower, and slope off into the plains of Lombardy. Near Arena, on the western side, is a large monastery, overlooking the lower part of the lake. Beside it, on a hill, is a colossal statue of San Carlo Borromeo, who gave his name to the lovely islands above.

After a seven hours' passage, we ran into Sesto Calende, at the foot of the lake. Here, passengers and baggage were tumbled promiscuously on shore, the latter gathered into the office to be examined, and the former left at liberty to ramble about an hour until their passports could be signed. We employed the time in trying the flavor the grapes and peaches of Lombardy, and looking at the groups of travelers who had come down from the Alps with the annual avalanche at this season. The custom house officers were extremely civil and obliging, as they did not think necessary to examine our knapsacks, and our passports being soon signed, we were at liberty to enter again into the dominions of His Majesty of Austria. Our companion, the German, whose feet could carry him no further, took a seat on the top of a diligence (stagecoach) for Milan; we left Sesto Calende on foot, and plunged into the cloud of dust which was whirling towards the capital of Northern Italy.

Being now really in the "sunny land," we looked on the scenery with a deep interest. The first thing that struck me was a resemblance to America in the fields of Indian corn, and the rank growth of weeds by the roadside. The mulberry trees and hedges, too, looked quite familiar, coming as we did, from fenceless and hedgeless Germany. But here the resemblance ceased. The people were coarse, ignorant and savage-looking, the villages remarkable for nothing except the contrast between splendid churches and miserable, dirty houses, while the luxurious palaces and grounds of the rich noblemen formed a still greater contrast to the poverty of the people. I noticed also that if the latter are as lazy as they are said to be, they make their horses work for them, as in a walk of a few hours yesterday afternoon, we saw two horses drawing heavy loads, drop down apparently dead, and several others seemed nearly ready to do the same.

We spent the night at the little village of Casina, about sixteen miles from Milan, and here made our first experience in the honesty of Italian inns. We had taken the precaution to inquire beforehand the price of a bed; but it seemed unnecessary and unpleasant, as well as evincing a mistrustful spirit, to do the same with every article we asked for, so we concluded to leave it to the host's conscience not to overcharge us. Imagine our astonishment, however, when at starting, a bill was presented to us, in which the smallest articles were set down at three or four times their value. We remonstrated, but to little purpose; the fellow knew scarcely any French, and we as little Italian, so rather than lose time or temper, we paid what he demanded and went on, leaving him to laugh at the successful imposition. The experience was of value to us, however, and it may serve as a warning to some future traveler.

About noon, the road turned into a broad and beautiful avenue of poplars, down which we saw, at a distance, the triumphal arch terminating the Simplon road, which we had followed from Sesto Calende. Beyond it rose the slight and airy pinnacle of the Duomo. We passed by the exquisite structure, gave up our passports at the gates, traversed the broad Piazza d'Armi, and found ourselves at liberty to choose one of the dozen streets that led into the heart of the city.

Chapter XXXI
MILAN

Aug. 21.—While finding our way at random to the "Pension Suisse," whither we had been directed by a German gentleman, we were agreeably impressed with the gaiety and bustle of Milan. The shops and stores are all open to the street, so that the city resembles a great bazaar. It has an odd look to see blacksmiths, tailors and shoemakers working unconcernedly in the open air, with crowds continually passing before them. The streets are filled with venders of fruit, who call out the names with a long, distressing cry, much like that of a person in great agony. Organ-grinders parade constantly about and snatches of songs are heard among the gay crowd, on every side.

In this lively, noisy Italian city, nearly all there is to see may be comprised in four things: the Duomo, the triumphal arch over the Simplon, La Scala and the Picture Gallery. The first alone is more interesting than many an entire city. We went there yesterday afternoon soon after reaching here. It stands in an irregular open place, closely hemmed in by houses on two sides, so that it can be seen to advantage from only one point. It is a mixture of the Gothic and Romanesque styles; the body of the structure is entirely covered with statues and richly wrought sculpture, with needle-like spires of white marble rising up from every corner. But of the exquisite, airy look of the whole mass, although so solid and vast, it is impossible to convey an idea. It appears like some fabric of frost-work which winter traces on the window-panes. There is a unity of beauty about the whole, which the eye takes in with a feeling of perfect and satisfied delight.

Ascending the marble steps which lead to the front, I lifted the folds of the heavy curtain and entered. What a glorious aisle!

The mighty pillars support a magnificent arched ceiling, painted to resemble fretwork, and the little light that falls through the small windows above, enters tinged with a dim golden hue. A feeling of solemn awe comes over one as he steps with a hushed tread along the colored marble floor, and measures the massive columns till they blend with the gorgeous arches above. There are four rows of these, nearly fifty in all, and when I state that they are eight feet in diameter, and sixty or seventy in height, some idea may be formed of the grandeur of the building. Imagine the Girard College, at Philadelphia, turned into one great hall, with four rows of pillars, equal in size to those around it, reaching to its roof, and you will have a rough sketch of the interior of the Duomo.

In the centre of the cross is a light and beautiful dome; he who will stand under this, and look down the broad middle aisle to the entrance, has one of the sublimest vistas to be found in the world. The choir has three enormous windows, covered with dazzling paintings, and the ceiling is of marble and silver. There are gratings under the high altar, by looking into which, I could see a dark, lonely chamber below, where one or two feeble lamps showed a circle of praying-places. It was probably a funeral vault, which persons visited to pray for the repose of their friends' souls. The Duomo is not yet entirely finished, the workmen being still employed in various parts, but it is said, that when completed there will be four thousand statues on the different parts of it.

The design of the Duomo is said to be taken from Monte Rosa, one of the loftiest peaks of the Alps. Its hundreds of sculptured pinnacles, rising from every part of the body of the church, certainly bear a striking resemblance to the splintered ice-crags of Savoy. Thus we see how Art, mighty and endless in her forms though she be, is in everything but the child of Nature. Her most divine conceptions are but copies of objects which we behold everyday. The faultless beauty of the Corinthian capital—the springing and intermingling arches of the Gothic aisle—the pillared portico or the massive and sky-piercing pyramid—are but attempts at reproducing, by the studied regularity of Art, the ever-varied and ever-beautiful forms of mountain, rock and forest.

But there is oftentimes a more thrilling sensation of enjoyment produced by the creations of man's hand and intellect than the grander effects of Nature, existing constantly before our eyes. It would seem as if man marvelled more at his own work than at the work of the Power which created him.

The streets of Milan abound with priests in their cocked hats and long black robes. They all have the same solemn air, and seem to go about like beings shut out from all communion with pleasure. No sight lately has saddened me so much as to see a bright, beautiful boy, of twelve or thirteen years, in those gloomy garments. Poor child! he little knows now what he may have to endure. A lonely, cheerless life, where every affection must be crushed as unholy, and every pleasure denied as a crime! And I knew by his fair brow and tender lip, that he had a warm and loving heart. I could not help regarding this class as victims to a mistaken idea of religious duty, and if I am not mistaken, I read on more than one countenance the traces of passions that burned within. It is mournful to see a people oppressed in the name of religion. The holiest aspirations of man's nature, instead of lifting him up to a nearer view of Christian perfection, are changed into clouds and shut out the light of heaven. Immense treasures, wrung drop by drop from the credulity of the poor and ignorant, are made use of to pamper the luxury of those who profess to be mediators between man and the Deity. The poor wretch may perish of starvation on a floor of precious mosaic, which perhaps his own pittance has helped to form, while ceilings and shrines of inlaid gold mock his dying eye with their useless splendor. Such a system of oppression, disguised under the holiest name, can only be sustained by the continuance of ignorance and blind superstition. Knowledge—Truth—Reason—these are the ramparts which Liberty throws up to guard the dominions from the usurpations of oppression and wrong.

We were last night in La Scala. Rossini's opera of William Tell was advertised, and as we had visited so lately the scene where that glorious historical drama was enacted, we went to see it represented in sound. It is a grand subject, which in the hands of a powerful composer, might be made very effective, but I must confess I was disappointed in the present case. The overture is, however, very beautiful. It begins low and mournful, like the lament of the Swiss over their fallen liberties. Occasionally a low drum is heard, as if to rouse them to action, and meanwhile the lament swells to a cry of despair. The drums now wake the land; the horn of Uri is heard pealing forth its summoning strain, and the echoes seem to come back from the distant Alps. The sound then changes for the roar of battle — the clang of trumpets, drums and cymbals. The whole orchestra did their best to represent this combat in music, which after lasting a short time, changed into the loud, victorious march of the conquerors. But the body of the opera, although it had several fine passages, was to me devoid of interest; in fact, unworthy the reputation of Rossini.

The theatre is perhaps the largest in the world. The singers are all good; in Italy it could not be otherwise, where everybody sings. As I write, a party of Italians in the house opposite have been amusing themselves with going through the whole opera of "*La fille du Regiment,*" with the accompaniment of the piano, and they show the greatest readiness and correctness in their performance. They have now become somewhat boisterous, and appear to be improvising. One young gentleman executes trills with amazing skill, and another appears to have taken the part of a despairing lover, but the lady has a very pretty voice, and warbles on and on, like a nightingale. Occasionally a group of listeners in the street below clap them applause, for as the windows are always open, the whole neighborhood can enjoy the performance.

This forenoon I was in the Picture Gallery. It occupies a part of the Library Building, in the Palazzo Cabrera. It is not large, and many of the pictures are of no value to anybody but antiquarians; still there are some excellent paintings, which render it well worthy a visit. Among these, a marriage, by Raphael, is still in a very good state of preservation, and there are some fine pictures by Paul Veronese and the Caracci. The most admired painting, is "Abraham sending away Hagar," by Guercino. I never saw a more touching expression of grief than in the face of Hagar. Her eyes are red with weeping, and as she listens in an agony of tears to the patriarch's command, she still seems doubting the reality of her doom. The countenance of Abraham is venerable and calm, and expresses little emotion; but one can read in that of Sarah, as she turns away, a feeling of pity for her unfortunate rival.

Next to the Duomo, the most beautiful specimen of architecture in Milan is the Arch of Peace, on the north side of the city, at the commencement of the Simplon Road. It was the intention of Napoleon to carry the road under this arch, across the Piazza d' Armi, and to cut a way for it directly into the heart of the city, but the fall of his dynasty prevented the execution of this magnificent design, as well as the completion of the arch itself. This has been done by the Austrian government, according to the original plan; they have inscribed upon it the name of Francis I., and changed the bas-reliefs of Lodi and Marengo into those of a few fields where their forces had gained the victory. It is even said that in many parts which were already finished, they altered the splendid Roman profile of Napoleon into the haggard and repulsive features of Francis of Austria.

The bronze statues on the top were made by an artist of Bologna, by Napoleon's order, and are said to be the finest works of modern times. In the centre is the goddess of Peace, in a triumphal car, drawn by six horses, while on the corners four angels, mounted, are starting off to convey the tidings to the four quarters of the globe. The artist has caught the spirit of motion and chained it in these moveless figures. One would hardly feel surprised if the goddess, chariot, horses and all, were to start off and roll away through the air.

With the rapidity usual to Americans we have already finished seeing Milan, and shall start tomorrow morning on a walk to Genoa.

Chapter XXXII
WALK FROM MILAN TO GENOA

It was finally decided we should leave Milan, so the next morning we arose at five o'clock for the first time since leaving Frankfort. The Italians had commenced operations at this early hour, but we made our way through the streets without attracting quite so much attention as on our arrival. Near the gate on the road to Pavia, we passed a long colonnade which was certainly as old as the times of the Romans. The pillars of marble were quite brown with age, and bound together with iron to keep them from falling to pieces. It was a striking contrast to see this relic of the past standing in the middle of a crowded thoroughfare and surrounded by all the brilliance and display of modern trade.

Once fairly out of the city we took the road to Pavia, along the banks of the canal, just as the rising sun gilded the marble spire of the Duomo. The country was a perfect level, and the canal, which was in many places higher than the land through which it passed, served also as a means of irrigation for the many rice-fields. The sky grew cloudy and dark, and before we reached Pavia gathered to a heavy storm. Torrents of rain poured down, accompanied with heavy thunder; we crept under an old gateway for shelter, as no house was near. Finally, as it cleared away, the square brown towers of the old city rose above the trees, and we entered the gate through a fine shaded avenue. Our passports were of course demanded, but we were only detained a minute or two. The only thing of interest is the University, formerly so celebrated; it has at present about eight hundred students.

We have reason to remember the city from another circumstance—the singular attention we excited. I doubt if Columbus was an object of greater curiosity to the simple natives of the new world, than we three Americans were to the good people of Pavia. I know not what part of our dress or appearance could have caused it, but we were watched like wild animals. If we happened to pause and look at anything in the street, there was soon a crowd of attentive observers, and as we passed on, every door and window was full of heads. We stopped in the marketplace to purchase some bread and fruit for dinner, which increased, if possible, the sensation. We saw eyes staring and fingers pointing at us from every door and alley. I am generally willing to contribute as much as possible to the amusement or entertainment of others, but such attention was absolutely embarrassing. There was nothing to do but to appear unconscious of it, and we went along with as much nonchalance as if the whole town belonged to us.

We crossed the Ticino, on whose banks near Pavia, was fought the first great battle between Hannibal and the Romans. On the other side, our passports were demanded at the Sardinian frontier and our knapsacks searched, which having proved satisfactory, we were allowed to enter the kingdom. Late in the afternoon we reached the Po, which in winter must be quarter of a mile wide, but the summer heats had dried it up to a small stream, so that the bridge of boats rested nearly its whole length in sand. We sat on the bank in the shade, and looked at the chain of hills which rose in the south, following the course of the Po, crowned with castles and villages and shining towers. It was here that I first began to realize Italian scenery. Although the hills were bare, they lay so warm and glowing in the sunshine, and the deep blue sky spread so calmly above, that it recalled all my dreams of the fair clime we had entered.

We stopped for the night at the little village of Casteggio, which lies at the foot of the hills, and next morning resumed our pilgrimage. Here a new delight awaited us. The sky was of a heavenly blue, without even the shadow of a cloud, and full and fair in the morning sunshine we could see the whole range of the Alps, from the blue hills of Friuli, which sweep down to Venice and the Adriatic, to the lofty peaks which stretch away to Nice and Marseilles! Like a summer cloud, except that they were far more dazzling and glorious, lay to the north of us the glaciers and untrodden snow-fields of the Bernese Oberland; a little to the right we saw the double peak of St. Gothard, where six days before we shivered in the region of eternal winter, while far to the north-west rose the giant dome of Mount Blanc. Monte Rosa stood near him, not far from the Great St. Bernard, and further to the south Mont Cenis guarded the entrance from Piedmont into France. I leave you to conceive the majesty of such a scene, and you may perhaps imagine, for I cannot describe the feelings with which I gazed upon it.

At Tortona, the next post, a great market was being held; the town was filled with country people selling their produce, and with vendors of wares of all kinds. Fruit was very abundant—grapes, ripe figs, peaches and melons were abundant, and for a trifle one could purchase a sumptuous banquet. On inquiring the road to Novi, the people made us understand, after much difficulty, that there was a nearer way across the country, which came into the post-road again, and we concluded to take it. After two or three hours' walking in a burning sun, where our only relief was the sight of the Alps and a view of the battlefield of Marengo, which lay just on our right, we came to a stand — the road terminated at a large stream, where workmen were busily engaged in making a bridge across. We pulled off our boots and waded through, took a refreshing bath in the clear waters, and walked on through by-lanes. The sides were lined with luxuriant vines, bending under the ripening vintage, and we often cooled our thirst with some of the rich bunches.

The large branch of the Po we crossed, came down from the mountains, which we were approaching. As we reached the post-road again, they were glowing in the last rays of the sun, and the evening vapors that settled over the plain concealed the distant Alps, although the snowy top of the Jungfrau and her companions the Wetterhorn and Schreckhorn, rose above it like the hills of another world. A castle or church of brilliant white marble glittered on the summit of one of the mountains near us, and as the sun went down without a cloud, the distant summits changed in hue to a glowing purple, amounting almost to crimson, which afterwards darkened into a deep violet. The western half of the sky was of a pale orange, and the eastern a dark red, which blended together in the blue of the zenith, that deepened as twilight came on. I know not if it was a fair specimen of an Italian sunset, but I must say, without wishing to be partial, that though certainly very soft and beautiful, there is no comparison with the splendor of such a scene in America. The day-sky of Italy better deserves its reputation. Although no clearer than our own, it is of a far brighter blue, arching above us like a dome of sapphire and seeming to sparkle all over with a kind of crystal transparency.

We stopped the second night at Arquato, a little village among the mountains, and after having bargained with the merry landlord for our lodgings, in broken Italian, took a last look at the plains of Piedmont and the Swiss Alps, in the growing twilight. We gazed out on the darkening scene till the sky was studded with stars, and went to rest with the exciting thought of seeing Genoa and the Mediterranean on the morrow. Next morning we started early, and after walking some distance made our breakfast in a grove of chestnuts, on the cool mountain side, beside a fresh stream of water. The sky shone like a polished gem, and the glossy leaves of the chestnuts gleamed in the morning sun. Here and there, on a rocky height, stood the remains of some knightly castle, telling of the Goths and Normans who descended through these mountain passes to plunder Rome.

As the sun grew high, the heat and dust became intolerable, and this, in connection with the attention we raised everywhere, made us somewhat tired of foot-traveling in Italy. I verily believe the people took us for pilgrims on account of our long white blouses, and had I a scallop shell I would certainly have stuck it into my hat to complete the appearance. We stopped once to ask a priest the road; when he had told us, he shook hands with us and gave us a parting benediction. At the common inns, where we stopped, we always met with civil treatment, though, indeed, as we only slept in them, there was little chance of practising imposition. We bought our simple meals at the baker's and grocer's, and ate them in the shade of the grape-bowers, whose rich clusters added to the repast. In this manner, we enjoyed Italy at the expense of a franc, daily. About noon, after winding about through the narrow passages, the road began ascending. The reflected heat from the hills on each side made it like an oven; there was not a breath of air stirring; but we all felt, although no one said it, that from the summit we could see the Mediterranean, and we pushed on as if life or death depended on it. Finally, the highest point came in sight — we redoubled our exertions, and a few minutes more brought us to the top, breathless with fatigue and expectation. I glanced down the other side — there lay a real sea of mountains, all around; the farthest peaks rose up afar and dim, crowned with white towers, and between two of them which stood apart like the pillars of a gateway, we saw the broad expanse of water stretching away to the horizon —

"To where the blue of heaven on bluer waves shut down!"

It would have been a thrilling sight to see any ocean, when one has rambled thousands of miles among the mountains and vales of the inland, but to behold this sea, of all others, was glorious indeed! This sea, whose waves wash the feet of Naples, Constantinople and Alexandria, and break on the hoary shores where Troy and Tyre and Carthage have mouldered away!—whose breast has been furrowed by the keels of a hundred nations through more than forty centuries —from the first rude voyage of Jason and his Argonauts, to the thunders of Navarino that heralded the second birth of Greece! You cannot wonder we grew romantic; but short space was left for sentiment in the burning sun, with Genoa to be reached before night. The mountain we crossed is called the Bochetta, one of the loftiest of the sea-Alps (or Apennines)—the road winds steeply down towards the sea, following a broad mountain rivulet, now perfectly dried up, as nearly every stream among the mountains is. It was a long way to us; the mountains seemed as if they would never unfold and let us out on the shore, and our weary limbs did penance enough for a multitude of sins. The dusk was beginning to deepen over the bay and the purple hues of sunset were dying away from its amphitheatre of hills, as we came in sight of the gorgeous city. Half the population were out to celebrate a festival, and we made our entry in the triumphal procession of some saint.

Chapter XXXIII
SCENES IN GENOA, LEGHORN AND PISA

Have you ever seen some grand painting of a city, rising with its domes and towers and palaces from the edge of a glorious bay, shut in by mountains—the whole scene clad in those deep, delicious, sunny hues which you admire so much in the picture, although they appear unrealized in Nature? If so, you can figure to yourself Genoa, as she looked to us at sunset, from the battlements west of the city. When we had passed through the gloomy gate of the fortress that guards the western promontory, the whole scene opened at once on us in all its majesty. It looked to me less like a real landscape than a mighty panoramic painting. The battlements where we were standing, and the blue mirror of the Mediterranean just below, with a few vessels moored near the shore, made up the foreground; just in front lay the queenly city, stretching out to the eastern point of the bay, like a great meteor — this point, crowned with the towers and dome of a cathedral representing the nucleus, while the tail gradually widened out and was lost among the numberless villas that reached to the top of the mountains behind. A mole runs nearly across the mouth of the harbor, with a tall lighthouse at its extremity, leaving only a narrow passage for vessels. As we gazed, a purple glow lay on the bosom of the sea, while far beyond the city, the eastern half of the mountain crescent around the gulf was tinted with the loveliest hue of orange. The impressions which one derives from looking on remarkable scenery, depend, for much of their effect, on the time and weather. I have been very fortunate in this respect in two instances, and shall carry with me through life, two glorious pictures of a very different character — the wild sublimity of the Brocken in cloud and storm, and the splendor of Genoa in an Italian sunset.

Genoa has been called the "city of palaces," and it well deserves the appellation. Row above row of magnificent structures rise amid gardens along the side of the hills, and many of the streets, though narrow and crooked, are lined entirely with the splendid dwellings of the Genoese nobles. All these speak of the republic in its days of wealth and power, when it could cope successfully with Venice, and Doria could threaten to bridle the horses of St. Mark. At present its condition is far different; although not so fallen as its rival, it is but a shadow of its former self — the life and energy it possessed as a republic, has withered away under the grasp of tyranny.

We entered Genoa, as I have already said, in a religious procession. On passing the gate we saw from the concourse of people and the many banners hanging from the windows or floating across the streets, that it was the day of a *festa*. Before entering the city we reached the procession itself, which was one of unusual solemnity. As it was impossible in the dense crowd, to pass it, we struggled through till we reached a good point for seeing the whole, and slowly moved on with it through the city. First went a company of boys in white robes; then followed a body of friars, dressed in long black cassocks, and with shaven crowns; then a company of soldiers with a band of music; then a body of nuns, wrapped from head to foot in blue robes, leaving only a small place to see out of—in the dusk they looked very solemn and ghost-like, and their low chant had to me something awful and sepulchral in it; then followed another company of friars, and after that a great number of priests in white and black robes, bearing the statue of the saint, with a pyramid of flowers, crosses and blazing wax tapers, while companies of soldiery, monks and music brought up the rear. Armed guards walked at intervals on each side of the procession, to keep the way clear and prevent disturbance; two or three hands played solemn airs, alternating with the deep monotonous chanting of the friars. The whole scene, dimly lighted by the wax tapers, produced in me a feeling nearly akin to fear, as if I were witnessing some ghostly, unearthly spectacle. To rites like these, however, which occur every few weeks, the people must be well accustomed.

Among the most interesting objects in Genoa, is the Doria palace, fit in its splendor for a monarch's residence. It stands in the *Strada Nova,* one of the three principal streets, and I believe is still in the possession of the family. There are many others through the city, scarcely less magnificent, among which that of the Durazzo family may be pointed out. The American consulate is in one of these old edifices, with a fine courtyard and ceilings covered with frescoes.

Mr. Moro, the Vice Consul, did us a great kindness, which I feel bound to acknowledge, although it will require the disclosure of some private and perhaps uninteresting circumstances. On leaving

Frankfort, we converted—for the sake of convenience—the greater part of our funds into a draft on a Saxon merchant in Leghorn, reserving just enough, as we supposed, to take us thither. As in our former case, in Germany, the sum was too small, which we found to our dismay on reaching Milan. Notwithstanding we had traveled the whole ninety miles from that city to Genoa for three francs each, in the hope of having enough left to enable one at least to visit Leghorn, the expenses for a passport in Genoa (more than twenty francs) prevented this plan. I went therefore to the Vice Consul to ascertain whether the merchant on whom the draft was drawn, had any correspondents there, who might advance a portion of it. His secretary made many inquiries, but without effect; Mr. Moro then generously offered to furnish me with means to reach Leghorn, whence I could easily remit a sufficient sum to my two comrades. This put an end to our anxiety, (for I must confess we could not help feeling some), and I prepared to leave that evening in the "Virgilio."

The feelings with which I look on this lovely land, are fast changing. What with the dust and heat, and cheating landlords, and the dull plains of Lombardy, my first experience was not very prepossessing. But the joyous and romantic anticipation with which I looked forward to realizing the dream of my earliest boyhood, is now beginning to be surpassed by the exciting reality. Every breath I drew in the city of Columbus and Doria, was deeply tinctured with the magic of history and romance. It was like entering on a new existence, to look on scenes so lovely by nature and so filled with the inspiring memories of old.

> "Italia too, Italia! looking on thee.
>   Full flashes on the soul the light of ages,
>   Since the fierce Carthagenian almost won thee,
>   To the last halo of the chiefs and sages
>   Who glorify thy consecrated pages!
>   Thou wert the throne and grave of empires."

The *Virgilio* was advertised to leave at six o'clock, and I accordingly went out to her in a little boat half an hour beforehand; but we
were delayed much longer, and I saw sunset again fade over the
glorious amphitheatre of palaces and mountains, with the same
orange glow—the same purple and crimson flush, deepening into
twilight — as before. An old blind man in a skiff, floated around
under the bows of the boat on the glassy water, singing to the violin
a plaintive air that appeared to be an evening hymn to the virgin.
There was something very touching in his venerable countenance,
with the sightless eyes turned upward to the sunset heaven whose
glory he could never more behold.

The lamps were lit on the tower at the end of the mole as we
glided out on the open sea; I stood on deck and watched the receding lights of the city, till they and the mountains above them were
blended with the darkened sky. The sea-breeze was fresh and cool,
and the stars glittered with a frosty clearness, which would have
made the night delicious had not a slight rolling of the waves obliged
me to go below. Here, besides being half seasick, I was placed at the
mercy of many voracious fleas, who obstinately stayed, persisting
in keeping me company. This was the first time I had suffered from
these cannibals, and such were my torments, I almost wished some
blood-thirsty Italian would come and put an end to them with his
stiletto.

The first ray of dawn that stole into the cabin sent me on deck.
The hills of Tuscany lay in front, sharply outlined on the reddening
sky; near us was the steep and rocky isle of Gorgona; and far to the
south-west, like a low mist along the water, ran the shores of Corsica
—the birth place of Columbus and Napoleon! (By recent registers
found in Corsica, it has been determined that this island also gave
birth to the discoverer of the new world.) As the dawn brightened
we saw on the southern horizon a cloud-like island, also imperish-
ably connected with the name of the latter—the prison-kingdom of
Elba! North of us extended the rugged mountains of Carrarra—that

renowned range whence has sprung many a form of almost breathing beauty, and where yet slumber, perhaps, in the unhewn marble,
the god-like-shapes of an age of art, more glorious than any the
world has ever yet beheld!

The sun rose from behind the Appenines and masts and towers
became visible through the golden haze, as we approached the
shore. On a flat space between the sea and the hills, not far from the
foot of Montenero, stands Leghorn. The harbor is protected by a
mole, leaving a narrow passage, through which we entered, and after
waiting two hours for the visit of the health and police officers, we
were permitted to go on shore. The first thing that struck me, was
the fine broad streets; the second, the motley character of the population. People were hurrying about noisy and bustling—Greeks in
their red caps and capotes; grave turbaned and bearded Turks; dark
Moors; the Corsair-looking natives of Tripoli and Tunis, and seamen
of nearly every nation. At the hotel where I stayed, we had a singular
mixture of nations at dinner:—two French, two Swiss, one Genoese,
one Roman, one American and one Turk—and we were waited on
by a Tuscan and an Arab! We conversed together in four languages,
all at once.

To the merchant, Leghorn is of more importance than to the
traveler. Its extensive trade, not only in the manufactures of Tuscany, but also in the productions of the Levant, makes it important
to the former, while the latter seeks in vain for fine buildings, galleries of art, or interesting historical reminiscences. Through the kind
attention of the Saxon Consul, to whom I had letters, two or three
days went by delightfully.

The only place of amusement here in summer is a drive along the
sea shore, called the Ardenza, which is frequented every evening by
all who can raise a vehicle. I visited it twice with a German friend.
We met one evening the Princess Corsini, wife of the Governor of
Leghorn, on horseback—a young, but not pretty woman. The road
leads out along the Mediterranean, past an old fortress, to a large

establishment for the sea bathers, where it ends in a large ring, around which the carriages pass and re-pass, until sunset has gone out over the sea, when they return to the city in a mad gallop, or as fast as the lean horses can draw them.

In driving around, we met two or three carriages of Turks, in one of which I saw a woman of Tunis, with a curious gilded head-dress, eighteen inches in height.

I saw one night a Turkish funeral. It passed me in one of the outer streets, on its way to the Turkish burying ground. Those following the coffin, which was covered with a heavy black pall, wore white turbans and long white robes — the mourning color of the Turks. Torches were borne by attendants, and the whole company passed on at a quick pace. Seen thus by night, it had a strange and spectral appearance.

There is another spectacle here which was exceedingly revolting to me. The condemned criminals, chained two and two, are kept at work through the city, cleaning the streets. They are dressed in coarse garments of a dirty red color, with the name of the crime for which they were convicted, painted on the back. I shuddered to see so many marked with the words *"omicidio premeditato,"* (premeditated murder). All day they are thus engaged, exposed to the scorn and contumely of the crowd, and at night dragged away to be incarcerated in damp, unwholesome dungeons, excavated under the public thoroughfares.

The employment of criminals in this way is common in Italy. Two days after crossing St. Gothard, we saw a company of abject-looking creatures, eating their dinner by the road-side, near Bellinzona. One of them had a small basket of articles of cotton and linen, and as he rose up to offer them to us, I was startled by the clank of fetters. They were all employed to labor on the road.

On going down to the wharf in Leghorn, in the morning, two or three days ago, I found F —— and B —— just stepping on shore from the steamboat, tired enough of the discomforts of the voyage, yet anxious to set out for Florence as soon as possible. After we had shaken off the crowd of porters, pedlars and vetturini, and taken a hasty breakfast at the *Café Americana,* we went to the Police Office to get our passports, and had the satisfaction of paying two francs for permission to proceed to Florence. The weather had changed since the preceding day, and the sirocco-wind which blows over from the coast of Africa, filled the streets with clouds of dust, which made walking very unpleasant. The clear blue sky had vanished, and a leaden cloud hung low on the Mediterranean, hiding the shores of Corsica and the rocky isles of Gorgona and Capraja.

The country between Leghorn and Pisa, is a flat marsh, inter-sected in several places by canals to carry off the stagnant water which renders this district so unhealthy. It is said that the entire plain between the mountains of Carrarra and the hills back of Leg-horn has been gradually formed by the deposits of the Arno and the receding of the Mediterranean, which is so shallow along the whole coast, that large vessels have to anchor several miles out. As we approached Pisa over the level marsh, I could see the dome of the Cathedral and the Leaning Tower rising above the gardens and groves which surround it.

Our baggage underwent another examination at the gate, where we were again assailed by the vetturini, one of whom hung on us like a leech till we reached a hotel, and there was finally no way of shak-ing him off except by engaging him to take us to Florence. The bar-gain having been concluded, we had still a few hours left and set off to hunt the Cathedral. We found it on an open square near the outer wall, and quite remote from the main part of the town. Emerging from the narrow and winding street, one takes in at a glance the Baptistery, the Campo Santo, the noble Cathedral and the Leaning Tower — forming altogether a view rarely surpassed in Europe for architectural effect. But the square is melancholy and deserted, and rank, untrampled grass fills the crevices of its marble pavement.

I was surprised at the beauty of the Leaning Tower. Instead of an old, black, crumbling fabric, as I always supposed, it is a light, airy, elegant structure, of white marble, and its declension, which is interesting as a work of art (or accident,) is at the same time pleasing from its novelty. There have been many conjectures as to the cause of this deviation, which is upwards of fourteen feet from the perpendicular; it is now generally believed that the earth having sunk when the building was half finished, it was continued by the architects in the same angle. The upper gallery, which is smaller than the others, shows a very perceptible inclination back towards the perpendicular, as if in some degree to counterbalance the deviation of the other part. There are eight galleries in all, supported by marble pillars, but the inside of the Tower is hollow to the very top.

We ascended by the same stairs which were trodden so often by Galileo in going up to make his astronomical observations; in climbing spirally around the hollow cylinder in the dark, it was easy to tell on which side of the Tower we were, from the proportionate steepness of the staircase. There is a fine view from the top, embracing the whole plain as far as Leghorn on one side, with its gardens and grain fields spread out like a vast map. In the valley of the Carrarrese Mountains to the north, we could see the little town of Lucca, much frequented at this season on account of its baths; the blue summits of the Appenines shut in the view to the east. In walking through the city I noticed two other towers, which had nearly as great a deviation from the perpendicular. We met a person who had the key of the Baptistery, which he opened for us. Two ancient columns covered with rich sculpture form the doorway, and the dome is supported by massive pillars of the red marble of Elba. The baptismal font is of the purest Parian marble. The most remarkable thing was the celebrated musical echo. Our cicerone stationed himself at the side of the font and sang a few notes. After a moment's pause they were repeated aloft in the dome, but with a sound of divine sweetness— as clear and pure as the clang of a crystal bell. Another pause—and we heard them again, higher, fainter and sweeter, followed by a dying note, as if they were fading far away into heaven. It seemed as if an angel lingered in the temple, echoing with his melodious lips the common harmonies of earth. Even thus does the music of good deeds, hardly noted in our grosser atmosphere, awake a divine echo in the far world of spirit.

The Campo Santo, on the north side of the Cathedral, was, until lately, the cemetery of the city; the space enclosed within its marble galleries is filled to the depth of eight or ten feet, with earth from the Holy Land. The vessels which carried the knights of Tuscany to Palestine were filled at Joppa, on returning, with this earth as ballast, and on arriving at Pisa it was deposited in the Cemetery. It has the peculiar property of decomposing all human bodies, in the space of two days. A colonnade of marble encloses it, with windows of the most exquisite sculpture opening on the inside. They reminded me of the beautiful Gothic oriels of Melrose. At each end are two fine, green cypresses, which thrive remarkably in the soil of Palestine. The dust of a German emperor, among others, rests in this conse-crated ground. There are other fine churches in Pisa, but the four buildings I have mentioned, are the principal objects of interest. The tower where Count Ugolino and his sons were starved to death by the citizens of Pisa, who locked them up and threw the keys into the Arno, has lately been destroyed.

An Italian gentleman having made a bargain in the meantime with our vetturino, we found everything ready on returning to the hotel. On the outside of the town we mounted into the vehicle, a rickety-looking concern, and as it commenced raining, I was afraid we would have a bad night of it. After a great deal of bargaining, the vetturino agreed to take us to Florence that night for five francs a piece, provided one person would sit on the outside with the driver. I accordingly mounted on front, protected by a blouse and umbrella, for it was beginning to rain dismally. The miserable, bare-boned horses were fastened with rope-traces, end the vetturino having taken the rope-lines in his hand, gave a flourish with his whip; one old horse tumbled nearly to the ground, but he jerked him up again and we rattled off.

After riding ten miles in this way, it became so wet and dreary, that I was fain to give the driver two francs extra, for the privilege of an inside seat. Our Italian companion was agreeable and talkative, but as we were still ignorant of the language, I managed to hold a scanty conversation with him in French. He seemed delighted to learn that we were from America; his polite reserve gave place to a friendly familiarity and he was loud in his praises of the Americans. I asked him why it was that he, and the Italians generally, appeared so friendly towards us. "I hardly know," he answered; "you are so different from any other nation; and then, too, you have so much sincerity!"

The Appenines were wreathed and hidden in thick mist, and the prospect over the flat cornfields bordering the road was not particularly interesting. We had made about one-third of the way as night set in, when on ascending a hill soon after dark, F —— happened to look out, and saw one of the axles bent and nearly broken off. We were obliged to get out and walk through the mud to the next village, when after two hours' delay, the vetturino came along with another carriage. Of the rest of the way to Florence, I cannot say much. Cramped up in the narrow vehicle, we jolted along in the dark, rumbling now and then through some silent village, where lamps were burning before the solitary shrines. Sometimes a blinding light crossed the road, where we saw the tile-makers sitting in the red glare of their kilns, and often the black boughs of trees were painted momentarily on the cloudy sky. If the jolting carriage had even permitted sleep, the horrid cries of the vetturino, urging on his horses, would have prevented it; and I decided, while trying to relieve my aching limbs, that three days' walking in sun and sand was preferable to one night of such travel.

Finally about four o'clock in the morning the carriage stopped; my Italian friend awoke and demanded the cause. "Signor," said the vetturino, *"we are in Florence!"* I blessed the man, and the city too. The good-humored officer looked at our passports and passed our baggage without examination; we gave the gatekeeper a paul and he admitted us. The carriage rolled through the dark, silent streets — passed a public square — came out on the Arno — crossed and entered the city again — and finally stopped at a hotel. The master of the "Lione Bianco" came down in an undress to receive us, and we shut the growing dawn out of our rooms to steal that repose from the day which the night had not given.

Chapter XXXIV
FLORENCE AND ITS GALLERIES

Sept. 11.—Our situation here is as agreeable as we could well desire. We have three large and handsomely furnished rooms, in the centre of the city, for which we pay Signor Lazzeri, a wealthy goldsmith, ten scudi per month — a scudo being a trifle more than an American dollar. We live at the *Cafés* and *Trattorie* very conveniently for twenty-five cents a day, enjoying moreover, at our dinner in the Trattoria del Cacciatore, the company of several American artists with whom we have become acquainted. The day after our arrival we met at the table d' hote of the "Lione Bianco," Dr. Boardman of New York, through whose assistance we obtained our present lodgings. There are at present ten or twelve American artists in Florence, and we promise ourselves much pleasure and profit from their acquaintance. B —— and I are so charmed with the place and the beautiful Tuscan dialect, that we shall endeavor to spend three or four months here. F —— returns to Germany in two weeks, to attend the winter term of the University at his favorite Heidelberg.

Our first walk in Florence was to the Royal Gallery — we wished to see the "goddess living in stone" without delay. Crossing the neighboring *Piazza del Granduca,* we passed Michael Angelo's colossal statue of David, and an open gallery containing, besides some antiques, the master-piece of John of Bologna. The palace of the *Uffizii,* fronting on the Arno, extends along both sides of an avenue running back to the Palazzo Vecchio. We entered the portico which passes around under the great building, and after ascending three or four flights of steps, came into a long hall, filled with paintings and ancient statuary. Towards the end of this, a door opened into the Tribune—that celebrated room, unsurpassed by any in the world for the number and value of the gems it contains. I pushed aside a crimson curtain and stood in the presence of the Venus.

It may be considered heresy, but I confess I did not at first go into raptures, nor perceive any traces of superhuman beauty. The predominant feeling, if I may so express it, was satisfaction; the eye dwells on its faultless outline with a gratified sense, that nothing is wanting to render it perfect. It is the ideal of a woman's form — a faultless standard by which all beauty may be measured, but without striking expression, except in the modest and graceful position of the limbs. The face, though regular, is not handsome, and the body appears small, being but five feet in height, which, I think, is a little below the average stature of women. On each side, as if to heighten its elegance by contrast with rude and unrefined nature, are the statues of the Wrestlers, and the slave listening to the conspiracy of Catiline, called also The Whetter.

As if to correspond with the value of the works it holds, the Tribune is paved with precious marbles and the ceiling studded, with polished mother-of-pearl. A dim and subdued light fills the hall, which throws over the mind that half-dreamy tone necessary to the full enjoyment of such objects. On each side of the Venus de Medici hangs a Venus by Titian, the size of life, and painted in that rich and gorgeous style of coloring which has been so often and vainly attempted since his time.

Here are six of Raphael's best preserved paintings, and I prefer the

"St. John in the Desert" to any other picture in the Tribune. His glorious form, in the fair proportions of ripening boyhood— the grace of his attitude, with the arm lifted eloquently on high—the divine inspiration which illumines his young features—chain the step irresistibly before it. It is one of those triumphs of the pencil which few but Raphael have accomplished—the painting of spirit in its loftiest and purest form. Near it hangs the Fornarina, which he seems to have painted in as deep a love as he entertained for the original. The face is modest and beautiful, and filled with an expression of ardent and tender attachment. I never tire looking upon either of these two.

Let me not forget, while we are in this peerless hall, to point out Guercino's Samian Sybil. It is a glorious work. With her hands clasped over her volume, she is looking up with a face full of deep and expressive sadness. A picturesque turban is twined around her head, and bands of pearls gleam amidst her rich, dark brown tresses. Her face bears the softness of dawning womanhood, and nearly answers my ideal of female beauty. The same artist has another fine picture here—a sleeping Endymion. The mantle has fallen from his shoulders, as he reclines asleep, with his head on his hand, and his crook beside him. The silver crescent of Dian looks over his shoulder from the sky behind, and no wonder if she should become enamored, for a lovelier shepherd has not been seen since that of King Admetus went back to drive his chariot in the heavens.

The "Drunken Bacchus" of Michael Angelo is greatly admired, and indeed it might pass for a relic of the palmiest times of Grecian art. The face, amidst its half-vacant, sensual expression, shows some traces of its immortal origin, and there is still an air of dignity preserved in the swagger of his beautiful form. It is, in a word, the ancient idea of a drunken god. It may be doubted whether the artist's talents might not have been employed better than in ennobling intoxication. If he had attempted to represent Bacchus as he really is—degraded even below the level of humanity—it might be more beneficial to the mind, though less beautiful to the eye. However, this is a question on which artists and moralists cannot agree. Perhaps the rich blood of the Falernian grape produced a more godlike delirium than the vulgar brandy which oversets the moderns!

At one end of the gallery is a fine copy in marble of the Laocoon, by Bandinelli, one of the rivals of Michael Angelo. When it was finished, the former boasted it was better than the original, to which Michael made the apt reply: "It is foolish for those who walk in the footsteps of others, to say they go before them!"

Let us enter the hall of Niobe. One starts back on seeing the many figures in the attitude of flight, for they seem at first about to spring from their pedestals. At the head of the room stands the afflicted mother, bending over the youngest daughter who clings to her knees, with an upturned countenance of deep and imploring agony. In vain! the shafts of Apollo fall thick, and she will soon be childless. No wonder the strength of that woe depicted on her countenance should change her into stone. One of her sons—a beautiful, boyish form,—is lying on his back, just expiring, with the chill langour of death creeping over his limbs. We seem to hear the quick whistling of the arrows, and look involuntarily into the air to see the hovering figure of the avenging god. In a chamber nearby is kept the head of a faun, made by Michael Angelo, at the age of fourteen, in the garden of Lorenzo de Medici, from a piece of marble given him by the workmen.

The portraits of the painters are more than usually interesting. Every countenance is full of character. There is the pale, enthusiastic face of Raphael, the stern vigor of Titian, the majesty and dignity of Leonardo da Vinci, and the fresh beauty of Angelica Kauffmann. I liked best the romantic head of Raphael Mengs. In one of the rooms there is a portrait of Alfieri, with an autograph sonnet of his own on the back of it. The house in which he lived and died, is on the north bank of the Arno, near the Ponte Caraja, and his ashes rest in Santa Croce.

Italy still remains the home of art, and it is but just she should keep these treasures, though the age that brought them forth has passed away. They are her only support now; her people are dependent for their subsistence on the glory of the past. The spirits of the old painters, living still on their canvas, earn from year to year the bread of an indigent and oppressed people. This ought to silence those utilitarians at home, who oppose the cultivation of the fine arts, on the ground of their being useless luxuries. Let them look to Italy, where a picture by Raphael or Correggio is a rich legacy for a whole city. Nothing is useless that gratifies that perception of beauty, which is at once the most delicate and the most intense of our mental sensations, binding us by an unconscious link nearer to nature and to Him, whose every thought is born of Beauty, Truth and Love. I envy not the one who looks with a cold and indifferent spirit on these immortal creations of the old masters—these poems written in marble and on the canvas. They who oppose everything which can refine and spiritualize the nature of man, by binding him down to the cares of the work-day world alone, cheat life of half its glory.

The eighth of this month was the anniversary of the birth of the Virgin, and the celebration, if such it might be called, commenced the evening before. It is the custom, and Heaven only knows how it originated, for the people of the lower class to go through the streets in a company, blowing little penny whistles. We were walking that night in the direction of the Duomo, when we met a band of these men, blowing with all their might on the shrill whistles, so that the whole neighborhood resounded with one continual, piercing, ear-splitting shriek. They marched in a kind of quick trot through the streets, followed by a crowd of boys, and varying the noise occasionally by shouts and howls of the most horrible character. They paraded through all the principal streets of the city, which for an hour sent up such an agonizing scream that you might have fancied it an enormous monster, expiring in great torment. The people seemed to take the whole thing as a matter of course, but it was to us a novel manner of ushering in a religious festival.

The sky was clear and blue, as it always is in this Italian paradise, when we left Florence a few days ago for Fiesole. In spite of many virtuous efforts to rise early, it was nine o'clock before we left the Porta San Gallo, with its triumphal arch to the Emperor Francis, striding the road to Bologna. We passed through the public walk at this end of the city, and followed the road to Fiesole along the dried-up bed of a mountain torrent. The dwellings of the Florentine nobility occupy the whole slope, surrounded with rich and lovely gardens. The mountain and plain are both covered with luxuriant olive orchards, whose foliage of silver gray gives the scene the look of a moonlight landscape.

At the base of the mountain of Fiesole we passed one of the great summer palaces of Lorenzo the Magnificent, and a little distance beyond, took a footpath overshadowed by magnificent cypresses, between whose dark trunks we looked down on the lovely Val d'Arno. But I will reserve all description of the view till we arrive at the summit.

The modern village of Fiesole occupies the site of an ancient city, generally supposed to be of Etrurian origin. Just above, on one of the peaks of the mountain, stands the Acropolis, formerly used as a fortress, but now untenanted save by a few monks. From the side of its walls, beneath the shade of a few cypresses, there is a magnificent view of the whole of Val d'Arno, with Florence—the gem of Italy—in the centre. Stand with me a moment on the height, and let us gaze on this grand panorama, around which the Apennines stretch with a majestic sweep, wrapped in a robe of purple air, through which shimmer the villas and villages on their sides! The lovely vale lies below us in its garb of olive groves, among which beautiful villas are sprinkled as plentifully as white anemones in the woods of May. Florence lies in front of us, the magnificent cupola of the Duomo crowning its clustered palaces. We see the airy tower of the Palazzo Vecchio—the new spire of Santa Croce—and the long front of the

Palazzo Pitti, with the dark foliage of the Boboli Gardens behind. Beyond, far to the south, are the summits of the mountains near Siena. We can trace the sandy bed of the Arno down the valley till it disappears at the foot of the Lower Apennines, which mingle in the distance with the mountains of Carrara.

Galileo was wont to make observations "at evening from the top of Fiesole," and the square tower of the old church is still pointed out as the spot. Many a night did he ascend to its projecting terrace, and watch the stars as they rolled around through the clearest heaven to which a philosopher ever looked up.

We passed through an orchard of fig trees, and vines laden with beautiful purple and golden clusters, and in a few minutes reached the remains of an amphitheatre, in a little nook on the mountain side. This was a work of Roman construction, as its form indicates. Three or four ranges of seats alone, are laid bare, and these have only been discovered within a few years. A few steps further we came to a sort of cavern, overhung with wild fig-trees. After creeping in at the entrance, we found ourselves in an oval chamber, tall enough to admit of our standing upright, and rudely but very strongly built. This was one of the dens in which the wild beasts were kept; they were fed by a hole in the top, now closed up. This cell communicates with four or five others, by apertures broken in the walls. I stepped into one, and could see in the dim, light, that it was exactly similar to the first, and opened into another beyond.

Further down the mountain we found the ancient wall of the city, without doubt of Etrurian origin. It is of immense blocks of stone, and extends more or less dilapidated around the whole brow of the mountain. In one place there stands a solitary gateway, of large stones, which looks as if it might have been me of the first attempts at using the principle of the arch. These ruins are all gray and ivied, and it startles one to think what a history Earth has lived through since their foundations were laid!

We sat all the afternoon under the cypress trees and looked down

on the lovely valley, practising Italian sometimes with two young
Florentines who came up to enjoy the *"bell' aria"* of Fiesole. Descending as sunset drew on, we reached the Porta San Gallo, as the
people of Florence were issuing forth to their evening promenade.

One of my first visits was to the church of Santa Croce. This is one
of the oldest in Florence, venerated alike by foreigners and citizens,
for the illustrious dead whose remains it holds. It is a plain, gloomy
pile, the front of which is still unfinished, though at the base, one
sees that it was originally designed to be covered with black marble.
On entering the door we first saw the tomb of Michael Angelo.
Around the marble sarcophagus which contains his ashes are three
mourning figures, representing Sculpture, Painting and Architecture, and his bust stands above—a rough, stern countenance, like
a man of vast but unrefined mind. Further on are the tombs of Alfieri
and Machiavelli and the colossal cenotaph lately erected to Dante.
Opposite reposes Galileo. What a world of renown in these few
names! It makes one venerate the majesty of his race, to stand beside the dust of such lofty spirits.

Dante's monument may be said to be only erected to his memory;
he sleeps at the place of his exile,

"Like Scipio, buried by the upbraiding shore!"

It is the work of Ricci, a Florentine artist, and has been placed
there within a few years. The colossal figure of Poetry weeping over
the empty urn, might better express the regret of Florence in being
deprived of his ashes. The figure of Dante himself, seated above, is
grand and majestic; his head is inclined as if in meditation, and his
features bear the expression of sublime thought. Were this figure
placed there alone, on a simple and massive pedestal, it would be
more in keeping with his fame than the lumbering heaviness of the
present monument.

Machiavelli's tomb is adorned with a female figure representing

History, bearing his portrait. The inscription, which seems to be somewhat exaggerated, is: *tanto nomini nullum par elogium.* Near lies Alfieri, the "prince of tragedy," as he is called by the Italians. In his life he was fond of wandering among the tombs of Santa Croce, and it is said that there the first desire and presentiment of his future glory stirred within his breast. Now he slumbers among them, not the least honored name of that immortal company.

Galileo's tomb is adorned with his bust. His face is calm and dignified, and he holds appropriately in his hands, a globe and telescope. Aretino, the historian, lies on his tomb with a copy of his works clasped to his breast; above that of Lanzi, the historian of painting, there is a beautiful fresco of the angel of fame; and opposite to him is the scholar Lamio. The most beautiful monument in the church is that of a Polish princess, in the transept. She is lying on the bier, her features settled in the repose of death, and her thin, pale hands clasped across her breast. The countenance wears that half-smile, "so coldly sweet and sadly fair," which so often throws a beauty over the face of the dead, and the light pall reveals the fixed yet graceful outline of the form.

In that part of the city, which lies on the south bank of the Arno, is the palace of the Grand Duke, known by the name of the Palazzo Pitti, from a Florentine noble of that name, by whom it was first built. It is a very large, imposing structure, preserving an air of lightness in spite of the rough, heavy stones of which it is built. It is another example of a magnificent failure. The Marquis Strozzi, having built a palace which was universally admired for its beauty, (which stands yet, a model of chaste and massive elegance,) his rival, the Marquis Pitti, made the proud boast that he would build a palace, in the courtyard of which could be placed that of Strozzi. These are the dimensions of the courtyard; but in building the palace, although he was liberally assisted by the Florentine people, he ruined himself, and his magnificent residence passed into other hands, while that of Strozzi is inhabited by his descendants to this very day.

The gallery of the Palazzo Pitti is one of the finest in Europe. It contains six or seven hundred paintings, selected from the best works of the Italian masters. By the praiseworthy liberality of the Duke, they are open to the public, six hours everyday, and the rooms are thronged with artists of all nations.

Among Titian's works, there is his celebrated "Bella," a half-length figure of a young woman. It is a masterpiece of warm and brilliant coloring, without any decided expression. The countenance is that of vague, undefined thought, as of one who knew as yet nothing of the realities of life. In another room is found his Magdalen, a large, voluptuous form, with her brown hair falling like a veil over her shoulders and breast, but in her upturned countenance one can sooner read a prayer for an absent lover than repentance for sins she has committed.

What could excel in beauty the *Madonna dela Sedia* of Raphael? It is another of those works of that divine artist, on which we gaze and gaze with a never-tiring enjoyment of its angelic beauty. To my eye it is faultless; I could not wish a single outline of form, a single shade of color changed. Like his unrivalled Madonna in the Dresden Gallery, its beauty is spiritual as well as earthly; and while gazing on the glorious countenance of the Jesus-child, I feel an impulse I can scarcely explain—a longing to tear it from the canvas as if it were a breathing form, and clasp it to my heart in a glow of passionate love. What a sublime inspiration Raphael must have felt when be painted it Judging from its effect on the beholder, I can conceive of no higher mental excitement than that required to create it.

Here are also some of the finest and best preserved pictures of Salvator Rosa, and his portrait—a wild head, full of spirit and genius. Besides several landscapes in his savage and stormy style, there are two large sea-views, in which the atmosphere is of a deep and exquisite softness, without impairing the strength and boldness of the composition. "A Battle Scene," is terrible. Hundreds of combatants are met in the shock and struggle of conflict. Horses, mailed knights, vassals are mixed together in wild confusion; banners are waving and lances flashing amid the dust and smoke, while the wounded and dying are trodden under foot in darkness and blood. I now first begin to comprehend the power and sublimity of his genius. From the wildness and gloom of his pictures, he might almost be called the Byron of painters.

There is a small group of the "Fates," by Michael Angelo, which is one of the best of the few pictures which remain of him. As is well known, he disliked the art, saying it was only fit for women. This picture shows, however, how much higher he might have gone, had he been so inclined. The three weird sisters are ghostly and awful—the one who stands behind, holding the distaff, almost frightful. She who stands ready to cut the thread as it is spun out, has a slight trace of pity on her fixed and unearthly lineaments. It is a faithful embodiment of the old Greek idea of the Fates. I have wondered why some artist has not attempted the subject in a different way. In the Northern Mythology they are represented as wild maidens, armed with swords and mounted on fiery coursers. Why might they not also be pictured as angels, with countenances of a sublime and mysterious beauty—one all radiant with hope and promise of glory, and one with the token of a better future mingled with the sadness with which it severs the links of life?

There are many, many other splendid works in this collection, but it is unnecessary to mention them. I have only endeavored, by taking a few of the best known, to give some idea of them as they appear to me. There are hundreds of pictures here, which, though gems in themselves, are by masters who are rarely heard of in America, and it would be of little interest to go through the Gallery, describing it in guide-book fashion. Indeed, to describe galleries, however rich and renowned they may be, is in general a work of so much difficulty, that I know not whether the writer or the reader is made most tired thereby.

This collection possesses also the celebrated statue of Venus, by

Canova. She stands in the centre of a little apartment, filled with the most delicate and graceful works of painting. Although undoubtedly a figure of great beauty, it by no means struck me as possessing that exquisite and classic perfection which has been ascribed to it. The Venus de Medici far surpasses it. The head is larger in proportion to the size of the body, than that of the fatter, but has not the same modest, virgin expression. The arm wrapped in the robe which she is pressing to her breast, is finely executed, but the fingers of the other hand are bad— looking, as my friend said, as if the ends were *whittled off!* The body is, however, of fine proportions, though, taken as a whole, the statue is inferior to many other of Canova's works.

Occupying all the hill in back of the Pitti Palace, are the Boboli Gardens, three times a week the great resort of the Florentines. They are said to be the most beautiful gardens in Italy. Numberless paths, diverging from a magnificent amphitheatre in the old Roman style, opposite the courtyard, lead either in long flights of steps and terraces, or gentle windings among beds sweet with roses, to the summit. Long avenues, entirely arched and interwoven with the thick foliage of the laurel, which here grows to a tree, stretch along the slopes or wind in the woods through thickets of the fragrant bay. Parterres, rich with flowers and shrubbery, alternate with delightful groves of the Italian pine, acacia and laurel-leaved oak, and along the hillside, gleaming among the foliage, are placed statues of marble, some of which are from the chisels of Michael Angelo and Bandinelli. In one part there is a little sheet of water, with an island of orange-trees in the centre, from which a broad avenue of cypresses and statues leads to the very summit of the hill.

We often go there to watch the sun set over Florence and the vale of the Arno. The palace lies directly below, and a clump of pine-trees on the hillside, that stand out in bold relief on the glowing sky, makes the foreground to one of the loveliest pictures this side of the Atlantic. I saw one afternoon the Grand Duke and his family get into their carriage to drive out. One of the little dukes, who seemed a mischievous imp, ran out on a projection of the portico, where considerable persuasion had to be used to induce him to jump into the arms of his royal papa. I turned from these titled infants to watch a group of American children playing, for my attention was drawn to them by the sound of familiar words, and I learned afterwards they were the children of the sculptor Hiram Powers. I contrasted involuntarily the destinies of each one to the enjoyment and proud energy of freedom, and one to the confining and vitiating atmosphere of a court. The merry voices of the latter, as they played on the grass, came to my ears most gratefully. There is nothing so sweet as to hear one's native tongue in a foreign land from the lips of children.

Chapter XXXV
A PILGRIMAGE TO VALLOMBROSA

A pilgramage to Vallombrosa! — in sooth it has a romantic sound. The phrase calls up images of rosaries, and crosses, and shaven-headed friars. Had we lived in the olden days, such things might verily have accompanied our journey to that holy monastery. We might then have gone barefoot, saying prayers as we toiled along the banks of the Arno and up the steep Appenines, as did Benevenuto Cellini, before he poured the melted bronze into the mould of his immortal Perseus. But we are pilgrims to the shrines of Art and Genius; the dwelling-places of great minds are our sanctuaries. The mean dwelling, in which a poet has battled down poverty with the ecstacy of his mighty conceptions, and the dungeon in which a persecuted philosopher has languished, are to us sacred; we turn aside from the palaces of kings and the battlefields of conquerors, to visit them. The famed miracles of San Giovanni Gualberto added little, in our eyes, to the interest of Vallombrosa, but there were indeed reverence and inspiration in the names of Dante, Milton, and Ariosto.

We left Florence early, taking the way that leads from the Porta della Croce, up the north bank of the Arno. It was a bright morning, but there was a shade of vapor on the hills, which a practised eye might have taken as a prognostic of the rain that too soon came on. Fiesole, with its tower and Acropolis, stood out brightly from the blue background, and the hill of San Miniato lay with its cypress groves in the softest morning light. The *Contadini* were driving into the city in their basket wagons, and there were some fair young faces among them, that made us think Italian beauty was not altogether in the imagination.

After walking three or four miles, we entered the Appenines, keeping along the side of the Arno, whose bed is more than half dried up from the long summer heats. The mountain sides were covered with vineyards, glowing with their wealth of white and purple grapes, but the summits were naked and barren. We passed through the little town of Ponte Sieve, at the entrance of a romantic valley, where our view of the Arno was made more interesting by the lofty range of the Appenines, amid whose forests we could see the white front of the monastery of Vallombrosa. But the clouds sank low and hid it from sight, and the rain came on so hard that we were obliged to take shelter occasionally in the cottages by the wayside. In one of these we made a dinner of the hard, black bread of the country, rendered palatable by the addition of mountain cheese and some chips of an antique Bologna sausage. We were much amused in conversing with the simple hosts and their shy, gypsy-like children, one of whom, a dark-eyed, curly-haired boy, bore the name of Raphael.

We also became acquainted with a shoemaker and his family, who owned a little olive orchard and vineyard, which they said produced enough to support them. Wishing to know how much a family of six consumed in a year, we inquired the yield of their property. They answered, twenty small barrels of wine, and ten of oil. It was nearly sunset when we reached Pellago, and the wet walk and coarse fare we were obliged to take on the road, well qualified us to enjoy the excellent supper the pleasant landlady gave us.

This little town is among the Appenines, at the foot of the magnificent mountain of Vallombrosa. What a blessing it was for Milton, that he saw its loveliness before his eyes closed on this beautiful earth, and gained from it another hue in which to dip his pencil, when he painted the bliss of Eden! I watched the hills all day as we approached them, and thought how often his eyes had rested on their outlines, and how he had carried their forms in his memory for many a sunless year. The banished Dante, too, had trodden them, flying from his ungrateful country; and many another, whose genius has made him a beacon in the dark sea of the world's history. It is one of those places where the enjoyment is all romance, and the blood thrills as we gaze upon it.

We started early next morning, crossed the ravine, and took the well-paved way to the monastery along the mountain side. The stones are worn smooth by the sleds in which ladies and provisions are conveyed up, drawn by the beautiful white Tuscan oxen. The hills are covered with luxuriant chestnut and oak trees, of those picturesque forms which they only wear in Italy one wild dell in particular is much resorted to by painters for the ready-made foregrounds it supplies. Further on, we passed the *Paterno,* a rich farm belonging to the Monks. The vines which hung from tree to tree, were almost breaking beneath clusters as heavy and rich as those which the children of Israel bore on staves from the Promised Land. Of their flavor, we can say, from experience, they were worthy to have grown in Paradise. We then entered a deep dell of the mountain, where little shepherd girls were sitting on the rocks tending their sheep and spinning with their fingers from a distaff, in the same manner, doubtless, as the Roman shepherdesses two thousand years ago. Gnarled, gray olive trees, centuries old, grew upon the bare soil, and a little rill fell in many a tiny cataract down the glen. By a mill, in one of the coolest and wildest nooks I ever saw, two of us acted the part of water-spirits under one of these, to the great astonishment of four peasants, who were watching us from a distance.

Beyond, our road led through forests of chestnut and oak, and a broad view of mountain and vale lay below us. We asked a peasant boy we met, how much land the Monks of Vallombrosa possessed. *"All that you see!"* was the reply. The dominion of the good fathers reached once even to the gates of Florence. At length, about noon, we emerged from the woods into a broad avenue leading across a lawn, at whose extremity stood the massive buildings of the monastery. On a rock that towered above it, was the *Paradisino,* beyond which rose the mountain, covered with forests —

"Shade above shade, a woody theatre
 Of stateliest view"

as Milton describes it. We were met at the entrance by a young monk in cowl and cassock, to whom we applied for permission to stay till the next day, which was immediately given. Brother Placido (for that was his name) then asked us if we would not have dinner. We replied that our appetites were none the worse for climbing the mountain; and in half an hour sat down to a dinner, the like of which we had not seen for along time. Verily, thought I, it must be a pleasant thing to be a monk, after all!— that is, a monk of Vallombrosa.

In the afternoon we walked through a grand pine forest to the western brow of the mountain, where a view opened which it would require a wonderful power of the imagination for you to see in fancy, as I did in reality. From the height where we stood, the view was uninterrupted to the Mediterranean, a distance of more than seventy miles; a valley watered by a branch of the Arne swept far to the east, to the mountains near the Lake of Thrasymene; northwestwards the hills of Carrara bordered the horizon; the space between these wide points was filled with mountains and valleys, all steeped in that soft blue mist which makes Italian landscapes more like heavenly visions than realities. Florence was visible afar off, and the current of the Arno flashed in the sun. A cool and almost chilling wind blew constantly over the mountain, although the country below basked in summer heat. We lay on the rocks, and let our souls luxuriate in the lovely scene till near sunset. Brother Placido brought us supper in the evening, with his ever-smiling countenance, and we soon after went to our beds in the neat, plain chambers, to get rid of the unpleasant coldness.

Next morning it was damp and misty, and thick clouds rolled down the forests towards the convent. I set out for the "Little Paradise," taking in my way the pretty cascade which falls some fifty feet down the rocks. The building is not now as it was when Milton lived here, having been rebuilt within a short time. I found no one there, and satisfied my curiosity by climbing over the wall and looking in at the windows. A little chapel stands in a cleft of the rock below, to mark the miraculous escape of St. John Gualberto, founder of the monastery. Being one day very closely pursued by the Devil, he took shelter under the rock, which immediately became soft and admitted him into it, while the fiend, unable to stop, was precipitated over the steep. All this is related in a Latin inscription, and we saw a large hollow in the rock near, which must have been intended for the imprint left by his sacred person.

One of the monks told us another legend, concerning a little chapel which stands alone on a wild part of the mountain, above a rough pile of crags, called the "Peak of the Devil." "In the time of San Giovanni Gualberto, the holy founder of our order," said he, "there was a young man, of a noble family in Florence, who was so moved by the words of the saintly father, that he forsook the world, wherein he had lived with great luxury and dissipation, and became a monk. But, after a time, being young and tempted again by the pleasures he had renounced, he put off the sacred garments. The holy San Giovanni warned him of the terrible danger in which he stood, and at length the wicked young man returned. It was not a great while, however, before he became dissatisfied, and in spite all holy counsel, did the same thing again. But behold what happened! As he was walking along the peak where the chapel stands, thinking nothing of his great crime, the devil sprang suddenly from behind a rock, and catching the young man in his arms, before he could escape, carried him with a dreadful noise and a great red flame and smoke over the precipice, so that he was never afterwards seen."

The church attached to the monastery is small, but very solemn and venerable. I went several times to muse in its still, gloomy aisle, and hear the murmuring chant of the Monks, who went through their exercises in some of the chapels. At one time I saw them all, in long black cassocks, march in solemn order to the chapel of St. John Gualberto, where they sang a deep chant, which to me had something awful and sepulchral in it. Behind the high altar I saw their black, carved chairs of polished oak, with ponderous gilded foliants lying on the rails before them. The attendant opened one of these, that we might see the manuscript notes, three or four centuries old, from which they sung.

We were much amused in looking through two or three Italian books, which were lying in the traveler's room. One of these which our friend Mr. Tandy, of Kentucky, read, described the miracles of the patron saint with an air of the most ridiculous solemnity. The other was a description of the Monastery, its foundation, history, etc. In mentioning its great and far-spread renown, the author stated than even an English poet, by the name of Milton, had mentioned it in the following lines, which I copied verbatim from the book,

> "Thick as autumnal scaves that strow she brooks
>   In vallombrosa, whereth Etruian Jades
>   Stigh over orch d'embrover!"

In looking over the stranger's book, I found among the names of my countrymen, that of S. V. Clevenger, the talented and lamented sculptor who died at sea on his passage home. There were also the names of Mrs. Shelley and the Princess Potemkin, and I saw written on the wall, the autograph of Jean Reboul, the celebrated modern French poet. We were so delighted with the place we would have stayed another day, but for fear of trespassing too much on the lavish and unceasing hospitality of the good fathers.

So in the afternoon we shook hands with Brother Placido, and turned our backs regretfully upon one of the loneliest and loveliest spots of which earth can boast. The sky became gradually clear as we descended, and the mist raised itself from the distant mountains. We ran down through the same chestnut groves, diverging a little to go through the village of Tosi, which is very picturesque when seen from a distance, but extremely dirty to one passing through. I stopped in the ravine below to take a sketch of the mill and bridge, and as we sat, the line of golden sunlight rose higher on the mountains above. On walking down the shady side of this glen, we were enraptured with the scenery. A brilliant yet mellow glow lay over the whole opposing height, lighting up the houses of Tosi and the white cottages half seen among the olives, while the mountain of Vallombrosa stretched far heavenward like a sunny painting, with only a misty wreath floating and waving around its summit. The glossy foliage of the chestnuts was made still brighter by the warm light, and the old olives softened down into a silvery gray, whose contrast gave the landscape a character of the mellowest beauty. As we wound out of the deep glen, the broad valleys and ranges of the Appenines lay before us, forests, castles and villages steeped in the soft, vapory blue of the Italian atmosphere, and the current of the Arno flashing like a golden belt through the middle of the picture.

The sun was nearly down, and the mountains just below him were of a deep purple hue, while those that ran out to the eastward wore the most aerial shade of blue. A few scattered clouds, floating above, soon put on the sunset robe of orange and a band of the same soft color encircled the western horizon. It did not reach half-way to the zenith, however; the sky above was blue, of such a depth and transparency, that to gaze upward was like looking into eternity. Then how softly and soothingly the twilight came on! How deep a hush sank on the chestnut glades, broken only by the song of the cicada, chirping its "goodnight carol!" The mountains, too, how majestic they stood in their deep purple outlines! Sweet, sweet Italy! I can feel now how the soul may cling to thee, since thou canst thus gratify its insatiable thirst for the Beautiful. Even thy plainest scene is clothed in hues that seem borrowed of heaven! In the twilight, more radiant than light, and the stillness, more eloquent than music, which sink down over the sunny beauty of thy shores, there is a silent, intense poetry that stirs the soul through all its impassioned depths. With warm, blissful tears filling the eyes and a heart overflowing with its own bright fancies, I wander in the solitude and calm of such a time, and love thee as if I were a child of thy soil!

Chapter XXXVI
WALK TO SIENA — INCIDENTS IN FLORENCE

October 16.—My cousin, being anxious to visit Rome, and reach Heidelberg before the commencement of the winter semester, set out towards the end of September, on foot. We accompanied him as far as Siena, forty miles distant. As I shall most probably take another road to the Eternal City, the present is a good opportunity to say something of that romantic old town, so famous throughout Italy for the honesty of its inhabitants.

We dined the first day, seventeen miles from Florence, at Tavenella, where, for a meagre dinner the hostess had the assurance to ask us seven pauls. We told her we would give but four and a half, and by assuming a decided manner, with a plentiful use of the word *"Signora"* she was persuaded to be fully satisfied with the latter sum.

From a height near, we could see the mountains coasting the Mediterranean, and shortly after, on descending a long hill, the little town of Poggibonsi lay in the warm afternoon light, on an eminence before us. It was soon passed with its dusky towers, then Stagia looking desolate in its ruined and ivied walls, and following the advice of a peasant, we stopped for the night at the inn of Querciola. As we knew something of Italian by this time, we thought it best to inquire the price of lodging, before entering. The *padrone* asked if we meant to take supper also. We answered in the affirmative; "then," said he, "you will pay half a paul (about five cents) apiece for a bed." We passed under the swinging bunch of boughs, which in Italy is the universal sign of an inn for the common people, and entered the bare, smoky room appropriated to travelers. A long table, with well-worn benches, were the only furniture; we threw our knapsacks on one end of it and sat down, amusing ourselves while supper was preparing, in looking at a number of grotesque charcoal drawings on the wall, which the flaring light of our tall iron lamp revealed to us. At length the hostess, a kindly-looking woman, with a white handkerchief folded gracefully around her head, brought us a dish of fried eggs, which, with the coarse black bread of the peasants and a basket-full of rich grapes, made us an excellent supper. We slept on mattresses stuffed with corn-husks, placed on square iron frames, which are the bedsteads most used in Italy. A brightly-painted caricature of some saint or a rough crucifix, trimmed with bay-leaves, hung at the head of each bed, and under their devout protection we enjoyed a safe and unbroken slumber.

Next morning we set out early to complete the remaining ten miles to Siena. The only thing of interest on the road, is the ruined wall and battlements of Castiglione, circling a high hill and looking as old as the days of Etruria. The towers of Siena are seen at some distance, but approaching it from this side, the traveler does not perceive its romantic situation until he arrives. It stands on a double hill, which is very steep on some sides; the hollow between the two peaks is occupied by the great public square, ten or fifteen feet lower than the rest of the city. We left our knapsacks at a *café* and sought the celebrated Cathedral, which stands in the highest part of the town, forming with its flat dome and lofty marble tower, an apex to the pyramidal mass of buildings.

The interior is rich and elegantly perfect. Every part is of black and white marble, in what I should call the striped style, which has a singular but agreeable effect. The inside of the dome and the vaulted ceilings of the chapels, are of blue, with golden stars; the pavement in the centre is so precious a work that it is kept covered with boards and only shown once a year. There are some pictures of great value in this Cathedral; one of "The Descent of the Dove," is worthy of the best days of Italian art. In an adjoining chamber, with frescoed walls, and a beautiful tesselated pavement, is the library, consisting of a few huge old volumes, which with their brown covers and brazen clasps, look as much like a collection of flat leather trunks as anything else. In the centre of the room stands the mutilated group of the Grecian Graces, found in digging the foundation of the Cathedral. The figures are still beautiful and graceful, with that exquisite curve of outline which is such a charm in the antique statues. Canova has only perfected the idea in his celebrated group, which is nearly a copy of this.

We strolled through the square and then accompanied our friend to the Roman gate, where we took leave of him for six months at least. He felt lonely at the thought of walking in Italy without a companion, but was cheered by the anticipation of soon reaching Rome. We watched him awhile, walking rapidly over the hot plain towards Radicofani, and then, turning our faces with much pleasure towards Florence, we commenced the return walk. I must not forget to mention the delicious grapes which we bought, begged and stole on the way. The whole country is like one vineyard—and the people live, in a great measure, on the fruit, during this part of the year. Would you not think it highly romantic and agreeable to sit in the shade of a cypress grove, beside some old weather-beaten statues, looking out over the vales of the Appenines, with a pile of white and purple grapes beside you, the like of which can scarcely be had in America for love or money, and which had been given you by a dark-eyed peasant girl? If so, you may envy us, for such was exactly our situation on the morning before reaching Florence.

Being in the Duomo, two or three days ago, I met a German traveler, who has walked through Italy thus far, and intends continuing his journey to Rome and Naples. His name is Von Raumer. He was well acquainted with the present state of America, and I derived much pleasure from his intelligent conversation. We concluded to ascend the cupola in company. Two black-robed boys led the way; after climbing an infinite number of steps, we reached the gallery around the foot of the dome. The glorious view of that paradise, the vale of the Arno, shut in on all sides by mountains, some bare and desolate, some covered with villas, gardens, and groves, lay in soft, hazy light, with the shadows of a few light clouds moving slowly across it. They next took us to a gallery on the inside of the dome, where we first saw the immensity of its structure. Only from a distant view, or in ascending it, can one really measure its grandeur. The frescoes, which from below appear the size of life, are found to be rough and monstrous daubs; each figure being nearly as many fathoms in length as a man is feet. Continuing our ascent; we mounted between the inside and outside shells of the dome. It was indeed a bold idea for Brunelleschi to raise such a mass in air. The dome of Saint Peter's, which is scarcely as large, was not made until a century after, and this was, therefore, the first attempt at raising one on so grand a scale. It seems still as solid as if just built.

There was a small door in one of the projections of the lantern, which the sacristan told us to enter and ascend still higher. Supposing there was a fine view to be gained, two priests, who had just come up, entered it; the German followed, and I after him. After crawling in at the low door, we found ourselves in a hollow pillar, little wider than our bodies. Looking up, I saw the German's legs just above my head, while the other two were above him, ascending by means of little iron bars fastened in the marble. The priests were very much amused, and the German said: — "This is the first time I ever learned chimney-sweeping!" We emerged at length into a hollow cone, hot and dark, with a rickety ladder going up—somewhere; we could not see where. The old priest, not wishing to trust himself to it, sent his younger brother up, and we shouted after him: — "What kind of a view have you?" He climbed up till the cone got so narrow he could go no further, and answered back in the darkness: — "I see nothing at all!" Shortly after he came down, covered with dust and cobwebs, and we all descended the chimney quicker than we went up. The old priest considered it a good joke, and laughed till his fat sides shook. We asked the sacristan why he sent us up, and he answered: — "To see the construction of the Church!"

I attended service in the Cathedral one dark, rainy morning, and was never before so deeply impressed with the majesty and grandeur of the mighty edifice. The thick, cloudy atmosphere darkened still more the light which came through the stained windows, and a solemn twilight reigned in the long aisles. The mighty dome sprang far aloft, as if it enclosed a part of heaven, for the light that struggled through the windows around its base, lay in broad bars on the blue, hazy air. I would not have been surprised at seeing a cloud float along within it. The lofty burst of the organ, that seemed like the pantings of a monster, boomed echoing away through dome and nave, with a chiming, metallic vibration, that shook the massive pillars which it would defy an earthquake to rend. All was wrapped in dusky obscurity, except where, in the side-chapels, crowns of tapers were burning around the images. One knows not which most to admire, the genius which could conceive, or the perseverance which could accomplish such a work. On one side of the square, the colossal statue of the architect, glorious old Brunelleschi, is most appropriately placed, looking up with pride at his performance.

The sunshine and genial airs of Italy have gone, leaving instead a cold, gloomy sky and chilling winds. The autumnal season has fairly commenced, and I suppose I must bid adieu to the brightness which made me in love with the land. The change has been no less sudden than unpleasant, and if, as they say, it will continue all winter with little variation, I shall have to seek a clearer climate. In the cold of these European winters, there is, as I observed last year in Germany, a dull, damp chill, quite different from the bracing, exhilarating frosts of America. It stagnates the vital principle and leaves the limbs dull and heavy, with a lifeless feeling which can scarcely be overcome by vigorous action. At least, that much has been my experience.

We lately made an excursion to Pratolino, on the Appenines, to see the vintage and the celebrated colossus, by John of Bologna. Leaving Florence in the morning, with a cool, fresh wind blowing down from the mountains, we began ascending by the road to Bologna. We passed Fiesole with its tower and acropolis on the right, ascending slowly, with the bold peak of one of the loftiest Appenines on our left. The abundant fruit of the olive was beginning to turn brown, and the grapes were all gathered in from the vineyards, but we learned front a peasant-boy that the vintage was not finished at Pratolino.

We finally arrived at an avenue shaded with sycamores, leading to the royal park. The vintagers were busy in the fields around, unloading the vines of their purple tribute, and many a laugh and jest among the merry peasants enlivened the toil. We assisted them in disposing of some fine clusters, and then sought the "Colossus of the Appenines." He stands above a little lake, at the head of a long mountain-slope, broken with clumps of magnificent trees. This remarkable figure, the work of John of Bologna, impresses one like a relic of the Titans. He is represented as half-kneeling, supporting himself with one hand, while the other is pressed upon the head of a dolphin, from which a little stream falls into the lake. The height of the figure when erect; would amount to more than sixty feet! We measured one of the feet, which is a single piece of rock, about eight feet long; from the ground to the top of one knee is nearly twenty feet. The limbs are formed of pieces of stone, joined together, and the body of stone and brick. His rough hair and eyebrows, and the beard, which reached nearly to the ground, are formed of stalactites, taken from caves, and fastened together in a dripping and crusted mass. These hung also from his limbs and body, and gave him the appearance of Winter in his mail of icicles. By climbing up the rocks at his back, we entered his body, which contains a small-sized room; it was even possible to ascend through his neck and look out at his ear! The face is in keeping with the figure—stern and grand, and the architect (one can hardly say sculptor) has given to it the majestic air and sublimity of the Appenines. But who can build up an image of the Alp?

We visited the factory on the estate, where wine and oil are made. The men had just brought in a cart-load of large wooden vessels, filled with grapes, which they were mashing with heavy wooden pestles. When the grapes were pretty well reduced to pulp and juice, they emptied them into an enormous tun, which they told us would be covered air-tight, and left for three or four weeks, after which the wine would be drawn off at the bottom. They showed us also a great stone mill for grinding olives; this estate of the Grand Duke produces five hundred barrels of wine and a hundred and fifty of oil, every year. The former article is the universal beverage of the laboring classes in Italy, or I might say of all classes; it is, however, the pure blood of the grape, and although used in such quantities, one sees little drunkenness— far less than in our own land.

Tuscany enjoys at present a more liberal government than any other part of Italy, and the people are, in many respects, prosperous and happy. The Grand Duke, although enjoying almost absolute privileges, is disposed to encourage every measure which may promote the welfare of his subjects. The people are, indeed, very heavily taxed, but this is less severely felt by them, than it would be by the inhabitants of colder climes. The soil produces with little labor all that is necessary for their support; though kept constantly in a state of comparative poverty, they appear satisfied with their lot, and rarely look further than the necessities of the present. In love with the delightful climate, they cherish their country, fallen as she is, and are rarely induced to leave her. Even the wealthier classes of the Italians travel very little; they can learn the manners and habits of foreigners nearly as well in their own country as elsewhere, and they prefer their own hills of olive and vine to the icy grandeur of the Alps or the rich and garden-like beauty of England.

But, although this sweet climate, with its wealth of sunlight and balmy airs, may enchant the traveler for awhile and make him wish at times that his whole life might be spent amid such scenes, it exercises a most enervating influence on those who are born to its enjoyment. It relaxes mental and physical energy, and disposes body and mind to dreamy inactivity. The Italians, as a race, are indolent and effeminate. Of the moral dignity of man they have little conception. Those classes who are engaged in active occupation seem even destitute of common honesty, practising all kinds of deceits in the most open manner and apparently without the least shame. The state of morals is lower than in any other country of Europe; what little virtue exists is found among the peasants. Many of the most sacred obligations of society are universally violated, and as a natural consequence, the people are almost entire strangers to that domestic happiness, which constitutes the true enjoyment of life.

This dark shadow in the moral atmosphere of Italy hangs like a curse on her beautiful soil, weakening the sympathies of citizens of freer lands with her fallen condition. I often feel vividly the sentiment which Percival puts into the mouth of a Greek in slavery:

"The spring may here with autumn twine
   And both combined may rule the year,

And fresh-blown flowers and racy wine
  In frosted clusters still be near—
Dearer the wild and snowy hills
Where hale and ruddy Freedom smiles."

No people can ever become truly great or free, who are not virtuous. If the soul aspires for liberty—pure and perfect liberty—it also aspires for everything that is noble in Truth, everything that is holy in Virtue. It is greatly to be feared that all those nervous and impatient efforts which have been made and are still being made by the Italian people to better their condition, will be of little avail, until they set up a better standard of principle and make their private actions more conformable and compatible with their ideas of political independence.

Oct. 22.—I attended today the fall races at the *Cascine.* This is a dairy farm of the Grand Duke on the Arno, below the city; part of it, shaded with magnificent trees, has been made into a public promenade and drive, which extends for three miles down the river. Towards the lower end, on a smooth green lawn, is the race-course. Today was the last of the season, for which the best trials had been reserved; on passing out the gate at noon, we found a number of carriages and pedestrians going the same way. It was the very perfection of autumn temperature, and I do not remember to have ever seen so blue hills, so green meadows, so fresh air and so bright sunshine combined in one scene before. All that gloom and coldness of which I lately complained has vanished.

Traveling increases very much one's capacity for admiration. Every beautiful scene appears as beautiful as if it had been the first; and although I may have seen a hundred times as lovely a combination of sky and landscape, the pleasure which it awakens is never diminished. This is one of the greatest blessings we enjoy—the freshness and glory which Nature wears to our eyes forever. It shows that the soul never grows old—that the eye of age can take in the impression of beauty with the same enthusiastic joy that leaped through the heart of childhood.

We found the crowd around the race-course but thin; half the people there, and all the horses, appeared to be English. It was a good place to observe the beauty of Florence, which however, may he done in a short time, as there is not much of it. There is beauty in Italy, undoubtedly, but it is either among the peasants or the higher class of nobility. I will tell our American women confidentially, for I know they have too much sense to be vain of it, that they surpass the rest of the world as much in beauty as they do in intelligence and virtue. I saw in one of the carriages the wife of Alexander Dumas, the French author. She is a large, fair complexioned woman, and is now, from what cause I know not, living apart from her husband.

The jockeys paced up and down the fields, preparing their beautiful animals for the approaching heat, and as the hour drew nigh the mounted dragoons busied themselves in clearing the space. It was a one-mile course, to the end of the lawn and back. At last the bugle sounded, and off went three steeds like arrows let fly. They passed us, their light limbs bounding over the turf, a beautiful dark-brown taking the lead. We leaned over the railing and watched them eagerly. The bell rang they reached the other end—we saw them turn and come dashing back, nearer, nearer; the crowd began to shout, and in a few seconds the brown one had won it by four or five lengths. The fortunate horse was led around in triumph, and I saw an English lady, remarkable for her betting propensities, come out from the crowd and kiss it in apparent delight.

After an interval, three others took the field—all graceful, spirited creatures. This was a more exciting race than the first; they flew past us nearly abreast, and the crowd looked after them in anxiety. They cleared the course like wild deer, and in a minute or two came back, the racer of an English nobleman a short distance ahead. The jockey threw up his hand in token of triumph as he approached the goal, and the people cheered him. It was a beautiful sight to see those noble animals stretching to the utmost of their speed, as they dashed down the grassy lawn. The lucky one always showed by his proud and erect carriage, his consciousness of success.

Florence is fast becoming modernized. The introduction of gas, and the construction of the railroad to Pisa, which is nearly completed, will make sad havoc with the air of poetry which still lingers in its silent streets. There is scarcely a bridge, a tower, or a street, which is not connected with some stirring association. In the Via San Felice, Raphael used to paint when a boy; near the Ponte Santa Trinita stands Michael Angelo's house, with his pictures, clothes, and painting implements, just as he left it three centuries ago; on the south side of the Arno is the house of Galileo, and that of Machiavelli stands in an avenue near the Ducal Palace. While threading my way through some dark, crooked streets in an unfrequented part of the city, I noticed an old, untenanted house, bearing a marble tablet above the door. I drew near and read: — "In this house of the Alighieri was born the Divine Poet!" It was the birthplace of Dante.

Nov. 1. — Yesterday morning we were apprised of the safe arrival of a new scion of the royal family in the world by the ringing of the city bells. Today, to celebrate the event, the shops were closed, and the people made a holiday of it. Merry chimes pealed out from every tower, and discharges of cannon thundered up from the fortress. In the evening the dome of the Cathedral was illuminated, and the lines of cupola, lantern, and cross were traced in flame on the dark sky, like a crown of burning stars dropped from Heaven on the holy pile. I went in and walked down the aisle, listening for awhile to the grand choral, while the clustered tapers under the dome quivered and trembled, as if shaken by the waves of music which burst continually within its lofty concave.

A few days ago Prince Corsini, Prime Minister of Tuscany, died at an advanced age. I saw his body brought in solemn procession by night, with torches and tapers, to the church of Santa Trinita.

Soldiers followed with revered arms and muffled drums, the band playing a funeral march. I forced myself through the crowd into the church, which was hung with black and gold, and listened to the long drawn chanting of the priests around the bier.

We lately visited the Florentine Museum. Besides the usual collection of objects of natural history, there is an anatomical cabinet, very celebrated for its preparations in wax. All parts of the human frame are represented so wonderfully exact, that students of medicine pursue their studies here in summer with the same facility as from real "subjects." Every bone, muscle, and nerve in the body is perfectly counterfeited, the whole forming a collection as curious as it is useful. One chamber is occupied with representations of the plague of Rome, Milan, and Florence. They are executed with horrible truth to nature, but I regretted afterwards having seen them. There are enough forms of beauty and delight in the world on which to employ the eye, without making it familiar with scenes which can only be remembered with a shudder.

We derive much pleasure from the society of the American artists who are now residing in Florence. At the houses of Powers, and Brown, the painter, we spend many delightful evenings in the company of our gifted countrymen. They are drawn together by a kindred, social feeling as well as by their mutual aims, and form among themselves a society so unrestrained, and American-like, that the traveler who meets them forgets his absence for a time. These noble representatives of our country, all of whom possess the true, inborn spirit of republicanism, have made the American name known and respected in Florence. Powers, especially, who is intimate with many of the principal Italian families, is universally esteemed. The Grand Duke has more than once visited his studio and expressed the highest admiration of his talents.

Chapter XXXVII
AMERICAN ART IN FLORENCE

I have seen Ibrahim Pacha, the son of old Mehemet Ali, driving in his carriage through the streets. He is here on a visit from Lucca, where he has been spending some time on account of his health. He is a man of apparently fifty years of age; his countenance wears a stern and almost savage look, very consistent with the character he bears and the political part he has played. He is rather portly in person, the pale olive of his complexion contrasting strongly with a beard perfectly white. In common with all his attendants, he wears the high red cap, picturesque blue tunic and narrow trousers of the Egyptians. There is scarcely a man of them whose face with its wild, oriental beauty, does not show to advantage among us civilized and prosaic Christians.

In Florence, and indeed through all Italy, there is much reason for our country to be proud of the high stand her artists are taking. The sons of our rude western clime, brought up without other resources than their own genius and energy, now fairly rival those, who from their cradle upwards have drawn inspiration and ambition from the glorious masterpieces of the old painters and sculptors. Wherever our artists are known, they never fail to create a respect for American talent, and to dissipate the false notions respecting our cultivation and refinement, which prevail in Europe. There are now eight or ten of our painters and sculptors in Florence, some of whom, I do not hesitate to say, take the very first rank among living artists.

I have been highly gratified in visiting the studio of Mr. G. L. Brown, who, as a landscape painter, is destined to take a stand second to few, since the days of Claude Lorraine. He is now without a rival in Florence, or perhaps in Italy, and has youth, genius and a plentiful stock of the true poetic enthusiasm for his art, to work for him far greater triumphs. His Italian landscapes have that golden mellowness and transparency of atmosphere which give such a charm to the real scenes, and one would think he used on his pallette, in addition to the more substantial colors, condensed air and sunlight and the liquid crystal of streams. He has wooed Nature like a lover, and she has not withheld her sympathy. She has taught him how to raise and curve her trees, load their boughs with foliage, and spread underneath them the broad, cool shadows—to pile up the shattered crag, and steep the long mountain range in the haze of alluring distance.

He has now nearly finished, a large painting of "Christ Preaching in the Wilderness," which is of surprising beauty. You look upon one of the fairest scenes of Judea. In front, the multitude are grouped on one side, at the edge of a magnificent forest; on the other side, towers up a rough wall of rock and foliage that stretches back into the distance, where some grand blue mountains are piled against the sky, and a beautiful stream, winding through the middle of the picture, slides away out of the foreground. Just emerging from the shade of one of the cliffs, is the benign figure of the Saviour, with the warm light which breaks from behind the trees, falling around him as he advances. There is a smaller picture of the "Shipwreck of St. Paul," in which he shows equal skill in painting a troubled sea and breaking storm. He is one of the young artists from whom we have most to hope.

I have been extremely interested in looking over a number of sketches made by Mr. Kellogg, of Cincinnati, during a tour through Egypt, Arabia Petræa and Palestine. He visited many places out of the general route of travelers, and beside the great number of landscape views, brought away many sketches of the characters and costumes of the Orient. From some of these he has commenced paintings, which, as his genius is equal to his practice, will be of no ordinary value. Indeed, some of these must give him at once an established reputation in America. In Constantinople, where he resided several months, he enjoyed peculiar advantages for the exercise of his art, through the favor and influence of Mr. Carr, the American, and Sir Stratford Canning, the British Minister. I saw a splendid diamond cup, presented to him by Riza Pacha, the late Grand Vizier. The sketches he brought from thence and from the valleys of Phrygia and the mountain solitudes of old Olympus, are of great interest and value. Among his later paintings, I might mention an angel, whose countenance beams with a rapt and glorious beauty. A divine light shines through all the features and heightens the glow of adoration to an expression all spiritual and immortal. If Mr. Kellogg will give us a few more of these heavenly conceptions, we will place him on a pedestal, little lower than that of Guido.

Greenough, who has been sometime in Germany, returned lately to Florence, where he has a colossal group in progress for the portico of the Capitol. I have seen part of it, which is nearly finished in the marble. It shows a backwoodsman just triumphing in the struggle with an Indian; another group to be added, will represent the wife and child of the former. The colossal size of the statues gives a grandeur to the action, as if it were a combat of Titans; there is a consciousness of power, an expression of lofty disdain in the expansion of the hunter's nostril and the proud curve of his lip, that might become a god. The spirit of action, of breathing, life-like exertion, so much more difficult to infuse into the marble than that of repose, is perfectly attained. I will not enter into a more particular description, as it will probably be sent to the United States in a year or two. It is a magnificent work; the best, unquestionably, that Greenough has yet made. The subject, and the grandeur he has given it in the execution, will ensure it a much more favorable reception than a false taste gave to his Washington.

Mr. C. B. Ives, a young sculptor from Connecticut, has not disappointed the high promise he gave before leaving home. I was struck with some of his busts in Philadelphia, particularly those of Mrs. Sigourney and Joseph R. Chandler, and it has been no common pleasure to visit his studio here in Florence, and look on some of his ideal works. He has lately made two models, which, when finished in marble, will be works of great beauty. They will contribute greatly to his reputation here and in America. One of these represents a child of four or five years of age, holding in his hand a dead bird, on which he is gazing, with childish grief and wonder, that it is so still and drooping. It is a beautiful thought; the boy is leaning forward as he sits, holding the lifeless playmate close in his hands, his sadness touched with a vague expression, as if he could not yet comprehend the idea of death.

The other is of equal excellence, in a different style; it is a bust of "Jephthah's daughter," when the consciousness of her doom first flashes upon her. The face and bust are beautiful with the bloom of perfect girlhood. A simple robe covers her breast, and her rich hair is gathered up behind, and bound with a slender fillet. Her head, of the pure classical mould, is bent forward, as if weighed down by the shock, and there is a heavy drooping in the mouth and eyelids, that denotes a sudden and sickening agony. It is not a violent, passionate grief, but a profound and almost paralyzing emotion—a shock from which, I think, the soul will finally rebound, strengthened to make the sacrifice.

Would it not be better for some scores of our rich merchants to lay out their money on great statues and pictures, instead of balls and spendthrift sons? A few such expenditures, properly directed, would do much for the advancement of the fine arts. An occasional golden blessing, bestowed on genius, might be returned on the giver, in the fame he had assisted in creating. There seems, however, to be at present a rapid increase in refined taste, and a better appreciation of artistic talent, in our country. And as an American, nothing has made me feel prouder than this, and the steadily increasing reputation of our artists.

Of these, no one has done more within the last few years, than Hiram Powers. With a tireless and persevering energy, such as could have belonged to few but Americans, he has already gained a name in his art, that posterity will pronounce in the same breath with Phidias, Michael Angelo and Thorwaldsen. I cannot describe the enjoyment I have derived from looking at his matchless works. I should hesitate in giving my own imperfect judgment of their excellence, if I had not found it to coincide with that of many others who are better versed in the rules of art. The sensation which his "Greek Slave" produced in England, has doubtless ere this been breezed across the Atlantic, and I see by the late American papers that they are growing familiar with his fame. When I read a notice seven or eight years ago, of the young sculptor of Cincinnati, whose busts exhibited so much evidence of genius, I little dreamed I should meet him in Florence, with the experience of years of toil added to his early enthusiasm, and everyday increasing his renown.

You would like to hear of his statue of Eve, which men of taste pronounce one of the finest works of modern times. A more perfect figure never filled my eye. I have seen the masterpieces of Thorwaldsen, Dannecker and Canova, and the Venus de Medici, but I have seen nothing yet that can exceed the beauty of this glorious statue. So completely did the first view excite my surprise and delight, and thrill every feeling that awakes at the sight of the Beautiful, that my mind dwelt intensely on it for days afterwards. This is the Eve of Scripture—the Eve of Milton—mother of mankind and fairest of all her race. With the full and majestic beauty of ripened womanhood, she wears the purity of a world as yet unknown to sin. With the bearing of a queen, there is in her countenance the softness and grace of a tender, loving woman:

"God-like erect, with native honor clad
  In naked majesty."

She holds the fatal fruit extended in her hand, and her face expresses the struggle between conscience, dread and desire. The serpent, whose coiled length under the leaves and flowers entirely surrounds her, thus forming a beautiful allegorical symbol, is watching her decision from an ivied trunk at her side. Her form is said to be fully as perfect as the Venus de Medici, and from its greater size, has an air of conscious and ennobling dignity. The head is far superior in beauty, and soul speaks from every feature of the countenance. I add a few stanzas which the contemplation of this statue called forth. Though unworthy the subject, they may perhaps faintly shadow the sentiment which Powers has so eloquently embodied in marble:

THE "EVE" OF POWERS

A faultless being from the marble sprung,
   She stands in beauty there!
As when the grace of Eden 'round her clung
   Fairest where all was fair!
Pure, as when first from God's creating hand
   She came on man to shine;
So seems she now, in living stone to stand —
   A mortal, yet divine!

The spark the Grecian from Olympus caught,
   Left not a loftier trace;
The daring of the sculptor's hand has wrought
   A soul in that sweet face!
He won as well the sacred fire from heaven,
   God-sent, not stolen down,
And no Promethean doom for him is given,
   But ages of renown!

The soul of beauty breathes around that form
   A more enchanting spell;

There blooms each virgin grace, ere yet the storm
    On blighted Eden fell!
The first desire upon her lovely brow,
    Raised by an evil power;
Doubt, longing, dread, are in her features now —
    It is the trial-hour!

How every thought that strives within her breast,
    In that one glance is shown!
Say, can that heart of marble be at rest,
    Since spirit warms the stone?
Will not those limbs, of so divine a mould,
    Move, when her thought is o'er —
When she has yielded to the tempters hold
    And Eden blooms no more?

Art, like a Phoenix, springs from dust again —
    She cannot pass away!
Bound down in gloom, she breaks apart the chain
    And struggles up to day!
The flame, first kindled in the ages gone,
    Has never ceased to burn,
And westward, now, appears the kindling dawn,
    Which marks the day's return!

The "Greek Slave" is now in the possession of Mr. Grant, of London, and I only saw the clay model. Like the Eve, it is a form that one's eye tells him is perfect, unsurpassed; but it is the budding loveliness of a girl, instead of the perfected beauty of a woman. In England it has been pronounced superior to Canova's works, and indeed I have seen nothing of his, that could be placed beside it.

Powers has now nearly finished a most exquisite figure of a fisher-boy, standing on the shore, with his net and rudder in one hand, while with the other he holds a shell to his ear and listens if it murmur to him of a gathering storm. His slight, boyish limbs are full of grace and delicacy—you feel that the youthful frame could grow up into nothing less than an Apollo. Then the head — how beautiful! Slightly bent on one side, with the rim of the shell thrust under his locks, lips gently parted, and the face wrought up to the most hushed and breathless expression, he listens whether the sound he deeper than its wont. It makes you hold your breath and listen, to look at it. Mrs. Jameson somewhere remarks that repose or suspended motion, should be always chosen for a statue that shall present a perfect, unbroken impression to the mind. If this be true, the enjoyment must be much more complete where not only the motion, but almost breath and thought are suspended, and all the faculties wrought into one hushed and intense sensation. In gazing on this exquisite conception. I feel my admiration filled to the utmost, without that painful, aching impression, so often left by beautiful works. It glides into my vision like a form long missed from the gallery of beauty I am forming in my mind, and I gaze on it with an ever new and increasing delight.

Now I come to the last and fairest of all—the divine Proserpine. Not the form, for it is but a bust rising from a capital of acanthus leaves, which curve around the breast and arms and turn gracefully outward, but the face, whose modest maiden beauty can find no peer among goddesses or mortals. So looked she on the field of Ennæ:—that "fairer flower," so soon to be gathered by "gloomy Dis." A slender crown of green wheat blades, showing alike her descent from Ceres and her virgin years, circles her head. Truly, if Pygmalion stole his fire to warm such a form as this, Jove should have pardoned him. Of Powers' busts it is unnecessary for me to speak. He has lately finished a very beautiful one of the Princess Demidoff, daughter of Jerome Bonaparte.

We will soon, I hope, have the "Eve" in America. Powers has generously refused many advantageous offers for it, that he might finally send it home; and his country, therefore, will possess this statue, his first ideal work. She may well be proud of the genius and native energy of her young artist, and she should repay them by a just and liberal encouragement.

Chapter XXXVIII
AN ADVENTURE ON THE GREAT ST. BERNARD — WALKS AROUND FLORENCE

Nov. 9. — A few days ago I received a letter from my cousin at Heidelberg, describing his solitary walk from Genoa over the Alps, and through the western part of Switzerland. The news of his safe arrival dissipated the anxiety we were beginning to feel, on account of his long silence, while it proved that our fears concerning the danger of such a journey were not altogether groundless. He met with a startling adventure on the Great St. Bernard, which will be best described by an extract from his own letter:

"... Such were my impressions of Rome. But leaving the 'Eternal City,' I must hasten on to give you a description of an adventure I met with in crossing the Alps, omitting for the present an account of the trip from Rome to Genoa, and my lonely walk through Sardinia. When I had crossed the mountain range north of Genoa, the plains of Piedmont stretched out before me. I could see the snowy sides and summits of the Alps more than one hundred miles, distant, looking like white, fleecy clouds on a summer day. It was a magnificent prospect, and I wonder not that the heart of the Swiss soldier, after years of absence in foreign service, beats with joy when he again looks on his native mountains.

"As I approached nearer, the weather changed, and dark, gloomy clouds enveloped them, so that they seemed to present an impassible barrier to the lands beyond them. At Ivrea, I entered the interesting valley of Aosta. The whole valley, some fifty miles in length, is inhabited by miserable looking people, nearly one half of them being afflicted with goitre and cretinism. They looked more idiotic and disgusting than any I have ever seen, and it was really painful to behold such miserable specimens of humanity dwelling amid the grandest scenes of nature. Immediately after arriving in the town of Aosta, situated at the upper end of the valley, I began, alone, the ascent of the Great St. Bernard. It was just noon, and the clouds on the mountains indicated rain. The distance from Aosta to the monastery or hospice of St. Bernard, is about twenty English miles.

"At one o'clock it commenced raining very hard, and to gain shelter I went into a rude hut; but it was filled with so many of those idiotic cretins, lying down on the earthy floor with the dogs and other animals, that I was glad to leave them as soon as the storm had abated in some degree. I walked rapidly for three hours, when I met a traveler and his guide descending the mountain. I asked him in Italian the distance to the hospice, and he undertook to answer me in French, but the words did not seem to flow very fluently, so I said quickly, observing then that he was an Englishman: 'Try some other language, if you please, sir!' He replied instantly in his vernacular: 'You have a damned long walk before you, and you'll have to hurry to get to the top before night!' Thanking him, we shook hands and hurried on, he downward and I upward. About eight miles from the summit, I was directed into the wrong path by an ignorant boy who was tending sheep, and went a mile out of the course, towards Mont Blanc, before I discovered my mistake. I hurried back into the right path again, and soon overtook another boy ascending the mountain, who asked me if he might accompany me as he was alone, to which I of course answered, yes; but when we began to enter the thick clouds that covered the mountains, he became alarmed, and said he would go no farther. I tried to encourage him by saying we had only five miles more to climb, but, turning quickly, he ran down the path and was soon out of sight.

"After a long and most toilsome ascent, spurred on as I was by the storm and the approach of night, I saw at last through the clouds a little house, which I supposed might be a part of the monastery, but it turned out to be a house of refuge, erected by the monks to take in travelers in extreme cases or extraordinary danger. The man who was staying there, told me the monastery was a mile and a half further, and thinking therefore that I could soon reach it, I started out again, although darkness was approaching. In a short time the storm began in good earnest, and the cold winds blew with the greatest fury. It grew dark very suddenly and I lost sight of the poles which are placed along the path to guide the traveler. I then ran on still higher, hoping to find them again, but without success. The rain and snow fell thick, and although I think I am tolerably courageous, I began to be alarmed, for it was impossible to know in what direction I was going. I could hear the waterfalls clashing and roaring down the mountain hollows on each side of me; in the gloom, the foam and leaping waters resembled streaming fires. I thought of turning back to find the little house of refuge again, but it seemed quite as dangerous and uncertain as to go forward. After the fatigue I had undergone since noon, it would have been dangerous to be obliged to stay out all night in the driving storm, which was every minute increasing in coldness and intensity.

"I stopped and shouted aloud, hoping I might be somewhere near the monastery, but no answer came—no noise except the storm and the roar of the waterfalls. I climbed up the rocks nearly a quarter of a mile higher, and shouted again. I listened with anxiety for two or three minutes, but hearing no response, I concluded to find a shelter for the night under a ledge of rocks. While looking around me, I fancied I heard in the distance a noise like the trampling of hoofs over the rocks, and thinking travelers might be near, I called aloud for the third time. After waiting a moment, a voice came ringing on my ears through the clouds, like one from Heaven in response to my own. My heart beat quickly; I hurried in the direction from which the sound came, and to my joy found two men— servants of the monastery—who were driving their mules into shelter. Never in my whole life was I more glad to hear the voice of man. These men conducted me to the monastery, one-fourth of a mile higher, built by the side of a lake at the summit of the pass, while on each side, the mountains, forever covered with snow, tower some thousands of feet higher.

"Two or three of the noble St. Bernard dogs barked a welcome as we approached, which brought a young monk to the door. I addressed him in German, but to my surprise he answered in broken English. He took me into a warm room and gave me a suit of clothes, such as are worn by the monks, for my dress, as well as my package of papers, were completely saturated with rain. I sat down to supper in company with all the monks of the Hospice, I in my monk's robe looking like one of the holy order. You would have laughed to have seen me in their costume. Indeed, I felt almost satisfied to turn monk, as everything seemed so comfortable in the warm supper room, with its blazing wood fire, while outside raged the storm still more violently. But when I thought of their voluntary banishment from the world, up in that high pass of the Alps, and that the affection of woman never gladdened their hearts, I was ready to renounce my monk's dress next morning, without reluctance.

"In the address book of the monastery, I found Longfellow's 'Excelsior' written on a piece of paper and signed 'America'. You remember the stanza:

'At break of day, as heavenward,
　The pious monks of St. Bernard
　Uttered the oft-repeated prayer,
　A voice cried through the startled air:
　　　　　　　　　Excelsior!'

"It seemed to add a tenfold interest to the poem, to read it on old St. Bernard. In the morning I visited the house where are kept the bodies of the travelers, who perish in crossing the mountain. It is filled with corpses, ranged in rows, and looking like mummies, for the cold is so intense that they will keep for years without decaying, and are often recognized and removed by their friends.

"Of my descent to Martigny, my walk down the Rhône, and along the shores of Lake Leman, my visit to the prison of Chillon and other wanderings across Switzerland, my pleasure in seeing the old river Rhine again, and my return to Heidelberg at night, with the bright moon shining on the Neckar and the old ruined castle, I can now say no more, nor is it necessary, for are not all these things 'written in my book of Chronicles,' to be seen by you when we meet again in Paris?

"Ever yours, Frank."

Dec. 16.—I took a walk lately to the tower of Galileo. In company with three friends, I left Florence by the *Porta Romana,* and ascended the *Poggie Imperiale.* This beautiful avenue, a mile and a quarter in length, leading up a gradual ascent to a villa of the Grand Duke, is bordered with splendid cypresses and evergreen oaks, and the grass banks are always fresh and green, so that even in winter it calls up a remembrance of summer. In fact, winter does not wear the scowl here that he has at home; he is robed rather in a threadbare garment of autumn, and it is only high up on the mountain tops, out of the reach of his enemy, the sun, that he dares to throw it off, and bluster about with his storms and scatter down his snowflakes. The roses still bud and bloom in the hedges, the emerald of the meadows is not a whit paler, the sun looks down lovingly as yet, and there are only the white helmets of some of the Appenines, with the leafless mulberries and vines, to tell us that we have changed seasons.

A quarter of an hour's walk, part of it by a path through an olive orchard, brought us to the top of a hill, which was surmounted by a square, broken, ivied tower, forming part of a storehouse for the produce of the estate. We entered, saluted by a dog, and passing through a courtyard, in which stood two or three carts full of brown olives, found our way to the rickety staircase. I spared my sentiment in going up, thinking the steps might have been renewed since Galileo's time, but the glorious landscape which opened around us when we reached the top, time could not change, and I gazed upon it with interest and emotion, as my eye took in those forms which had once been mirrored in the philosopher's. Let me endeavor to describe the features of the scene.

Fancy yourself lifted to the summit of a high hill, whose base slopes down to the valley of the Arno, and looking northward. Behind you is a confusion of hill and valley, growing gradually dimmer away to the horizon. Before and below you is a vale, with Florence and her great domes and towers in its lap, and across its breadth of five miles the mountain of Fiesole. To the west it stretches away unbroken for twenty miles, covered thickly with white villas — like a meadow of daisies, magnified. A few miles to the east the plain is rounded with mountains, between whose interlocking bases we can see the brown current of the Arno. Some of their peaks, as well as the mountain of Vallombrosa, along the eastern sky, are tipped with snow. Imagine the air filled with a thick blue mist, like a semi-transparent veil, which softens everything into dreamy indistinctness, the sunshine falling slantingly through this in spots, touching the landscape here and there as with a sudden blaze of fire, and you will complete the picture. Does it not repay your mental flight across the Atlantic?

One evening, on coming out of the café, the moon was shining so brightly and clearly, that I involuntarily bent my steps towards the river; I walked along the *Lung' Arno,* enjoying the heavenly moonlight—"the night of cloudless climes and starry skies!" A purer silver light never kissed the brow of Endymion. The brown Arno took into his breast "the redundant glory," and rolled down his pebbly bed with a more musical ripple; opposite stretched the long mass of buildings—the deep arches that rose from the water were filled with black shadow, and the irregular fronts of the houses touched with a mellow glow. The arches of the upper bridge were in shadow, cutting their dark outline on the silvery sweep of the Appenines, far up the stream. A veil of luminous gray covered the hill of San Miniato, with its towers and cypress groves, and there was a crystal depth in the atmosphere, as if it shone with its own light. The whole scene affected me as something too glorious to be real—painful from the very intensity of its beauty. Three moons ago, at the foot of Vallombrosa, I saw the Appenines flooded with the same silvery gush, and thought also, then, that I had seen the same moon amid far dearer scenes, but never before the same dreamy and sublime glory showered down from her pale orb. Some solitary lights were burning along the river, and occasionally a few Italians passed by, wrapped in their mantles. I went home to the Piazza del Granduca as the light, pouring into the square from behind the old palace, fell over the fountain of Neptune and sheathed in silver the back of the colossal god.

Whoever looks on the valley of the Arno from San Miniato, and observes the Appenine range, of which Fiesole is one, bounding it on the north, will immediately notice to the northwest a double peak rising high above all the others. The bare, brown forehead of this, known by the name of *Monte Morello,* seemed so provokingly to challenge an ascent, that we determined to try it. So we started early, the day before yesterday, from the Porta San Gallo, with nothing but the frosty grass and fresh air to remind us of the middle of December. Leaving the Prato road, at the base of the mountain, we passed Careggi, a favorite farm of Lorenzo the Magnificent, and entered a narrow glen where a little brook was brawling down its rocky channel. Here and there stood a rustic mill, near which women were busy spreading their washed clothes on the grass. Following the footpath, we ascended a long eminence to a chapel where some boys were amusing themselves with a common country game. They have a small wheel, around which they wind a rope, and, running a little distance to increase the velocity, let it off with a sudden jerk. On a level road it can be thrown upwards of a quarter of a mile.

From the chapel, a gradual ascent along the ridge of a hill brought us to the foot of the peak, which rose high before us, covered with bare rocks and stunted oaks. The wind blew coldly from a snowy range to the north, as we commenced ascending with a good will. A few shepherds were leading their flocks along the sides, to browse on the grass and withered bushes, and we started up a large hare occasionally from his leafy covert. The ascent was very toilsome; I was obliged to stop frequently on account of the painful throbbing of my heart, which made it difficult to breathe. When the summit was gained, we lay down on the leeward side to recover ourselves.

We looked on the great valley of the Arno, perhaps twenty-five miles long, and five or six broad, lying like a long elliptical basin sunk among the hills. I can liken it to nothing but a vast sea; for a dense, blue mist covered the level surface, through which the domes of Florence rose up like a craggy island, while the thousands of scattered villas resembled ships, with spread sails, afloat on its surface. The sharp, cutting wind soon drove us down, with a few hundred bounds, to the path again. Three more hungry mortals did not dine at the *Cacciatore* that day.

The chapel of the Medici, which we visited, is of wonderful beauty. The walls are entirely encrusted with *pietra dura* and the most precious kinds of marble. The ceiling is covered with gorgeous frescoes by Benevenuto, a modern painter. Around the sides, in magnificent sarcophagi of marble and jasper, repose the ashes of a few Cosmos and Ferdinands. I asked the sacristan for the tomb of Lorenzo the Magnificent. "Oh!" said he, "he lived during the republic—he has no tomb; these are only for Dukes!" I could not repress a sigh at the lavish waste of labor and treasure on this one princely chapel. They might have slumbered unnoted, like Lorenzo, if they had done as much for their country and Italy.

December 19.—It is with a heavy heart, that I sit down tonight to make my closing note in this lovely city and in the journal which has recorded my thoughts and impressions since leaving America. I should find it difficult to analyze my emotions, but I know that they oppress me painfully. So much rushes at once over the mind and heart—memories of what has passed through both, since I made the first note in its pages—alternations of hope and anxiety and aspiration, but never despondency—that it resembles in a manner, the closing of a life. I seem almost to have lived through the common term of a life in this short period. Much spiritual and mental experience has crowded into a short time the sensations of years. Painful though some of it has been, it was still welcome. Difficulty and toil give the soul strength to crush, in a loftier region, the passions which draw strength only from the earth. So long as we listen to the purer promptings within us, there is a Power invisible, though not unfelt, who protects us — amid the toil and tumult and soiling struggle, there is ever an eye that watches, ever a heart that overflows with Infinite and Almighty Love! Let us trust then in that Eternal Spirit, who pours out on us his warm and boundless blessings, through the channels of so many kindred human hearts!

Chapter XXXIX
WINTER TRAVELING AMONG THE APPENINES

Valley of the Arno, Dec. 22 — It is a glorious morning after our two days' walk, through rain and mud, among these stormy Appenines. The range of high peaks, among which is the celebrated monastery of Camaldoli, lie just before us, their summits dazzling with the new fallen snow. The clouds are breaking away, and a few rosy flushes announce the approach of the sun. It has rained during the night, and the fields are as green and fresh as on a morning in spring.

We left Florence on the 20th, while citizens and strangers were vainly striving to catch a glimpse of the Emperor of Russia. He is, from some cause, very shy of being seen, in his journeys from place to place, using the greatest art and diligence to prevent the time of his departure and arrival from being known. On taking leave of Powers, I found him expecting the Autocrat, as he had signified his intention of visiting his studio; it was a cause of patriotic pride to find that crowned heads know and appreciate the genius of our sculptor. The sky did not promise much, as we set out; when we had entered the Appenines and taken a last look of the lovely valley behind us, and the great dome of the city where we had spent four delightful months, it began to rain heavily. Determined to conquer the weather at the beginning, we kept on, although before many miles were passed, it became too penetrating to be agreeable. The mountains grew nearly black under the shadow of the clouds, and the storms swept drearily down their passes and passages, till the scenery looked more like the Hartz than Italy. We were obliged to stop at Ponte Sieve and dry our saturated garments; when, as the rain slackened somewhat, we rounded the foot of the mountain of Vallombrosa, above the swollen and noisy Arno, to the little village of Cucina.

We entered the only inn in the place, followed by a crowd of wondering boys, for two such travelers had probably never been seen there. They made a blazing fire for us in the broad chimney, and after the police of the place satisfied themselves that we were not dangerous characters, they asked many questions about our country. I excited the sympathy of the women greatly on our behalf by informing them we had three thousand miles of sea between us and our homes. They then exclaimed in the most sympathising tones: "Poverini! so far to go!—three thousand miles of water!"

The next morning we followed the right bank of the Arno. At Incisa, a large town on the river, the narrow pass broadens into a large and fertile plain, bordered on the north by the mountains. The snow storms were sweeping around their summits the whole day, and I then thought of the desolate situation of the good monks who had so hospitably entertained us three months before. It was weary traveling; but at Levane our fatigues were soon forgotten. Two or three peasants were sitting last night beside the blazing fire, and we were amused to hear them talking about us. I overheard one asking another to converse with us awhile. "Why should I speak to them?" said he; "they are not of our profession—we are swineherds, and they do not care to talk with us." However, his curiosity prevailed at last, and we had a long conversation together. It seemed difficult for them to comprehend how there could be so much water to cross, without any land, before reaching our country. Finding we were going to Rome, I overheard one remark we were pilgrims, which seemed to be the general supposition, as there are few foot-travelers in Italy. The people said to one another as we passed along the road: — "They are making a journey of penance!" These peasants expressed themselves very well for persons of their station, but they were remarkably ignorant of everything beyond their own olive orchards and vine fields.

Perugia, Dec. 24.—On leaving Levane, the morning gave a promise, and the sun winked at us once or twice through the broken clouds, with a watery eye; but our cup was not yet full.

After crossing one or two shoulders of the range of hills, we descended to the great upland plain of Central Italy, watered by the sources of the Arno and the Tiber. The scenery is of a remarkable character. The hills appear to have been washed and swept by some mighty flood. They are worn into every shape—pyramids, castles, towers—standing desolate and brown, in long ranges, like the ruins of mountains. The plain is scarred with deep gulleys, adding to the look of decay which accords so well with the Cyclopean relics of the country.

A storm of hail which rolled away before us, disclosed the city of Arezzo, on a hill at the other end of the plain, its heavy cathedral crowning the pyramidal mass of buildings. Our first care was to find a good trattoria, for hunger spoke louder than sentiment, and then we sought the house where Petrarch was born. A young priest showed it to us on the summit of the hill. It has not been changed since he lived in it.

On leaving Florence, we determined to pursue the same plan as in Germany, of stopping at the inns frequented by the common people. They treated us here, as elsewhere, with great kindness and sympathy, and we were freed from the outrageous impositions practised at the greater hotels. They always built a large fire to dry us, after our day's walk in the rain, and placing chairs in the hearth, which was raised several feet above the floor, stationed us there, like the giants Gog and Magog, while the children, assembled below, gazed up in open-mouthed wonder at our elevated greatness. They even invited us to share their simple meals with them, and it was amusing to hear their good-hearted exclamations of pity at finding we were so far from home. We slept in the great beds (for the most of the Italian beds are calculated for a man, wife, and four children!) without fear of being assassinated, and only met with banditti in dreams.

This is a very unfavorable time of the year for foot-traveling. We were obliged to wait three or four weeks in Florence for a remittance from America, which not only prevented our leaving as soon as was desirable, but, by the additional expense of living, left us much smaller means than we required. However, through the kindness of a generous countryman, who unhesitatingly loaned us a considerable sum, we were enabled to start with thirty dollars each, which, with care and economy, will be quite sufficient to take us to Paris, by way of Rome and Naples, if these storms do not prevent us from walking. Greece and the Orient, which I so ardently hoped to visit, are now out of the question. We walked till noon today, over the Val di Chiana to Camuscia, the last post-station in the Tuscan dominions. On a mountain near it is the city of Cortona, still enclosed within its Cyclopean walls, built long before the foundation of Rome.

Here our patience gave way, melted down by the unremitting rains, and while eating dinner we made a bargain for a vehicle to bring us to this city. We gave a little more than half of what the vetturino demanded, which was still an exorbitant price—two scudi each for a ride of thirty miles.

In a short time we were called to take our seats; I beheld with consternation a rickety, uncovered, two-wheeled vehicle, to which a single lean horse was attached. "What!" said I; "is that the carriage you promised?" "You bargained for a *calesino*," said he, "and there it is!" adding, moreover, that there was nothing else in the place. So we clambered up, thrust our feet among the hay, and the machine rolled off with a kind of saw-mill motion, at the rate of five miles an hour.

Soon after, in ascending the mountain of the Spelunca, a sheet of blue water was revealed below us—the Lake of Thrasymene! From the eminence around which we drove, we looked on the whole of its broad surface and the mountains which encompass it. It is a magnificent sheet of water, in size and shape somewhat like New York Bay, but the heights around it are far higher than the hills of Jersey or Staten Island. Three beautiful islands lie in it, near the eastern shore.

While our *calesino* was stopped at the papal custom-house, I gazed on the memorable field below us. A crescent plain, between the mountain and the lake, was the arena where two mighty empires met in combat. The place seems marked by nature for the scene of some great event. I experienced a thrilling emotion, such as no battle plain has excited, since, when a schoolboy, I rambled over the field of Brandywine. I looked through, the long arcades of patriarchal olives, and tried to cover the field with the shadows of the Roman and Carthaginian myriads. I recalled the shock of meeting legions, the clash of swords and bucklers, and the waving standards amid the dust of battle, while stood on the mountain amphitheatre, trembling and invisible, the protecting deities of Rome.

"Far other scene is Thrasymene now"

We rode over the plain, passed through the dark old town of Passignano, built on a rocky point by the lake, and dashed along the shore. A dark, stormy sky bent over us, and the roused waves broke in foam on the rocks. The winds whistled among the bare oak boughs, and shook the olives till they twinkled all over. The vetturino whipped our old horse into a gallop, and we were borne on in unison with the scene, which would have answered for one of Hoffman's wildest stories.

Ascending a long hill, we took a last look in the dusk at Thrasymene, and continued our journey among the Appenines. The vetturino was to have changed horses at Magione, thirteen miles from Perugia, but there were none to be had, and our poor beast was obliged to perform the whole journey without rest or food. It grew very dark, and a storm, with thunder and lightning, swept among the hills. The clouds were of pitchy darkness, and we could see nothing beyond the road, except the lights of peasant cottages trembling through the gloom. Now and then a flash of lightning revealed the black masses of the mountains, on which the solid sky seemed to rest. The wind and cold rain swept wailing past us, as if an evil spirit were abroad on the darkness. Three hours of such nocturnal travel brought us here, wet and chilly, as well as our driver, but I pitied the poor horse more than him.

When we looked out the window, on awaking, the clustered house-tops of the city, and the summits of the mountains near were covered with snow. But on walking to the battlements we saw that the valleys below were green and untouched. Perugia, for its "pride of place," must endure the storms, while the humbler villages below escape them. As the rain continues, we have taken seats in a country diligence (stagecoach) for Foligno and shall depart in a few minutes.

Dec. 28. — We left Perugia in a close but covered vehicle, and descending the mountain, crossed the muddy and rapid Tiber in the valley below. All day we rode slowly among the hills; where the ascent was steep, two or four large oxen were hitched before the horses. I saw little of the scenery, for our Italian companions would not bear the windows open. Once, when we stopped, I got out and found we were in the region of snow, at the foot of a stormy peak, which towered sublimely above. At dusk, we entered Foligno, and were driven to the "Croce Bianca"— glad to be thirty miles further on our way to Rome.

After some discussion with a vetturino, who was to leave next morning, we made a contract with him for the remainder of the journey, for the rain, which fell in torrents, forbade all thought of pedestrianism. At five o'clock we rattled out of the gate, and drove by the waning moon and morning starlight, down the vale of the Clitumnus. As the dawn stole on, I watched eagerly the features of the scene. Instead of a narrow glen, as my fancy had pictured, we were in a valley, several miles broad, covered with rich orchards and fertile fields. A glorious range of mountains bordered it on the north, looking like Alps in their winter garments. A rosy flush stole over the snow, which kindled with the growing morn, till they shone like clouds that float in the sunrise. The Clitumnus, beside us, was the purest of streams. The heavy rains which had fallen, had not soiled in the least its limpid crystal.

When it grew light enough, I looked at our companions for the three days' journey. The two other inside seats were occupied by a tradesman of Trieste, with his wife and child; an old soldier, and a young dragoon going to visit his parents after seven years' absence, occupied the front part. Persons traveling together in a carriage are not long in becoming acquainted — close companionship soon breeds familiarity. Before night, I had made a fast friend of the young soldier, learned to bear the perverse humor of the child with as much patience as its father, and even drawn looks of grim kindness from the crusty old vetturino.

Our midday resting place was Spoleto. As there were two hours given us, we took a ramble through the city, visited the ruins of its Roman theatre and saw the gate erected to commemorate the victory gained here over Hannibal, which stopped his triumphal march towards Rome. A great part of the afternoon was spent in ascending among the passages of Monte Somma, the highest pass on the road between Ancona and Rome. Assisted by two yoke of oxen we slowly toiled up through the snow, the mountains on both sides covered with thickets of box and evergreen oaks, among whose leafy screens the banditti hide themselves. It is not considered dangerous at present, but as the dragoons who used to patrol this pass have been sent off to Bologna, to keep down the rebellion, the robbers will probably return to their old haunts again. We saw many suspicious looking coverts, where they might have hidden.

We slept at Terni and did not see the falls—not exactly on Wordsworth's principle of leaving Yarrow "unvisited," but because under the circumstances, it was impossible. The vetturino did not arrive there till after dark; he was to leave before dawn; the distance was five miles, and the roads very bad. Besides, we had seen falls quite as grand, which needed only a Byron to make them as renowned— we had been told that those of Tivoli, which we shall see, were equally fine. The Velino, which we crossed near Terni, was not a large stream—in short, we hunted as many reasons as we could find, why the falls need not be seen.

Leaving Terni before day, we drove up the long vale towards Narni. The roads were frozen hard; the ascent becoming more difficult, the vetturino was obliged to stop at a farm-house and get another pair of horses, with which, and a handsome young *contadino* as postillion, we reached Narni in a short time. In climbing the hill, we had a view of the whole valley of Terni, shut in on all sides by snow-crested Appenines, and threaded by the Nar, whose waters flow "with many windings, through the vale!"

At Otricoli, while dinner was being prepared, I walked around the crumbling battlements to look down into the valley and trace the far windings of the Tiber. In rambling through the crooked streets, we saw everywhere the remains of the splendor which this place boasted in the days of Rome. Fragments of fluted pillars stood here and there in the streets; large blocks of marble covered with sculpture and inscriptions were built into the houses, defaced statues were used as door-ornaments, and the stepping stone to our rude inn, worn everyday by the feet of grooms and vetturini, contained some letters of an inscription which may have recorded the glory of an emperor.

Traveling with a vetturino, is unquestionably the pleasantest way of seeing Italy. The easy rate of the journey allows time for becoming well acquainted with the country, and the tourist is freed from the annoyance of quarrelling with cheating landlords. A translation of our written contract, will best explain this mode of traveling

CARRIAGE FOR ROME

Our contract is, to be conducted to Rome for the sum of twenty francs each, say 20f. and the *buona mano,* if we are well served. We must have from the vetturino, Giuseppe Nerpiti, supper each night, a free chamber with two beds, and fire, until we shall arrive at Rome.

I, Geronymo Sartarelli, steward of the Inn of the White Cross, at Foligno, in testimony of the above contract.

Beyond Otricoli, we passed through some relics of an age anterior to Rome. A few soiled masses of masonry, black with age, stood along the brow of the mountain, on whose extremity were the ruins of a castle of the Middle Ages. We crossed the Tiber on a bridge built by Augustus Cæsar, and reached Borghetto as the sun was gilding with its last rays the ruined citadel above. As the carriage with its four horse was toiling slowly up the hill, we got out and walked before, to gaze on the green meadows of the Tiber.

On descending from Narni, I noticed a high, prominent mountain, whose ridgy back, somewhat like the profile of a face, reminded me of the Traunstein, in Upper Austria. As we approached, its form gradually changed, until it stood on the Campagna

"Like a long-swept wave about to break,
     That on the curl hangs pausing"

and by that token of a great bard, I recognized Monte Soracte. The dragoon took us by the arms, and away we scampered over the Campagna, with one of the loveliest sunsets before us, that ever painted itself on my retina. I cannot portray in words the glory that flooded the whole western heaven. It was like a sea of melted ruby, amethyst and topaz — deep, dazzling and of crystal transparency. The color changed in tone every few minutes, till in half an hour it sank away before the twilight to a belt of deep orange along the west.

We left Civita Castellana before daylight. The sky was red with dawn as we approached Nepi, and we got out to walk, in the clear, frosty air. A magnificent Roman aqueduct, part of it a double row of arches, still supplies the town with water. There is a deep ravine, appearing as if rent in the ground by some convulsion, on the eastern side of the city. A clear stream that steals through the arches of the aqueduct, falls in a cascade of sixty feet down into the chasm, sending up constant wreaths of spray through the evergreen foliage that clothes the rocks. In walking over the desolate Campagna, we saw many deep chambers dug in the earth, used by the charcoal burners; the air was filled with sulphureous exhalations, very offensive to the smell, which rose from the ground in many places.

Miles and miles of the dreary waste, covered only with flocks of grazing sheep, were passed,—and about noon we reached Baccano, a small post station, twenty miles from Rome. A long hill rose before us, and we sprang out of the carriage and ran ahead, to see Rome from its summit. As we approached the top, the Campagna spread far before and around us, level and blue as an ocean. I climbed up a high bank by the roadside, and the whole scene came in view.

Perhaps eighteen miles distant rose the dome of St. Peter's, near the horizon—a small spot on the vast plain. Beyond it and further east, were the mountains of Albano — on our left Soracte and the Appenines, and a blue line along the west betrayed the Mediterranean. There was nothing peculiarly beautiful or sublime in the landscape, but few other scenes on earth combine in one glance such a myriad of mighty associations, or bewilder the mind with such a crowd of confused emotions.

As we approached Rome, the dragoon, with whom we had been walking all day, became anxious and impatient. He had not heard from his parents for a long time, and knew not if they were living. His desire to be at the end of his journey finally became so great, that he hailed a peasant who was driving by in a light vehicle, left our slow carriage and went out of sight in a gallop.

As we descended to the Tiber in the desk of evening, the domes and spires of Rome came gradually into view, St. Peter's standing like a mountain in the midst of them. Crossing the yellow river by the Ponte Molle, two miles of road, straight as an arrow, lay before us, with the light of the *Porta del Popolo* at the end. I felt strangely excited as the old vehicle rumbled through the arch, and we entered a square with fountains and an obelisk of Egyptian granite in the centre. Delivering up our passports, we waited until the necessary examinations were made, and then went forward. Three streets branch out from the square, the middle one of which, leading directly to the Capitol, is the Corso, the Roman Broadway. Our vetturino chose that to the left, the Via della Scrofa, leading off towards the bridge of St. Angelo. I looked out the windows as we drove along, but saw nothing except butcher-shops, grocer-stores, etc.—horrible objects for a sentimental traveler!

Being emptied out on the pavement at last, our first care was to find rooms; after searching through many streets, with a coarse old Italian who spoke like an angel, we arrived at a square where the music of a fountain was heard through the dusk and an obelisk cut out some of the starlight. At the other end I saw a portico through the darkness, and my heart gave a breathless bound on recognizing the *Pantheon* — the matchless temple of Ancient Rome! And now while I am writing, I hear the gush of the fountain — and if I step to the window, I see the time-worn but still glorious edifice.

On returning for our baggage, We met the funeral procession of the Princess Altieri. Priests dressed in white and gold carried flaming torches, and the coffin, covered with a magnificent golden pall, was borne in a splendid hearse, guarded by four priests. As we were settling our account with the vetturino, who demanded much more *buona mano* than we were willing to give, the young dragoon returned. He was greatly agitated. "I have been at home!" said he, in a voice trembling with emotion. I was about to ask him further concerning his family, but he kissed and embraced us warmly and hurriedly, saying he had only come to say "addio!" and to leave us.

I stop writing to ramble through Rome. This city of all cities to me — this dream of my boyhood — giant, god-like, fallen Rome — is around me, and I revel in a glow of anticipation and exciting thought that seems to change my whole state of being.

Chapter XL
ROME

Dec. 29. — One day's walk through Rome — how shall I describe it? The Capitol, the Forum, St. Peter's, the Coliseum — what few hours' ramble ever took in places so hallowed by poetry, history and art? It was a golden leaf in my calendar of life. In thinking over it now, and drawing out the threads of recollection from the varied woof of thought I have woven today, I almost wonder how I dared so much at once; but within reach of them all, how was it possible to wait? Let me give a sketch of our day's ramble.

Hearing that it was better to visit the ruins by evening or moonlight, (alas! there is no moon now) we started out to hunt St. Peter's. Going in the direction of the Corso, we passed the ruined front of the magnificent Temple of Antoninus, now used as the Papal Custom House. We turned to the right on entering the Corso, expecting to have a view of the city from the hill at its southern end. It is a magnificent street, lined with palaces and splendid edifices of every kind, and always filled with crowds of carriages and people. On leaving it, however, we became bewildered among the narrow streets — passed through a market of vegetables, crowded with beggars and contadini—threaded many by-ways between dark old buildings— saw one or two antique fountains and many modern churches, and finally arrived at a hill.

We ascended many steps, and then descending a little towards the other side, saw suddenly below us the *Roman Forum!* I knew it at once—and those three Corinthian columns that stood near us— what could they be but the remains of the temple of Jupiter Stator? We stood on the Capitoline Hill; at the foot was the Arch of Septimus Severus, brown with age and shattered; near it stood the majestic front of the Temple of Fortune, its pillars of polished granite glistening in the sun, as if they had been erected yesterday, while on the left the rank grass was waving from the arches and mighty walls of the Palace of the Cæsars! In front, ruin upon ruin lined the way for half a mile, where the Coliseum towered grandly through the blue morning mist, at the base of the Esquiline Hill!

Good heavens, what a scene! Grandeur, such as the world never saw, once rose through that blue atmosphere; splendor inconceivable, the spoils of a world, the triumphs of a thousand armies had passed over that earth; minds which for ages moved the ancient world had thought there, and words of power and glory, from the lips of immortal men, had been syllabled on that hallowed air. To call back all this on the very spot, while the wreck of what once was, rose mouldering and desolate around, aroused a sublimity of thought and feeling too powerful for words.

Returning at hazard through the streets, we came suddenly upon the column of Trajan, standing in an excavated square below the level of the city, amid a number of broken granite columns, which formed part of the Forum dedicated to him by Rome, after the conquest of Dacia. The column is one hundred and thirty-two feet high, and entirely covered with bas-reliefs representing his victories, winding about it in a spiral line to the top. The number of figures is computed at two thousand five hundred, and they were of such excellence that Raphael used many of them for his models. They are now much defaced, and the column is surmounted by a statue of a saint. The inscription on the pedestal has been erased, and the name of Sixtus V. substituted. Nothing can exceed the vanity of the old popes in thus mutilating the finest monuments of ancient art. You cannot look upon any relic of antiquity in Rome, but your eyes are assailed by the words "PONTIFEX MAXIMUS," in staring modern letters. Even the magnificent bronzes of the Pantheon were stripped to make the baldachin under the dome of St. Peter's.

Finding our way back again, we took a fresh start, happily in the right direction, and after walking some time, came out on the Tiber, at the Bridge of St. Angelo. The river rolled below in his muddy glory, and in front, on the opposite bank, stood "the pile which Hadrian reared on high" — now, the Castle of St. Angelo. Knowing that St. Peter's was to be seen from this bridge, I looked about in search of it. There was only one dome in sight, large and of beautiful proportions. I said at once, "surely that cannot be St. Peter's!" On looking again, however, I saw the top of a massive range of building near it, which corresponded so nearly with the pictures of the Vatican, that I was unwillingly forced to believe the mighty dome was really before me. I recognized it as one of those we saw from the Capitol, but it appeared so much smaller when viewed from a greater distance, that I was quite deceived. On considering we were still three fourths of a mile from it, and that we could see its minutest parts distinctly, the illusion was explained.

Going directly down the *Borgo Vecchio,* towards it, it seemed a
quite a long time before we arrived at the square of St. Peter's; when
at length we stood in front with the majestic colonnade sweeping
around — the fountains on each side sending up their showers of
silvery spray—the mighty obelisk of Egyptian granite piercing the
sky—and beyond, the great front and dome of the Cathedral, I confessed my unmingled admiration. It recalled to my mind the grandeur of ancient Rome, and mighty as her edifices must have been,
I doubt if there were many views more overpowering than this. The
façade of St. Peter's seemed close to us, but it was a third of a mile
distant, and the people ascending the steps dwindled to pygmies.

I passed the obelisk, went up the long ascent, crossed the portico,
pushed aside the heavy leathern curtain at the entrance, and stood
in the great nave. I need not describe my feelings at the sight, but I
will tell the dimensions, and you may then fancy what they were.
Before me was a marble plain six hundred feet long, and under the
cross four hundred and seventeen feet wide! One hundred and fifty
feet above, sprang a glorious arch, dazzling with inlaid gold, and in
the centre of the cross there were four hundred feet of air between
me and the top of the dome! The sunbeam, stealing through the lofty
window at one end of the transept, made a bar of light on the blue
air, hazy with incense, one-tenth of a mile long, before it fell on the
mosaics and gilded shrines of the other extremity. The grand cupola
alone, including lantern and cross, is two hundred and eighty-five
feet high, or sixty feet higher than the Bunker Hill Monument, and
the four immense pillars on which it rests are each one hundred and
thirty-seven feet in circumference! It seems as if human art had
outdone itself in producing this temple — the grandest which the
world ever erected for the worship of the Living God! The awe felt
in looking up at the giant arch of marble and gold, did not humble
me; on the contrary, I felt exalted, ennobled—beings in the form I
wore planned the glorious edifice, and it seemed that in godlike
power and perseverance, they were indeed but "a little lower than

the angels!" I felt that, although fallen, my race was still mighty and immortal.

The Vatican is only open twice a week, on days which are not *festas;* most fortunately, today happened to be one of these, and we took a run through its endless halls. The extent and magnificence of the gallery of sculpture is perfectly amazing. The halls, which are filled to overflowing with the finest works of ancient art, would, if placed side by side, make a row more than two miles in length! You enter at once into a hall of marble, with a magnificent arched ceiling, a third of a mile long; the sides are covered for a great distance with inscriptions of every kind, divided into compartments according to the era of the empire to which they refer. One which I examined, appeared to be a kind of index of the roads in Italy, with the towns on them; and we could decipher on that time-worn block, the very route I had followed from Florence hither.

Then came the statues, and here I am bewildered, how to describe them. Hundreds upon hundreds of figures — statues of citizens, generals, emperors and gods—fauns, satyrs and nymphs—children, cupids and tritons—in fact, the store seemed inexhaustible. Many of them, too, were forms of matchless beauty; there were Venuses and nymphs, born of the loftiest dreams of grace; fauns on whose faces shone the very soul of humor, and heroes and divinities with an air of majesty worthy the "land of lost gods and godlike men!"

I am lost in astonishment at the perfection of art attained by the Greeks and Romans. There is scarcely a form of beauty, "has ever met my eye, which is not to be found in this gallery." I should almost despair of such another blaze of glory on the world, were it not my devout belief that what has been done may be done again, and had I not faith that the dawn in which we live will bring another day equally glorious. And why should not America, with the experience and added wisdom which three thousand years have slowly yielded to the old world, joined to the giant energy of her youth and freedom, re-bestow on the world the divine creations of art?

Let Powers answer!

But let us step on to the hemicycle of the Belvidere, and view some works greater than any we have yet seen, or even imagined. The adjoining gallery is filled with masterpieces of sculpture, but we will keep our eyes unwearied and merely glance along the rows. At length we reach a circular court with a fountain flinging up its waters in the centre. Before us is an open cabinet; there is a beautiful, manly form within, but you would not for an instant take it for the Apollo. By the Gorgon head it holds aloft, we recognize Canova's Perseus—he has copied the form and attitude of the Apollo, but he could not breathe into it the same warming fire. It seemed to me particularly lifeless, and I greatly preferred his Boxers, who stand on either side of it. One, who has drawn back in the attitude of striking, looks as if he could fell an ox with only a single blow of his powerful arm. The other is a more lithe and agile figure, and there is a quick fire in his countenance which might overbalance the massive strength of his opponent.

Another cabinet—this is the far-famed Antinous. A countenance of perfect Grecian beauty, with a form such as we would imagine for one of Homer's heroes. His features are in repose, and there is something in their calm, settled expression, strikingly like life.

Now we look on a scene of the deepest physical agony. Mark how every muscle of old Laocoon's body is distended to the utmost in the mighty struggle! What intensity of pain in the quivering, distorted features! Every nerve, which despair can call into action, is excited in one giant effort, and a scream of anguish seems just to have quivered on those marble lips. The serpents have rolled their strangling coils around father and sons, but terror has taken away the strength of the latter, and they make but feeble resistance. After looking with indifference on the many casts of this group, I was the more moved by the magnificent original. It deserves all the admiration that has been heaped upon it.

I absolutely trembled on approaching the cabinet of the Apollo.

I had built up in fancy a glorious ideal, drawn from all that bards have sung or artists have rhapsodized about its divine beauty. I feared disappointment—I dreaded to have my ideal displaced and my faith in the power of human genius overthrown by a form less than perfect. However, with a feeling of desperate excitement, I entered and looked upon it.

Now what shall I say of it? How to make you comprehend its immortal beauty? To what shall I liken its glorious perfection of form, or the fire that imbues the cold marble with the soul of a god? Not with sculpture, for it stands alone and above all other works of art—nor with men, for it has a majesty more than human. I gazed on it, lost in wonder and joy— joy that I could, at last, take into my mind a faultless ideal of godlike, exalted manhood. The figure appears actually to possess a spirit, and I looked on it, not as on a piece of marble, but a being of loftier mould, and half expected to see him step forward when the arrow had reached its mark. I would give worlds to feel one moment the sculptor's mental triumph when his work was completed; that one exulting thrill must have repaid him for every ill he might have suffered on earth! With what divine inspiration has he wrought its faultless lines! There is a spirit in every limb which mere toil could not have given. It must have been caught in those lofty moments:

> "When each conception was a heavenly guest—
> A ray of immortality—and stood
> Star-like, around, until they gathered to a god?"

We ran through a series of halls, roofed with golden stars on a deep blue, midnight sky, and filled with porphyry vases, black marble gods, and mummies. Some of the statues shone with the matchless polish they had received from a Theban artisan before Athens was founded, and are, apparently, as fresh and perfect as when looked upon by the vassals of Sesostris. Notwithstanding their stiff, rough-hewn limbs, there were some figures of great beauty, and they gave me a much higher idea of Egyptian sculpture. In an adjoining hall, containing colossal busts of the gods, is a vase forty-one feet in circumference, of one solid block of red porphyry.

The "Transfiguration" is truly called the first picture in the world. The same glow of inspiration which created the Belvidere, must have been required to paint the Saviour's aerial form. The three figures hover above the earth in a blaze of glory, seemingly independent of all material laws. The terrified Apostles on the mount, and the wondering group below, correspond in the grandeur of their expression to the awe and majesty of the scene. The only blemish in the sublime perfection of the picture is the introduction of the two small figures on the left hand; who, incidentally, were Cardinals, inserted there by command. Some travelers say the color is all lost, but I was agreeably surprised to find it well preserved. It is, undoubtedly, somewhat imperfect in this respect, as Raphael died before it was entirely finished; but "take it all in all," you may search the world in vain to find its equal.

January 1, 1846. — New Year's Day in the Eternal City! It will be something to say in after years, that I have seen one year open in Rome—that while my distant friends were making up for the winter without, with good cheer around the merry board, I have walked in sunshine by the ruins of the Coliseum, watched the orange groves gleaming with golden fruitage in the Farnese gardens, trodden the daisied meadow around the sepulchre of Cams Cestius, and mused by the graves of Shelley, Keats and Salvator Rosa! The Palace of the Cæsars looked even more mournful in the pale, slant sunshine, and the yellow Tiber, as he flowed through the "marble wilderness," seemed sullenly counting up the long centuries during which degenerate slaves have trodden his banks. A leaden-colored haze clothed the seven hills, and heavy silence reigned among the ruins, for all work was prohibited, and the people were gathered in their churches.

Rome never appeared so desolate and melancholy as today.

In the morning I climbed the Quirinal Hill, now called Monte Cavallo, from the colossal statues of Castor and Pollux, with their steeds, supposed to be the work of Phidias and Praxiteles. They stand on each side of an obelisk of Egyptian granite, beside which a strong stream of water gushes up into a magnificent bronze basin, found in the old Forum. The statues, entirely browned by age, are considered masterpieces of Grecian art, and whether or not from the great masters, show in all their proportions, the conceptions of lofty genius.

We kept on our way between gardens filled with orange groves, whose glowing fruit reminded me of Mignon's beautiful reminiscence — "Im dunkeln Laub die Gold Orangen glühn!" Rome, although subject to cold winds from the Appenines, enjoys so mild a climate that oranges and palm trees grow in the open air, without protection. Daisies and violets bloom the whole winter, in the meadows of never-fading green. The basilic of the Lateran equals St. Peter's in splendor, though its size is much smaller. The walls are covered with gorgeous hangings of velvet embroidered with gold, and before the high altar, which glitters with precious stones, are four pillars of gilt bronze, said to be those which Augustus made of the spars of Egyptian vessels captured at the battle of Actium.

We descended the hill to the Coliseum, and passing under the Arch of Constantine, walked along the ancient triumphal way, at the foot of the Palatine Hill, which is entirely covered with the ruins of the Cæsars' Palace. A road, rounding its southern base towards the Tiber, brought us to the Temple of Vesta — a beautiful little relic which has been singularly spared by the devastations that have overthrown so many mightier fabrics. It is of circular form, surrounded by nineteen Corinthian columns, thirty-six feet in height; a clumsy tiled roof now takes the place of the elegant cornice which once gave the crowning charm to its perfect proportions. Close at hand are the remains of the temple of Fortuna Virilis, of which some

Ionic pillars alone are left, and the house of Cola di Rienzi—the last Tribune of Rome.

As we approached the walls, the sepulchre of Caius Cestius came in sight—a single solid pyramid, one hundred feet in height. The walls are built against it, and the light apex rises far above the massive gate beside it, which was erected by Belisarius. But there were other tombs at hand, for which we had more sympathy than that of the forgotten Roman, and we turned away to look for the graves of Shelley and Keats.

They lie in the Protestant burying ground, on the side of a mound that slopes gently up to the old wall of Rome, beside the pyramid of Cestius. The meadow around is still verdant and sown thick with daisies, and the soft green of the Italian pine mingles with the dark cypress above the slumberers. Huge aloes grow in the shade, and the sweet bay and bushes of rosemary make the air fresh and fragrant. There is a solemn, mournful beauty about the place, green and lonely as it is, beside the tottering walls of ancient Rome, that takes away the gloomy associations of death, and makes one wish to lie there, too, when his thread shall be spun to the end.

We found first the simple head-stone of Keats, alone, in the grassy meadow. Its inscription states that on his death-bed, in the bitterness of his heart, at the malice of his enemies, he desired these words to be written on his tombstone: *"Here lies one whose name was written in water."* Not far from him reposes the son of Shelley.

Shelley himself lies at the top of the shaded slope, in a lonely spot by the wall, surrounded by tall cypresses. A little hedge of rose and bay surrounds his grave, which bears the simple inscription— "PERCY BYSSHE SHELLEY; *Cor Cordium."*

> "Nothing of him that doth fade,
> But doth suffer a sea-change
> Into something rich and strange"

Glorious, but misguided Shelley! He sleeps calmly now in that silent nook, and the air around his grave is filled with sighs from those who mourn that the bright, erratic star should have been blotted out ere it reached the zenith of its mounting fame. I plucked a leaf from the fragrant bay, as a token of his fame, and a sprig of cypress from the bough that bent lowest over his grave; and passing between tombs shaded with blooming roses or covered with unwithered garlands, left the lovely spot.

Amid the excitement of continually changing scenes, I have forgotten to mention our first visit to the Coliseum. The day after our arrival we set out with two English friends, to see it by sunset. Passing by the glorious fountain of Trevi, we made our way to the Forum, and from thence took the road to the Coliseum, lined on both sides with the remains of splendid edifices. The grass-grown ruins of the Palace of the Cæsars stretched along on our right; on our left we passed in succession the granite front of the Temple of Antoninus and Faustina, the three grand arches of the Temple of Peace and the ruins of the Temple of Venus and Rome. We went under the ruined triumphal arch of Titus, with broken friezes representing the taking of Jerusalem, and the mighty walls of the Coliseum gradually rose before us. They grew in grandeur as we approached them, and when at length we stood in the centre, with the shattered arches and grassy walls rising above and beyond one another, far around us, the red light of sunset giving them a soft and melancholy beauty, I was fain to confess that another form of grandeur had entered my mind, of which I before knew not.

A majesty like that of nature clothes this wonderful edifice. Walls rise above walls, and arches above arches, from every side of the grand arena, like a sweep of craggy, pinnacled mountains around an oval lake. The two outer circles have almost entirely disappeared, torn away by the rapacious nobles of Rome, during the Middle Ages, to build their palaces. When entire, and filled with its hundred thousand spectators, it must have exceeded any pageant which the world can now produce. No wonder it was said:

"While stands the Coliseum, Rome shall stand;
When falls the Coliseum, Rome shall fall;
And when Rome falls, the world!"

—a prediction, which time has not verified. The world is now going forward, prouder than ever, and though we thank Rome for the legacy she has left us, we would not wish the dust of her ruin to encumber our path.

While standing in the arena, impressed with the spirit of the scene around me, which grew more spectral and melancholy as the dusk of evening began to fill up the broken arches, my eye was assailed by the shrines ranged around the space, doubtless to remove the pollution of paganism. In the middle stands also a cross, with an inscription, granting an absolution of forty days to all who kiss it. Now, although a simple cross in the centre might be very appropriate, both as a token of the heroic devotion of the martyr Telemachus and the triumph of a true religion over the barbarities of the Past, this congregation of shrines and bloody pictures mars very much the unity of association so necessary to the perfect enjoyment of any such scene.

We saw the flush of sunset fade behind the Capitoline Hill, and passed homeward by the Forum, as its shattered pillars were growing solemn and spectral through the twilight. I intend to visit them often again, and "meditate amongst decay." I begin already to grow attached to their lonely grandeur. A spirit, almost human, speaks from the desolation, and there is something in the voiceless oracles it utters, that strikes an answering chord in my own breast.

In the *Via de' Pontefici,* not far distant from the Borghese Palace, we saw the Mausoleum of Augustus. It is a large circular structure somewhat after the plan of that of Hadrian, but on a much smaller scale. The interior has been cleared out, seats erected around the walls, and the whole is now a summer theatre, for the amusement of the peasantry and tradesmen. What a commentary on greatness! Harlequin playing his pranks in the tomb of an Emperor, and the spot which nations approached with reverence, resounding with the mirth of beggars and degraded vassals!

I visited lately the studio of a young Philadelphian, Mr. W. B. Chambers, who has been here two or three years. In studying the legacies of art which the old masters left to their country, he has caught some of the genuine poetic inspiration which warmed them. But he is modest as relented, and appears to undervalue his works, so long as they do not reach his own mental ideal. He chooses principally subjects from the Italian peasant life, which abounds with picturesque and classic beauty. His pictures of the shepherd boy of the Albruzzi, and the brown maidens of the Campagna are fine illustrations of this class, and the fidelity with which he copies nature, is an earnest of his future success.

I was in the studio of Crawford, the sculptor; he has at present nothing finished in marble. There were many casts of his former works, which, judging from their appearance in plaster, must be of no common excellence—for the sculptor can only be justly judged in marble. I saw some fine bas-reliefs of classical subjects, and an exquisite group of Mercury and Psyche, but his masterpiece is undoubtedly the Orpheus. There is a spirit in this figure which astonished me. The face is full of the inspiration of the poet, softened by the lover's tenderness, and the whole fervor of his soul is expressed in the eagerness with which he gazes forward, on stepping past the sleeping Cerberus. Crawford is now engaged on the statue of an Indian girl, pierced by an arrow, and dying. It is a simple and touching figure, and will, I think, be one of his best works.

We are often amused with the groups in the square of the Pantheon, which we can see from our chamber-window. Shoemakers and tinkers carry on their business along the sunny side, while the venders of oranges and roasted chestnuts form a circle around the

Egyptian obelisk and fountain. Across the end of an opposite street we get a glimpse of the vegetable-market, and now and then the shrill voice of a pedlar makes its nasal solo audible above the confused chorus. As the beggars choose the Corso, St. Peter's, and the ruins for their principal haunts, we are now spared the hearing of their lamentations. Every time we go out we are assailed with them. *"Maladetta sia la vostra testa!"*—"Curses be upon your head!"—said one whom I passed without notice. The priests are, however, the greatest beggars. In every church are kept offering boxes, for the support of the church or some unknown institution; they even go from house to house, imploring support and assistance in the name of the Virgin and all the saints, while their bloated, sensual countenances and capacious frames tell of anything but fasts and privations. Once, as I was sitting among the ruins, I was suddenly startled by a loud, rattling sound; turning my head, I saw a figure clothed in white from head to foot, with only two small holes for the eyes. He held in his hand a money-box, on which was a figure of the Virgin, which he held close to my lips, that I might kiss it. This I declined doing, but dropped a baiocco into his box, when, making the sign of the cross, he silently disappeared.

Our present lodging (Trattoria del Sole) is a good specimen of an Italian inn for mechanics and common tradesmen. Passing through the front room, which is an eating-place for the common people—with a barrel of wine in the corner, and bladders of lard hanging among orange boughs in the window—we enter a dark courtyard filled with heavy carts, and noisy with the neighing of horses and singing of grooms, for the stables occupy part of the house. An open staircase, running all around this hollow square leads to the second, third, and fourth stories.

On the second story is the dining-room for the better class of travelers, who receive the same provisions as those below for double the price, and the additional privilege of giving the waiter two baiocchi. The sleeping apartments are in the fourth story, and are named according to the fancy of a former landlord, in mottos above each door. Thus, on arriving here, the Triester, with his wife and child, more fortunate than our first parents, took refuge in "Paradise," while we Americans were ushered into the "Chamber of Jove." We have occupied it ever since, and find a paul (ten cents) apiece cheap enough for a good bed and a window opening on the Pantheon.

Next to the Coliseum, the baths of Caracalla are the grandest remains of Rome. The building is a thousand feet square, and its massive walls look as if built by a race of giants. These Titan remains are covered with green shrubbery, and long, trailing vines sweep over the cornice, and wave down like tresses from architrave and arch. In some of its grand halls the mosaic pavement is yet entire. The excavations are still carried on; from the number of statues already found, this would seem to have been one of the most gorgeous edifices of the olden time.

I have been now several days loitering and sketching among the ruins, and I feel as if I could willingly wander for months beside these mournful relics, and draw inspiration from the lofty yet melancholy lore they teach. There is a spirit haunting them, real and undoubted. Every shattered column, every broken arch and mouldering wall, but calls up more vividly to mind the glory that has passed away. Each lonely pillar stands as proudly as if it still helped to bear up the front of a glorious temple, and the air seems scarcely to have ceased vibrating with the clarions that heralded a conqueror's triumph.

"—the old majestic trees
Stand ghost-like in the Cæsar's home,
    As if their conscious roots were set
In the old graves of giant Rome,
    And drew their sap all kingly yet!"

"There every mouldering stone beneath
  Is broken from some mighty thought,
And sculptures in the dust still breathe
  The fire with which their lines were wrought,
And sunder'd arch and plundered tomb
  Still thunder back the echo — 'Rome!' "

In Rome, there is no need that the imagination be excited to call up thrilling emotion or poetic reverie—they are forced on the mind by the sublime spirit of the scene. The roused bard might here pour forth his thoughts in the wildest climates, and I could believe he felt it all. This is like the Italy of my dreams—that golden realm whose image has been nearly chased away by the earthly reality. I expected to find a land of light and beauty, where every step crushed a flower or displaced a sunbeam—whose very air was poetic inspiration, and whose every scene filled the soul with romantic feelings. Nothing is left of my picture but the far-off mountains, robed in the sapphire veil of the Ausonian air, and these ruins, amid whose fallen glory sits triumphant the spirit of ancient song.

I have seen the flush of morn and eve rest on the Coliseum; I have seen the noon-day sky framed in its broken loopholes, like plates of polished sapphire; and last night, as the moon has grown into the zenith, I went to view it with her. Around the Forum all was silent and spectral—a sentinel challenged us at the Arch of Titus, under which we passed and along the Cæsar's wall, which lay in black shadow. Dead stillness brooded around the Coliseum; the pale, silvery lustre streamed through its arches, and over the grassy walls, giving them a look of shadowy grandeur which day could not bestow. The scene will remain fresh in my memory forever.

Chapter XLI
TIVOLI AND THE ROMAN CAMPAGNA

Jan. 9.—A few days ago we returned from an excursion to Tivoli, one of the loveliest spots in Italy. We left the Eternal City by the Gate of San Lorenzo, and twenty minutes walk brought us to the bare and bleak Campagna, which was spread around us for leagues in every direction. Here and there a shepherd-boy in his woolly coat, with his flock of browsing sheep, were the only objects that broke its desert-like monotony.

At the fourth mile we crossed the rapid Anio, the ancient Teverone, formerly the boundary between Latium and the Sabine dominions, and at the tenth, came upon some fragments of the old Tiburtine way, formed of large irregular blocks of basaltic lava. A short distance further, we saw across the plain the ruins of the bath of Agrippa, built by the side of the Tartarean Lake. The wind, blowing from it, bore us an overpowering smell of sulphur; the waters of the little river Solfatara, which crosses the road, are of a milky blue color, and carry those of the lake into the Anio. A fragment of the old bridge over it still remains.

Finding the water quite warm, we determined to have a bath. So we ran down the plain, which was covered with a thick coat of sulphur, and sounded hollow to our tread, till we reached a convenient place, where we threw off our clothes, and plunged in. The warm wave was delightful to the skin, but extremely offensive to the smell, and when we came out, our mouths and throats were filled with the stifling gas.

It was growing dark as we mounted through the narrow streets of Tivoli, but we endeavored to gain some sight of the renowned beauties of the spot, before going to rest. From a platform on a brow of the hill, we looked down into the passage, at whose bottom the Anio was roaring, and caught a sideward glance of the Cascatelles, sending up their spray amid the evergreen bushes that fringe the rocks. Above the deep glen that curves into the mountain, stands the beautiful temple of the Sybil—a building of the most perfect and graceful proportion. It crests the "rocky brow" like a fairy dwelling, and looks all the lovelier for the wild caverns below. Gazing downward from the bridge, one sees the waters of the Anio tumbling into the picturesque grotto of the Sirens; around a rugged corner, a cloud of white spray whirls up continually, while the boom of a cataract rumbles down the glen. All these we marked in the deepening dusk, and then hunted an albergo.

The shrill-voiced hostess gave us a good supper and clean beds; in return we diverted the people very much by the relation of our sulphur bath. We were awakened in the night by the wind shaking the very soul out of our loose casement. I fancied I heard torrents of rain dashing against the panes, and groaned in bitterness of spirit on thinking of a walk back to Rome in such weather. When morning came, we found it was only a hurricane of wind which was strong enough to tear off pieces of the old roofs. I saw some capuchins nearly overturned in crossing the square, by the wind seizing their white robes.

I had my fingers frozen and my eyes filled with sand, in trying to draw the Sybil's temple, and therefore left it to join my companions, who had gone down into the glen to see the great cascade. The Anio bursts out of a cavern in the mountain-side, and like a prisoner giddy with recovered liberty, reels over the edge of a precipice more than two hundred feet deep. The bottom is hid in a cloud of boiling spray, that shifts from side to side, and driven by the wind, sweeps whistling down the narrow pass. It stuns the ear with a perpetual boom, giving a dash of grandeur to the enrapturing beauty of the scene. I tried a footpath that appeared to lead down to the Cascatelles, but after advancing some distance along the side of an almost perpendicular precipice, I came to a corner that looked so dangerous, especially as the wind was nearly strong enough to carry me off, that it seemed safest to return. We made another vain attempt to get down, by creeping along the bed of a torrent, filled with briars. The Cascatelles are formed by that part of the Anio, which is used in the iron works, made out of the ruins of Mecænas' villa. They gush out from under the ancient arches, and tumble more than a hundred feet down the precipice, their white waters gleaming out from the dark and feathery foliage. Not far distant are the remains of the villa of Horace.

We took the road to Frascati, and walked for miles among cane-swamps and over plains covered with sheep. The people we saw, were most degraded and ferocious-looking, and there were many I would not willingly meet alone after nightfall. Indeed, it is still considered quite unsafe to venture without the walls of Rome, after dark. The women, with their yellow complexions, and the bright red blankets they wear folded around the head and shoulders, resemble Indian Squaws.

I lately spent three hours in the Museum of the Capitol, on the summit of the sacred hill. In the hall of the Gladiator I noticed an exquisite statue of Diana. There is a pure, virgin grace in the classic outlines of the figure that keeps the eye long upon it. The face is full of cold, majestic dignity, but it is the ideal of a being to be worshipped, rather than loved. The Faun of Praxiteles, in the same room, is a glorious work; it is the perfect embodiment of that wild, merry race the Grecian poets dreamed of. One looks on the Gladiator with a hushed breath and an awed spirit. He is dying; the blood flows more slowly from the deep wound in his side; his head is sinking downwards, and the arm that supports his body becomes more and more nerveless. You feel that a dull mist is coming over his vision, and almost wait to see his relaxing limbs sink suddenly on his shield. That the rude, barbarian form has a soul, may be read in his touchingly expressive countenance. It warms the sympathies like reality to look upon it. Yet how many Romans may have gazed on this work, moved nearly to tears, who have seen hundreds perish in the arena without a pitying emotion! Why is it that Art has a voice frequently more powerful than Nature?

How cold it is here! I was forced to run home tonight, nearly at full speed, from the Café delle *Belle Arti* through the Corso and the Piazza Colonna, to keep warm. The clear, frosty moon threw the shadow of the column of Antoninus over me as I passed, and it made me shiver to look at the thin, falling sheet of the fountain. Winter is winter everywhere, and even the sun of Italy cannot always scorch his icy wings.

Two days ago we took a ramble outside the walls. Passing the Coliseum and Caracalla's Baths, we reached the tomb of Scipio, a small sepulchral vault, near the roadside. The ashes of the warrior were scattered to the winds long ago, and his mausoleum is fast falling to decay. The old arch over the Appian way is still standing, near the modern *Porta San Sebastiano* through which we entered on the far-famed road. Here and there it is quite entire, and we walked over the stones once worn by the feet of Virgil and Horace and Cicero. After passing the temple of Romulus—a shapeless and ivy-grown ruin—and walking a mile or more beyond the walls, we reached the Circus of Caracalla, whose long and shattered walls fill the hollow of one of the little dells of the Campagna. The original structure must have been of great size and splendor, but those twin Vandals—Time and Avarice—have stripped away everything but the lofty brick masses, whose nakedness the ivy strives to cover.

Further, on a gentle slope, is the tomb of "the wealthiest Roman's wife," familiar to everyone through Childe Harold's musings. It is a round, massive tower, faced with large blocks of marble, and still bearing the name of Cecilia Metella. One side is much ruined, and the top is overgrown with grass and wild bushes. The wall is about thirty feet thick, so that but a small round space is left in the interior, which is open to the rain and filled with rubbish. The echoes pronounced hollowly after us the name of the dead for whom it was built, but they could tell us nothing of her life's history —

"How lived, how loved, how died she?"

I made a hurried drawing of it, and we then turned to the left, across the Campagna, to seek the grotto of Egeria. Before us, across the brown plain, extended the Sabine Mountains; in the clear air the houses of Tivoli, twenty miles distant, were plainly visible. The giant aqueduct stretched in a long line across the Campagna to the mountain of Albano, its broken and disjointed arches resembling the vertebrae of some mighty monster. With the ruins of temples and tombs strewing the plain for miles around it, it might be called the spine to the skeleton of Rome.

We passed many ruins, made beautiful by the clinging ivy, and reached a solemn grove of evergreen oak, overlooking a secluded valley. I was soon in the meadow, leaping ditches, rustling through cane-brakes, and climbing up to mossy arches to find out the fountain of Numa's nymph; while my companion, who had less taste for the romantic, looked on complacently from the leeward side of the hill. At length we found an arched vault in the hillside, overhung with wild vines, and shaded in summer by umbrageous trees that grow on the soil above. At the further end a stream of water gushed out from beneath a broken statue, and an aperture in the wall revealed a dark cavern behind. This, then, was "Egeria's grot." The ground was trampled by the feet of cattle, and the taste of the water was anything but pleasant. But it was not for Numa and his nymph alone, that I sought it so ardently. The sunbeam of another mind lingers on the spot. See how it gilds the ruined and neglected fount!

"The mosses of thy fountain still are sprinkled
    With thine Elysian water-drops; the face
Of thy cave-guarded spring, with years unwrinkled,
    Reflects the meek-eyed genius of the place,

Whose wild, green margin, now no more erase
   Art's works; no more its sparkling waters sleep,
Prisoned in marble; bubbling from the base
   Of the cleft statue, with a gentle leap,
The rill runs o'er, and 'round, fern, flowers and ivy creep,
   Fantastically tangled."

I tried to creep into the grotto, but it was unpleasantly dark, and no nymph appeared to that could chase away the shadow with her lustrous eyes. The whole hill is pierced by subterranean chambers and passages.

I spent another Sunday morning in St. Peter's. High mass was being celebrated in one of the side Chapels, and a great number of the priesthood were present. The music was simple, solemn, and very impressive, and a fine effect was produced by the combination of the full, sonorous voices of the priests, and the divine sweetness of that band of mutilated unfortunates (castratoes), who sing here. They sang with a full, clear tone, sweet as the first lispings of a child, but it was painful to hear that melody, purchased at the expense of manhood.

Near the dome is a bronze statue of St. Peter, which seems to have a peculiar atmosphere of sanctity. People say their prayers before it by hundreds, and then kiss its toe, which is nearly worn away by the application of so many thousand lips. I saw a crowd struggle most irreverently to pay their devotion to it. There was a great deal of jostling and confusion; some went so far as to thrust the faces of others against the toe as they were about to kiss it. What is more remarkable, it is an antique statue of Jupiter, taken, I believe, from the Pantheon. An English artist, showing it to a friend, just arrived in Rome, remarked very wittily that it was the statue of *Jew-Peter*.

I went afterwards to the Villa Borghese, outside the Porta del Popolo. The gardens occupy thirty or forty acres, and are always thronged in the afternoon with the carriages of the Roman and foreign nobility. In summer, it must be a heavenly place; even now, with its musical fountains, long avenues, and grassy slopes, crowned with the fan-like branches of the Italian pine, it reminds one of the fairy landscapes of Boccaccio. We threaded our way through the press of carriages on the Pincian hill, and saw the enormous bulk of St. Peter's looming up against the sunset sky. I counted forty domes and spires in that part of Rome that lay below us— but on what a marble glory looked that sun eighteen centuries ago! Modern Rome—it is in comparison, a den of filth, cheats and beggars!

Yesterday, while taking a random stroll through the city, I visited the church of St. Onofrio, where Tasso is buried. It is not far from St. Peter's, on the summit of a lonely hill. The building was closed, but an old monk admitted us on application. The interior is quite small, but very old, and the floor is covered with the tombs of princes and prelates of a past century. Near the end I found a small slab with the inscription:

TORQUATI TASSI

OSSA

IIIC JACENT

That was all—but what more was needed? Who knows not the name and fame and sufferings of the glorious bard? The pomp of gold and marble are not needed to deck the slumber of genius. On the wall, above, hangs an old and authentic portrait of him, very similar to the engravings in circulation. A crown of laurel encircles the lofty brow, and the eye has that wild, mournful expression, which accords so well with the mysterious tale of his love and madness.

Owing to the mountain storms, which imposed on us the expense of a carriage-journey to Rome, we shall be prevented from going further. One great cause of this is the heavy fee required for passports in Italy. In most of the Italian cities, the cost of the different visés amounts to $4 or $5; a few such visits as these reduce our funds very materially. The American Consul's fee is $2, owing to the illiberal course of our government, in withholding all salary from her Consuls in Europe. Mr. Brown, however, in whose family we spent last evening very pleasantly, on our requesting that he would deduct something from the usual fee, kindly declined accepting anything. We felt this kindness the more, as from the character which some of our late Consuls bear in Italy, we had not anticipated it. We shall remember him with deeper gratitude than many would suppose, who have never known what it was to be a *foreigner.*

Tomorrow, therefore, we leave Rome—here is, at last, the limit of our wanderings. We have spent much toil and privation to reach here, and now, after two weeks' rambling and musing among the mighty relics of past glory, we turn our faces homeward. The thrilling hope I cherished during the whole pilgrimage—to climb Parnassus and drink from Castaly, under the blue heaven of Greece (both far easier than the steep hill and hidden fount of poesy, I worship afar off)—to sigh for fallen art, beneath the broken friezes of the Parthenon, and look with a pilgrim's eye on the isles of Homer and of Sappho—must be given up, unwillingly and sorrowfully though it be. These glorious anticipations—among the brightest that blessed my boyhood—are slowly wrung from me by stern necessity. Even Naples, the lovely Parthenope, where the Mantuan bard sleeps on the sunny shore, by the bluest of summer seas, with the disinterred Pompeii beyond, and Pæstum amid its roses on the lonely Calabrian plain—even this, almost within sight of the cross of St. Peter's, is barred from me. Farewell then, clime of "fame and eld," since it must be! A pilgrim's blessing for the lore ye have taught him!

Chapter XLII
PALO, CIVITA VECCHIA AND MARSEILLES

Palo. —The sea is breaking in long swells below the window, and a glorious planet shines in the place of the sunset that has died away. This is our first resting-place since leaving Rome. We have been walking all day over the bare and dreary Campagna, and it is a relief to look at last on the broad, blue expanse of the Tyrrhene Sea.

When we emerged from the cool alleys of Rome, and began to climb up and down the long, barren swells, the sun beat down on us with an almost summer heat. On crossing a ridge near Castel Guido, we took our last look of Rome, and saw from the other side the sunshine lying like a dazzling belt on the far Mediterranean. The country is one of the most wretched that can be imagined. Miles and miles of uncultivated land, with scarcely a single habitation, extend on either side of the road, and the few shepherds who watch their flocks in the marshy hollows, look wild and savage enough for any kind of crime. It made me shudder to see every face bearing such a villainous stamp.

Civita Vecchia, Jan. 11. —We left Palo just after sunrise, and walked in the cool of the morning beside the blue Mediterranean. On the right, the low outposts of the Appenines rose, bleak and brown, the narrow plain between them and the shore resembling a desert, so destitute was it of the signs of civilized life. A low, white cloud that hung over the sea, afar off, showed us the locality of Sardinia, though the land was not visible. The sun shone down warmly, and with the blue sky and bluer sea we could easily have imagined a milder season. The barren scenery took a new interest in my eyes, when I remembered that I was spending amidst it that birthday which removes me, in the eyes of the world, from dependant youth to responsible manhood.

In the afternoon we found a beautiful cove in a curve of the shore, and went to bathe in the cold surf. It was very refreshing, but not quite equal to the sulphur-bath on the road to Tivoli. The mountains now ran closer to the sea, and the road was bordered with thickets of myrtle. I stopped often to beat my staff into the bushes, and inhale the fragrance that arose from their crushed leaves. The hills were covered with this poetical shrub, and any acre of the ground would make the fortune of a florist at home.

The sun was sinking in a sky of orange and rose, as Civita Vecchia came in sight on a long headland before us. Beyond the sea there stretched the dim hills of Corsica. We walked nearly an hour in the clear moonlight, by the sounding shore, before the gate of the city was reached. We have found a tolerable inn, and are now enjoying the pleasures of supper and rest.

Marseilles, Jan. 16. — At length we tread the shore of France — of sunny Provence — the last unvisited realm we have to roam through before returning home. It is with a feeling of more than common relief that we see around us the lively faces and hear the glib tongues of the French. It is like an earnest that the "roughing" we have undergone among Bohemian boors and Italian savages is well nigh finished, and that, henceforth, we shall find civilized sympathy and politeness, if nothing more, to make the way smoother. Perhaps the three woeful days which terminated at half past two yesterday afternoon, as we passed through the narrow strait into the beautiful harbor which Marseilles encloses in her sheltering heart, make it still pleasenter.

Now, while there is time, I must describe those three days, for who could write on the wet deck of a steamboat, amid all the sights and smells which a sea voyage creates? Description does not flourish when the bones are sore with lying on planks, and the body shivering like an aspen leaf with cold.

About the old town of Civita Vecchia there is not much to be said, except that it has the same little harbor which Trajan dug for it, and is as dirty and disagreeable as a town can well be. We saw nothing except a little church, and the prison-yard, full of criminals, where the celebrated bandit, Gasparoni, has been now confined for eight years.

The Neapolitan Company's boat was advertised to leave the 12th, so, after procuring our passports, we went to the office to take passage. The official, however, refused to give us tickets for the third place, because we were not servants or common laborers! and words were wasted in trying to convince him that it would make no difference. As the second cabin fare was nearly three times as high, and entirely too dear for us, we went to the office of the Tuscan Company, whose boat was to leave in two days. Through the influence of an Italian gentleman, secretary to Bartolini, the American Consul, whom we met, they agreed to take us for forty-five francs, on deck, the price of the Neapolitan boat being thirty.

Rather than stay two days longer in the dull town, we went again to the latter Company's office and offered them forty-five francs to go that day in their boat. This removed the former scruples, and tickets were immediately made out. After a plentiful dinner at the albergo, to prepare ourselves for the exposure, we filled our pockets with a supply of bread, cheese, and figs, for the voyage. We then engaged a boatman, who agreed to row us out to the steamer for two pauls, but after he had us on board and an oar's length from the quay, he said two pauls *apiece* was his bargain. I instantly refused, and, summoning the best Italian I could command, explained our agreement; but he still persisted in demanding double price. The dispute soon drew a number of persons to the quay, some of whom, being boatmen, sided with him. Finding he had us safe in his boat, his manner was exceedingly calm and polite. He contradicted me with a "pardon, Signore!" accompanying the words with a low bow and a graceful lift of his scarlet cap, and replied to my indignant accusations in the softest and most silvery-modulated Roman sentences. I found, at last, that if I was in the right, I cut the worse figure of the two, and, therefore, put an end to the dispute by desiring him to row on at his own price.

The hour of starting was two, but the boat lay quietly in the harbor till four, when we glided out on the open sea, and went northward, with the blue hills of Corsica far on our left. A gorgeous sunset faded away over the water, and the moon rose behind the low mountains of the Italian coast.

Having found a warm and sheltered place near the chimney, I drew my beaver further over my eyes, to keep out the moonlight, and lay down on the deck with my knapsack under my head. It was a hard bed, indeed; and the first time I attempted to rise, I found myself glued to the floor by the pitch which was smeared along the seams of the boards! Our fellow-sufferers were a company of Swiss soldiers going home after a four years' service under the King of Naples, but they took to their situation more easily than we.

Sleep was next to impossible, so I paced the deck occasionally looking out on the moonlit sea and the dim shores on either side. A little after midnight we passed between Elba and Corsica. The dark crags of Elba rose on our right, and the bold headlands of Napoleon's isle stood opposite, at perhaps twenty miles' distance. There was something dreary and mysterious in the whole scene, viewed at such a time — the grandeur of his career, who was born on one and exiled to the other, gave it a strange and thrilling interest.

We made the lighthouse before the harbor of Leghorn at dawn, and by sunrise were anchored within the mole. I sat on the deck the whole day, watching the picturesque vessels that skimmed about with their lateen sails, and wondering how soon the sailors, on the deck of a Boston brig anchored near us, would see my distant country. Leaving at four o'clock, we dashed away, along the mountain coast of Carrara, at a rapid rate. The wind was strong and cold, but I lay down behind the boiler, and though the boards were as hard as ever, slept two or three hours. When I awoke at half past two in the morning, after a short rest, Genoa was close at hand. We glided between the two revolving lights on the mole, into the harbor, with the amphitheatre on which the superb city sits, dark and silent around us. It began raining soon, the engine-fire sank down, and as there was no place of shelter, we were shortly wet to the skin.

How long those dreary hours seemed, till the dawn came! All was cold and rainy and dark, and we waited in a kind of torpid misery for daylight. The entire day, I passed sitting in a coil of rope under the stern of the cabin, and even the beauties of the glorious city scarce affected me. We lay opposite the Doria palace, and the constellation of villas and towers still glittered along the hills; but who, with his teeth chattering and limbs numb and damp, could feel pleasure in looking on Elysium itself?

We got under way again at three o'clock. The rain very soon hid the coast from view, and the waves pitched our boat about in a manner not at all pleasant. I soon experienced seasickness in all its horrors. We had accidentally made the acquaintance of one of the Neapolitan sailors, who had been in America. He was one of those rough, honest natures I like to meet with — their blunt kindness, is better than refined and oily-tongued suavity. As we were standing by the chimney, reflecting dolefully how we should pass the coming night, he came up and said; "I am in trouble about you, poor fellows! I don't think I shall sleep three hours tonight, to think of you. I shall tell all the cabin they shall give you beds, because they shall see you are gentlemen!" Whether he did so or the officers were moved by spontaneous commiseration, we knew not, but in half an hour a servant beckoned us into the cabin, and berths were given us.

I turned in with a feeling of relief not easily imagined, and forgave the fleas willingly, in the comfort of a shelter from the storm. When I awoke, it was broad day. A fresh breeze was drying the deck, and the sun was half-visible among breaking clouds. We had passed the Isle of the Titan, one of the *Isles des Hyères,* and the bay of Toulon opened on our right. It was a rugged, rocky coast, but the hills of sunny Provence rose beyond. The sailor came up with a smile of satisfaction on his rough countenance, and said: "You did sleep better, I think; I did tell them all!" coupling his assertion with a round curse on the officers.

We ran along, beside the brown, bare crags till nearly noon, when we reached the eastern point of the Bay of Marseilles. A group of small islands, formed of bare rocks, rising in precipices three or four hundred feet high, guards the point; on turning into the Gulf, we saw on the left the rocky islands of Pomegues, and If, with the castle crowning the latter, in which Mirabeau was confined. The ranges of hills which rose around the great bay, were spotted and sprinkled over with thousands of the country cottages of the Marseilles merchants, called *Bastides;* the city itself was hidden from view. We saw apparently the whole bay, but there was no crowd of vessels, such as would befit a great sea-port; a few spires peeping over a hill, with some fortifications, were all that was visible. At length we turned suddenly aside and entered a narrow strait, between two forts. Immediately a broad harbor opened before us, locked in the very heart of the hills on which the city stands. It was covered with vessels of all nations; on leaving the boat, we rowed past the Aristides, bearing the blue cross of Greece, and I searched eagerly and found, among the crowded masts, the starry banner of America.

I have rambled through all the principal parts of Marseilles, and am quite favorably impressed with its appearance. Its cleanliness and the air of life and business which marks the streets, are the more pleasant after coming from the dirty and depopulated Italian cities. The broad avenues, lined with trees, which traverse its whole length, must be delightful in summer. I am often reminded, by its spacious and fairly crowded thoroughfares, of our American cities. Although founded by the Phoceans, three thousand years ago, it has scarcely an edifice of greater antiquity than three or four centuries, and the tourist must content himself with wandering through the narrow streets of the old town, observing the Provençal costumes, or strolling among Turks and Moors on the *Quai d'Orleans.*

We have been detained here a day longer than was necessary, owing to some misunderstanding about the passports. This has not been favorable to our reduced circumstances, for we have now but twenty francs each, left, to take us to Paris. Our boots, too, after serving us so long, begin to show signs of failing in this hour of adversity. Although we are somewhat accustomed to such circumstances, I cannot help shrinking when I think of the solitary napoleon and the five hundred miles to be passed. Perhaps, however, the coin will do as much as its great namesake, and achieve for us a Marengo in the war with fate.

Chapter XLIII
PILGRIMAGE TO VAUCLUSE AND JOURNEY UP THE RHÔNE

We left Marseilles about nine o'clock, on a dull, rainy morning, for Avignon and the Rhône, intending to take in our way the glen of Vaucluse. The dirty *faubourgs* stretch out along the road for a great distance, and we trudged through them, past foundries, furnaces and manufactories, considerably disheartened with the prospect. We wound among the bleak stony hills, continually ascending, for nearly three hours. Great numbers of *cabarets,* frequented by the common people, lined the roads, and we met continually trains of heavy laden wagons, drawn by large mules. The country is very wild and barren, and would have been tiresome, except for the pine groves with their beautiful green foliage. We got something to eat with difficulty at an inn, for the people spoke nothing but the Provençal dialect, and the place was so cold and cheerless we were glad to go out again into the storm. It mattered little to us, that we heard the language in which the gay troubadours of king René sung their songs of love. We thought more of our dripping clothes and numb, cold limbs, and would have been glad to hear instead, the strong, hearty German tongue, full of warmth and kindly sympathy for the stranger. The windswept drearily among the hills; black, gusty clouds covered the sky, and the incessant rain filled the road with muddy pools. We looked at the country chateaux, so comfortable in the midst of their sheltering poplars, with a sigh, and thought of homes afar off, whose doors were never closed to us.

This was all forgotten, when we reached Aix, and the hostess of the Café d'Afrique filled her little stove with fresh coal, and hung our wet garments around it, while her daughter, a pale faced, crippled child, smiled kindly on us and tried to talk with us in French. Putting on our damp, heavy coats again, B —— and I rambled through the streets, while our frugal supper was preparing. We, saw the statue of the *Bon Roi René,* who held at Aix his court of shepherds and troubadours—the dark Cathedral of St. Saveur—the ancient walls and battlements, and gazed down the valley at the dark, precipitous mass of Mont St. Victor, at whose base Marius obtained a splendid victory over the barbarians.

After leaving next morning, we saw at some distance to the south, the enormous aqueduct now being erected for the canal from the Rhône to Marseilles. The shallow, elevated valleys we passed in the forenoon's walk were stony and barren, but covered with large orchards of almond trees, the fruit of which forms a considerable article of export. This district borders an the desert of the Crau, a vast plain of stones, reaching to the mouth of the Rhône and almost entirely uninhabited. We caught occasional glimpses of its sea-like waste, between the summits of the hills. At length, after threading a high ascent, we saw the valley of the Durance suddenly below us. The sun, breaking through the clouds, shone on the mountain wall, which stood on the opposite side, touching with his glow the bare and rocky precipices that frowned far above the stream. Descending to the valley, we followed its course towards the Rhône, with the ruins of feudal bourgs crowning the crags above us.

It was dusk, when we reached the village of Senas, tired with the day's march. A landlord, standing in his door, on the lookout for customers, invited us to enter, in a manner so polite and pressing, we could not choose but do so. This is a universal custom with the country innkeepers. In a little village which we passed towards evening, there was a tavern, with the sign *"The Mother of Soldiers."* A portly woman, whose face beamed with kindness and cheerfulness, stood in the door and invited us to stop there for the night. "No, mother!" I answered; "we must go much further today." "Go, then," said she, "with good luck, my children! a pleasant journey!" On entering the inn at Senas, two or three bronzed soldiers were sitting by the table. My French vocabulary happening to give out in the middle of a consultation about eggs and onion-soup, one of them came to my assistance and addressed me in German. He was from Fulda, in Hesse Cassel, and had served fifteen years in Africa. Two other young soldiers, from the western border of Germany, came during the evening, and one of them being partly intoxicated, created such a tumult, that a quarrel arose, which ended in his being beaten and turned out of the house.

We met, everyday, large numbers of recruits in companies of one or two hundred, on their way to Marseilles to embark for Algiers. They were mostly youths, from sixteen to twenty years of age, and seemed little to forebode their probable fate. In looking on their fresh, healthy faces and bounding forms, I saw also a dim and ghastly vision of bones whitening on the desert, of men perishing with heat and fever, or stricken down by the aim of the savage Bedouin.

Leaving next morning at day-break, we walked on before breakfast to Orgon, a little village in a corner of the cliffs which border the Durance, and crossed the muddy river by a suspension bridge a short distance below, to Cavaillon, where the country people were holding a great market. From this place a road led across the meadow-land to L'Isle, six miles distant. This little town is so named, because it is situated on an island formed by the crystal Sorgues, which flows from the fountains of Vaucluse. It is a very picturesque and pretty place. Great mill-wheels, turning slowly and constantly, stand at intervals in the stream, whose grassy banks are now as green as in spring-time. We walked along the Sorgues, which is quite as beautiful and worthy to be sung as the Clitumnus, to the end of the village, to take the road to Vaucluse. Beside its banks stands a dirty, modern "Hôtel de Petrarque et Laure." Alas, that the names of the most romantic and impassioned lovers of all history should be desecrated to a sign-post to allure gormandizing tourists!

The bare mountain in whose heart lies the poet's solitude, now rose before us, at the foot of the lofty Mont Ventoux, whose summit of snows extended beyond. We left the river, and walked over a barren plain, across which the wind blew most drearily. The sky was rainy and dark, and completed the desolateness of the scene, which in no wise heightened our anticipations of the renowned glen. At length we rejoined the Sorgues and entered a little green valley running up into the mountain. The narrowness of the entrance entirely shut out the wind, and except the rolling of the waters over their pebbly bed, all was still and lonely and beautiful. The sides of the dell were covered with olive trees, and a narrow strip of emerald meadow lay at the bottom. It grew more hidden and sequestered as we approached the little village of Vaucluse. Here, the mountain towers far above, and precipices of grey rock, many hundred feet high, hang over the narrowing glen. On a crag over the village are the remains of a castle; the slope below this, now rugged and stony, was once graced by the cottage and garden of Petrarch. All traces of them have long since vanished, but a simple column, bearing the inscription, "À PETRARQUE," stands beside the Sorgues.

We ascended into the passage by a path among the rocks, overshadowed by olive and wild fig trees, to the celebrated fountains of Vaucluse. The glen seems as if struck into the mountain's depths by one blow of an enchanter's wand; and just at the end, where the rod might have rested in its downward sweep, is the fathomless well whose overbrimming fulness gives birth to the Sorgues. We climbed up over the mossy rocks and sat down in the grot, beside the dark, still pool. It was the most absolute solitude. The rocks towered above and over us, to the height of six hundred feet, and the gray walls of the wild glen below shut out all appearance of life. I leaned over the rock and drank of the blue crystal that grew gradually darker towards the centre, till it became a mirror, and gave back a perfect reflection of the crags above it. There was no bubbling—no gushing up from its deep bosom—but the wealth of sparkling waters continually welled over, as from a too-full goblet.

It was with actual sorrow that I turned away from the silent spot. I never visited a place to which the fancy clung more suddenly and fondly. There is something holy in its solitude, making one envy Petrarch the years of calm and unsullied enjoyment which blessed him there. As some persons, whom we pass as strangers, strike a hidden chord in our spirits, compelling a silent sympathy with them, so some landscapes have a character of beauty which harmonizes thrillingly with the mood in which we look upon them, till we forget admiration in the glow of spontaneous attachment. They seem like abodes of the Beautiful, which the soul in its wanderings long ago visited, and now recognizes and loves as the home of a forgotten dream. It was thus I felt by the fountains of Vaucluse; sadly and with weary steps I turned away, leaving its loneliness unbroken as before.

We returned over the plain in the wind, under the gloomy sky, passed L' Isle at dusk, and after walking an hour with a rain following close behind us, stopped at an *auberge* in Le Thor, where we rested our tired frames and broke our long day's fasting. We were greeted in the morning with a dismal rain and wet roads, as we began the march. After a time, however, it poured down in such torrents, that we were obliged to take shelter in a *remise* by the roadside, where a good woman, who addressed us in the unintelligible Provençal, kindled up a blazing fire. On climbing along hill, when the storm had abated, we experienced a delightful surprise. Below us lay the broad valley of the Rhône, with its meadows looking fresh and spring-like after the rain. The clouds were breaking away; clear blue sky was visible over Avignon, and a belt of sunlight lay warmly along the mountains of Languedoc. Many villages, with their tall, picturesque towers, dotted the landscape, and the groves of green olive enlivened the barrenness of winter. Two or three hours' walk over the plain, by a road fringed with willows, brought us to the gates of Avignon.

We walked around its picturesque turreted wall, and rambled through its narrow streets, washed here and there by streams which turn the old mill-wheels lazily around. We climbed up to the massive palace, which overlooks the city from its craggy seat, attesting the splendor it enjoyed, when for thirty years the Papal Court was held there, and the gray, weather-beaten, irregular building, resembling a pile of precipitous rocks, echoed with the revels of licentious prelates. We could not enter to learn the terrible secrets of the Inquisition, here unveiled, but we looked up at the tower, from which the captive Rienzi was liberated at the intercession of Petrarch.

After leaving Avignon, we took the road up the Rhône for Lyons, turning our backs upon the rainy south. We reached the village of Sorgues by dusk, and accepted the invitation of an old dame to lodge at her inn, which proved to be a *blacksmith's shop!* It was nevertheless clean and comfortable, and we sat down in one corner, out of the reach of the showers of sparks, which flew hissing from a red-hot horseshoe, that the smith and his apprentice were hammering. A Piedmontese pedlar, who carried the "Song of the Holy St. Philomène" to sell among the peasants, came in directly, and bargained for a sleep on some hay, for two sons. For a bed in the loft over the shop, we were charged five sous each, which, with seven sous for supper, made our expenses for the night about eleven cents! Our circumstances demanded the greatest economy, and we began to fear whether even this spare allowance would enable us to reach Lyons. Owing to a day's delay in Marseilles, we had left that city with but fifteen francs each; the incessant storms of winter and the worn-out state of our shoes, which were no longer proof against water or mud, prolonged our journey considerably, so that by starting before dawn and walking till dark, we were only able to make thirty miles a day. We could always procure beds for five sous, and as in the country inns one is only charged for what he chooses to order, our frugal suppers cost us but little. We purchased bread and cheese in the villages, and made our breakfasts and dinners on a bank by the roadside, or climbed the rocks and sat down by the source of some trickling rill. This simple fare had an excellent relish, and although we walked in wet clothes from morning till night, often laying down on the damp, cold earth to rest, our health was never affected.

It is worth all the toil and privation we have as yet undergone, to gain, from actual experience, the blessed knowledge that man always retains a kindness and brotherly sympathy towards his fellow — that under all the weight of vice and misery which a grinding oppression of soul and body brings on the laborers of earth, there still remain many bright tokens of a better nature. Among the starving mountaineers of the Hartz—the degraded peasantry of Bohemia —the savage *contadini* of Central Italy, or the dwellers on the hills of Provence and beside the swift Rhône, we almost invariably found kind, honest hearts, and an aspiration for something better, betokening the consciousness that such brute-like, obedient existence was not their proper destiny. We found few so hardened as to be insensible to a kind look or a friendly word, and nothing made us forget we were among strangers so much as the many tokens of sympathy which met us when least looked for. A young Englishman, who had traveled on foot from Geneva to Rome, enduring many privations on account of his reduced circumstances, said to me, while speaking on this subject: "A single word of kindness from a stranger would make my heart warm and my spirits cheerful, for days afterwards." There is not so much evil in man as men would have us believe; and it is a happy comfort to know and feel this.

Leaving our little inn before day-break next morning, we crossed the Sorgues, grown muddy since its infancy at Vaucluse, like many a young soul, whose mountain purity goes out into the soiling world and becomes sullied forever. The road passed over broad, barren ranges of hills, and the landscape was destitute of all interest, till we approached Orange. This city is built at the foot of a rocky height, a great square projection of which seemed to stand in its midst. As we approached nearer, however, arches and lines of cornice could be discerned, and we recognized it as the celebrated amphitheatre, one of the grandest Roman relics in the south of France.

I stood at the foot of this great fabric, and gazed up at it in astonishment. The exterior wall, three hundred and thirty-four feet in length, and rising to the height of one hundred and twenty one feet, is still in excellent preservation, and through its rows of solid arches one looks on the broken ranges of seats within. On the crag above, and looking as if about to topple down on it, is a massive fragment of the fortress of the Princes of Orange, razed by Louis XIV. Passing through the city, we came to the beautiful Roman triumphal arch, which to my eye is a finer structure than that of Constantine at Rome. It is built of a rich yellow marble and highly ornamented with sculptured trophies. From the barbaric shields and the letters MARIO, still remaining, it has been supposed to commemorate the victory of Marius over the barbarians, near Aix. A frieze, running along the top, on each side, shows, although broken and much defaced by the weather, the life and action which once marked the struggling figures. These Roman ruins, scattered through Provence and Languedoc, though inferior in historical interest, equal in architectural beauty the greater part of those in the Eternal City itself.

The rest of the day the road was monotonous, though varied somewhat by the tall crags of Mornas and Mont-dragon, towering over the villages of the same name. Night came on as the rock of Pierrelatte, at whose foot we were to sleep, appeared in the distance, rising like a Gibraltar from the plain, and we only reached it in time to escape the rain that came down the valley of the Rhône.

Next day we passed several companies of soldiers on their way to Africa. One of them was accompanied by a young girl, apparently the wife of the recruit by whose side she was marching. She wore the tight blue jacket of the troop, and a red skirt, reaching to the knees, over her soldier pantaloons; while her pretty face showed to advantage beneath a small military cap. It was a "Fille du Regiment" in real life. Near Montelimart, we lost sight of Mont Ventoux, whose gleaming white crest had been visible all the way from Vaucluse, and passed along the base of a range of hills running near to the river. So went our march, without particular incident, till we bivouacked for the night among a company of soldiers in the little village of Loriol.

Leaving at six o'clock, wakened by the trumpets which called up the soldiery to their day's march, we reached the river Drome at dawn, and from the bridge over its rapid current, gazed at the dim, ash-colored masses of the Alps of Dauphine, piled along the sky, far up the valley. The coming of morn threw a yellow glow along their snowy sides, and lighted up, here and there, a flashing glacier. The peasantry were already up and at work, and caravans of pack-wagons rumbled along in the morning twilight We trudged on with them, and by breakfast-time had made some distance of the way to Valence. The road, which does not approach the Rhône, is devoid of interest and tiresome, though under a summer sky, when the bare vine-hills are latticed over with green, and the fruit-trees covered with blossoms and foliage, it might be a scene of great beauty.

Valence, which we reached towards noon, is a commonplace city on the Rhône; and my only reasons for traversing its dirty streets in preference to taking the road, which passes without the walls, were to get something for dinner, and because it might have been the birthplace of Aymer de Valence, the valorous Crusader, chronicled in "Ivanhoe," whose tomb I had seen in Westminster Abbey. One of the streets which was marked "*Rue Bayard,*" shows that my valiant namesake—the knight without fear and reproach—is still remem-

bered in his native province. The ruins of his chateau are still standing among the Alps near Grenoble.

In the afternoon we crossed the Isère, a swift, muddy river, which
rises among the Alps of Dauphiné. We saw their icy range, among
which is the desert solitude of the Grand Chartreuse, far up the
valley; but the thick atmosphere hid the mighty Mont Blanc, whose
cloudy outline, eighty miles distant in a "bee line," is visible in fair
weather. At Tain, we came upon the Rhône again, and walked along
the base of the hills which contract its current. Here, I should call
it beautiful. The scenery has a wildness that approaches to that of
the Rhine. Rocky, castellated heights frown over the rushing waters,
which have something of the majesty of their "exulting and abounding" rival. Winding around the curving hills, the scene is constantly
varied, and the little willowed islets clasped in the embrace of the
stream, mingle a trait of softened beauty with its sterner character.

After passing the night at a village on its banks, we left it again at
St. Vallier, the next morning. At sunset, the spires of Vienne were
visible, and the lofty Mont Pilas, the snows of whose riven summits
feed the springs of the Loire on its western side, stretched majesti-
cally along the opposite bank of the Rhône. In a meadow, near
Vienne, stands a curious Roman obelisk, seventy-six feet in height.
The base is composed of four pillars, connected by arches, and the
whole structure has a barbaric air, compared with the more elegant
monuments of Orange and Nismes. Vienne, which is mentioned by
several of the Roman historians under its present name, was the
capital of the Allobroges, and I looked upon it with a new and
strange interest, on calling to mind my school-boy days, when I had
become familiar with that war-like race, in toiling over the pages of
Cæsar. We walked in the mud and darkness for what seemed a great
distance, and finally took shelter in a little inn at the northern end
of the city. Two Belgian soldiers, coming from Africa, were already
quartered there, and we listened to their tales of the Arab and the
desert, while supper was preparing.

The morning of the 25th was dull and rainy; the road, very muddy and unpleasant, led over the hills, avoiding the westward curve of the Rhône, directly towards Lyons. About noon, we came in sight of the broad valley in which the Rhône first clasps his Burgundian bride —the Saone, and a cloud of impenetrable coal-smoke showed us the location of Lyons.

A nearer approach revealed a large flat dome, and some ranges of tall buildings near the river. We soon entered the suburb of La Guillotière, which has sprung up on the eastern bank of the Rhône. Notwithstanding our clothes were like sponges, our boots entirely worn out, and our bodies somewhat thin with nine days exposure to the wintry storms in walking two hundred and forty miles, we entered Lyons with suspense and anxiety. But one franc apiece remained out of the fifteen with which we left Marseilles. B ——— wrote home some time ago, directing a remittance to be forwarded to a merchant at Paris, to whom he had a letter of introduction, and in the hope that this had arrived, he determined to enclose the letter in a note, stating our circumstances, and requesting him to forward a part of the remittance to Lyons. We had then to wait at least four days; people are suspicious and mistrustful in cities, and if no relief should come, what was to be done?

After wading through the mud of the suburbs, we chose a common-looking inn near the river, as the comfort of our stay depended wholly on the kindness of our hosts, and we hoped to find more sympathy among the laboring classes. We engaged lodgings for four or five days; after dinner the letter was dispatched, and we wandered about through the dark, dirty city until night. Our landlord, Monsieur Ferrand, was a rough, vigorous man, with a gloomy, discontented expression; his words were few and blunt, but a certain restlessness of manner, and a secret flashing of his cold, forbidding eye betrayed to me some strong hidden excitement. Madame Ferrand was kind and talkative, though passionate; but the appearance of the place gave me an unfavorable impression, which was heightened by the thought that it was now impossible to change our lodgings until relief should arrive.

When bed-time came, a ladder was placed against a sort of high platform along one side of the kitchen; we mounted and found a bed, concealed from the view of those below by a dusty muslin curtain. We lay there, between heaven and earth—the dirty earth of the brick floor and the sooty heaven of the ceiling—listening until midnight to the boisterous songs, and loud, angry disputes in the room adjoining. Thus ended our first day in Lyons.

Five weary days, each of them containing a month of torturing suspense, have since passed. Our lodging-place grew so unpleasant that we preferred wandering all day through the misty, muddy, smoky streets, taking refuge in the covered bazaars when it rained heavily. The gloom of everything around us, entirely smothered down the lightness of heart which made us laugh over our embarrassments at Vienna. When at evening, the dull, leaden hue of the clouds seemed to make the air dark and cold and heavy, we walked beside the swollen and turbid Rhône, under an avenue of leafless trees, the damp soil chilling our feet and striking an unpleasant numbness through our frames, and then I knew what those must feel who have no hope in their destitution, and not a friend in all the great world, who is not wretched as themselves. I prize the lesson, though the price of it is hard.

"This morning," I said to B ——, "will terminate our suspense." I felt cheerful in spite of myself; and this was like a presentiment of coming good luck. To pass the time till the mail arrived we climbed to the chapel of Fourvières, whose walls are covered with votive offerings to a miraculous picture of the Virgin. But at the precise hour we were at the Post Office. What an intensity of suspense can be felt in that minute, while the clerk is looking over the letters! And what a lightning-like shock of joy when it did come, and was opened with eager, trembling hands, revealing the relief we had almost despaired of! The city itself did not seem less gloomy, for that was impossible, but the faces of the crowd which had appeared cold and suspicious, were now kind and cheerful. We came home to our lodgings with changed feelings, and Madame Ferrand must have seen the joy in our faces, for she greeted us with an unusual smile.

We leave tomorrow morning for Chalons. I do not feel disposed to describe Lyons particularly, although I have become intimately acquainted with every part of it, from *Presqu' isle Perrache* to *Croix Rousse.* I know the contents of every shop in the Bazaar, and the passage of the Hôtel Dieu — the title of every volume in the bookstores in the Place Belcour — and the countenance of every bootblack and apple-woman on the Quais on both sides of the river. I have walked up the Saone to *Pierre Scise*—down the Rhône to his muddy marriage — climbed the Heights of *Fourvières,* and promenaded in the *Cours Napoleon!* Why, men have been presented with the freedom of cities, when they have had far less cause for such an honor than this.

Chapter XLIV
TRAVELING IN BURGUNDY — THE MISERIES OF A COUNTRY DILIGENCE

Paris, Feb. 6, 1846. — Every letter of the date is traced with an emotion of joy, for our dreary journey is over. There was a magic in the name that revived us during a long journey, and now the thought that it is all over — that these walls which enclose us, stand in the heart of the gay city—seems almost too joyful to be true. Yesterday I marked with the whitest chalk, on the blackest of all tablets to make the contrast greater, for I got out of the diligence (stagecoach) at the Barrière de Charenton, and saw before me in the morning twilight, the immense grey mass of Paris. I forgot my numbed and stiffened frame, and every other of the thousand disagreeable feelings of diligence traveling, in the pleasure which that sight afforded.

We arose in the dark at Lyons, and after bidding adieu to morose Monsieur Ferrand, traversed the silent city and found our way in the mist and gloom to the steamboat landing on the Saone. The waters were swollen much above their usual level, which was favorable for the boat, as long as there was room enough left to pass under the bridges. After a great deal of bustle we got under way, and were dashing out of Lyons, against the swift current, before day-break. We passed *L'Isle Barbe,* once a favorite residence of Charlemagne, and now the haunt of the Lyonnaise on summer holidays, and going under the suspension bridges with levelled chimneys, entered the picturesque hills above, which are covered with vineyards nearly to the top; the villages scattered over them have those square, pointed towers, which give such a quaintness to French country scenery.

The stream being very high, the meadows on both sides were deeply overflowed. To avoid the strong current in the centre, our boat ran along the banks, pushing aside the alder thickets and poplar shoots; in passing the bridges, the pipes were always brought down flat on the deck. A little after noon, we passed the large town of Macon, the birthplace of the poet Lamartine. The valley of the Saone, no longer enclosed among the hills, spread out to several miles in width. Along the west lay in sunshine the vine-mountains of Côte d'Or, and among the dark clouds in the eastern sky, we could barely distinguish the outline of the Jura. The waters were so much swollen as to cover the plain for two or three miles. We seemed to be sailing down a lake, with rows of trees springing up out of the water, and houses and villages lying like islands on its surface. A sunset that promised better weather tinged the broad brown flood, as Chalons came in sight, looking much like a city built along the shore of a lake. We squeezed through the crowd of porters and diligence men, declining their kind offers, and hunted quarters to suit ourselves.

We left Chalons on the morning of the 1st, in high spirits at the thought that there were but little more than two hundred miles between us and Paris. In walking over the cold, muddy plain, we passed a family of strolling musicians, who were sitting on a heap of stones by the roadside. An ill-dressed, ill-natured man and woman, each carrying a violin, and a thin, squalid girl, with a tamborine, composed the group. Their faces bore that unfeeling stamp, which springs from depravity and degradation. When we had walked somewhat more than a mile, we overtook a little girl, who was crying bitterly. By her features, from which the fresh beauty of childhood had not been worn, and the steel triangle which was tied to her belt, we knew she belonged to the family we had passed. Her dress was thin and ragged and a pair of wooden shoes but ill protected her feet from the sharp cold. I stopped and asked her why she cried, but she did not at first answer. However, by questioning, I found her unfeeling parents had sent her on without food; she was sobbing with hunger and cold. Our pockets were full of bread and cheese which we had bought for breakfast, and we gave her half a loaf, which stopped her tears at once. She looked up and thanked us, smiling; and sitting down on a bank, began to eat as if half-famished.

The physiognomy of this region is very singular. It appears as if the country had been originally a vast elevated plain, and some great power had scooped out, as with a hand, deep circular valleys all over its surface. In winding along the high ridges, we often looked down, on either side, into such hollows, several miles in diameter, and sometimes entirely covered with vineyards.

At La Rochepot, a quaint, antique village, lying in the bottom of one of these dells, we saw the finest ruin of the Middle Ages that I have met with in France. An American lady had spoken to me of it in Rome, and I believe Willis mentions it in his "Pencillings," but it is not described in the guide books, nor could we learn what feudal lord had ever dwelt in its halls. It covers the summit of a stately rock, at whose foot the village is crouched, and the green ivy climbs up to the very top of its gray towers.

As the road makes a wide curve around the side of the hill, we descended to the village by the nearer footpath, and passed among its low, old houses, with their pointed gables and mossy roofs. The path led close along the foot of the rock, and we climbed up to the ruin, and stood in its grass-grown courtyard. Only the outer walls and the round towers at each corner are left remaining; the inner part has been razed to the ground, and where proud barons once marshalled their vassals, the villagers now play their holiday games. On one side, several Gothic windows are left standing, perfect, though of simple construction, and in the towers we saw many fireplaces and doorways of richly cut stone, which looked as fresh as if just erected.

We passed the night at Ivry (not the Ivry which gained Henri Quatre his kingdom) and then continued our march over roads which I can only compare to our country roads in America during the spring thaw. In addition to this, the rain commenced early in the morning and continued all day, so that we were completely wet the whole time. The plains, too high and cold to produce wine, were varied by forests of beech and oak, and the population was thinly scattered over them in small villages.

Travelers generally complain very much of the monotony of this part of France, and, with such dreary weather, we could not disagree with them.

As the day wore on, the rain increased, and the sky put on that dull, gray cast, which denotes a lengthened storm. We were inclined to stop at nightfall, but there was no inn near at hand—not even a hovel of a *cabaret* in which to shelter ourselves, and, on enquiring of the wagoners, we received the comforting assurance that there was yet a league and a half to the nearest stopping place. On, then, we went, with the pitiless storm beating in our faces and on our breasts, till there was not a dry spot left, except what our knapsacks covered. We could not have been more completely saturated if we had been dipped in the Yonne. At length, after two hours of slipping and sliding along in the mud and wet and darkness, we reached

Saulieu, and, by the warm fire, thanked our stars that the day's dismal tramp was over.

By good or bad luck (I have not yet decided which) a vehicle was to start the next morning for Auxerre, distant sixty miles, and the fare being but five francs, we thought it wisest to take places. It was always with reluctance that we departed from our usual mode of traveling, but, in the present instance, the circumstances absolutely compelled it.

Next morning, at sunrise, we took our seats in a large, square vehicle on two wheels, calculated for six persons and a driver, with a single horse. But, as he was fat and round as an elephant, and started off at a brisk pace, and we were well protected from the rain, it was not so bad after all, barring the jolts and jarred vertebræ. We drove on, over the same dreary expanse of plain and forest, passing through two or three towns in the course of the day, and by evening had made somewhat more than half our journey. Owing to the slowness of our fresh horse, we were jolted about the whole night, and did not arrive at Auxerre until six o'clock in the morning. After waiting an hour in a hotel beside the rushing Yonne, a lumbering diligence was got ready, and we were given places to Paris for seven francs. As the distance is one hundred and ten miles, this would be considered cheap, but I should not want to travel it again and be paid for doing so. Twelve persons were packed into a box not large enough for a cow, and no cabinet-maker ever dove-tailed the corners of his bureaus tighter than we did our knees and nether extremities. It is my lot to be blessed with abundance of stature, and none but tall persons can appreciate the misery of sitting for hours with their joints in an immovable vice. The closeness of the atmosphere — for the passengers would not permit the windows to be opened for fear of taking cold — combined with loss of sleep, made me so drowsy that my head was continually falling on my next neighbor, who, being a heavy country lady, thrust it indignantly away. I would then try my best to keep it up awhile, but it would droop gradually, till the crash of a bonnet or a smart bump against some other head would recall me, for a moment, to consciousness.

We passed Joigny, on the Yonne, Sens, with its glorious old cathedral, and at dusk reached Montereau, on the Seine. This was the scene of one of Napoleon's best victories, on his return from Elba. In driving over the bridge, I looked down on the swift and swollen current, and hoped that its hue might never be darkened again so fearfully as the last sixty years have witnessed. No river in Europe has such an association connected with it. We think of the Danube, for its majesty, of the Rhine, for its wild beauty, but of the Seine—for its blood!

In coming thus to the last famed stream I shall visit in Europe, I might say, with Barry Cornwall:

"We've sailed through banks of green,
  Where the wild waves fret and quiver;
And we've down the Danube been —
  The dark, deep, thundering river!
We've thridded the Elbe and Rhône,
  The Tiber and blood-dyed Seine,
And we've been where the blue Garonne
  Goes laughing to meet the main!"

All that night did we endure squeezing and suffocation, and no morn was ever more welcome than that which revealed to us Paris. With matted hair, wild, glaring eyes, and dusty and dishevelled habiliments, we entered the gay capital, and blessed every stone upon which we placed our feet, in the fulness of our joy.

In paying our fare at Auxerre, I was obliged to use a draft on the banker, Rougemont de Löwenberg. The ignorant conductor hesitated to change this, but permitted us to go, on condition of keeping it until we should arrive. Therefore, on getting out of the diligence, after forty-eight hours of sleepless and fasting misery, the *facteur* of the office went with me to get it paid, leaving B —— to wait for us. I knew nothing of Paris, and this merciless man kept me for three hours at his heels, following him on all his errands, before he did mine, in that time traversing the whole length of the city, in order to leave a *chèvre-feuille* at an aristocratic residence in the Faubourg St. Germain. Yet even combined weariness and hunger could not prevent me from looking with vivid interest down a long avenue, at the Column of the place Vendòme, in passing, and gazing up in wonder at the splendid portico of the Madeleine. But of anything else I have a very faint remembrance. "You can eat breakfast, now, I think," said he, when we returned, "we have walked more than four leagues!"

I know we will be excused, that, instead of hurrying away to Notre Dame or the Louvre, we sat down quietly to a most complete breakfast. Even the most romantic must be forced to confess that admiration does not sit well on an empty stomach. Our first walk was to a bath, and then, with complexions several shades lighter, and limbs that felt as if lifted by invisible wings, we hurried away to the Post Office. I seized the welcome missives from my far home, with a beating heart, and hastening back, read till the words became indistinct in the twilight.

Chapter XLV
POETICAL SCENES IN PARIS

What a gay little world in miniature this is! I wonder not that the French, with their exuberant gaiety of spirit, should revel in its ceaseless tides of pleasure, as if it were an earthly Elysium. I feel already the influence of its cheerful atmosphere, and have rarely threaded the crowds of a stranger city, with so light a heart as I do now daily, on the thronged banks of the Seine. And yet it would be difficult to describe wherein consists this agreeable peculiarity. You can find streets as dark and crooked and dirty anywhere in Germany, and squares and gardens as gay and sunny beyond the Alps, and yet they would affect you far differently. You could not, as here, divest yourself of every particle of sad or serious thought and be content to gaze for hours on the showy scene, without an idea beyond the present moment. It must be that the spirit of the crowd is magnetically contagious.

The evening of our arrival we walked out past the massive and stately *Hôtel de Ville,* and took a promenade along the Quais. The shops facing the river presented a scene of great splendor. Several of the Quais on the north bank of the Seine seem to be occupied almost entirely by jewellers, the windows of whose shops, arranged in a style of the greatest taste, make a dazzling display. Rows of gold watches and chains are carefully arranged across the crystal panes, and heaped in pyramids on long glass slabs; cylindrical wheels of wire, hung with jewelled breastpins and earrings, turn slowly around by some invisible agency, displaying row after row of their glittering treasures.

From the centre of the Pont Neuf, we could see for a long distance up and down the river. The different bridges traced on either side a dozen starry lines through the dark air, and a continued blaze lighted the two shores in their whole length, revealing the outline of the Isle de la Cité. I recognized the Palaces of the Louvre and the Tuileries in the dusky mass beyond. Eastward, looming against the dark sky, I could faintly trace the black towers of Notre Dame. The rushing of the swift waters below mingled with the rattling of a thousand carts and carriages, and the confusion of a thousand voices, till it seemed like some grand nightly festival.

I first saw Notre Dame by moonlight. The shadow of its stupendous front was thrown directly towards me, hiding the innumerable lines of the ornamental sculpture which cover its tall, square towers. I walked forward until the interlacing, Moorish arches between them stood full against the moon, and the light, struggling through the quaint openings of the tracery, streamed in silver lines down into the shadow. The square before it was quite deserted, for it stands on a lonely part of the Isle de la Cité, and it looked thus far more majestic and solemn than in the glaring daylight.

The great quadrangle of the Tuileries encloses the Place du Carrousel, in the centre of which stands a triumphal arch, erected by Napoleon after his Italian victories. Standing in the middle of this arch, you look through the open passage in the central building of the palace, into the Gardens beyond. Further on, in a direct line, the middle avenue of the Gardens extends away to the *Place de la Concorde,* where the Obelisk of Luxor makes a perpendicular line through your vista; still further goes the broad avenue through the Elysian Fields, until afar off, the Arc de l'Etoile, two miles distant, closes this view through the palace doorway.

Let us go through it, and on, to the Place de la Concorde, reserving the Gardens for another time. What is there in Europe—no, in the world,—equal to this? In the centre, the mighty obelisk of red granite pierces the sky, — on either hand showers of silver spray are thrown up from splendid bronze fountains—statues and pillars of gilded bronze sweep in a grand circle around the square, and on each side magnificent vistas lead the eye off, and combine the distant with the near, to complete this unparalleled view! Eastward, beyond the tall trees in the garden of the Tuileries, rises the long front of the Palace, with the tricolor floating above; westward, in front of us, is the Forest of the Elysian Fields, with the arch of triumph nearly a mile and a half distant, looking down from the end of the avenue, at the Barriere de Neuilly. To the right and left are the marble fronts of the Church of the Madeleine and the Chamber of Deputies, the latter on the other side of the Seine. Thus the groves and gardens of Paris—the palace of her kings—the proud monument of her sons' glory—and the masterpieces of modern French architecture are all embraced in this one splendid *coup d'œil.*

Following the motley multitude to the bridge, I crossed and made my way to the Hôtel des Invalides. Along the esplanade, playful companies of children were running and tumbling in their sports over the green turf, which was as fresh as a meadow; while, not the least interesting feature of the scene, numbers of scarred and disabled veterans, in the livery of the Hospital, basked in the sunshine, watching with quiet satisfaction the gambols of the second generation they have seen arise. What tales could they not tell, those wrinkled and feeble old men! What visions of Marengo and Austerlitz and Borodino shift still with a fiery vividness through their fading memories! Some may have left a limb on the Lybian desert; and the sabre of the Cossack may have scarred the brows of others. They witnessed the rising and setting of that great meteor, which intoxicated France with such a blaze of power and glory, and now, when the recollection of that wonderful period seems almost like a stormy dream, they are left to guard the ashes of their ancient General, brought back from his exile to rest in the bosom of his own French people. It was to me a touching and exciting thing, to look on those whose eyes had witnessed the filling up of such a fated leaf in the world's history.

Entrance is denied to the tomb of Napoleon until it is finished, which will not be for three or four years yet. I went, however, into the "Church of the Banners" — a large chapel, hung with two or three hundred flags taken by the armies of the Empire. The greater part of them were Austrian and Russian. It appeared to be empty when I entered, but on looking around, I saw an old gray-headed soldier kneeling at one side. His head was bowed over his hands, and he seemed perfectly absorbed in his thoughts. Perhaps the very tattered banners which hung down motionless above his head, he might have assisted in conquering. I looked a moment on those eloquent trophies, and then noiselessly withdrew.

There is at least one solemn spot near Paris; the laughing winds that come up from the merry city sink into sighs under the cypress boughs of Père Lachaise. And yet it is not a gloomy place, but full of a serious beauty, fitting for a city of the dead. I shall never forget the sunny afternoon when I first entered its gate and walked slowly up the hill, between rows of tombs, gleaming white amid the heavy foliage, while the green turf around them was just beginning to be starred by the opening daisies. From the little chapel on its summit I looked back at the blue spires of the city, whose roar of life dwindled to a low murmur. Countless pyramids, obelisks and urns, rising far and wide above the cedars and cypresses, showed the extent of the splendid necropolis, which is inhabited by pale, shrouded emigrants from its living sister below. The only sad part of the view, was the slope of the hill alloted to the poor, where legions of plain black crosses are drawn up into solid squares on its side and stand alone and gloomy—the advanced guard of the army of Death! I mused for awhile over the tombs of Molière and La Fontaine; Massena, Mortier and Lefebre; General Fey and Casimir Périer; and finally descended to the shrine where Abelard reposes by the side of his Heloise. The old sculptured tomb, brought away from the Paraclete, still covers their remains, and pious hands (of lovers, perhaps) keep fresh the wreaths of *immortelles* above their marble effigies.

In the Theatre Français, I saw Rachel, the actress. She appeared in the character of "Virginia," in a tragedy of that name, by the poet Latour. Her appearance as she came upon the stage alone, convinced me she would not belie her renown. She is rather small in stature, with dark, piercing eyes and rich black hair; her lips are full, but delicately formed, and her features have a marked yet flexible outline, which conveys the minutest shades of expression. Her voice is clear, deep and thrilling, and like some grand strain of music, there is power and meaning in its slightest modulations. Her gestures embody the very spirit of the character; she has so perfectly attained that rare harmony of thought, sound and action, or rather, that unity of feeling which renders them harmonious, that her acting seems the unstudied, irrepressible impulse of her soul. With the first sentence she uttered, I forgot Rachel. I only saw the innocent Roman girl; I awaited in suspense and with a powerful sympathy, the development of the oft-told tragedy. My blood grew warm with indignation when the words of Appius roused her to anger, and I could scarcely keep back my tears, when, with a voice broken by sobs, she bade farewell to the protecting gods of her father's hearth.

Among the bewildering variety of ancient ornaments and implements in the Egyptian Gallery of the Louvre, I saw an object of startling interest. A fragment of the Iliad, written nearly three thousand years ago! One may even dare to conjecture that the torn and half-mouldered slip of papyrus, upon which he gazes, may have been taken down from the lips of the immortal Chian. The eyes look on those faded characters, and across the great gulf of Time, the soul leaps into the Past, brought into shadowy nearness by a mirage of the mind. There, as in the desert, images start up, vivid, yet of a vague and dreamy beauty. We can see the olive groves of Greece—white-robed youths and maidens sit in the shade of swaying boughs—and one of them reads aloud, in words that sound like the clashing of shields, the deeds of Achilles.

As we step out the western portal of the Tuileries, a beautiful scene greets us. We look on the palace garden, fragrant with flowers and classic with bronze copies of ancient sculpture. Beyond this, broad gravel walks divide the flower-bordered lawns and ranks of marble demigods and heroes look down on the joyous crowd. Children troll their hoops along the avenues or skip the rope under the clipped lindens, whose boughs are now tinged a pale yellow by the bursting buds. The swans glide about on a pond in the centre, begging bread of the bystanders, who watch a miniature ship which the soft breeze carries across. Paris is unseen, but *heard,* on every side; only the Column of Luxor and the Arc de Triomphe rise blue and grand above the top of the forest. What with the sound of voices, the merry laughter of the children and a host of smiling faces, the scene touches a happy chord in one's heart, and one mingles with it, lost in pleasant reverie, till the sounds fade away with the fading light.

Just below the Baths of the Louvre, there are several floating barges belonging to the washer-women, anchored at the foot of the great stone staircase leading down to the water. They stand there day after day, beating their clothes upon flat boards and rinsing them in the Seine. One day there seemed to have been a wedding or some other cause of rejoicing among them, for a large number of the youngest were talking in great glee on one of the platforms of the staircase, while a handsome, German-looking youth stood near, with a guitar slung around his neck. He struck up a lively air, and the girls fell into a droll sort of a dance. They went at it heavily and roughly enough, but made up in good humor what they lacked in grace; the older members of the craft looked up from their work with satisfaction and many shouts of applause were sent down to them from the spectators on the Quai and the Pont Neuf. Not content with this, they seized on some luckless men who were descending the steps, and clasping them with their powerful right arms, spun them around like so many tops and sent them whizzing off at a tangent. Loud bursts of laughter greeted this performance, and the stout river maidens returned to their dance with redoubled spirit.

Yesterday, the famous procession of the *"bœuf gras"* took place for the second time, with great splendor. The order of march had been duly announced beforehand, and by noon all the streets and squares through which it was to pass, were crowded with waiting spectators. Mounted gens d'armes rode constantly to, and fro, to direct the passage of vehicles and keep an open thoroughfare. Thousands of country peasants poured into the city, the boys of whom were seen in all directions, blowing distressingly through hollow ox-horns. Altogether, the spirit of nonsense which animated the crowd, displayed itself very amusingly.

A few mounted guards led the procession, followed by a band of music. Then appeared Roman lictors and officers of sacrifice, leading Dagobert, the famous bull of Normandy, destined to the honor of being slaughtered as the Carnival beef. He trod rather tenderly, finding, no doubt, a difference between the meadows of Caen and the pavements of Paris, and I thought he would have been willing to forego his gilded horns and flowery crown, to get back there again. His weight was said to be four thousand pounds, and the bills pompously declared that he had no rival in France, except the elephant in the *Jardin des Plantes.*

After him came the farmer by whom he was raised, and M. Roland, the butcher of the carnival, followed by a hundred of the same craft, dressed as cavaliers of the different ages of France. They made a very showy appearance, although the faded velvet and soiled tinsel of their mantles were rather too apparent by daylight.

After all these had gone by, came an enormous triumphal car, very profusely covered with gilding and ornamental flowers. A fellow with long woollen hair and beard, intended to represent Time, acted as driver. In the car, under a gilded canopy, reposed a number of persons, in blue silk smocks and yellow "flesh-tights," said to be Venus, Apollo, the Graces, &c. but I endeavored in vain to distinguish one divinity from another. However, three children on the back seat, dressed in the same style, with the addition of long flaxy ringlets, made very passable Cupids. This closed the march; which passed onward towards the Place de la Concorde, accompanied by the sounds of music and the shouts of the mob. The broad, splendid line of Boulevards, which describe a semicircle around the heart of the city, were crowded, and for the whole distance of three miles, it required no slight labor to make one's way. People in masks and fancy costumes were continually passing and re-passing, and I detected in more than one of the carriages, cheeks rather too fair to suit the slouched hunter's hats which shaded them. It seemed as if all Paris was taking a holiday, and resolved to make the most of it.

Chapter XLVI
A GLIMPSE OF NORMANDY

After a residence of five weeks, which, in spite of some few troubles, passed away quickly and delightfully, I turned my back on Paris. It was not regret I experienced on taking my seat in the cars for Versailles, but that feeling of reluctance with which we leave places whose brightness and gaiety force the mind away from serious toil. Steam, however, cuts short all sentiment, and in much less time than it takes to bid farewell to a German, we had whizzed past the Place d'Europe, through the barrier, and were watching the spires start up from the receding city, on the way to St. Cloud.

At Versailles I spent three hours in a hasty walk through the palace, which allowed but a bare glance at the gorgeous paintings of Horace Vernet. His "Taking of Constantine" has the vivid look of reality. The white houses shine in the sun, and from the bleached earth to the blue and dazzling sky, there seems to hang a heavy, scorching atmosphere. The white smoke of the artillery curls almost visibly off the canvas, and the cracked and half-sprung walls look as if about to topple down on the besiegers. One series of halls is devoted to the illustration of the knightly chronicles of France, from the days of Charlemagne to those of Bayard and Gaston de Foix. Among these pictured legends, I looked with the deepest interest on that of the noble girl of Orléans. Her countenance—the same in all these pictures and in a beautiful statue of her, which stands in one of the corridors—is said to be copied from an old and well-authenticated portrait. United to the sweetness and purity of peasant beauty, she has the lofty brow and inspired expression of a prophetess. There is a soft light in her full blue eye that does not belong to earth. I wonder not the soldiery deemed her chosen by God to lead them to successful battle; had I lived in those times I could have followed her consecrated banner to the ends of the earth. In the statue, she stands musing, with her head drooping forward, as if the weight of the breastplate oppressed her woman's heart; the melancholy soul which shines through the marble seems to forebode the fearful winding-up of her eventful destiny.

The afternoon was somewhat advanced, by the time I had seen the palace and gardens. After a hurried dinner at a restaurant, I shouldered my knapsack and took the road to St. Germain. The day was gloomy and cheerless, and I should have felt very lonely but for the thought of soon reaching England. There is no time of the year more melancholy than a cold, cloudy day in March; whatever may be the beauties of pedestrian traveling in fairer seasons, my experience dictates that during winter storms and March glooms, it had better be dispensed with. However, I pushed on to St. Germain, threaded its long streets, looked down from the height over its magnificent tract of forest and turned westward down the Seine. Owing to the scantiness of villages, I was obliged to walk an hour and a half in the wind and darkness, before I reached a solitary inn. As I opened the door and asked for lodging, the landlady inquired if I had the necessary papers. I answered in the affirmative and was admitted. While I was eating supper, they prepared their meal on the other end of the small table and sat down together. They fell into the error, so common to ignorant persons, of thinking a foreigner could not understand them, and began talking quite unconcernedly about me. "Why don't he take the railroad?" said the old man: "he must have very little money—it would be bad for us if he had none." "Oh!" remarked his son, "if he had none, he would not be sitting there so quiet and unconcerned." I thought there was some knowledge of human nature in this remark. "And besides," added the landlady, "there is no danger for us, for we have his passport." Of course I enjoyed this in secret, and mentally pardoned their suspicions, when I reflected that the high roads between Paris and London are frequented by many imposters, which makes the people naturally mistrustful. I walked all the next day through a beautiful and richly cultivated country. The early fruit trees were bursting into bloom, and the farmers led out their cattle to pasturage in the fresh meadows. The scenery must be delightful in summer — worthy of all that has been said or sung about lovely Normandy. On the morning of the third day, before reaching Rouen, I saw at a distance the remains of Chateau Galliard, the favorite castle of Richard Cœur de Lion. Rouen breathes everywhere of the ancient times of Normandy. Nothing can be more picturesque than its quaint, irregular wooden houses, and the low, mossy mills, spanning the clear streams which rush through its streets. The Cathedral, with its four towers, rises from among the clustered cottages like a giant rock, split by the lightning and worn by the rains of centuries is into a thousand fantastic shapes.

Resuming my walk in the afternoon, I climbed the heights west of the city, and after passing through a suburb four or five miles in length, entered the vale of the Cailly. This is one of the sweetest scenes in France. It lies among the woody hills like a Paradise, with its velvet meadows and villas and breathing gardens. The grass was starred with daisies and if I took a step into the oak and chestnut woods, I trampled on thousands of anemones and fragrant daffodils. The upland plain, stretching inward from the coast, wears a different character. As I ascended, towards evening, and walked over its monotonous swells, I felt almost homesick beneath its saddening influence. The sun, hazed over with dull clouds, gave out that cold and lifeless light which is more lonely than complete darkness. The wind, sweeping dismally over the fields, sent clouds of blinding dust down the road, and as it passed through the forests, the myriads of fine twigs sent up a sound as deep and grand as the roar of a roused ocean. Every chink of the Norman cottage where I slept, whistled most drearily, and as I looked out the little window of my room, the trees were swaying in the gloom, and long, black clouds scudded across the sky. Though my bed was poor and hard, it was a sublime sound that cradled me into slumber. Homer might have used it as the lullaby of Jove.

My last day on the continent came. I rose early and walked over the hills towards Dieppe. The scenery grew more bleak as I approached the sea, but the low and sheltered valleys preserved the pastoral look of the interior. In the afternoon, as I climbed a long, elevated ridge, over which a strong northwester was blowing, I was struck with a beautiful rustic church, in one of the dells below me. While admiring its neat tower I had gained unconsciously the summit of the hill, and on turning suddenly around, lo! there was the glorious old Atlantic stretching far before and around me! A shower was sweeping mistily along the horizon and I could trace the white line of the breakers that foamed at the foot of the cliffs. The scene came over me like a vivid electric shock, and I gave an involuntary shout, which might have been heard in all the valleys around. After a year and a half of wandering over the continent, that gray ocean was something to be revered and loved, for it clasped the shores of my native America.

I entered Dieppe in a heavy shower, and after finding an inn suited to my means and obtaining a *permis d'embarquement* from the police office, I went out to the battlements and looked again on the sea. The landlord promised to call me in time for the boat, but my anxiety waked me sooner, and mistaking the strokes of the cathedral bell, I shouldered my knapsack and went down to the wharf at one o'clock. No one was stirring on board the boat, and I was obliged to pace the silent, gloomy streets of the town for two hours. I watched the steamer glide out on the rainy channel, and turning into the topmost berth, drew the sliding curtain and strove to keep out cold and sea-sickness. But it was unavailing; a heavy storm of snow and rain rendered our passage so dreary that I did not stir until we were approaching the chain pier of Brighton.

I looked out on the foggy shores of England with a feeling of relief; my tongue would now be freed from the difficult bondage of foreign languages, and my ears be rejoiced with the music of my own. After two hours' delay at the Custom House, I took my seat in an open car for London. The day was dull and cold; the sun resembled a milky blotch in the midst of a leaden sky. I sat and shivered, as we flew onward, amid the rich, cultivated English scenery. At last the fog grew thicker; the road was carried over the tops of houses; the familiar dome of St. Paul's stood out above the spires; and I was again in London.

Chapter XLVII
LOCKHART, BERNARD BARTON AND CROLY—LONDON CHIMES AND GREENWICH FAIR

My circumstances, on arriving at London, were again very reduced. A franc and a half constituted the whole of my funds. This, joined to the knowledge of London expenses, rendered instant exertion necessary, to prevent still greater embarrassment. I called on a printer the next morning, hoping to procure work, but found, as I had no documents with me to show I had served a regular apprenticeship, this would be extremely difficult, although workmen were in great demand. Mr. Putnam, however, on whom I had previously called, gave me employment for a time in his publishing establishment, and thus I was fortunately enabled to await the arrival of a remittance from home.

Mrs. Trollope, whom I met in Florence, kindly gave me a letter to Murray, the publisher, and I visited him soon after my arrival. In his library I saw the original portraits of Byron, Moore, Campbell and the other authors who were intimate with him and his father.

A day or two afterwards I had the good fortune to breakfast with Lockhart and Bernard Barton, at the house of the former. Mr. Murray, through whom the invitation was given, accompanied me there. As it was late when we arrived at Regent's Park, we found them waiting, and sat down immediately to breakfast.

I was much pleased with Lockhart's appearance and manners. He has a noble, manly countenance—in fact, the handsomest English face I ever saw—a quick, dark eye and an ample forehead, shaded by locks which show, as yet, but few threads of gray. There is a peculiar charm in his rich, soft voice; especially when reciting poetry, it has a clear, organ-like vibration, which thrills deliciously on the ear. His daughter, who sat at the head of the table, is a most lovely and amiable girl.

Bernard Barton, who is now quite an old man, is a very lively and sociable Friend. His head is gray and almost bald, but there is still plenty of fire in his eyes and life in his limbs. His many kind and amiable qualities endear him to a large circle of literary friends. He still continues writing, and within the last year has brought out a volume of simple, touching "Household Verses." A picture of cheerful and contented old age has never been more briefly and beautifully drawn, than in the following lines, which he sent me, in answer to my desire to possess one of his poems in his own hand:

STANZAS

I feel that I am growing old,
  Nor wish to hide that truth;
Conscious my heart is not more cold
  Than in my by-gone youth.

I cannot roam the country round,
  As I was wont to do;
My feet a scantier circle bound,
  My eyes a narrower view.

But on my mental vision rise
  Bright scenes of beauty still

Morn's splendor, evening's glowing skies,
    Valley, and grove, and hill.

Nor can infirmities o'erwhelm
    The purer pleasures brought
From the immortal spirit's realm
    Of Feeling and of Thought!

My heart! let not dismay or doubt
    In thee an entrance win!
Thou hast enjoyed thyself *without* —
    Now seek thy joy within!

During breakfast he related to us a pleasant anecdote of Walter Scott. He once wrote to the poet on behalf of a young lady, who wished to have the description of Melrose, in the "Lay of the last Minstrel," in the poet's own writing. Scott sent it, but added these lines to the conclusion:

"Then go, and muse with deepest awe
    On what the writer never saw;
Who would not wander 'neath the moon
    To see what he could see at noon"

We went afterwards into Lockhart's library, which was full of interesting objects. I saw the private diary of Scott, kept until within a short time of his death. It was melancholy to trace the gradual failing of all his energies in the very wavering of the autograph. In a large volume of his correspondence, containing letters from Campbell, Wordsworth, Byron, and all the distinguished characters of the age, I saw Campbell's "Battle of the Baltic" in his own hand. I was highly interested and gratified with the whole visit; the more so, as Mr. Lockhart had invited me voluntarily, without previous acquaintance. I have since heard him spoken of in the highest terms of esteem.

I went one Sunday to the Church of St. Stephen, to hear George Croly, the poet. The service, read by a drowsy clerk, was long and monotonous; I sat in a side-aisle, looking up at the dome, and listening to the rain which dashed in torrents against the windowpanes. At last, a tall, gray-haired man came down the passage. He bowed with a sad smile, so full of benevolence and resignation, that it went into my heart at once, and I gave him an involuntary tribute of sympathy. He has a heavy affliction to bear — the death of his gallant son, one of the officers slain in the late battle of Ferozeshaw. His whole manner betrays the tokens of subdued but constant grief.

His sermon was peculiarly finished and appropriate; the language was clear and forcible, without that splendor of thought and dazzling vividness of imagery which mark "Salathiel." Yet I could not help noticing that he delighted to dwell on the spiritualities of religion, rather than its outward observances, which he seemed inclined to hurry over as lightly as possible. His mild, gray eye and lofty forehead are more like the benevolent divine than the poet. I thought of Salathiel, and looked at the dignified, sorrowful man before me. The picture of the accursed Judean vanished, and his own solemn lines rang on my ear:

"The mighty grave
　Wraps lord and slave,
　Nor pride, nor poverty dares come
　Within that prison-house, that tomb!"

Whenever I hear them, or think of them again, I shall see, in memory, Croly's calm, pale countenance.

"The chimes, the chimes of Mother-land,
　Of England, green and old;

That out from thane and ivied tower
  A thousand years have tolled!"

I often thought of Coxe's beautiful ballad, when, after a day spent
in Waterloo Place, I have listened, on my way homeward, to the
chimes of Mary-le-bone Chapel, sounding sweetly and clearly above
all the din of the Strand. There is something in their silvery vibration,
which is far more expressive than the ordinary tones of a bell. The
ear can become weary of a continued toll—the sound of some bells
seems to have nothing more in it than the ordinary clang of metal
—but these simple notes, following one another so melodiously, fall
on the ear, stunned by the ceaseless roar of carriages or the mingled
cries of the mob, as gently and gratefully as drops of dew. Whether
it be morning, and they ring out louder and deeper through the mist,
or midnight, when the vast ocean of being beneath them surges less
noisily than its wont, they are alike full of melody and poetry. I have
often paused, deep in the night, to hear those clear tones, dropping
down from the darkness, thrilling, with their full, tremulous sweetness, the still air of the lighted Strand, and winding away through
dark, silent lanes and solitary courts, till the ear of the care-worn
watcher is scarcely stirred with their dying vibrations. They seemed
like those spirit-voices, which, at such times, speak almost audibly
to the heart. How delicious it must be, to those who dwell within the
limits of their sound, to wake from some happy dream and hear
those chimes blending in with their midnight fancies, like the musical echo of the promised bliss. I love these eloquent bells, and I
think there must be many, living out a life of misery and suffering,
to whom their tones come with an almost human consolation. The
natures of the very cockneys who never go without the horizon of
their vibrations, is, to my mind, invested with one hue of poetry!
  A few days ago, an American friend invited me to accompany him
to Greenwich Fair. We took a penny steamer from Hungerford Market to London Bridge, and jumped into the cars, which go every five

minutes. Twelve minutes' ride above the chimneys of London and the vegetable-fields of Rotherhithe and Deptford brought us to Greenwich, and we followed the stream of people which was flowing from all parts of the city into the Park.

Here began the merriment. We heard on every side the noise of the "scratchers," or, as the venders of these articles denominated them—"the fun of the fair," By this is meant a little notched wheel, with a piece of wood fastened on it, like a miniature watchman's rattle. The "fun" consists in drawing them down the back of anyone you pass, when they make a sound precisely like that of ripping cloth. The women take great delight in this, and as it is only deemed politeness to return the compliment, we soon had enough to do. Nobody seemed to take the diversion amiss, but it was so irresistibly droll to see a large crowd engaged in this singular amusement, that we both burst into hearty laughter.

As we began ascending Greenwich Hill, we were assailed with another kind of game. The ground was covered with smashed oranges, with which the people above and below were stoutly pelting each other. Half a dozen heavy ones whizzed uncomfortably near my head as I went up, and I saw several persons get the full benefit of a shot on their backs and breasts. The young country lads and lasses amused themselves by running at full speed down the steep side of a hill. This was, however, a feat attended with some risk; for I saw one luckless girl describe an arc of a circle, of which her feet was the centre and her body the radius. All was noise and nonsense. They ran to and fro under the long, hoary boughs of the venerable oaks that crest the summit, and clattered down the magnificent forest-avenues, whose budding foliage gave them little shelter from the passing April showers.

The view from the top is quite splendid. The stately Thames curves through the plain below, which loses itself afar off in the mist; Greenwich, with its massive hospital, lies just at one's feet, and in a clear day the domes of London skirt the horizon. The wood of the

Park is entirely oak—the majestic, dignified, English oak — which covers, in picturesque clumps, the sides and summits of the two billowy hills. It must be a sweet place in summer, when the dark, massive foliage is heavy on every mossy arm, and the smooth and curving sward shines with thousands of field-flowers.

Owing to the showers, the streets were coated with mud, of a consistence as soft and yielding as the most fleecy Persian carpet. Near the gate, boys were holding scores of donkeys, which they offered us at threepence for a ride of two miles. We walked down towards the river, and came at last to a group of tumblers, who with muddy hands and feet were throwing somersets in the open street. I recognized them as old acquaintances of the Rue St. Antoine and the Champs Elysées; but the little boy who cried before, because he did not want to bend his head and feet into a ring, like a hoop-snake, had learned his part better by this time, so that he went through it all without whimpering and came off with only a fiery red face. The exercises of the young gentlemen were of course very graceful and classic, and the effect of their poses of strength was very much heightened by the muddy foot-marks which they left on each other's orange-colored skins.

The avenue of booths was still more diverting. Here under sheets of leaky awning, were exposed for sale rows of gilded gingerbread kings and queens, and I cannot remember how many men and women held me fast by the arms, determined to force me into buying a pound of them. We paused at the sign: "Signor Urbani's Grand Magical Display." The title was attractive, so we paid the penny admission, and walked behind the dark, mysterious curtain. Two bare brick walls, three benches and a little boy appeared to us. A sheet hung before us upon which quivered the shadow of some terrible head. At my friend's command, the boy (also a spectator) put out the light, when the awful and grinning face of a black woman became visible. While we were admiring this striking production, thus mysteriously revealed, Signor Urbani came in, and seeing no hope of any more spectators, went behind the curtain and startled our sensitive nerves with six or seven skeleton and devil apparitions, winding up the wonderful entertainment with the same black head. We signified our entire approbation by due applause and then went out to seek further novelties.

The centre of the square was occupied by swings, where some eight or ten boat-loads of persons were flying topsy-turvy into the air, making one giddy to look at them, and constant fearful shrieks arose from the lady swingers, at finding themselves in a horizontal or inverted position, high above the ground.

One of the machines was like a great wheel, with four cars attached, which mounted and descended with their motley freight. We got into the boat by way of experiment. The starting motion was pleasant, but very soon it flew with a swiftness and to a height rather alarming. I began to repent having chosen such a mode of amusement, but held on as well as I could, in my uneasy place. Presently we mounted till the long beam of our boat was horizontal; at one instant, I saw three young ladies below me, with their heads downward, like a shadow in the water — the next I was turned heels up, looking at them as a shadow does at its original. I was fast becoming sea-sick, when, after a few minutes of such giddy soaring, the ropes were slackened and we all got out, looking somewhat pale, and feeling nervous, if nothing else.

There were also many great tents, hung with boughs and lighted with innumerable colored lamps, where the people danced their country dances in a choking cloud of dry sawdust. Conjurors and gymnastic performers were showing off on conspicuous platforms, and a continual sound of drums, cymbals and shrill trumpets called the attention of the crowd to some "Wonderful Exhibition" — some infant phenomenon, giant, or three-headed pig. A great part of the crowd belonged evidently to the very worst part of society, but the watchfulness of the police prevented any open disorder. We came away early and in a quarter of an hour were in busy London, leaving far behind us the revel and debauch, which was prolonged through the whole night.

London has the advantage of one of the most gloomy atmospheres in the world. During this opening spring weather, no light and scarcely any warmth can penetrate the dull, yellowish gray mist, which incessantly hangs over the city. Sometimes at noon we have for an hour or two a sickly gleam of sunshine, but it is soon swallowed up by the smoke and drizzling fog. The people carry umbrellas at all times, for the rain seems to drop spontaneously out of the very air, without waiting for the usual preparation of a gathering cloud. Professor Espy's rules would be of little avail here.

A few days ago we had a real fog — a specimen of November weather, as the people said. If November wears such a mantle, London, during that sober month, must furnish a good idea of the gloom of Hades. The streets were wrapped in a veil of dense mist, of a dirty yellow color, as if the air had suddenly grown thick and mouldy. The houses on the opposite sides of the street were invisible, and the gas-lamps, lighted in the shops, burned, with a white and ghastly flame. Carriages ran together in the streets, and I was kept constantly on the look-out, lest someone should come suddenly out of the cloud around me, and we should meet with a shock like that of two knights at a tournament. As I stood in the centre of Trafalgar Square, with every object invisible around me, it reminded me, (hoping the comparison will not be accepted in every particular) of Satan resting in the middle of Chaos. The weather sometimes continues thus for whole days together.

April 26.—An hour and a half of land are still allowed us, and then we shall set foot on the back of the oak-ribbed leviathan, which will be our home until a thousand leagues of blue ocean are crossed. I shall hear the old Aldgate clock strike for the last time—I shall take a last walk through the Minories and past the Tower yard, and as we glide down the Thames, St. Pauls, half-hidden in mist and coal-smoke, will probably be my last glimpse of London.

Chapter XLVIII
HOMEWARD BOUND—CONCLUSION

We slid out of St. Katharine's Dock at noon on the appointed day, and with a pair of sooty steamboats hitched to our vessel, moved slowly down the Thames in mist and drizzling rain. I stayed on the wet deck all afternoon, that I might more forcibly and joyously feel we were again in motion on the waters and homeward bound! My attention was divided between the dreary views of Blackwall, Greenwich and Woolwich, and the motley throng of passengers who were to form our ocean society. An English family, going out to settle in Canada, were gathered together in great distress and anxiety, for the father had gone ashore in London at a late hour, and was left behind. When we anchored for the night at Gravesend, their fears were quieted by his arrival in a skiff from the shore, as he had immediately followed us by railroad.

My cousin and B —— had hastened on from Paris to join me, and a day before the sailing of the "Victoria," we took berths in the second cabin, for twelve pounds ten shillings each, which in the London line of packets, includes coarse but substantial fare for the whole voyage. Our funds were insufficient to pay even this; but Captain Morgan, who was less mistrustful than my Norman landlord, generously agreed that the remainder of the fare should be paid in America. B —— and I, with two young Englishmen, took possession of a state-room of rough boards, lighted by a bull's eye, which in stormy weather leaked so much that our trunks swam in water. A narrow mattress and blanket, with a knapsack for a pillow, formed a passable bed. A long entry between the rooms, lighted by a feeble swinging lamp, was filled with a board table, around which the thirty-two second cabin passengers met to discuss politics and salt pork, favorable winds and hard sea-biscuit.

We lay becalmed opposite Sheerness the whole of the second day. At dusk a sudden squall came up, which drove us foaming towards the North Foreland. When I went on deck in the morning, we had passed Dover and Brighton, and the Isle of Wight was rising dim ahead of us. The low English coast on our right was bordered by long reaches of dazzling chalky sand, which glittered along the calm blue water.

Gliding into the Bay of Portsmouth, we dropped anchor opposite the romantic town of Ryde, built on the sloping shore of the green Isle of Wight. Eight or nine vessels of the Experimental Squadron were anchored near us, and over the houses of Portsmouth, I saw the masts of the Victory—the flag-ship in the battle of Trafalgar, on board of which Nelson was killed. The wind was not strong enough to permit the passage of the Needles, so at midnight we succeeded in wearing back again into the channel, around the Isle of Wight. A head wind forced us to tack away towards the shore of France. We were twice in sight of the rocky coast of Brittany, near Cherbourg, but the misty promontory of Land's End was our last glimpse of the old world.

On one of our first days at sea, I caught a curlew, which came flying on weary wings towards us, and alighted on one of the boats. Two of his brethren, too much exhausted or too timid to do likewise, dropped flat on the waves and resigned themselves to their fate without a struggle. I slipped up and caught his long, lank legs, while he was resting with flagging wings and half-shut eyes. We fed him, though it was difficult to get anything down his reed-shaped bill; but he took kindly to our force-work, and when we let him loose on the deck, walked about with an air quite tame and familiar. He died, however, two days afterwards. A French pigeon, which was caught in the rigging, lived and throve during the whole of the passage.

A few days afterwards, a heavy storm came on, and we were all sleepless and sea-sick, as long as it lasted. Thanks, however, to a beautiful law of memory, the recollection of that dismal period soon lost its unpleasantness, while the grand forms of beauty the vexed ocean presented, will remain forever, as distinct and abiding images. I kept on deck as long as I could stand, watching the giant waves over which our vessel took her course. They rolled up towards us, thirty or forty feet in height—dark gray masses, changing to a beautiful vitriol tint, wherever the light struck through their countless and changing crests. It was a glorious thing to see our good ship mount slowly up the side of one of these watery hills, till her prow was lifted high in air, then, rocking over its brow, plunge with a slight quiver downward, and plough up a briny cataract, as she struck the vale. I never before realized the terrible sublimity of the sea. And yet it was a pride to see how man—strong in his almost godlike will—could bid defiance to those whelming surges, and brave their wrath unharmed.

We swung up and down on the billows, till we scarcely knew which way to stand. The most grave and sober personages suddenly found themselves reeling in a very undignified manner, and not a few measured their lengths on the slippery decks. Boxes and barrels were affected in like manner; everything danced around us. Trunks ran out from under the berths; packages leaped down from the shelves; chairs skipped across the rooms, and at table, knives, forks and mugs engaged in a general waltz and break down. One incident of this kind was rather laughable. One night, about midnight, the gale, which had been blowing violently, suddenly lulled, "as if," to use a sailor's phrase, "it had been chopped off!" Instantly the ship gave a tremendous lurch, which was the signal for a general breaking loose. Two or three others followed, so violent, that for a moment I imagined the vessel had been thrown on her beam ends. Trunks, crockery and barrels went banging down from one end of the ship to the other. The women in the steerage set up an awful scream, and the German emigrants, thinking we were in terrible danger, commenced praying with might and main. In the passage near our room stood several barrels, filled with broken dishes, which

394 Views of Old Europe

at every lurch went banging from side to side, jarring the board partition and making a horrible din. I shall not soon forget the Babel which kept our eyes open that night.

The 19th of May, a calm came on. Our white wings flapped idly on the mast, and only the top-gallant sails were bent enough occasionally to lug us along at a mile an hour. A barque from Ceylon, making the most of the wind, with every rag of canvas set, passed us slowly on the way eastward. The sun went down unclouded, and a glorious starry night brooded over us. Its clearness and brightness were to me indications of America. I longed to be on shore. The forests about home were then clothed in the delicate green of their first leaves, and that bland weather embraced the sweet earth like a blessing of heaven. The gentle breath from out the west seemed made for the odor of violets, and as it came to me over the slightly-ruled deep, I thought how much sweeter it were to feel it, while "wasting in wood-paths the voluptuous hours."

Soon afterwards a fresh wind sprung up, which increased rapidly, till every sail was bent to the full. Our vessel parted the brine with an arrowy glide, the ease and grace of which it is impossible to describe. The breeze held on steadily for two or three days, which brought us to the southern extremity of the Banks. Here the air felt so sharp and chilling, that I was afraid we might be under the lee of an iceberg, but in the evening the dull gray mass of clouds lifted themselves from the horizon, and the sun set in clear, American beauty away beyond Labrador. The next morning we were enveloped in a dense fog, and the wind which bore us onward was of a piercing coldness. A sharp look-out was kept on the bow, but as we could see but a short distance, it might have been dangerous had we met one of the Arctic squadron. At noon it cleared away again, and the bank of fog was visible a long time astern, piled along the horizon, reminding me of the Alps, as seen from the plains of Piedmont.

On the 31st, the fortunate wind which carried us from the Banks, failed us about thirty-five miles from Sandy Hook. We lay in the midst of the mackerel fishery, with small schooners anchored all around us. Fog, dense and impenetrable, weighed on the moveless ocean, like an atmosphere of wool. The only incident to break the horrid monotony of the day, was the arrival of a pilot, with one or two newspapers, detailing the account of the Mexican war. We heard in the afternoon the booming of the surf along the low beach of Long Island—hollow and faint, like the murmur of a shell. When the mist lifted a little, we saw the faint line of breakers along the shore. The Germans gathered on deck to sing their old, familiar songs, and their voices blended beautifully together in the stillness.

Next morning at sunrise we saw Sandy Hook; at nine o'clock we were telegraphed in New York by the station at Coney Island; at eleven the steamer "Hercules" met us outside the Hook; and at noon we were gliding up the Narrows, with the whole ship's company of four hundred persons on deck, gazing on the beautiful shores of Staten Island and agreeing almost universally, that it was the most delightful scene they had ever looked upon.

And now I close the story of my long wandering, as I began it— with a lay written on the deep.

HOMEWARD BOUND

Farewell to Europe!   Days have come and gone
Since misty England set behind the sea.
Our ship climbs onward o'er the lifted waves,
That gather up in ridges, mountain-high,
And like a sea-god, conscious in his power,
Buffets the surges. Storm-arousing winds
That sweep, unchecked, from frozen Labrador,
Make wintry music through the creaking shrouds.
Th' horizon's ring, that clasps the dreary view,
Lays mistily upon the gray Atlantic's breast,

Shut out, at times, by bulk of sparry blue,
That, rolling near us, heaves the swaying prow
High on its shoulders, to descend again
Ploughing a thousand cascades, and around
Spreading the frothy foam. These watery gulfs,
With storm, and winds far-sweeping, hem us in,
Alone upon the waters!

               Days must pass —
Many and weary—between sea and sky.
Our eyes, that long e'en now for the fresh green
Of sprouting forests, and the far blue stretch
Of regal mountains piled along the sky,
Must see, for many an eve, the level sun
Sheathe, with his latest gold, the heaving brine,
By thousand ripples shivered, or Night's pomp
Brooding in silence, ebon and profound,
Upon the murmuring darkness of the deep,
Broken by flashings, that the parted wave
Sends white and star-like through its bursting foam.

Yet not more dear the opening dawn of heaven
Poured on the earth in an Italian May,
When souls take wings upon the scented air
Of starry meadows, and the yearning heart
Pains with deep sweetness in the balmy time,
Than these gray morns, and days of misty blue,
And surges, never-ceasing; — for our prow
Points to the sunset like a morning ray,
And o'er the waves, and through the sweeping storms,
Through day and darkness, rushes ever on,
Westward and westward still! What joy can send
The spirit thrilling onward with the wind,

In untamed exultation, like the thought
That fills the Homeward Bound?

     Country and home!
Ah! not the charm of silver-tongued romance,
Born of the feudal time, nor whatsoe'er
Of dying glory fills the golden realms
Of perished song, where heaven-descended Art
Still boasts her later triumphs, can compare
With that one thought of liberty inherited—
Of free life giv'n by fathers who were free,
And to be left to children freer still!
That pride and consciousness of manhood, caught
From boyish musings on the holy graves
Of hero-martyrs, and from every form
Which virgin Nature, mighty and unchained,
Takes in an empire not less proudly so—
Inspired in mountain airs, untainted yet
By thousand generations' breathing—felt
Like a near presence in the awful depths
Of unhewn forests, and upon the steep
Where giant rivers take their maddening plunge—
Has grown impatient of the stifling damps
Which hover close on Europe's shackled soil.

Content to tread awhile the holy steps
Of Art and Genius, sacred through all time,
The spirit breathed that dull, oppressive air—
Which, freighted with its tyrant-clouds, o'erweighs
The upward throb of many a nation's soul—
Amid those olden memories, felt the thrall,
But kept the birth-right of its freer home.
Here, on the world's blue highway, comes again

The voice of Freedom, heard amid the roar
Of sundered billows, while above the wave
Rise visions of the forest and the stream.
Like trailing robes the morning mists uproll,
Torn by the mountain pines; the flashing rills
Shout downward through the hollows of the vales;
Down the great river's bosom shining sails
Glide with a gradual motion, while from all—
Hamlet, and bowered homestead, and proud town—
Voices of joy ring far up into heaven!

Yet louder, winds! Urge on our keel, ye waves,
Swift as the spirit's yearnings! We would ride
With a loud stormy motion o'er your crests,
With tempests shouting like a sudden joy—
Interpreting our triumph! 'Tis your voice,
Ye unchained elements, alone can speak
The sympathetic feeling of the free—
The arrowy impulse of the Homeward Bound!

I shall not attempt to describe the excitement of that afternoon. After thirty-seven days between sky and water, any shore would have been beautiful, but when it was home, after we had been two years absent, during an age when time is always slow, it required a powerful effort to maintain any propriety of manner. The steward prepared a parting dinner, much better than any we had had at sea; but I tried in vain to eat. Never were trees such a glorious green as those around the Quarantine Buildings, where we lay to for half an hour, to be visited by the physician. The day was cloudy, and thick mist hung on the tops of the hills, but I felt as if I could never tire looking at the land.

At last we approached the city. It appeared smaller than when I left, but this might have been because I was habituated to the broad distances of the sea. Our scanty baggage was brought on deck, for the inspection of the custom-house officer, but we were neither annoyed nor delayed by the operation. The steamer by this time had taken us to the pier at Pine-street wharf, and the slight jar of the vessel as she came alongside, sent a thrill of delight through our frames. But when finally the ladder was let down, and we sprang upon the pier, it was with an electric shock, as if of recognition from the very soil. It was about four o'clock in the afternoon, and we were glad that night was so near at hand. After such strong excitement, and even bewilderment of feeling as we had known since morning, the prospect of rest was very attractive.

But no sooner were we fairly deposited in a hotel, than we must see the city again. How we had talked over this hour! How we had thought of the life, the neatness, the comfort of our American cities, when rambling through some filthy and depopulated capital of the Old World! At first sight, our anticipations were not borne out; there had been heavy rains for a week or two, and the streets were not re-markably clean; houses were being built up or taken down, on all sides, and the number of trees in full foliage, everywhere visible, gave us the idea of an immense unfinished country town. I took this back, it is true, the next morning, when the sun was bright and the streets were thronged with people. But what activity, what a restless eagerness and even keenness of expression on every countenance! I could not have believed that the general cast of the American face was so sharp; yet nothing was so remarkable as the perfect inde-pendence of manner which we noticed in all, down to the very chil-dren. I can easily conceive how this should jar with the feelings of a stranger, accustomed to the deference, not to say servility, in which the largest class of the people of Europe is trained; but it was a most refreshing change to us.

Life at sea sharpens one's sensibilities to the sounds and scents of land, in a very high degree. We noticed a difference in the atmo-sphere of different streets, and in the scent of leaves and grass, which a land friend who was with us failed entirely to distinguish. The next day, as we left New York, and in perfect exultation of spirit sped across New Jersey, (which I admit was never half so beautiful to our eyes,) I could feel nothing but one continued sensation of the country—fragrant hay-field and wild clearing, garden and marshy hollow, and the cool shadow of the woodlands — I was by turns possessed with the spirit of them all. The twilight deepened as we passed down the Delaware; I stood on the promenade deck and watched the evening star kindling through the cloudless flush of sunset, while the winds that came over the glassy river bore me the odor of long-remembered meadow flowers. We asked each other what there was in the twilights of Florence and Vallambrosa more delicious than this?

A night in neat, cheerful, home-like Philadelphia, whose dimensions were also a little shrunken in our eyes, and a glorious June morning broke on the last day of our pilgrimage. Again we were on the Delaware, pacing the deck in rapture at the green, luxuriant beauty of its shores. Is it not worth years of absence, to learn how to love one's land as it should be loved? Two or three hours brought us to Wilmington, in Delaware, and within twelve miles of home. Now came the realization of a plan we had talked over a hundred times, to keep up our spirits when the weather was gloomy, or the journey lay through some waste of barren country. Our knapsacks, which had been laid down in Paris, were again taken up, slouched German hats substituted for our modern black cylinders, belt and blouse donned, and the pilgrim staff grasped for the rest of our journey. But it was part of our plan, that we should not reach home till after nightfall; we could not think of seeing anyone we knew before those who were nearest to us; and so it was necessary to wait a few hours before starting.

The time came; that walk of three or four hours seemed longer than many a day's tramp of thirty miles, but every step of the way was familiar ground. The people we met stared, laughed, or looked suspiciously after us, but we were quite insensible to any observation. We only counted the fields, measured the distance from hill to hill, and watched the gradual decline of the broad, bright sun. It went down at last, and our homes were not far off. When the twilight grew deeper, we parted, and each thought what an experience lay between that moment and the next morning. I took to the fields, plunged into a sea of dewy clover, and made for a light which began to glimmer as it grew darker. When I reached it and looked with the most painful excitement through the window at the unsuspecting group within, there was not one face missing.

Postscript
ADVICE AND INFORMATION FOR PEDESTRIANS

Although the narrative of my journey, "with knapsack and staff" is now strictly finished, a few more words of explanation seem necessary, to describe more fully the method of traveling which we adopted. I add them the more willingly, as it is my belief that many, whose circumstances are similar to mine, desire to undertake the same romantic journey. Some matter-of-fact statements may be to them useful as well as interesting.

To see Europe as a pedestrian requires little preparation, if the traveler is willing to forego some of the refinements of living to which he may have been accustomed, for the sake of the new and interesting fields of observation which will be opened to him. He must be content to sleep on hard beds, and partake of coarse fare; to undergo rudeness at times from the officers of the police and the porters of palaces and galleries; or to travel for hours in rain and storm, without finding a shelter. The knapsack will at first be heavy upon the shoulders, the feet will be sore and the limbs weary with the day's walk, and sometimes the spirit will begin to flag under the general fatigue of body. This, however, soon passes over. In a week's time, if the pedestrian does not attempt too much on setting out, his limbs are stronger, and his gait more firm and vigorous; he lies down at night with a feeling of refreshing rest, sleeps with a soundness undisturbed by a single dream, that seems almost like death, if he has been accustomed to restless nights; and rises invigorated in heart and frame for the next day's journey. The coarse black bread of the peasant inns, with cheese no less coarse, and a huge mug of milk or the nourishing beer of Germany, have a relish to his keen appetite, which excites his own astonishment. And if he is willing to regard all incivility and attempts at imposition as valuable lessons in the study of human nature, and to keep his temper and cheerfulness in any situation which may try them, he is prepared to walk through the whole of Europe, with more real pleasure to himself, and far more profit, than if he journeyed in style and enjoyed the constant services of *couriers* and *valets de place.*

Should his means become unusually scant, he will find it possible to travel on an amazingly small pittance, and with more actual bodily comfort than would seem possible, to one who has not tried it. I was more than once obliged to walk a number of days in succession, on less than a franc a day, and found that by far the greatest drawback to my enjoyment was the fear that I might be without relief when this allowance should be exhausted. One observes, admires, wonders and learns quite as extensively, under such circumstances, as if he had unlimited means. Perhaps some account of this truly pilgrim-like journeying, may possess a little interest for the general reader.

The only expense that cannot be reduced at will, in Europe, is that for sleeping. You may live on a crust of bread a day, but lower than four cents for a bed you cannot go! In Germany this is the regular price paid by traveling journeymen, and no one need wish for a more comfortable resting place, than those massive boxes, (when you have become accustomed to their shortness,) with their coarse but clean linen sheets, and healthy mattresses of straw. In Italy the price varies from half a paul to a paul, (ten cents,) but a person somewhat familiar with the language would not often be asked more than the former price, for which he has a bed stuffed with corn-husks, large enough for at least three men. I was asked in France, five sous in all the village inns, from Marseilles to Dieppe. The pedestrian cares far more for a good rest, than for the quality of his fare, and a walk of thirty miles prepares him to find it, on the hardest couch.

I usually rose before sunrise, and immediately began the day's journey, the cost of lodging having been paid the night before, a universal custom among the common inns, which are frequented by the peasantry. At the next village, I would buy a loaf of the hard brown bread, with some cheese, or butter, or whatever substantial addition could be made at trifling cost, and breakfast up on a bank by the roadside, lying at full length on the dewy grass, and using my knapsack as a table. I might also mention that a leathern pouch, fastened to one side of this table, contained a knife and fork, and one or two solid tin boxes, for articles which could not be carried in the pocket. A similar pouch at the other side held pen and ink, and a small bottle, which was filled sometimes with the fresh water of the streams, and sometimes with the common country wine, of the year's vintage, which costs from three to six sous the quart.

After walking more than half the distance to be accomplished, with half an hour's rest, dinner would be made in the same manner, and while we rested the full hour allotted to the midday halt, guide-books would be examined, journals written, a sketch made of the landscape, or our minds refreshed by reading a passage in Milton or Childe Harold. If it was during the cold, wet days of winter, we sought a rock, or sometimes the broad abutment of a chance bridge, upon which to lie; in summer, it mattered little whether we rested in sun or shade, under a bright or rainy sky. The vital energy which this life in the open air gives to the constitution, is remarkable. The very sensation of health and strength becomes a positive luxury, and the heart overflows with its buoyant exuberance of cheerfulness. Every breath of the fresh morning air was like a draught of some sparkling elixir, gifted with all the potency of the undiscovered Fountain of Youth. We felt pent and oppressed within the walls of a dwelling; it was far more agreeable to march in the face of a driving shower, under whose beating the blood grew fresh and warm, than to sit by a dull fireplace, waiting for it to cease. Although I had lived mainly upon a farm till the age of seventeen, and was accustomed to outdoor exercise, I never before felt how much life one may draw from air and sunshine alone.

Thus, what at first was borne as a hardship, became at last an enjoyment, and there seemed to me no situation so extreme, that I did not possess some charm to my mind, which made me unwilling to shrink from the experience. Still, as one depth of endurance after another was reached, the words of Cicero would recur to me as encouragement— "Perhaps even this may hereafter be remembered with pleasure." Once only, while waiting six days at Lyons, in gloomy weather and among harsh people, without a sous, and with a strong doubt of receiving any relief, I became indifferent to what might happen, and would have passively met any change for the worse— as men who have been exposed to shipwreck for days, scarce make an effort to save themselves when the vessel strikes at last.

One little experience of this kind, though less desperate, may be worth relating. It happened during my stay in Florence; and what might not a man bear, for the sake of living in the midst of such a paradise?

My comrade and I had failed to receive a remittance at the expected time, and our funds had gone down to zero. The remaining one of our trio of Americans, who had taken a suite of rooms in company, a noble-hearted Kentuckian, shared his own means with us, till what he had in Florence was nearly exhausted. His banker lived in Leghorn, and he concluded to go there and draw for more, instead of having it sent through a correspondent. B —— decided to accompany him, and two young Englishmen, who had just arrived on foot from Geneva, joined the party. They resolved on making an adventure out of the expedition, and it was accordingly agreed that they should take one of the market-boats of the Arno, and sail down to Pisa, more than fifty miles distant, by the river. We paid one or two visits to the western gate of the city, where numbers of these craft always lie at anchor, and struck a bargain with a sturdy boatman, that he should take them for a scudo (about one dollar) each.

The hour of starting was nine o'clock in the evening, and I accompanied them to the starting place. The boat had a slight canvas covering, and the crew consisted only of the owner and his son Antonio, a boy of ten. I shall not recount their voyage all that night, (which was so cold, that they tied each other up in the boatman's meal-bags, around the neck, and lay down in a heap on the ribbed bottom of the boat,) nor their adventures in Pisa and Leghorn. They were to be absent three or four days, and had left me money enough to live upon in the meantime, but the next morning an unexpected expense consumed nearly the whole of it. I had about four crazie (three cents) a day for my meals, and by spending one of these for bread, and the remainder for ripe figs, of which one crazie will purchase fifteen or twenty, I managed to make a diminutive breakfast and dinner, but was careful not to take much exercise, on account of the increase of hunger. As it happened, my friends remained two days longer than I had expected, and the last two crazie I had were expended for one day's provisions. I then decided to try the next day without any thing, and actually felt a curiosity to know what one's sensations would be, on experiencing two or three days of starvation. I knew that if the feeling should become insupportable, I could easily walk out to the mountain of Fiesole, where a fine fig orchard shaded the old Roman amphitheatre. But the experiment was broken off in its commencement, by the arrival of the absent ones, in the middle of the night. Such is the weakness of human nature, that on finding I should not want for breakfast, I arose from bed, and ate two or three figs which, by a strong exertion, I had saved from the scanty allowance of the day. I only relate this incident to show that the severest deprivation is very easily borne, and that it is worth bearing for what it teaches.

So also, when a storm came up at nightfall, while we were a league distant from the end of our journey, after the first natural shrinking from its violence was over, there was a sublime pleasure in walking in the midst of darkness and dashing rain. There have been times when the sky was black, just revealing its deeps of whelming cloud, and the winds full of the cold, fresh, saddening spirit of the storm, which I would not have exchanged for the brightness of a morning beside the sea.

A few words in relation to a pedestrian's (hiker's) equipment may be of some practical value. I adopted, as the most serviceable and agreeable, the traveling costume of a German student, but there are many small particulars, in addition, which I have often been asked to give. It is the best plan to take no more clothing than is absolutely required, as the traveler will not desire to carry more than fifteen pounds on his back, knapsack included. A single suit of good dark cloth, with a supply of linen, will be amply sufficient. The strong linen blouse, confined by a leather belt, will protect it from the dust, and when this is thrown aside on entering a city, the traveler makes a very respectable appearance. The slouched hat of finely-woven felt, is a delightful covering to the head, serving at the same time as umbrella or nightcap, traveling dress or visiting costume. No one should neglect a good cane, which, besides its feeling of companionship, is equal to from three to five miles a day, and may serve as a defence against banditti, or savage Bohemian dogs. In the Alps, the tall staves, pointed with iron, and topped with a curved chamois horn, can be bought for a franc apiece, and are of great assistance in crossing ice-fields, or sustaining the weight of the body in descending steep and difficult passes.

An umbrella is rather inconvenient, unless it is short and may be strapped on the knapsack, but even then, an ample cape of oiled silk or India rubber cloth is far preferable. The pedestrian need not be particular in this respect; he will soon grow accustomed to an occasional drenching, and I am not sure that men, like plants, do not thrive under it, when they have outgrown the hot-house nature of civilization, in a life under the open heaven. A portfolio, capable of hard service, with a guide-book or two, pocket-compass and spyglass, completes the contents of the knapsack, though if there is still a small corner to spare, I would recommend that it be filled with pocket editions of one or two of the good old English classics. It is a rare delight to sit down in the gloomy fastnesses of the Hartz, or in the breezy valleys of Styria, and read the majestic measures of our glorious Saxon bards. Milton is first fully appreciated, when you look up from his page to the snowy ramparts of the Alps, which shut out all but the Heaven of whose beauty he sang; and all times and places are fitting for the universal Shakespeare. Childe Harold bears such a glowing impress of the scenery on which Byron's eye has dwelt, that it spoke to me like the answering heart of a friend, from the crag of Drachenfels, in the rushing of the arrowy Rhône, and beside the breathing marbles of the Vatican and the Capitol.

A little facility in sketching from nature is a most useful and delightful accomplishment for the pedestrian. He may bring away the features of wild and unvisited landscapes, the picturesque fronts of peasant cottages and wayside shrines, or the simple beauty of some mountain child, watching his herd of goats. Though having little knowledge and no practice in the art, I persevered in my awkward attempts, and was soon able to take a rough and rapid, but tolerably correct outline of almost any scene. These memorials of two years of travel have now a value to me, which I would not exchange for the finest engravings, however they might excel in faithful representation. Another article of equipment, which I had almost forgotten to mention, is a small bottle of the best Cognac, with which to bathe the feet, morning and evening, for the first week or two, or as long as they continue tender with the exercise. It was also very strengthening and refreshing, when the body was unusually weary with a long day's walking or climbing, to use as an outward stimulant; for I never had occasion to apply it internally. Many of the German students wear a wicker flask, slung over their shoulder, containing kirschwasser, which they mix with the water of the mountain streams, but this is not at all necessary to the traveler's health and comfort.

These students, with all their irregularities, are a noble, warmhearted class, and make the best companions in the world. During the months of August and September, hundreds of them ramble through Switzerland and the Tyrol, extending their route sometimes to Venice and Rome. With their ardent love for everything republican, they will most always receive an American heartily, consecrate him as a bursch, and admit him to their fellowship. With most of them, an economy of expense is part of the habit of their student-life, and they are only spendthrifts on the articles of beer and tobacco. A month's residence in Heidelberg, the most beautiful place in Germany, will serve to make the young American acquainted with their habits, and able to join them for an adventurous foot-journey, with the greatest advantage to himself.

We always accepted a companion, of whatever kind, while walking — from chimney-sweeps to barons. In a strange country one can learn something from every peasant, and we neglected no opportunity, not only to obtain information, but to impart it. We found everywhere great curiosity about America, and we were always glad to tell them all they wished to know. In Germany, we were generally taken for Germans from some part of the country where the dialect was a little different, or, if they remarked on our foreign peculiarities, they supposed we were either Poles, Russians, or Swiss. The greatest ignorance in relation to America, prevails among the common people. They imagine we are a savage race, without intelligence and almost without law.

Persons of education, who had some slight knowledge of our history, showed a curiosity to know something of our political condition. They are taught by the German newspapers (which are under a strict censorship in this respect) to look only at the evil in our country, and they almost invariably began by adverting to *Slavery* and *Repudiation*. While we admitted, often with shame and mortification, the existence of things so totally inconsistent with true republicanism, we endeavored to make them comprehend the advantages enjoyed by the *free* citizen — the complete equality of birth—which places America, despite her sins, far above any other nation on earth. I could plainly see, by the kindling eye and half-suppressed sigh, that they appreciated a freedom so immeasurably greater than that which they enjoyed.

In large cities we always preferred to take the second or third-rate hotels, which are generally visited by merchants and persons who travel on business; for, with the same comforts as the first rank, they are nearly twice as cheap. A traveler, with a guidebook and a good pair of eyes, can also dispense with the services of a *courier,* whose duty it is to conduct strangers about the city, from one area to another. We chose rather to find out and view the "sights" at our leisure. In small villages, where we were often obliged to stop, we chose the best hotels, which, particularly in Northern Germany and in Italy, are none too good. But if it was a post, that is, a town where the post-chaise stops to change horses, we usually avoided the post-hotel, where one must pay high for having curtains before his windows and a more elegant cover on his bed. In the less splendid country inns, we always found neat, comfortable lodging, and a pleasant, friendly reception from the people. They saluted us on entering, with "Be you welcome," and on leaving, wished us a pleasant journey and good fortune. The host, when he brought us supper or breakfast, lifted his cap, and wished us a good appetite—and when he lighted us to our chambers, left us with "May you sleep well!" We generally found honest, friendly people; they delighted in telling us about the country around; what ruins there were in the neighborhood—and what strange legends were connected with them. The only part of Europe where it is unpleasant to travel in this manner, is Bohemia. We could scarcely find a comfortable inn; the people all spoke an unknown language, and were not particularly celebrated for their honesty. Beside this, travelers rarely go on foot in those regions; we were frequently taken for traveling handwerker, and subjected to imposition.

With regard to passports, although they were vexatious and often expensive, we found little difficulty when we had acquainted ourselves with the regulations concerning them. In France and Germany they are comparatively little trouble; in Italy they are the traveler's greatest annoyance. Americans are treated with less strictness, in this respect, than citizens of other nations, and, owing to the absence of rank among us, they also enjoy greater advantages of acquaintance and intercourse.

The expenses of traveling in England, although much greater than in our own country, may, as we learned by experience, be brought, through economy, within the same compass. Indeed, it is my belief, from observation, that, with few exceptions, throughout Europe, where a traveler enjoys the same comfort and abundance as in America, he must pay the same prices. The principal difference is, that he only pays for what he gets, so that, if he be content with the necessities of life, without its luxuries, the expense is in proportion.

The best coin for the traveler's purpose, is English gold, which passes at a considerable premium on the Continent, and is readily accepted at all the principal hotels. Having to earn my means as I went along, I was obliged to have money forwarded in small remittances, generally in drafts on the house of Hottingeur & Co., in Paris, which could be cashed in any large city of Europe. If only a short tour is intended, and the pedestrian's means are limited, he may easily carry the necessary amount with him. There is little danger of robbery for those who journey in such an humble style. I never lost a single article in this manner, and rarely had any feeling but that of perfect security. No part of our own country is safer in this respect than Germany, Switzerland or France. Italy still bears an unfortunate reputation for dishonesty; the narrow passages of the Apennines and the hollows of the Roman Campagna are haunted by banditti, and persons who travel in their own carriages are often plundered. I saw the caves and hiding-places of these outlaws among the evergreen shrubbery, in the pass of Monte Somma, near Spoleto, but as we had a dragoon in the crazy old vehicle, we feared no hindrance from them. A Swedish gentleman in Rome told me he had walked from Ancona, through the mountains to the Eternal City, partly by night, but that, although he met with many meaning faces, he was not disturbed in any way. An English artist of my acquaintance walked from Leghorn along the Tuscan and Tyrrhene coast to Civita Vecchia, through a barren and savage district, overgrown with aloes and cork-trees, without experiencing any trouble, except from the extreme curiosity of the ignorant inhabitants. The fastnesses of the Abruzzi have been explored with like facility by daring pedestrians; indeed, the sight of a knapsack seems to serve as a free passport with all highwaymen.

I have given, at times, through the foregoing chapters, the cost of portions of my journey and residence in various cities of Europe.

The cheapest country for traveling, as far as my experience extended, is Southern Germany, where one can travel comfortably on twenty-five cents a day. Italy and the south of France come next in order, and are but little more expensive; then follow Switzerland and Northern Germany, and lastly, Great Britain. The cheapest city, and one of the pleasantest in the world, is Florence, where we breakfasted on five cents, dined sumptuously on twelve, and went to a good opera for ten. A man would find no difficulty in spending a year there, for about $250. This fact may be of some importance to those whose health requires such a stay, yet are kept back from attempting the voyage through fear of the expense. Counting the passage to Leghorn at fifty or sixty dollars, it will be seen how little is necessary for a year's enjoyment of the sweet atmosphere of Italy. In addition to these particulars, the following connected estimate will better show the *minimum* expense of a two years' pilgrimage:

Voyage to Liverpool, in the second cabin	$24.00
Three weeks' travel in Ireland and Scotland	25.00
A week in London, at three shillings a day	4.50
From London to Heidelberg	15.00
A month at Heidelberg, and trip to Frankfort	20.00
Seven months in Frankfort, at $10 per month	70.00
Fuel, passports, excursions and other expenses	30.00
Tour through Cassel, the Hartz, Saxony, Austria, Bavaria, &c.	40.00
A month in Frankfort	10.00
From Frankfort through Switzerland, and over the Alps to Milan	15.00
From Milan to Genoa	.50
Expenses from Genoa to Florence	14.00
Four months in Florence	50.00
Eight days' journey from Florence to Rome, two weeks in Rome, voyage to Marseilles, and journey to Paris	40.00
Five weeks in Paris	15.00
From Paris to London	8.00
Six weeks in London, at three shillings a day	31.00
Passage home	60.00
	$472.00

The cost for places of amusement, guides' fees, and other small expenses, not included in this list, increase the sum total to $500, for which the tour may be made.

Now having, I hope, established this to the reader's satisfaction, I respectfully take leave of him.

Index

quaint, 36, 48, 61, 75, 95, 107, 204, 219, 366, 372, 380

Quais, 364, 371

Quarantine Buildings, 398

Querciola, 284

questions, 37, 104, 110, 202, 213, 312

Rachel, 374

railroad, 50, 51, 123, 127, 142, 175, 208, 215, 293, 379, 391

rains, 18, 19, 76, 114, 315, 317, 380, 399

rambling, 142, 163, 175, 319, 345, 399

Random, Roderick, 16

rank and status, 26, 105, 147, 177, 240, 242, 260, 295, 323, 410, 411

Raphael, 128, 158, 201, 247, 266–268, 273, 277, 293, 324, 329

Rapperschwyl, 224, 225

rapture, 145, 171, 172, 207, 219, 223, 400

Rasselas, 218

Ratisbon, 175, 202

ravines, 19, 134, 183, 278, 282, 320

reasons, 36, 47, 85, 150, 246, 249, 295

Reboul, Jean, 282

recollections, 107, 145, 190, 322, 373, 392

recreation, 62, 222

Red Fisherman, 80, 86

Red Water, 36

refreshing, 67, 184, 232, 251, 347, 399, 402, 408

refuge, 19, 224, 305, 336, 363

Regent Circus, 46

Regent's Park, 47, 156, 382

Rehberger Graben, 115

relics, 28, 160, 163, 313, 319, 336, 345, 359

religion, 61, 144, 245, 333, 385: apostles, 329; bible, 204; bishops, 58, 92, 120; churches, 10, 36, 42, 48, 53, 66, 114, 124, 145, 156–158, 185, 192–194, 201, 214, 226, 242, 251, 262, 270–272, 281, 293, 323, 329, 344, 372, 381, 385; idolatry, 143; Jesus Christ, 88, 89, 128, 141, 164, 174, 273, 296; priests, 92, 143, 144, 150, 151, 245, 252, 255, 286, 287, 294, 314, 322, 335, 343; saints, 50, 52, 66, 143, 193, 335; shrines, 45, 143, 144, 148, 151, 174, 186, 227, 229, 374

remittance, 87, 212, 314, 362, 382, 405

René, King, 352

renown, 93, 180, 271, 299, 300, 374

reputation, 213, 246, 296, 298, 411

resemblance, 11, 12, 14, 27, 103, 156, 242, 245

Reuss, 230–232

reverence, 126, 148, 149, 158, 207, 276, 334

Rhine, 35, 54–57, 59, 61, 65, 69, 140,